THE CONSEQUENCES
OF HUMILIATION

THE CONSEQUENCES OF HUMILIATION

Anger and Status in World Politics

Joslyn Barnhart

CORNELL UNIVERSITY PRESS   ITHACA AND LONDON

Copyright © 2020 by Cornell University

Cornell University Press gratefully acknowledges receipt of a grant from Wesleyan University, which aided in the publication of this book.

All rights reserved. Except for brief quotations in a review, this book, or parts thereof, must not be reproduced in any form without permission in writing from the publisher. For information, address Cornell University Press, Sage House, 512 East State Street, Ithaca, New York 14850. Visit our website at cornellpress.cornell.edu.

First published 2020 by Cornell University Press

Library of Congress Cataloging-in-Publication Data

Names: Barnhart, Joslyn, author.
Title: The consequences of humiliation : anger and status in world politics / Joslyn Barnhart.
Description: Ithaca : Cornell University Press, 2020. | Includes bibliographical references and index.
Identifiers: LCCN 2019027231 (print) | LCCN 2019027232 (ebook) | ISBN 9781501748042 (cloth) | ISBN 9781501748684 (epub) | ISBN 9781501748691 (pdf)
Subjects: LCSH: International relations—Psychological aspects. | World politics—Psychological aspects. | Humiliation—Political aspects. | Anger—Political aspects. | Aggressiveness—Political aspects. | Public opinion—Political aspects.
Classification: LCC JZ1253 .B37 2020 (print) | LCC JZ1253 (ebook) | DDC 327.101/9—dc23
LC record available at https://lccn.loc.gov/2019027231
LC ebook record available at https://lccn.loc.gov/2019027232

*To Tom, Joy,
and Francesca*

Contents

Introduction	1
1. National Failure and International Disregard	15
2. Withdrawal, Opposition, and Aggression	36
3. National Humiliation at the Individual Level	57
4. The Cross-National Consequences of Humiliating International Events	78
5. Soothing Wounded Vanity: French and German Expansion in Africa from 1882 to 1885	108
6. "Our Honeymoon with the U.S. Came to an End": Soviet Humiliation at the Height of the Cold War	138
Conclusion: The Attenuation and Prevention of National Humiliation	164
Acknowledgments	185
Appendix	187
Notes	209
References	233
Index	253

THE CONSEQUENCES
OF HUMILIATION

Introduction

Political references to national humiliation span time and place, often uttered in conjunction with predictions of violence. In 1925, Adolf Hitler, for instance, infamously decried the "inhuman barbarity" of the arbitrary dictates of the Treaty of Versailles, a treaty he deemed an "instrument of blackmail and shameful humiliation." He presciently warned that the "sadist cruelty" of the treaty could, in the right hands, be used to arouse national sentiment to "its highest pitch . . . such that the souls of sixty million Germans would be aflame with a feeling of rage" and a "spirit of dauntless resistance."[1] Hitler would deliberately invoke the specter of Germany's humiliation fifteen years later when he arranged to sign the 1940 Armistice with France while sitting in the same chair, in the same railway car—removed from a local museum for the occasion—in the village of Compiègne where Ferdinand Foch had signed the Armistice marking Germany's defeat in 1918.[2]

In 1871, the British Lord Salisbury had similarly predicted that French humiliation engendered by the outcome of the Franco-Prussian War would have lasting consequences on French foreign policy. The loss of the French provinces of Alsace and Lorraine would, he argued, serve as a "constant memorial of [French] humiliation," pushing the French toward renewed aggression against Germany.[3] The desire to expunge the humiliation of the lost French provinces remained a prominent focus within French political rhetoric up until the eve of World War I and the provinces' eventual return.

Past humiliating events have also been offered as an explanation for revisionist foreign policies. In arguing for Iran's right to possess nuclear weapons, for instance, Iranian representatives referenced Western unilateral intervention in 1953, declaring, "You humiliated us more than fifty years ago, but you will not be able to repeat it today."[4] Russian leaders have repeatedly invoked national humiliation at the hands of the West when discussing their motivation for recent acts of aggression within the former Soviet sphere. Russian president Dmitry Medvedev in 2008 pushed back against the U.S. bombing of Serbia and a NATO newly expanded up to Russian borders, declaring to a Western audience, "[Russia] will not tolerate any more humiliation and we are not joking."[5] Less than a month later, Russian troops marched into Georgia in flagrant disregard of U.S. pleas for restraint. Six years later, President Vladimir Putin cited Western failure to consult with Russia over the admission of Ukraine to the European Union as one in a long line of humiliations at the hands of the West, noting that "It is impossible to keep humiliating one's partners forever in such a way. That kind of relationship eventually breaks down."[6]

These, and countless other, references by decision makers suggest that national and group-based humiliation can have a broad, significant, and lasting impact on international behavior. What is the exact nature of this effect? This book shows that Germany's catastrophic reaction to humiliation engendered by the outcome of World War I was not an anomaly but was representative of a broader pattern of international behavior in which states that have experienced certain humiliating events are more likely to engage in international aggression and intentionally defiant foreign policies. Such states will be more apt to pursue territorial conquest, to intervene in the affairs of other states, to engage in diplomatic hostility and verbal discord, and to pursue advanced weaponry and other symbols of national resurgence. Humiliated states engage in these behaviors because these acts define high international status and because participating in them enables those who identify with the state to overcome humiliation and to thereby regain a sense of collective efficacy and authority. Furthermore, the acts promise to bolster the image of the state in the eyes of others because they demonstrate the state's distinctive capabilities as well as its intention to restore prior status.

Simply establishing the relationship between national humiliation and aggressive, status-seeking behaviors leaves many important questions about the role of national humiliation in international relations unanswered. I address three specific questions about the role of national humiliation in international politics in detail: What types of international events do we expect to engender the greatest sense of national humiliation? How exactly do we expect particularly humiliating international events to shape the foreign policies of states and how should we expect these responses to change over time? And under what conditions is humiliation-fueled aggression most likely to occur?

The Book's Argument in Brief

The historical and contemporary cases mentioned above point to numerous potential sources of national humiliation. French humiliation stemmed in part from France's unexpected defeat by Prussia in 1871 but also from the loss of French heartland territory, a loss that represented the extent of France's inability to successfully defend its interests and thereby its status as a preeminent world power. Hitler rooted German humiliation not in defeat at the hands of the Allied powers in World War I but in the post-war treaty, which he believed relegated Germany to permanent second-rate status. For Iranian diplomats, humiliation was engendered by direct infringement on Iranian sovereignty while for Russian leaders, the source of humiliation was in the West's disrespect for Russia's prior sphere of influence.

What do these seemingly disparate experiences have in common? The answer to this question is rooted in the nature of humiliation. "Humiliation" is the emotional response to the perceived undeserved decline of one's status in the eyes of others.[7] Humiliation is a complex and negative self-conscious emotion, which combines the sense that one has been mistreated with a painful sense of self-doubt and helplessness in the face of this injustice. A state of "national humiliation" arises when individuals who identify as members of the state experience humiliation as the overwhelming emotional response to an international event, which they believe has undeservedly threatened the state's image on the world stage.

This definition enables us to make a priori assumptions about the types of international events that are likely to inflict the deepest sense of national humiliation and to have the most significant effects on international behavior. I argue that two broad types of humiliating events exist. The first type involves the failure of the state to live up to international expectations of how it should perform, given its perceived status. Failure of this sort can take the form of rapid defeat to a state with lesser military capability or the involuntary loss of homeland territory. Such public failures are often perceived as undeserved threats to the status of the state and thereby serve as deep sources of collective outrage and impotence. The second type of humiliating event involves the treatment of the state by others. States whose rights and expected privileges are denied by others are also likely to perceive that the state's image in the eyes of others has been unfairly undermined by ill-intended others. Allowing others to disrespect one's sovereignty or to interfere in one's sphere of influence can generate common knowledge that a state is undeserving of high status while simultaneously engendering a pervasive and potentially constraining sense of powerlessness within the disrespected state.

How exactly should we expect the behavior of states that have experienced such events to differ from those that have not? Above, I suggested that humiliated states are more likely to engage in several different foreign policy behaviors intended to bolster the image of the state in its eyes and the eyes of others. These behaviors include, for instance, diplomatic opposition, the pursuit of symbols of high status such as nuclear weapons or colonies abroad, and the use of force against the state responsible for one's humiliation or against third-party states that were not involved in the original humiliating event. Which of these numerous assertive strategies will humiliated states pursue?

The answer to this question depends in part on the capabilities of the state. Humiliated states seek to reestablish their status in the eyes of others. To do this, they engage in actions that define the status they seek to hold. Great powers might project their power and maintain extensive spheres of influence abroad. Those states seeking to assert their regional power status might engage in similar status-seeking actions, but would be expected to do so over more circumscribed areas and for less sustained periods.[8] Humiliated states that already hold low status, by contrast, have fewer options for restoring their sense of efficacy.

The behavior of all humiliated states, including great powers, will be constrained by the need for success. Humiliation, like anger, involves a sense of injustice. Humiliation is distinct from anger in that humiliated parties question their ability to assert themselves and to successfully defend their image in the eyes of others. Overcoming humiliation requires the elimination of self-doubt. Humiliated states are motivated by the desire to reestablish both their confidence as well as their image in the eyes of others, and they will seek to prove to themselves and others that they are effective actors on the world stage. They will generally avoid rash actions and will prioritize favorable outcomes. Thus, though revenge might offer the most satisfying path toward status renewal, states may avoid revanchism if they believe repeated humiliation is likely. States that possess sufficient capabilities are more likely to bolster their image in other ways through the projection of power abroad at the expense of weaker, third-party states. Such acts demonstrate the state's distinctive capabilities as well as its intention to be viewed as a high status state. Most important, such acts serve to demonstrate these qualities to those within the state itself, thereby bolstering confidence in the state.

The cases above, and many others, also suggest that national humiliation can have significant staying power. Indeed, leaders frequently invoke instances of national humiliation that occurred long in the past. Slobodan Milosevic marked with great fanfare the 600th anniversary of the humiliating loss of the Serbs at the hands of the Ottoman Empire in 1989. China's oft-referenced "Century of Humiliation," commemorated annually in September on National Humiliation Day, began with the defeat of Chinese forces in the First Opium War in 1842 and ended, according to national narratives, with the Chinese Communist Revolution in 1949.

What explains the longevity of humiliation? Research in social psychology provides insight into this question. Experiments have shown that of all emotions, humiliation is felt the most intensely, generating sensations akin to physical pain that can be conjured with unreduced intensity decades after the original humiliating event.[9] On a national level, a sense of humiliation can persist across generations if humiliation becomes ingrained within national narratives and the self-concept of the state.

States often do not respond immediately to a humiliating event with assertive status-seeking acts. The effects of Germany's humiliation in 1919 arguably became palpable in 1933 with the election of Adolf Hitler on a platform of vengeance-seeking against the Allied powers. We are possibly now experiencing the most intense effects of Russian humiliation first engendered by the fall of the Soviet Union and subsequent Western declarations of victory over the Russian foe. This prompts the question of when exactly humiliation's effects on international behavior will be most keenly felt.

I argue that the timing of assertive responses to humiliation depends on whether the state has sufficiently recovered from losses incurred as a result of the humiliating event. The political instability and loss of material capabilities that often follow significant humiliating events, such as defeat in war, limit the state's ability to achieve success in the aftermath of a humiliating event. They also further erode collective confidence within the state. The restoration of political stability and material wherewithal is a necessary step toward the elimination of national self-doubt. Once states fully achieve domestic recovery, they will be far more likely to engage in assertive acts on the world stage intended to announce their intentions to regain previous status. States that never regain the level of material wealth and political stability they possessed before the humiliating event will be far less likely to assert their status and capabilities following a humiliating event.

The renewal of national confidence, therefore, occurs in two stages. Domestic recovery serves as the first step toward the renewed collective confidence of the state. The second stage of recovery takes place at the international level once the humiliated state engages in repeated successful international assertions of its status. Although domestic recovery may provide sufficient self-confidence for states to reassert themselves, only success at these international acts fully enables members of the state to overcome the sense of helplessness, and thereby the humiliation, that the original status-threatening event engendered.

Material recovery and political stability are not the only two factors that affect collective self-esteem. Strong and charismatic leaders may be able to instill a stronger sense of authority in their people than material and political recovery might support. Even in these cases, however, the desire of the state to prove itself on the world stage will be constrained by the fear of repeated humiliation. Such repetition suggests that the original failure of the state was not a fluke but instead accurately represented the state's appropriate status. Repeated failure would arguably induce more discomfort than a single humiliating event, eventually forcing the state to downgrade its own status expectations, its identity, and its sense of place in the world. States are therefore willing to sit and wait before reasserting themselves on the world stage, biding their time until a sufficient sense of collective efficacy returns.

Contribution: Humiliation and Status in World Affairs

This book is not the first to highlight the substantial impact of national humiliation in international relations. It is, however, the first to systematically analyze a common assumption within the humiliation literature: that violent acts of revenge, targeted at one's "humiliator" are the most likely consequence of humiliating events. The book shows that a desire to right the wrongs of the past is not the only, or even the most, prominent motivator of post-humiliation foreign policy for acts of direct military revenge are in fact quite rare, at least among great powers, in the years immediately following a humiliating event. Rather, humiliated states often seek to overcome their sense of helplessness by demonstrating their efficacy through acts of aggression targeting third-party states that played no role in the original humiliating event. These third-party targets are often far weaker than the humiliated states targeting them. They are also often perceived to be of little strategic or material benefit to the humiliated state. Yet aggression against them promises to bolster national confidence while also signaling to international observers that the state intends to maintain its high status.

This book is also the first to focus significant attention on the timing of aggressive responses to humiliating international events. Many equate emotionality with recklessness and haste. In fact, humiliated states are deliberate and productive in their attempts to reestablish their status and esteem after a humiliating event. They bide their time for years until they recover sufficient resources and regain confidence that they will be able to successfully reassert themselves on the world stage in a way that comports with their desired status. Humiliation's most destabilizing international effects can, therefore, take place many years into the future.

My argument and findings also contribute to a substantial and growing literature on the role that status plays in international affairs. First, the book provides insight into the conditions under which status concerns are most likely to shape state behavior. Prior work on this topic has convincingly demonstrated that states care significantly about their relative standing within international hierarchies. Somewhat less consensus exists, however, about when exactly status concerns are most likely to drive state behavior. The most common explanation of why status concerns vary over time points to discrepancies between the status a state expects, expectations typically based in the state's relative military capabilities, and the status others attribute to the state. States are said to be in the domain of "status inconsistency" when their material rank outpaces the relative degree of international influence and privilege they wield.[10] Status inconsistency is proposed to be most likely among rising states experiencing substantial material growth but which are denied an increasing share of global influence.

It is likely true that rising states often fight for status concessions from higher status states. I demonstrate, however, that the denial of status to rising states accounts for only a portion of status-motivated behavior. Status inconsistency results from a lack of sufficient status recognition by others. But non-recognition is only one source of status threat. International status is a function of how others see the state as well as how the state performs on the world stage. Events in which a state fails to live up to expectations associated with its desired status also have the potential to engender significant humiliation among citizens within the low-achieving state, thereby increasing the likelihood that the state engages in acts aimed at bolstering its image in the eyes of others and the eyes of its citizens.

William Callahan has argued that the humiliation of a country provides the impetus for its material regrowth and rejuvenation.[11] Humiliating events may motivate the rapid relative material growth that characterizes rising states and can give rise to a condition of status inconsistency. Humiliating events and the status concerns they engender may, however, have little to do with the relative material rank or trajectory of the state. An additional contribution of this book is the demonstration that the effects of status concerns are not limited to rising states. States of any rank can experience a humiliating international event. This includes world powers that reside at the top of both material and status rankings as well as lower status states who may be in relative material decline.

Third, prior work on the effects of status seeking has typically examined the relationship between status concerns and one particular type of assertive status-seeking behavior, such as the pursuit of status symbols like nuclear weapons or the initiation of international disputes.[12] We know little about why states would select one assertive status-seeking act over another. The incorporation of humiliation and confidence helps flesh out a more precise predictive model. Such behaviors involve different levels of risk to the self-conception and status of humiliated states. Seemingly less risky acts, like diplomatic defiance, do involve some risk. It is possible that the humiliated state's defiance may be ignored or even mocked on the world stage, highlighting the fecklessness of the state. Such acts are, however, far less risky than initiating and losing a military conflict. States will only be willing to take on the risks that the projection of power abroad involves once a sufficient level of collective esteem has been restored.

Finally, while other work has typically considered status-seeking acts of states in isolation, I demonstrate that humiliation-triggered aggression can have profound effects on the stability of the international system. I show that, under certain conditions, responses to humiliating events can lead to periods of heightened international competition, which I call *international races* for status. At the heart of the logic of an international race is the fact that status is a zero-sum good. Status investments by one state inevitably threaten a decline in the status and influence of others, who then have an incentive to make investments they likely would not have otherwise made in defense of their own status. International races for status emerge when the value of the good states compete over becomes endogenous to the competition itself—states come to value a good only as much as they believe others do.

This logic of status competitions helps us understand unusually competitive periods of international history, including the Scramble for Africa and the race for nuclear parity that occurred in the middle of the Cold War. These cases show that the focal point of competitions for status can change over time as symbols of international status change. Colonies were pursued as the ultimate symbols of great power status around the turn of the nineteenth century. Decades later, colonies were deemed unacceptable while large nuclear arsenals were seen to be essential to great power status. Yet the general logic of status competition remained. By incorporating these dynamics into our understanding of international status, we see that the effects of status in international relations extend far beyond those states that have themselves been denied status recognition and include states that have come to believe that the status-seeking acts of others could potentially lead to their own status decline.

In demonstrating the significant degree to which national humiliation shapes world affairs, this book expands our understanding of how past events shape current state behavior. There are many theories of how reputation, and in particular a reputation for lack of resolve, functions within international relations. Scholars have shown that states that have backed down in the past are more likely to face future challengers, the theory being that the credibility of states which have backed down in the past will be diminished and their threats will go unbelieved.[13]

However, this is not the only past event that can have significant repercussions long into the future. Humiliating events can affect state behavior not only immediately after they occur, but for many decades into the future. Humiliated states are more likely to engage in aggression and to pursue territorial gains than states that have not been humiliated. This suggests that current theories of state behavior dramatically underestimate the effect of the past on the present. Just as we assume, however, that individuals' responses to circumstances are shaped in part by their past experiences, the history of a state's humiliating interactions with others is bound to shape its present and future behavior in ways that have been unaccounted for in existing theories of state behavior.

Level of Analysis

National humiliation, as defined above, is ultimately experienced as a painful physical sensation within individuals who identify with the state. We expect those who most closely identify with the state to experience the most intense emotions in reaction to events involving the state; those who do not identify with the state may feel little emotional reaction at all. It is not exactly accurate, however, to describe these emotions as existing solely at the individual level. Some researchers argue that the nature and level of emotions felt by individuals who identify with the state are strongly influenced by the sharing and validation of these feelings by others who are also strong identifiers.[14] The theory of national humiliation presented here does not exist at either the individual or state level but at the level of those who identify with their state.

The notion that individuals can have shared, significant emotional reactions to events affecting their states has strong foundations within personal experience. Anyone who has ever been filled with pride when a citizen of their state performed well on the world stage knows that members of social groups frequently experience shared emotional reactions to events that affect their group but in which they did not personally participate. The same is true of Americans who were not directly affected by the events of September 11, 2001 but who nevertheless responded with great sadness, or of those who felt ashamed viewing photos documenting the denigration of prisoners by U.S. soldiers at Abu Ghraib.[15] The "rally around the flag effect" in fact relies on the idea that successful military conflict with a rival will generate predictable emotional responses of pride and enthusiasm among the state's citizens.[16] As I discuss in Chapter 1, these intuitions have found consistent support within both social psychology and international relations research.[17]

One significant premise of this book is that these individual but shared reactions to events affecting the state with which they identify can have significant effects on the foreign policy of the state. As I show in Chapter 3, individual emotions in response to humiliating events affecting one's state explain individual-level variation in support for aggressive foreign policies. This has two primary implications on foreign policy. The first exists at the level of elites. It is safe to assume that elites, as representatives of their state, are among those who most closely identify as members of the state. Elites are also therefore likely to experience strong emotional reactions to humiliating international events. We can then assume that leader foreign policy preferences would shift in ways that mimic average foreign policy shifts within the broader populace.

The second implication exists at the level of the broader populace. Because individuals who feel humiliated on behalf of their state prioritize ameliorating the sense of helplessness and inferiority they feel, they will be more susceptible, on average, to leaders' or candidates' rallying cries for the resurgence of the state in an effort to avoid "second-rate" status. These individuals will be more supportive, on average, of politicians who speak in confident terms about the states' ability to restore the image of the state in the eyes of others. Leaders are, therefore, less likely to experience political constraints as they pursue aggressive agendas.

The Scope of the Book

The book examines the relationship between national humiliation and assertive status-seeking strategies like the acquisition of status symbols and direct military conflict. It does not address the relationship between humiliation and other more pacific status-seeking strategies like social creativity or imitation.[18] Instead, it focuses on aggressive status-seeking acts. Most crucially, such acts have the largest potential implications for international stability. The acquisition of nuclear arms as symbols of international status, for instance, can trigger an international arms race which destabilizes the international system. The projection of power abroad often comes at the expense of weaker states and can, in turn, engender a sense of national humiliation within the targeted state, which can subsequently motivate aggressive behavior.

There is also reason to believe that states are more likely to respond to humiliating events with aggressive rather than imitative or creative strategies. Humiliated states seek to restore their sense of efficacy and authority. Aggressive, status-seeking acts best enable states to overcome their sense of helplessness and empower them on the world stage. Because humiliating events often fuel anger once states have recovered their confidence, these events tend to serve as triggers for aggressive action. Finally, competitive strategies enable status-threatened states to send more targeted signals to states which have humiliated them than do imitation and creativity. These signals often involve vigorously exercising the right or pursuing the exact interest the humiliated state was originally denied.

The analysis of the causes and effects of national humiliation that follows pays particular attention to symbols of great power status, like nuclear arsenals and empires. Territory—its loss and its gain—tends to play a unique role in national humiliation. Territorial loss not only signals that a state was unable to protect its territorial integrity. The territory itself also comes to symbolize and embody the humiliation of the state, making it more difficult for elites to compromise over territorial disputes. Territorial gain, or the ability to maintain a sphere of influence and to project power abroad, has also long been seen as an act that distinguishes greater powers from lesser powers. The reunification of national territories most clearly symbolizes national resurgence and signifies that past humiliation has finally been overcome.

The theory of humiliation offered in the coming chapter addresses the impact of international humiliation on all states, but I predominantly focus on the behavior of those states with expectations of great power status. Not only are great powers the states with the greatest capability to engage in observable and measurable responses to humiliating events. Great power aspirants also expect more substantial rights and privileges which other great powers for various reasons may be more reluctant to grant them, engendering a perception of disrespect. The expectations for the performance of these states on the world stage are high and the public failure to perform up to these expectations can threaten the great power standing of the state.

Measurement and Methods

The core concepts at the heart of my analysis, including national humiliation and self-esteem, are difficult to measure. Both concepts reside within the collective perceptions of individuals within the state. One can detect useful and informative empirical patterns even if, however, one's measures are rough. This is evidenced by the many statistical studies of international status, which rely on diplomatic exchange data as a proxy measure of state influence.[19] Few scholars would argue that this measure completely captures a state's relative international influence. From the numerous analyses that utilize this measure, however, we know that those states whose diplomatic rank is inconsistent with their military rank are on average more likely to engage in aggressive acts.

While Chapter 3 measures collective humiliation induced within an experimental setting, the statistical analysis in Chapter 4 does not rely on direct measures of national humiliation. Instead, the analysis examines the impact of two types of events that, by definition, we should expect to engender a sense of national humiliation—defeat to a weaker state and involuntary territorial loss. The selection of these two events was based on a priori assumptions about the nature of humiliating international events, though qualitative evidence in Chapters 5, 6, and 7 demonstrates the strong probabilistic relationship between these events and a sense of national humiliation.

Some readers may argue that such complex psychological concepts cannot be captured by such blunt measures or that we could never be sure that the impact of such events on future behavior is truly driven by any humiliating effects they might have. So how can we be sure that these measures are serving as reliable proxies for national humiliation? To bolster confidence, the analysis in Chapter 4 examines in detail the plausibility of several alternative explanations that might explain the relationship between past defeat or territorial loss and future aggression, including those rooted in concerns about security, material capabilities, and reputation. I outline a set of hypotheses about how we would expect each category of concerns to shape future conflict behavior and then test its validity against hypotheses rooted in the logic of national humiliation. I also compare the effects of defeat and involuntary territorial loss to other potential outcomes, like a stalemate in war or the voluntary loss of territory, that we would expect by definition to pose less threat to the status of the state but which we would also expect to have similar material consequences for the state. Through these comparisons, we can further isolate the effect of undeserved status threat from alternative hypotheses that might explain the relationship between past losses and future aggression.

The results show robust support for the idea that increases in future conflict following defeat and territorial loss are driven to a more substantial degree by a desire to ameliorate the psychological impact of these events than by any material, strategic, or domestic concerns these events might elicit. The analysis shows, for instance, that while recently defeated states are 42 percent more likely to initiate conflict in the ten years following defeat than great powers that have not recently experienced defeat, great powers that have recently experienced stalemate are no more likely to initiate conflict than states that have not. Similarly, states that have recently lost territory through involuntary means are 88 percent more likely to engage in territorial aggression than states that have not recently experienced involuntary territorial loss. Voluntary loss, which is often accompanied by similar material costs, is not associated with significant shifts in rates of territorial aggression.

Chapters 5 and 6 examine four particular humiliating international events in significant detail—the defeat and loss of territory for France in the Franco-Prussian War in 1881, the British denial of German colonial interests within

Africa in 1884, the U.S.' failure to apologize for persistent disrespect of Soviet airspace in 1960, and, finally, the perception of Soviet failure at the end of the Cuban Missile Crisis in 1962. The contribution of these cases to the overall objective of this book is to further establish and illustrate the causal relationship between humiliating events and subsequent shifts in foreign policy. These cases were chosen because they provide insight into the exact nature of the potential events that can engender a strong sense of humiliation and because they allow us to further assess the plausibility of the book's theory regarding the exact timing and nature of state responses to humiliating events. The cases also attest to the particularly dramatic effects that state responses to humiliation can have on the foreign policies of other states and the stability of the international system more broadly.

Plan of the Book

The next chapter further defines key terms, discussing the relationship between humiliation and other emotions like shame, embarrassment, and anger, and explores the features of humiliating international events in more detail. Chapter 2 discusses why exactly we should expect humiliating events to alter state behavior and then outlines the various responses that states may have to humiliating events, ranging from withdrawal to direct military conflict. The chapter addresses how these responses to humiliating events can affect the behaviors of other states as well as the overall stability of the international system.

Chapters 3 and 4 examine how national humiliation plays out at the individual and cross-national levels, respectively. Chapter 3 examines the effects of international events on individuals' emotions and foreign policy preferences using a set of survey experiments conducted within the United States. This experimental approach enables us to 1) test our assumptions about the types of international events that are likely to engender national humiliation; 2) demonstrate a clear link between a sense of helplessness and humiliation in a way that distinguishes humiliation from anger; 3) assess the degree to which these events might shift foreign policy preferences for aggressive foreign policy behaviors; and 4) assess the degree to which emotional concerns mediate the relationship between humiliating international events and support for aggression relative to security and instrumental concerns. Chapter 4 presents statistical evidence in support of the book's model of humiliation. The cross-national and within-country approaches used in this chapter shed light on the degree to which the behavior of recently humiliated states differs from that of states that have not experienced recent humiliation.

Chapters 5 and 6 turn to the qualitative analysis of humiliation's effects. These chapters enable us to plot more precisely the nature and effect of national humiliation and national confidence across time and place and to assess the impact of humiliation-motivated aggression on the behavior of other states. Chapter 5 focuses on national humiliation and the triggering in the 1880s of the Scramble for Africa, an unprecedented land grab by European great powers. Chapter 6 examines the significant role that national humiliation played in shaping Soviet policy during the most dangerous period of the Cold War, defining the relationship between the Soviets' sense of humiliation perpetuated by U.S. surveillance flyovers between 1957 and 1961 through Soviet airspace and Khrushchev's decision shortly thereafter to break ties with the Americans and place missiles in Cuba.

The book concludes by placing the findings into the broader context of international politics and international relations theory. It demonstrates the utility of the theory for understanding the contemporary foreign policies of China and Russia and, in doing so, sheds light on why the effects of humiliation may linger in some states longer than others. The conclusion draws key distinctions between the theory and predictions of humiliation and more material and security-based explanations of international behavior. Finally, the chapter addresses the policy implications of the book's findings. If humiliating events often lead states to engage in assertive and often aggressive acts, what can be done to ameliorate or even prevent national humiliation? And why are these ameliorative strategies often not employed by other states, much to the detriment of international stability and cooperation?

1
NATIONAL FAILURE AND INTERNATIONAL DISREGARD

National humiliation can arise in response to a wide variety of events. Defeat is an oft-cited source of humiliation as are post-war treaties like the Treaty of Versailles, which has become virtually synonymous with national humiliation. Yet not all defeats or treaties humiliate to the same degree. The Six-Day War and the First Italo-Ethiopian War are frequently referred to as sources of deep humiliation for the defeated Arab states and for Italy while other instances of defeat, like the Anglo-Egyptian War in 1882, are less often cited as causes of humiliation for the defeated state. Similarly, the 1895 Treaty of Shimonoseki is rarely invoked without reference to its humiliating effects while other treaties, such as The Potsdam Agreement at the end of World War II, are less often blamed for inciting national humiliation.

This chapter characterizes the features of the international events that are likely to arouse the deepest forms of national humiliation and are therefore the most likely to significantly affect world affairs. These events can assume two general forms: 1) those in which a state fails to perform in accordance with its status and 2) those in which a state is attributed fewer rights and privileges than expected. Though seemingly distinct in nature, events of both types engender the two key characteristic features of humiliation: a sense of other-directed outrage and a sense of self-doubt and impotence.

Definitions

The last chapter defined humiliation as the emotional response to the perceived undeserved decline of one's status in the eyes of others. To develop a clearer understanding of the nature of humiliation, it is useful to distinguish this emotional response from the similar negative emotional states of anger, shame, and embarrassment. Like anger, humiliation involves a strong sense of other-directed outrage at the party deemed responsible for treating one unfairly.[1] Humiliation is distinct from anger in that anger is associated with a sense of empowerment and authority, whereas humiliation melds outrage with a sense of powerlessness that stems from one's inability to defend against injustice. Humiliation is like shame in that both emotions involve the internalization of a lowered estimation of the self.[2] Those who feel shame believe that they deserve their inferior position. Humiliated actors, by contrast, believe that the threat to their status is undeserved and unjust.

Humiliation is thought to differ from embarrassment by a matter of degree. Embarrassment attaches to more superficial experiences, which are unlikely to have long-term effects on self-image, while humiliation involves a deeper sense of mortification at the prolonged loss of one's self-esteem and status.[3] Of all negative emotional states, social threat and humiliation have been shown to have some of the most deleterious physiological and psychological effects. Status threat has been shown to lead to high blood pressure, elevated levels of cortisol, and to increased harm to the cardiovascular, autonomic, endocrine, and immune systems.[4] These negative physiological effects are conjoined with negative self-evaluations and lowered self-esteem that can persist over long periods.

Two related and important features of humiliation are directly implied by the definition. First, because humiliation resides in subjective experience, actors do not need confirmation that an event has eroded their social image to perceive the event as humiliating. They need only fear erosion of their social position as a likely repercussion of the event and to perceive this erosion as unjust. Second, the intention to humiliate is not necessary for others to arrive at the perception that they have been unjustly demeaned.[5] Actors who feel they have been wronged may erroneously assign negative intention to others. Moreover, actors that fail to live up to social expectations in ways that threaten their status may blame others for their failure. Such actors likely fear the decline of their image in the eyes of others and themselves just as do actors who are intentionally victimized.

As the definition of humiliation conveys, humiliation and status are intertwined. "Status" refers to one's position vis-à-vis a comparison group.[6] While one maintains expectations about the status they think they should hold, the amount of status an actor ultimately holds resides in the perceptions of others. These perceptions are shaped in part by estimations of how an actor's characteristics rank relative to others but also by estimations of how other actors estimate the actor's relative ranking.[7] Collective and intersubjective perceptions of status inform patterns of deference and expectations of behavior and rights.[8] It is important to note that the effects of humiliation are not limited to concerns about what others think of us. Humiliating events have significant implications on how actors see themselves.[9] Even though humiliated actors do not believe they deserve inferior treatment, they experience a loss of self-esteem associated with the perception that they have been unable to prevent others from degrading their image.

National Humiliation and Status

How do we extrapolate from this discussion of humiliation at the individual level to humiliation felt at the level of the state? Humiliation at the individual level arises in response to perceived undeserved threats to one's own status while national humiliation emerges in reaction to perceived undeserved threats to the status of one's state. What then constitutes an undeserved threat to the status of a state? The answer to this question stems directly from the nature of international status and its relationship to humiliation.

High international status commonly has been attributed to those states that possess distinctive military, economic, technological, and organizational capacities and that use these material capacities in service of an assertive foreign policy intended to promote a state's interests in far-flung regions.[10] Because precise estimations of the relative degree to which states possess a composite of such diverse characteristics are difficult to form, however, status estimations are also based on one's beliefs about others' beliefs about the status that each state should hold.[11] Beliefs about others' estimations of a state's rightful position are shaped by the amount of influence other states bestow on the state in question. Acknowledging that a state is deserving of the rights and privileges it expects to hold signals to others that you find the state to be worthy of its desired status. This signal may, in turn, shape what others perceive to be the rightful privileges of the state.

A state's status is secured when two sets of expectations are met. The first set of expectations, held by the international community, involves how states of a particular status are expected to behave on the world stage and the characteristics they are expected to embody. High status states, for instance, are typically expected to succeed in military contests against lower status actors and to project more influence and power abroad. The second set of expectations, held by each individual state, involves the rights, privileges, and influence they expect to hold as a function of their expected status.[12]

States are likely to perceive an unjust challenge to their status when either of these two sets of expectations is not met. First, a state may fail to perform as would be expected of a state of its desired status. The failure to perform as expected given one's perceived status threatens to generate the common perception that the state lacks the capacities needed to distinguish itself from lower status states and that the state does not deserve the status it has held. The failure to meet the expectations associated with one's status threatens to generate common knowledge that the state lacks the capacities needed to distinguish itself from lower status states. The resulting threat to the state's status evokes self-doubt as well as other-directed outrage. Why the latter? As Van Evera puts it, states confronting painful national circumstances will be "'more willing to believe that others are responsible" for these public failings than they will be to accept blame for the failure of the state.[13] The acceptance of blame forces reconciliation with lower status expectations and inferiority. State elites also have a clear domestic incentive to generate a national narrative that shifts blame to outside parties and triggers a sense of outrage directed at those seen to have been responsible for or to have profited from one's failure.

Second, a state is likely to perceive an undeserved threat to its status if other states fail to acknowledge the rights and privileges the state expects to hold as a function of its status. For instance, lower status states may expect the respect of only those states' rights that are codified within international law—the right to sovereignty, to bear arms, and to defend one's waterways and airspace.[14] Higher status states, by contrast, expect to exercise a set of privileges, or unique sets of rights attached to different strata of regional or global status hierarchies, without challenge.[15] Great powers expect the right to maintain an uncontested sphere of influence within their geographic region and beyond, the right to disproportionate influence within international institutions, and the right to more deferential diplomatic treatment.[16] Regional powers may expect similar privileges but on a more local scale.[17]

States that do not receive the rights and privileges they believe they deserve confront the non-recognition of their status. As Honneth notes, rights represent social standing.[18] The respect and recognition of another's rights are important because they represent the implicit acceptance of an actor's rank.[19] The denial of another's rights deprecates the status of the other and is, by definition, humiliating. It also threatens the state's status by shaping the beliefs of others about the status the state should rightfully hold. Failure to recognize another's rights and privileges or to sufficiently attend to the state's interests presents an image of the state on the world stage as inferior and weak.

Like instances of state failure, a lack of acknowledgment by others can lead to an internalization of a sense of impotence, which stems from the state's inability to successfully demand the recognition it believes it deserves. Perhaps even more so than acts of state failure, disrespectful acts have the power to create a sense of injustice accompanied by outrage directed at the state responsible for one's humiliation. Indeed, in cases in which an instance of disrespect is not accompanied by material loss or political instability, it is likely that the sense of inefficacy induced by acts of disrespect will be relatively short-lived and that humiliation will quickly morph into anger and soon thereafter be followed by confident acts of assertiveness.

This discussion begs the question of how states form collective beliefs about their rightful position within regional and global hierarchies. These beliefs are rooted in the state's national identity, which is constituted by a set of ideas accepted by a majority within the state that define "what the collectivity is and the general rules under which it operates."[20] I argue that national identity and collective status expectations are based primarily on the relative capabilities of the state and the state's historical status, but also in part on the domestic political rhetoric of elites. States form subjective estimates of how they compare to other states on measurable status dimensions such as demography, military capabilities, and economic productivity. These estimations provide states with a baseline expectation of the standing they believe they deserve in the international hierarchy.[21]

In addition, identity and status expectations stem from temporal comparisons made with the state's own historical status.[22] National narratives about the state's past greatness and accomplishments can instill a sense of national pride leading states that once held high status to seek it again in the future.[23] Negative estimations of the current status of the state with historic peaks in the past can also negatively impact collective self-esteem. States that once held high status states will want to stabilize their identity and to erase the resulting damages to self-esteem by restoring their image in the eyes of others. Those states will be reluctant to fully relinquish their claims to that high status if they believe their decline has been the result of injustices by others. It is typically only after repeated failures or the substantial and seemingly permanent decline in relative resources that national conceptions are restructured around lower status identities.[24]

Finally, domestic elites can play some role in shaping collective status expectations and the national identity of the state. Elites may hold divergent ideas about appropriate national identity and may often self-consciously attempt to shape collective ideas and national narratives about the status that the state should hold and thus about how the state should be treated by others. These ideas often compete for dominance within domestic political discourse.[25] I argue that the degree to which leaders can shape the status expectations of the state is constrained by the state's relative capabilities and historical status. It is unlikely that leaders will seek to shape national identity around great power status in states with few material resources and without a model of past national grandeur to build on.

Before turning to the conditions under which international events are likely to induce the greatest degree of humiliation, it is important to highlight that not all status decline will arouse intense humiliation. Some transitions within status hierarchies come in the form of the slow and gradual accretion or decline of relative capabilities and international influence. For example, the scale of China's recent economic growth has in many ways been historically unprecedented, but talk of China's (re)emergence as a great power has been ongoing for decades, prompted significantly by the gradual rise in the size of the Chinese population. Another example is the dismantling of the Ottoman Empire, which occurred abruptly at the end of World War I, though the empire had arguably been experiencing a slow decline for centuries. States that have experienced repeated instances of internal and external failure or defeat may, over time, be forced to downgrade their status expectations. Less and less will they perceive each additional failure as an undeserved and inaccurate reflection of their rightful status. The declining state can often adapt to such gradual shifts without dramatic or violent state action.

By contrast, threats to social standing that come in the form of one-time sudden shocks, such as surprising defeat, are more likely to be perceived as unfair and inaccurate reflections of the relative capacities of the state. Defeated states in such cases will be less likely to immediately downgrade their status expectations even as others question their appropriate status rank and even as the state itself suffers from questions about its efficacy. This tendency to hold on to past status expectations, even in the face of international failure, is likely to give rise to an incongruity between how a state sees itself and how others see it, paving the way for the state to experience further humiliation since the attributed status the state may receive may well depend on how it has recently performed on the world stage.

What Factors Heighten National Humiliation?

The discussion so far has described two broad sources of national humiliation—international failure and international disrespect. My goal, however, is to move toward a predictive model of the specific events that are likely to inflict the most severe humiliation on states. One could argue that instances of international disrespect and failure abound within international relations. Yet they do not all have the potential to destabilize world affairs to the same degree.

Above all, the size of the discrepancy between expectations and reality will determine the degree of national humiliation that results from international events. States that are expected to handily defeat a foe in conflict but which instead lose the war quickly are likely to internalize a deeper sense of inferiority and outrage. States that expect to be afforded great power privileges but that are denied basic sovereign rights are similarly likely to be affected by a propulsive and galvanizing form of humiliation.

National Failure

States commonly fall short of achieving their international objectives. They pursue losing military and diplomatic strategies. They back down in the face of others' threats. In many cases, the inability to generate favorable outcomes does not have deleterious effects on the status of the state. In some instances, however, the failure to successfully achieve one's international aims can significantly undermine the image of the state in the eyes of others.

Of all forms of international failure, defeat in international conflict threatens to have the most deleterious effects on national status. Because military conflict provides insight into the relative underlying military capabilities of the states involved, it threatens to humiliate states at all rungs of the status hierarchy. I argue that the degree to which defeat arouses national humiliation depends on four primary factors: the relative military capabilities of the defeated state prior to the war, the locus of war initiation, the duration of the war, and whether the defeated party lost territory.

First, because status rank is in part predicated on perceptions of relative military rank and power, defeat in conflict is far more likely to engender national humiliation if a state is defeated by an opponent that was thought to possess fewer capabilities in the lead up to the war. The greater the perceived military advantage of the defeated state leading up to the war, the more intense the humiliation. In the lead up to what would be called the Six-Day War, the Arab states, for instance, possessed roughly six times the estimated military capacity of their opponent Israel.[26] Moreover, they had the backing of the Soviet Union. Yet the Arab states surrendered in only six days, their militaries decimated. The defeat was cited for causing "wounds which remain open and deep in the subconscious."[27] According to Khashan, the war engendered humiliation and the lowering of self-respect among Arabs because it not only highlighted the military inferiority of the Arab states but also demonstrated that the secular Arab states were unable to protect their citizens.[28] Because the war was intended to redress not only the Arab losses of 1948 but also to avenge three centuries of humiliation by the West, the defeat of 1967 only redoubled Arab humiliation.[29]

On this basis, we would also successfully predict the profound sense of humiliation induced by the United States' surprising loss in Vietnam. Though U.S. forces dropped three times the number of bombs in Vietnam than they had dropped in Europe and Asia during World War II, the superpower remained unable over the course of a decade to coerce the North Vietnamese who relied at first solely on American weapons captured from the battlefield. U.S. politicians throughout the war recognized the implications of failure. As U.S. secretary of defense Robert McNamara's assistant John McNaughton summarized in 1965, the United States had no good strategies for success. But withdrawal was unacceptable because it would be "tainted by the humiliation likely to follow."[30] In listing U.S. war objectives, McNaughton prioritized "avoiding a humiliating US defeat" far ahead of the other two objectives—limiting China's sphere of influence and improving life for the South Vietnamese. Indeed, the unambiguous military defeat that followed engendered a deep national trauma characterized by severe self-doubt and a sense of impotence on the world stage.[31] McNamara regretted in hindsight that the war had "warped the lives" not only of those on the ground but of a full generation of Americans at home.[32] That the United States had gone into the war with high expectations bolstered by a sense of near invincibility further heightened the sense and longevity of the emotional trauma.[33]

Finland's loss to the Soviet Union in the Winter War offers a stark contrast to these cases of surprising and humiliating defeat. In November 1939, Finnish soldiers were outnumbered two to one by the Soviet soldiers amassed on their border. Finland possessed a tiny fraction of the men, planes, guns, and tanks. Nikita Khrushchev, who was responsible for Soviet war planning, anticipated victory within weeks.[34] Carl Gustaf Mannerheim, Finland's greatest general, argued against fighting back, predicting that the Finnish army would cave quickly to the largest and most well-equipped army in Europe. One German attaché pronounced that if it came to a fight, "nothing might remain of Finland except a tale of heroism."[35] Yet the war lasted over three months. The Finns endured significant territorial losses and the loss of roughly 25,000 lives but maintained their independence. The Soviets lost over 200,000 men and gained only "enough ground to bury" their dead. Far from humiliating, the story of a nation of 3.7 million battling against a nation roughly fifty times its size was depicted at home and abroad as the basis of glorified legend. Unified and heroic, Finland had protected its independence in a way that no one had expected.

The pattern represented by these three cases is reflected within text analysis of descriptions of wars presented within academic history journals.[36] Those defeats in which the losing state possessed more than 60 percent of the total military capabilities of all states involved in the year before the war are roughly six times more likely to be referred to as "humiliating" or as a source of "national humiliation" in history journals than are defeats in which the losing party possessed 40 percent or less of the total military capabilities.[37] The left graph in Figure 1.1 depicts this comparison.

Although the characterizations of historians may not be a perfect measure of the internal perceptions and emotional responses of states to instances of defeat, in most cases, they are based on the statements of leaders of defeated countries or the work of other historians who have cited such statements.[38]

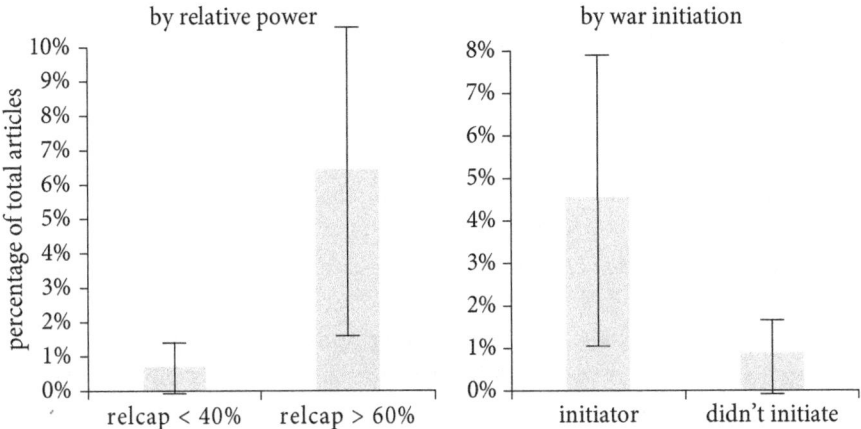

FIGURE 1.1 Proportion of articles in history journals labeling defeat as humiliation. This analysis includes forty-two cases of defeat, as coded by the Correlates of War Military Interstate Dispute dataset. Because it is difficult to form meaningful comparisons of military capabilities in wars with many participations, only those wars with five or fewer participants are included. The two percentages on the left can be distinguished at the $p < .05$ level. The values on the right can be distinguished at $p < .01$.

The accuracy of these characterizations can also be validated through the analysis of cases at each end of the spectrum of relative pre-war capabilities. The defeats that are most frequently referred to as "humiliating" are China's defeat to Japan in 1895, Italy's defeat to a much weaker Ethiopia in 1896, Russia's defeat to Japan in 1905, and the Arab states' defeat in the Six-Day War in 1967. In each of these cases, the defeated party is coded to have more than 75 percent of the material capabilities leading into war and, in each case, a strong argument can be made that the defeat engendered a notable degree of national humiliation. Denmark's defeat by Germany and Austria in 1864, Egypt's loss to England in 1882, and Cyprus's defeat by Turkey in 1974 are, by contrast, far less likely to be referred to as humiliating. In each of these cases, the defeated state is estimated to have had less than 10 percent of the total dyadic capabilities before the war. While these defeats may have aroused other collective emotional responses within the defeated state, they were unlikely to arouse humiliation largely because they did not fundamentally shift perceptions about the rightful status of the state.

The relative capabilities of the victor are not the only factor in determining how humiliating defeat will be. The humiliation one suffers from defeat is often worse among those who initiated the war. A willingness to initiate conflict can be interpreted by others as a signal of a state's resolve and preparedness. Because initiators may be expected to fully engage their capabilities to ensure victory, the failure to achieve victory in such a fight may be understood as an even more accurate reflection of the state's military capabilities. Thus, we would expect that defeat in a war that one has initiated and in which one was thought to have a military advantage would be more humiliating than a lost war that had a similar balance of power but which one did not start. One can imagine, for example, the First Italo-Ethiopian War would have been less humiliating for Italy if it had not initiated the war.

That initiation is likely to serve as its own source of humiliation also finds support within analysis of history journals similar to that described above but which compares two different sets of defeats: defeats in wars that the losing state initiated and defeats in wars that were started by one's opponent.[39] The graph on the right in Figure 1.1 shows that the likelihood that a defeat will be referred to as "humiliating" or as a source of "national humiliation" is roughly 4.5 times higher if the losing state initiated the war than if it did not. And though the stronger state is on average more likely to initiate a conflict, the analysis also shows that defeat following initiation increases the likelihood of references to humiliation by 650 percent even among those states that have less than 40 percent of total military capabilities before the war.[40] References to humiliation are three times more common for states with more capabilities that were defeated in wars they initiated than for stronger states defeated in wars they did not.[41]

Third, I argue that the duration of conflict can exacerbate the humiliation of defeat. International perceptions of relative status and capabilities not only shape expectations about the outcome of conflict but also expectations about how quickly that outcome will come to pass. Defeat to a weaker state alone can be sufficient for humiliation, but defeat to a weaker state in rapid fashion can heighten both the sense of surprise at defeat and the sense that the state must be weaker than it first appeared. Again, one can imagine that the defeat of the Arab states would have been at least minimized if the states had managed to engage Israel in a longer struggle.

Finally, the humiliation of defeat is likely to be heightened if defeat is accompanied by the loss of territory, which often comes to symbolize national humiliation. The loss of contiguous territory often leaves the most searing emotional marks on the state. The loss of East Jerusalem, for instance, was viewed as a particularly salient cause of humiliation for the Arab states in 1967. The loss of the French provinces of Alsace and Lorraine to the Prussians in 1871 proved to elicit palpable humiliation among the French population until it was retrieved in World War I. The Bolivians still seek to regain territory painfully lost to Chile in the War of the Pacific in 1883. States confronting territorial losses are expected to dedicate all resources in an effort to maintain ownership, and the failure to defend one's territory can be understood as highly indicative of the state's ultimate capabilities. As I discuss in Chapter 4, some instances of territorial loss occur outside of the course of direct military conflict, resulting instead from annexation or the threat of force. Such was the case with many instances of territorial loss by great powers in colonial spheres. Though the loss of non-contiguous territory abroad may engender less humiliation than the loss of contiguous territory following a defeat, the loss still represents a failure of high status states to successfully project power abroad, thereby threatening the state's image on the world stage.

While international defeat is likely to engender the gravest and most lasting form of national humiliation, international failure need not involve defeat in full-scale war or the actual loss of territory to be perceived as humiliating. Backing down in the face of aggression by others has also been the source of significant national humiliation as has the failure to protect one's citizens abroad. The same factors described above—degree of relative military advantage, the locus of crisis initiation, and even the duration of the crisis—also play a role here in determining how grave the resulting humiliation will be. The number of days Iranian college students held hostages during the Iranian Hostage Crisis, for instance, served as a measure of increasing humiliation felt by U.S. citizens and leaders alike.[42] In his call for action, the then national security adviser Zbigniew Brzezinski cited the need to consider "the deleterious effects of a protracted stalemate ... and the international humiliation of the U.S."[43]

Just days after America's humiliating military withdrawal in Somalia, President Bill Clinton ordered the retreat of the USS *Harlan County*, a navy vessel sent to pave the way for UN intervention in Haiti in 1993, in the face of violent protests and out of fear that the ship would be fired on. The event created a sense of humiliation both at home and abroad. Senator Tom Harkin described the feeling at the time, decrying "The mightiest nation on Earth, one that just beat Saddam Hussein, being faced down by a rag-tag element of no more than 100 drug traffickers ... and we tucked our tail and ran." UN secretary-general Boutros Boutros-Ghali was concerned by the damage of the "humiliation" brought about by the incoherence of U.S. policy.[44] Clinton was so outraged that he reportedly struggled to find the words to accurately describe the nature of the humiliation that he felt.[45]

President John Kennedy and his advisers appear to have experienced a similar sense of humiliation following the Bay of Pigs fiasco in 1961. The operation would come to be synonymous with failure. The United States had failed to impose its will on a small island nation of 7,000,000 inhabitants, leading one American general to describe it as the "greatest American defeat since the War of 1812." The experience reportedly left the president and his advisers "tired, frustrated and personally humiliated," as well as concerned about the implications of the debacle on the status of the United States.[46] Kennedy sought to avoid similar humiliation a year later when he acknowledged during EXComm discussions that the United States would suffer deep humiliation if the Soviets were allowed to place missiles in Cuba.[47]

In these instances, states failed to live up to the expectations of performance associated with their expected status and failed to accomplish the state's original goals. Failed attempts to protect one's citizens and failed interventions in the affairs of other states, and in particular much smaller and weaker states, demonstrate the limitations of a state's influence. As stated, influence is a measure of status. A failure to influence outcomes in situations that one has selected to play a role indicates that the state lacked either the resolve or the capabilities to follow through on its intended mission. In both cases, states which have made claims to great power status are subject to the potential downgrading of their standings in the eyes of others.

In summary, we should not expect all instances in which states fail to accomplish their political or military objectives to engender similar degrees of humiliation. We can expect four features of military failure—relative capabilities, the locus of initiation, the duration of the dispute, and territorial loss—to interact in ways that enable us to place events along a spectrum of humiliation. We would not expect losses like that of Germany in World War I after five years of fighting against a much stronger consolidated force to induce an intense sense of national humiliation.[48] By contrast, defeats like that of the Arab states in the First and Second Israel Wars in which the state or states with more military resources initiated a fight they quickly lost, also losing valued territory in the process, would be expected to humiliate a great deal.

International Disrespect

Just as we would not expect all instances of international failure to induce national humiliation to the same degree, we should also not expect all acts intended to convey disrespect of another state's interests, rights, and privileges to engender severe and motivating humiliation.[49] As stated, the depth of humiliation induced by a lack of recognition depends on the size of the discrepancy between how one expects to be treated and the treatment a state receives. The greatest disparity would, therefore, likely occur in the case that a state expecting the privileges associated with great power status is denied basic rights expected by all states, such as the right to possess an army, to dictate affairs within its own borders, or to govern its own airspace. While the denial of such rights would undoubtedly instill a sense of humiliation within lower status states, it would arguably do so to a lesser degree.

Beyond this fundamental basis, additional factors serve to exacerbate the degree of humiliation inflicted by a lack of recognition. First, humiliation does not require intentionality on the part of the disrespectful actor. A state need only assume that others' disrespectful acts were intended to signal its inferiority in order for humiliation to take root. In cases in which the intentionality of the disrespectful actor is undeniable or verified in some way, the extent of humiliation is often far more severe in large part because any plausible deniability that might have mitigated a sense of outrage and inefficacy has been removed. For example, French humiliation following the Franco-Prussian War was exacerbated by Bismarck's decision to proclaim a new German Empire and crown its new emperor in the Hall of Mirrors at the Palace of Versailles, an act that is hard to read as anything but a pointed signal of France's newfound inferiority and relative impotence. The verification of Eisenhower's intentions, as we will see in Chapter 6, also played an important role in exacerbating Soviet humiliation stemming from U.S. U2 flyovers through Soviet airspace in the 1960s.

The intensity of national humiliation also depends on another related factor: the perceived longevity of disrespect. Some acts of denial, such as the infringement of one's airspace, may be one-time events that could be explained away as unintentional. Isolated cases are likely to induce outrage, but are less likely to arouse a sense of impotence unless the act is perceived to represent a broader policy of denial. The prolonged or repeated denial of rights, by contrast, is more likely to be perceived as intentional and to engender a sense of inefficacy. The codification of inferiority within formalized treaties also serves to further inflame a sense of humiliation. For, as we will see below, treaties can create a permanent register of inequality that demonstrates to a world audience that a state was unable to shape its own fate. Unequal treaties are often perceived and are indeed often intended, to be punitive and aimed at highlighting the inferiority of the punished. As long as formalized inequality goes unchallenged, it serves as a constant reminder of a state's inferiority, often fueling persistent outrage and self-doubt over long periods.

Third, the level of publicity surrounding a disrespectful event affects the level of humiliation that follows. Because status is rooted in social perception, events that receive wide attention pose an intensified threat to the status of the state.[50] The more international attention a threat to one's status garners, the more likely common knowledge will evolve that the state is undeserving of the status and resulting influence it expects to hold. Citizens of the state will recognize that the state's inefficacy and potential inferiority have been highlighted on the world stage, augmenting their desire to prove to international observers and themselves that they do indeed deserve the high status they expect to hold.

Finally, acts of disrespect by states of equal or higher status are also on average more likely to induce a heightened sense of humiliation. Because self-concept is more deeply predicated on one's image in the eyes of equals superiors, higher status states have the ability to inflict the most significant blow to the esteem of others.[51] Moreover, only states of equal status can be accused of enforcing double standards by denying supposed equal privileges one has recently exercised. The signal that one is perceived as inferior tends to be seen as unjust and unfair and as a result induces significant outrage. It also serves as a reminder of a state's impotence until such time that it is able to directly challenge the state responsible for its humiliation, often through engagement in the prohibited act. Lower status states may engage in the denial of rights, though they will likely possess fewer capabilities to do so, than higher status states, but these acts of denial are less likely to induce a sense of impotence and inferiority unless they are repeated or to generate meaningful shifts in others' perceptions of the target's status.

This basic framework enables us to predict which instances of international disrespect are going to be humiliating and to what degree. We would expect one-time denial of rights by lower status states to engender humiliation to a far lesser extent than the permanent and codified denial of the rights and privileges of states that expect great power status treatment. Many post-war treaties in the pre–World War II era indeed fit the latter description to differing degrees. Among the most befitting examples of this is the Treaty of Versailles. Germany was forced to agree to permanent concessions that not only substantiated Germany's loss of great power privileges but also permanently robbed Germany of many rights associated with sovereign statehood. The German army was capped at 100,000 and the country was stripped of its colonies, the truest symbols of great power status at the time, as well as 25,000 additional square miles of German territory containing the contested provinces of Alsace and Lorraine. Perhaps the most humiliating was the War Guilt Clause, which forced Germany to assume full responsibility for the war. That Germany was forced to accept what it perceived to be patently untrue and to bear the shame and guilt the clause implied only emphasized the degree to which Germany had lost all influence in world affairs.[52]

Though British and American statesmen recognized the potentially humiliating consequences of overly exacting measures, they ultimately failed to avoid them.[53] The Germans perceived a clear punitive intent in the treaty. What other purpose could be served, the Germans questioned, by the War Guilt Clause or the complete exclusion of Germany from the League of Nations? Moreover, German statesmen were given no voice within the negotiation process. In German eyes, the treaty was unilaterally imposed by high status states seeking to permanently enforce German inferiority.

The emotional reaction among German elites and citizens to these "arbitrary dictates" was immediate. German statesmen sought to strongly protest the violation of German honor embodied in early drafts of the treaty. The sense of collective self-doubt and outrage evoked by the treaty within a large segment of the German population was broadly felt during the Weimar years.[54] These feelings reached their peak under Hitler, who deemed the institutionalization of the "permanent inequality" of Germany a "scandal and a disgrace." As he saw it, the treaty signaled that the rest of the world looked on Germany "only as its valet, or as a kindly dog that will lick its master's hand after he has been whipped."[55]

The Treaty of Shimonoseki in 1895, which formalized Japanese superiority over China at the end of the Sino-Japanese War and which was one in a line of repeated humiliations for China, foreshadowed both the tenets of the Treaty of Versailles and its emotional impact.[56] With its defeat and the post-war treaty, China was forced to accept a fate handed down by Japan, a country over which China had maintained dominance for centuries. China was forced to cede valuable Chinese ports and other territories including Taiwan, marking the end of 200 years of Qing dynasty rule over the island. China was stripped of all influence in Korea, traditionally a tributary state of the Qing Empire, and was forced to pay a war indemnity equal to three times the government's annual revenue.[57] Chiang Kai-Shek viewed China's defeat by Japan and the vastly unequal post-war treaty that followed to represent the most significant catastrophe within a long chronology of China's Century of Humiliation.[58] As in the German case, Japanese leaders failed to heed their own concerns about the humiliating effects of the treaty, instead taking highly symbolic territories, the loss of which continues to structure Chinese foreign policy in the contemporary period.[59]

As these examples suggest, humiliating post-war treaties may compound humiliation already aroused by unexpected defeat. In other cases, the unequal treaty itself may be the primary source of humiliation. Germany, for instance, had little cause for humiliation in its military performance in World War I. It had been defeated by three large and powerful states, two of which were at its borders. Hitler acknowledged this when suggesting that Germany's military defeat in 1918 had been self-induced and therefore deserved.[60] German leaders exited the war with the expectation that they would be afforded the basic post-war right of playing a role in Germany's fate, a right that they were ultimately denied. The Treaty of Paris imposed on Russia following the Crimean War represents a similar case. While Russians were not significantly humiliated by Russia's defeat at the hands of three powerful states, both Alexander Gorchakov, the Russian foreign minister, and the tsar viewed the post-war Treaty of Paris to be unequal and intentionally disrespectful of Russian rights as a sovereign state in part because it prohibited

Russia from building warships or erecting forts on its own territory along the Black Sea. Count Karl Nesselrode commented to the tsar in 1856 that the treaty itself represented the "diminution of Russian possessions and Russian prestige as a Great Power."[61] Russian elites believed more broadly that the treaty reflected the "instinctive hatred" of Russia by the West.[62]

It is also possible for treaties and international agreements to be deeply humiliating even when they do not follow war. For example, the Washington Conference of 1921, a conference aimed at minimizing a naval race in the Pacific, formalized a permanent inferior role for Japan vis-à-vis the United States and Britain. The United States' insistence on a tonnage displacement ratio between Japanese and American battleships of 6:10 represented to the Japanese a clear codification of superiority and a refusal to recognize the privileges that Japan expected as an emerging great power. That the unequal treaty was "dictated" proved to be an "unbearable humiliation" for Japan and its leader Hara Takashi, who, following the signing of the treaty, declared that "war with America" would start now and that revenge would be forthcoming.[63] Similarly, the Twenty-One Demands made by Japan of China in 1915 did not immediately follow a Japanese military victory but were accompanied by warnings of dire consequences if the Chinese were to reject them. The demands, deemed highly humiliating by the Chinese, robbed China of many rights associated with sovereignty and extended Japanese control over Manchuria as well as China's railways, ports, and raw materials. The treaty aroused significant humiliation within China and led to an upsurge in anti-Japanese protests.[64]

The instances of intensely humiliating treaties described above share similar features. All except for the 1921 Naval Conference codify the long-term denial of basic rights to states with great power expectations. The treaties were imposed, and the intention of their authors to formalize the inferiority of the disrespected state was difficult to deny. The features of these treaties can be contrasted to those of others that have induced national humiliation to a far lesser degree. The Potsdam Agreement at the end of World War II, for example, did not engender similar levels of national humiliation within Germany as the Treaty of Versailles, despite the fact that German leaders were tried and convicted in highly public hearings and German territory was temporarily occupied by Allied forces. What explains the difference in German reactions to the two post-war settlements? I argue that the perceived intention of the winners as well as the duration of the denial of rights and privileges account for their differential emotional effects. The impact of the Treaty of Versailles was almost omnipresent in the minds of the key Allied leaders responsible for designing the post–World War II settlement. Secretary of War Henry Stimson argued strongly at almost every turn that a punitive and vengeful approach like that of the Treaty of Versailles would only lead to long-term anger and repeated violence.[65]

These concerns led Allied leaders to intentionally pursue acts that would minimize the challenge to German status after 1945. Unlike the aftermath of World War I, when Germany was stripped of its colonies abroad and 20 percent of its territory at home, the territorial occupation of Germany after World War II was intended as temporary. Stimson and President Harry Truman, as well as numerous British leaders, sought to shift blame for wartime atrocities away from the German people and onto the German leaders who could be portrayed as having led their people astray. In doing so, allied leaders sought to avoid the implication that the German state was morally inferior and therefore deserving of lower status.[66] The decision about how many German leaders to try in court was constrained by concerns about spreading the blame around too broadly. The British argued that only ten Nazi leaders should be tried, the Soviets wanted more—they ultimately decided on twenty-four.

U.S. and British post-war policy toward Germany was based on the assumption that peace would best be preserved if Germany were a productive and wealthy democratic state that, most important, would be eventually integrated with other European states as an equal. This goal prompted the eventual push for the European Coal and Steel Commission, which ultimately treated its founding members as equal signatories. The Allies hoped that a sense of outrage, helplessness, and inferiority could be avoided by ensuring that Germany maintained a voice and influence in European affairs.

Long-term codified forms of disrespect are likely to be the most emotionally searing and to have the most extreme effects on the behavior of the disrespected state. Not all forms of disrespect exist, however, at this codified extreme. The repeated denial of a great power's basic rights, even if un-formalized, would also serve as a potent source of national humiliation that can have significantly destabilizing effects on the world affairs, though to a lesser and perhaps more temporary degree. According to the framework above, we would expect the repeated denial of the privileges of status to also induce humiliation, but again to a lesser degree. That the denial of great power privileges remains, however, a potent source of humiliation is evidenced by Russian reactions to Western efforts to minimize Russian influence within the ex-Soviet sphere through the expansion of NATO. Acts such as the unilateral American intervention within Serbia, a former client state of the Soviet Union, was perceived within Russia as an act intended to highlight Russian inferiority and undermine its image on the world stage. As will be discussed in the Conclusion, these perceived acts of disrespect by the West continue to affect Russian foreign policy in the contemporary era.

The forms of disrespect described here are not exhaustive. International disrespect can take many shapes, ranging from small diplomatic slights to the denial of basic rights. Each instance will, however, share one common feature.

The "victim" will receive a signal that suggests to them that another "humiliator" state views them as inferior and unworthy of the influence and deference they expect. The degree to which these signals are likely to induce lasting collective humiliation within a state depends on 1) the size of the discrepancy between status expectations and the extent of recognized rights and privileges a state receives, 2) the intentionality of the disrespectful state, 3) the longevity or persistence of the denial, 4) the level of attention the event receives, and 5) the status of the state engaging in disrespect. With these conditions in mind, and others likely at the margins, I argue that we can predict with relative accuracy the types of disrespectful events that are most likely to impact world affairs.

Variability in National Responses

The discussion so far has focused on establishing the conditions under which certain types of events are likely to engender the most extreme degrees of national humiliation. The discussion has primarily assumed that the same event is likely to evoke similar emotional reactions across all states. States may, however, differ in their emotional reactions to potentially humiliating acts.

A particularly important factor in explaining different reactions across states is whether a state has recently experienced a humiliating event or has already incorporated some notion of national humiliation within its national narrative. Such states, I argue, will be more sensitive to potential implications of their inferiority because they already possess a sense of powerlessness and are more likely to feel powerless, and therefore humiliated, in the face of another slight than they are to feel empowered and angry.[67] The perception of the state as a victim can exacerbate both collective outrage and the sense of impotence if the state does not respond with a vigorous defense of its status.[68] Recently humiliated states will often maintain a heightened sensitivity to status threat in the future and may, therefore, attribute negative intentions to states that others might not. Such was the case of the U.S. bombing of the Chinese embassy in Belgrade during the 1999 intervention in Yugoslavia. Though the U.S. leaders apologized for what they claimed was the accidental targeting of the embassy, a large majority of Chinese leaders and citizens believed the bombing had been intentional and perceived it as just another in a long line of humiliations that China has suffered at the hands of the West.[69]

It is also likely that culture plays a role both in shaping the degree to which states are likely to experience national humiliation in response to certain international events.[70] Numerous scholars have demonstrated that the concept of honor, defined as a person's value both in his own eyes and the eyes of others, is more central to some cultures than others.[71] Within states dominated by honor cultures, interactions are more likely to be interpreted as slights to one's honor, which in turn are more likely to lead to acts of violence as well as public expressions of anger, shame, and pride. Many have noted the central importance in China of "face," or *mien-tzu*—defined as "social status or prestige acquired by one's accomplishments."[72] Chinese society is defined by a hierarchical network of social relations, referred to as *guanxi*, in which position is often obtained by manipulating symbols of face.[73] Cultural variation in the value of concepts like social status and image would arguably closely correlate with the probability that states will perceive negative intentions in the acts of others and in turn experience national humiliation in response to the treatment of their state on the world stage.

It can be difficult to determine the direction of the relationship between culture and humiliation. Although it is likely that culture shapes reactions to humiliation, traumatic international events that challenge state identity can affect the culture of that state, leading to deeply ingrained societal narratives of national humiliation and increasing the likelihood that members of that state will perceive future international events to be humiliating. In some cases, it may be clear that culture has a primary independent effect on reactions to international events. U.S. missionaries to China, for instance, noted in the early 1800s, prior to Chinese humiliation at the hands of British forces, the extreme degree to which the Chinese appeared to care about their social status.[74] In other cases, international events appear to be a primary shaper of national culture, as was the case with a defeated France following the Franco-Prussian War.

The current status of the state also may affect the degree to which it experiences national humiliation.[75] Great powers arguably will be disproportionately subject to the effects of humiliation when they fail to achieve their foreign policy objectives or to project the domestic and economic strength that others would expect.[76] Great powers that are forced to make dramatic concessions will likely experience a far more severe threat to their identity and status than will lower status states which entered into the losing side of a conflict with far fewer rights and privileges to lose. This is in part because such events involving great powers are more likely to gain wider attention, but also because falling from higher status positions poses a greater challenge to self-concept than when starting from lower status positions.[77] Humiliating failures contradict the image of the state as an effective and influential actor in world affairs.[78] The expectations of state performance are proportional to the status of the state. Lower status states are less likely to expect to be influential or effective; international failure will not be in such stark contrast to the self-image of the state.

Domestic political processes can also play a role in shaping collective perceptions of the intentions of other states. Leaders may have little desire to focus on foreign policy failures that occur on their watch, but those in charge may benefit domestically from highlighting acts of disrespect by others. Such references can mobilize public sentiment in support of the regime's effort to defend the status of the state in the face of unjust humiliation by others. Strong candidates may also emerge after humiliating events that proffer more explicit narratives about the continued humiliation of the state and that promise to restore the state to its rightful position within the status hierarchy. Yet, I argue, elites cannot conjure a sense of national humiliation out of nothing. They have direct control over state responses to humiliation, and they often have control over the degree to which a narrative of national humiliation is passed down to future generations through institutionalized cultural and educational practices. The degree to which elite humiliation rhetoric comes to dominate national political narratives is dependent, however, on the degree to which such political messages resonate within a society which in turn is dependent on existing emotional currents within a society.

Finally, to speak of national humiliation and its effects is not to presume that all members of the state will be equivalently humiliated by the same event. As we will see in Chapter 3, not all individuals respond to potentially humiliating events affecting their states in the same way. Such events will have the most detrimental psychological effects on those citizens who most strongly identify with the state. Those who do not strongly identify with the state are more likely to be ashamed of the state than they are to experience other-directed outrage on the state's behalf. To discuss national responses to national humiliation is to only temporarily ignore this intrastate variation. As I will show, however, a significant degree of public consensus exists about the degree to which certain international events like defeat and the denial of rights are perceived to be humiliating.

Many events would seemingly fall within these broad categories of humiliating events described in this chapter, some of which would likely have only shallow and fleeting effects on the collective emotion, or foreign policy, of the state. It is the acute forms of national humiliation, however, those that become ingrained more deeply, that are of greatest interest to international relations scholars. This chapter has argued that the size of the discrepancy between expectations—about how a state should perform or about the rights and privileges a state should hold—and reality will correlate with the degree of induced humiliation. Beyond this basic relationship, numerous additional features can be used to predict the degree of humiliation a state will experience. The relative capability of one's victory, whether a state starts the war it loses, the duration of the fight and, significantly, whether a state loses territory can all exacerbate the sense of humiliation stemming from international failure. The duration, publicity, and persistence of disrespect as well as the intentions and relative status of the disrespectful actor can all serve to inflame the humiliation instilled by the denial of recognition.

Unexpected failure and the formalized denial of rights are, in many ways, very distinct types of international events. Yet they are alike in the emotional impact they can have on those who identify with the "victimized" state. They threaten the status of the state in ways that are perceived as unjust, and this sense of injustice evokes other-directed outrage. The state's inability to prevent the status threat sparks painful self-doubt about the authority and capabilities of the state. These events can also have significant negative instrumental repercussions for the humiliated state, which, as a result of the decline in its status, can lose international influence. As we will see in the next chapter, the desire to shore up the image of the state in its own eyes as well as the eyes of others can, under certain conditions, lead states to pursue more aggressive foreign policies and to engage in costly status-seeking measures they likely would not have otherwise. These status-seeking measures can have broad and significant effects on world order.

2
WITHDRAWAL, OPPOSITION, AND AGGRESSION

> **I think that what is called an "Act of Vigour" is required to soothe the wounded vanity of the nation. It does not much matter which of our numerous foes we defy but we ought to defy someone.**
> —British colonial secretary Joseph Chamberlain, 1895

> **Evils which are patiently endured when they seem inevitable become intolerable once the idea of escape from them is suggested.**
> —Alexis de Tocqueville

Prior accounts of humiliation's effects in international relations have focused almost exclusively on the relationship between humiliation and revenge.[1] This chapter argues, and empirical analysis in later chapters shows, that the effects of national humiliation on state behavior are not so straightforward. Not all states respond to humiliating events in the same ways. Some states pursue direct military revenge, whereas others may pursue symbols of high status or initiate conflict against third-party states. Humiliation may also conversely lead to withdrawal from the international stage within states that become constrained by the sense of powerlessness that humiliating events engender. This chapter first addresses why exactly humiliating events affect international behavior and then turns to discussing possible reactions to national humiliation, laying out the conditions under which we should expect humiliation to engender aggression.

Humiliation as a Motivation

Why do humiliating events motivate states to engage in assertive and aggressive acts they would not have otherwise? Psychologists have established that humiliation at the individual level increases aggression.[2] But why does it do so? Aggression by humiliated actors is motivated both by outrage and by the psychological desire to overcome the pain of helplessness.[3] Outrage can serve as a potent motivator of individual and collective behavior.[4] Outraged actors seek the psychological salve of righting wrongs and of asserting one's rights in the face of injustice. Humiliated actors also seek to overcome the sometimes-crippling sense of powerlessness and self-doubt that stems from being unable to defend oneself against an undeserved status threat.[5] To restore self-esteem and thereby assuage wounded vanity, humiliated actors seek opportunities to vigorously demonstrate their capabilities, influence, and efficacy on the international stage through acts that will bolster their image in the eyes of others and in the eyes of those who identify with the state.

This framework implies that the primary behavioral driver of humiliated states can change over time. Assertive acts taken in the immediate aftermath of a humiliating event are typically driven by a desire to re-instill a collective sense of efficacy among those who identify with the humiliated states as well as by a desire to enact justice. As the sense of efficacy within the state is restored through successful acts demonstrating the abilities and influence of the state, humiliated states may be increasingly motivated by outrage and the desire to push back against unfair treatment. Not all humiliating events will engender a sense of impotence and self-doubt to the same degree. One-time humiliating events that do not involve material loss may induce a far lesser sense of impotence than repeated humiliations or those that involve significant material losses, such as the loss of territory, military personnel, or economic wherewithal. When less impotence is initially aroused, we would expect outrage to be a more prominent driver of state behavior following a humiliating event than the desire to prove bolster self-esteem.

Evidence in this book illustrates the validity of these claims. As the epigraph to this chapter shows, Colonial Secretary Joseph Chamberlain expressed the need to "soothe the wounded vanity" of the British following Britain's defeat in a key raid during the South African War. The need to improve the image of the state in its own eyes was a key driver of state behavior among those that had experienced severe or repeated instances of humiliation. Such states seek to enhance their amour propre through actions that prove they have the capabilities, influence, and resolve to successfully assert themselves on the world stage. We will see that other states that experienced humiliating events that called the efficacy of the state into question to a lesser degree typically acted more quickly to assert their rights in the face of unjust constraints by others.

To focus on the psychological impact of status-challenging events is not to suggest that such events do not also motivate state behavior through their broader instrumental repercussions. Because high-status actors are accorded greater deference by others, events that threaten the status of the state in the eyes of others also threaten the degree of influence the state holds. Leaders have indeed expressed concern about the instrumental effects of humiliating events, as Russian foreign minister Karl Nesselrode did when blaming the 1856 Treaty of Paris for leaving Russia "belittled in the eyes of public opinion and weakened in its political capacity."[6] Humiliated states have an instrumental incentive to engage in status-seeking actions that promise to bolster their status in the eyes of others in order to shore up their existing influence.[7] They also have an incentive to prevent further erosion of their status by engaging in costly aggression directed at the state who disrespected them, not out of a desire to punish, but to demonstrate the costs that other states will pay if they engage in disrespectful acts.[8]

While this book focuses on the psychological motives that play a crucial role in shaping the behavior of states that have experienced an undeserved threat to their status, demonstrating the relative import of psychological and instrumental factors is difficult to do. Indeed, the effort to distinguish their relative impact may be futile.[9] It is unlikely that a single humiliating event will sufficiently threaten the status of the state without also engendering a negative emotional reaction to status decline. Conversely, for states to experience collective humiliation, they must experience an event that they believe threatens the status of the state and therefore is likely to have negative instrumental repercussions. The emotional and instrumental repercussions of status-threatening events are therefore arguably impossible to disentangle.[10]

This discussion of why humiliation motivates state behavior also sheds light on how long we should expect national humiliation to last and when we should expect its effects to dissipate. Numerous features of humiliation foster its longevity. First, scholars have shown that it is difficult to remember humiliating events without again experiencing humiliation's painful physiological effects, even long into the future.[11] Second, humiliation increases sensitivity to slights, thereby fueling its existence. But humiliation does not permanently motivate behavior once it has been evoked. For humiliation to dissipate, it is necessary for self-doubt about the efficacy of the group to pass or for other-directed outrage to be assuaged. The collective confidence of the state can increase when states successfully engage in actions intended to assert and defend their interests in world affairs. The extent of assertive actions required to increase the positive identity of the state is dependent on the extent of the original humiliation.

Reactions to Humiliating Events

Humiliation has been labeled one of the most powerful motivators of collective human behavior.[12] But what behaviors does it lead states to engage in? Drawing on existing work in social psychology and status in international relations, this section describes five broad potential policies that humiliated states may be more likely to adopt than states that haven't recently experienced a humiliating event.

First, humiliated states may not engage in reassertions of status at all but may instead engage in increasing avoidance and passivity in the face of repeated status threats. Social psychologists Jeremy Ginges and Scott Atran demonstrate the existence of this somewhat counterintuitive response to status-threatening events, which they label the "inertia effect," within the Palestinian population. The more humiliated Palestinian respondents reportedly felt in response to events that threatened the status of the Palestinian people, the less likely they were to support violent policies against Israel.[13] It is important to note that this decrease in support for political violence is not synonymous with increased support for cooperation since in-group humiliation also correlated with decreased support for acts aimed at intergroup compromise and conflict resolution. This avoidant reaction is logically motivated by an extreme sense of powerlessness evoked by repeated acts of disrespect or failure and by the decline in material capabilities and political stability that often accompanies humiliating events.

In some cases, this avoidant reaction will be temporary. Some states are able to turn their attention inward in order to restore a minimal sense of efficacy and confidence through the recovery of national capabilities and the restoration of domestic stability.[14] Humiliated states frequently engage in extensive domestic restructuring, often imitating the political, economic, and military policies and institutions of the "victor" state in hopes of minimizing the status gap and to prepare for the reassertion of the state on the world stage.[15] Some states are, however, unable to successfully restore their material capabilities or, as a result, the collective confidence of the state. For these states, withdrawal from the international stage is likely to be more permanent, weighted with a lingering sense of inefficacy eventually combined with downgraded status expectations.

Second, states seeking to bolster the image of the state in the eyes of its people and the eyes of others following a humiliating event may engage in diplomatic practices aimed at displaying collective outrage and at publicly opposing the interests of other states seen to have been responsible for one's humiliation. The display of collective anger plays a role in shaping others' impressions of how the humiliated state will behave and contributes to a heightened sense of authority and efficacy within those who identify with the humiliated state.[16] Provocative diplomatic policies may take a variety of forms. Humiliated states may demand an apology from the victor. Although apologies may promote reconciliation between previously warring states, the public demand for an apology is also an attempt to force another state to publicly take responsibility for an unjust act and to recognize the equal status of the victim.[17] The demand for an apology, even if unmet, can boost self-esteem and restore the image of the disrespected state.[18]

Humiliated states may also engage in the diplomatic opposition of the policies of their "humiliator" on the world stage in hopes of undermining perceptions of the victor's influence in the eyes of others and increasing the domestic sense of efficacy and esteem within their state.[19] Larson and Shevchenko show, for instance, that Russia diplomatically opposed U.S. interventions in the Balkans and Iraq following the humiliating demise of the Soviet Union with the intention of highlighting not only the limitations of U.S. influence but also the extent of Russian influence on the world stage, with Russia playing the role of informal leader of an oppositional coalition.[20] Humiliated states may also engage in diplomatic opposition by choosing to ally with and support a victor's rivals. Such counter alliances serve to publicly portray the humiliated state as an equal counterforce to the victor with the expectation that such acts will bolster state confidence and enhance the state's image in the eyes of others. Though acts of diplomatic opposition do not involve acts of direct military conflict, they can have significant effects on international alliances and the stability of the international system.

Third, humiliated states seeking to bolster their status and self-concept may also engage in material practices intended to signal a state's technological and organizational capacity as well as the state's status expectations. Material practices involve the acquisition of goods that have come to symbolize high status in the hope of being admitted to a high status club.[21] At different points in history, dreadnought battleships, nuclear weapons, aircraft carriers, space programs, and colonial empires have all been pursued by states because of their symbolism of great power status, even when their acquisition came at significant material or strategic costs.[22] The successful pursuit of these goods can engender national pride in the state's capabilities, thereby improving collective morale within the state. It can also demonstrate to others that the state deserves and expects high status.

Symbols of high status are determined by their exclusivity.[23] As the number of states possessing a symbol grows, the less symbolic of high status the good becomes, leaving those states seeking to distinguish themselves in search of new exclusive goods. Material practices may also entail competitions to determine preeminence within the high status club, as defined by which state has more of a symbolic good. As we will see, this was the case between Britain and France toward the end of the nineteenth century as they competed over who could possess more colonial holdings within Africa. It was also the case between the United States and the Soviet Union as the two states competed over the possession of the largest nuclear arsenal. In these cases, exclusivity was limited by the fact that only one could claim to possess the most.[24]

Fourth, humiliated states in search of ways to alter others' perceptions of them can choose to engage in more aggressive and provocative acts aimed not at the state responsible for their humiliation, but at third-party states that were not involved in the original humiliating event. A state pursuing a strategy of third-party aggression may engage in highly visible displays aimed at demonstrating its competence and intention to pursue an independent, expansive foreign policy as would befit a state of its desired status. Throughout much of history, such acts often took the form of imperial expansion abroad. The acquisition of colonies allowed states to demonstrate their ability to project power abroad and their expectations that they should have influence in far-flung regions of the world. In the contemporary era, in which colonies are no longer normatively acceptable, similar displays of power against third parties are more likely to assume the form of temporary military intervention.

Finally, states may be motivated to engage in acts of direct military revenge against the state they deem responsible for their humiliation. This response to humiliating events has received significant attention within prior studies of humiliation and its effects on international behavior.[25] Revenge, if successful, arguably offers the best path to renewed status and self-concept. Attempts at military revenge also, however, come with significant risks as further military failure could solidify the perception of the state's decline in the eyes of others and could have a lasting detrimental impact on how members of the state see themselves. For this reason, states willing to pursue a strategy of revenge must be willing to accept the significant risk of seeking revenge and failing.

As this discussion suggests, each of these policies can be expected to offer some degree of psychological solace as well as the promise of heightened status in the eyes of others, though to varying degrees. Transforming domestic institutions and imitating the value and norms of higher status states, for instance, can lead to moderate status gains, as higher status states come to view the status-seeker as more similar and admirable. It may also mildly improve collective pride and confidence in the state that has now come to look more like higher status states. Such acts of imitation do not force the eye of others; they do not publicly demand rights and privileges in the way that more assertive and provocative strategies do. Imitation therefore is likely to provide lower status gains than would, for example, successful interventions abroad. Moreover, unless a state is willing to also imitate the cultural and normative characteristics of high status states, strategies of imitation are not likely to lead to sustained status gains.[26]

Diplomatic victories and the successful pursuit of status goods promise to raise esteem and pride in one's state as well as the image of the state in the eyes of others, though also to a lesser degree than the successful use of force abroad. Research has shown that generally engaging in prideful or self-confident acts raises the esteem and social assertiveness of actors.[27] Adolf Hitler explicitly noted the positive effect that large-scale domestic projects can have on the esteem of a humiliated state's citizens, noting that such acts make a state's people feel that they are "the complete equals of every other nation."[28] Moreover, the acquisition of particular symbols of status, such as nuclear weapons or colonies, can gain the state a seat at the table with other high status states.[29]

Third-party aggression also offers the psychological benefit of ameliorating collective self-doubt. At the state level, successful military ventures and displays of power, even if directed against third-party states, typically provide a large boost to citizen's opinions about the state and their leaders as citizens gain a sense of authority and efficacy.[30] In seeking an opportunity to boost morale and confidence following the United States' unexpected defeat in Vietnam more than a decade earlier, Ronald Reagan, for instance, opted to intervene on the small island of Grenada, believing that there the United States would be able to "purge itself" of its lingering self-doubt. Success in Grenada, Reagan remarked afterward, "mark[ed] a turning point." "Our days of weakness are over," he proclaimed. "Our military forces are back on their feet and standing tall."[31] Through its intervention in Grenada, the United States—in Reagan's view had begun to fully regain its confidence while also demonstrating to other states that it would once again be assuming the role of a great power by establishing its will abroad at the expense of weaker, third-party state.[32]

The notion that psychological benefits can be gained from targeting third-party actors following humiliating events is not new. This pattern of redirected aggression is so prevalent among vertebrate species as to have been deemed "a near-universal tendency" by biologists.[33] Researchers have found evidence that aggression redirected toward third parties is associated with reductions in the psychological strain engendered by humiliating events.[34] As one biologist put it, such aggression seems intended to signal that a humiliated actor "may be down, but not out."[35]

Third-party aggression promises to boost the state's image in the eyes of others. Because status resides in social perceptions, states seeking to shore up their image in the eyes of others can engage in highly visible actions that befit and define their desired international strata. In successfully doing so, the humiliated state establishes common knowledge that it meets the qualifications of high status, that it currently possesses sufficient international influence to pursue an expansive and aggressive policy without being stymied by other high status states, and that it intends to maintain high status.[36] If others allow the state to exercise the prerogatives associated with its desired status, this serves as a signal that others must perceive the state as deserving of high status. In this way, highly visible status-reasserting acts can shape higher order beliefs about a state's status and generate common knowledge that the state is not in decline but rather is an important player on the world stage.[37]

It is also possible that assertive acts involving the use of force will be judged unwarranted and normatively unacceptable within the contemporary international order and will fail to bolster the state's image and status in the eyes of others.[38] Even if, however, states fail to bolster their image in others' eyes through aggressive status-seeking acts, these acts invariably promise the emotional satisfaction that comes from successful assertions of state identity, capabilities, and status expectations on the world stage. In that the redressing of negative psychological states can be an end in itself, the process of asserting one's interests and capabilities may be more important than the foreign policy result it achieves.[39]

Finally, the restoration of justice by punishing those responsible for the undeserved threat to status arguably offers the greatest improvements to the self-image of the state and the greatest boost to the perception of the state in the eyes of others.[40] Successful military revenge in cases in which humiliation stems from defeat most clearly demonstrates that the initial failure was an improbable fluke, thus shoring up any doubts about the state's efficacy and rightful position. The costs of failed attempts at revenge can be high, for failure to successfully seek revenge provides the greatest confirmation that the initial humiliating event was not a statistical improbability. The potential status gains that a strategy might provide and the risks it poses are directly proportional. Humiliated states must individually weigh this tradeoff when choosing how to respond to humiliating events.

Before moving on, it is important to note that the foreign policy of humiliated states can, in addition to the direct effects described above, be affected by humiliating events in more indirect ways. The outrage conjured by humiliating events often fosters a deep mistrust of those who are blamed for one's humiliation.[41] Trust is the willingness to "place the fate of one's interests under the control of others."[42] Because those responsible for one's past humiliation are perceived to have treated one unjustly, humiliated actors will be inclined in the future to perceive that "humiliators" will continue to act in ways that undermine their best interest. This degree of mistrust tends to be proportional to the original extent and intent of the perceived humiliation. Once mistrust has become ingrained, it can be difficult to shake. If you believe that an actor has intentionally subjected you to injustice in the past, you will be more likely to erroneously attribute ill intent to their future actions and to perceive broader conspiracies aimed at undermining your image and self-respect.[43]

A state of mistrust between international actors can have numerous important implications. The potential for cooperation between states declines with trust just as the potential for conflict increases.[44] Mistrust also augments concerns about relative gains, which typically arise when a state believes that a partner will use gains obtained through cooperation to increase its relative military advantage.⁴⁵ Attribution errors rooted in mistrust also increase the probability of international crises. Humiliated states often respond to actions by the humiliator state in ways that appear to be disproportional to the event simply because they are more likely to ascribe intentionality. These disproportional reactions, often expressed through public anger and demands for apology or recognition of equality, are often misperceived by victor states as unprovoked threats to state security to which they often respond with greater obstinacy and aggression. A dynamic of unusual escalation often persists between humiliator and victim states long after the original humiliating event.⁴⁶

Hypotheses about Strategy Selection

The policies described above are distributed along a spectrum of assertiveness, with avoidance at one end and initiation of war at the other. This section outlines a set of conditions under which states are more or less likely to engage in aggression in their quest to overcome humiliation and when these aggressive acts are most likely to target the state responsible for their humiliation. National recovery, the capabilities of the humiliated state vis-à-vis its victor, and the status of the humiliated state each play a central role in defining how states will behave in the aftermath of a humiliating event.

Because humiliation is engendered by status threats that are perceived as undeserved, few states will accept a downgrade of their status after a single, or even sometimes after numerous, humiliating events. They will instead maintain an interest in redressing the psychological burdens associated with humiliation through the reassertion of their status on the world stage. This basic theoretical framework provides a basis for the primary and most general prediction in this book:

> *H1: States that have recently experienced a humiliating event will be more likely on average to engage in assertive and aggressive behaviors in the years after the event than will those states that have not.*

These behaviors include the status-seeking strategies described above, including acts of diplomatic opposition, the acquisition of material symbols of status, and the initiation of conflict and use of force. States need not select only one of these strategies. They may engage in several simultaneously or they may have varied reactions as time passes after a humiliating event. Humiliated states will engage in one or a set of these acts in large part because of the psychological solace they provide and because they promise to bolster the image of the state in the eyes of others.

This general prediction, however, masks distinctions within the behavior of humiliated states and the timing of their responses to humiliating events. As described, some states initially become avoidant while others are motivated by humiliating events to engage in acts of aggression immediately afterward. When and how should we expect states to respond in the years following a humiliating event? The answers to both questions depend significantly on the degree to which the humiliated state manages to overcome political instability and recover from an economic and military decline caused by the humiliating events. Events like defeat, territorial loss, or backing down often result in the loss of economic or military resources or personnel. In the wake of the Franco-Prussian War, for instance, France faced the incapacitation of roughly 30 percent of its fighting forces.[47] Russia lost roughly 60 percent of its army in the fray of the Crimean War. Such events often give rise to significant political instability and unrest within the humiliated state as the leaders seen to be responsible for allowing the humiliation are challenged by other elites or are forcefully removed from office. The lack of political order and stability and material capacities can seriously constrain states in their desire to reassert their status in the immediate aftermath of humiliating events. This provides the basis for two complementary predictions:

> H2a: *Humiliated states that recover from material and political losses incurred during the humiliating event will be more likely to engage in assertive status-seeking acts than humiliated states that do not and than states that have not recently been humiliated.*
> H2b: *Humiliated states that suffer sufficiently severe losses from which they have not recovered will adopt more avoidant strategies than states that have not recently experienced a humiliating event*

Political stability and material recovery are essential in shaping the behavior of humiliated states because they better facilitate the successful pursuit of aggressive international policies. Recovery in these two arenas is also influential because of its relationship to national confidence and collective morale within the state. Humiliating events, by definition, instill a sense of self-doubt about state efficacy. Military theorist Carl von Clausewitz noted as such in 1812 when speaking of the "the shameful blot of cowardly submission [that] can never be erased"—a decline in morale following international failure, which constrains the will and resolve of the people to engage in aggressive actions abroad. Clausewitz likened submissive defeat to a "drop of poison in the blood of a nation . . . passed on to posterity . . . crippling and eroding the strength of future generations."[48] Hitler similarly noted in 1939 the long-term detrimental effects that defeat can have on the morale and esteem of the defeated people, observing that Germans had not been able to restore their national honor in the years after World War I because "they lacked those energies which spring from the instinct of national preservation and the will to hold on to one's own."[49]

For Clausewitz, the impetus for national resurgence laid within the humiliation itself. "The loss of liberty after a sanguinary and honourable struggle assures the resurgence of the nation," he argued, "and is the vital nucleus from which one day a new tree can draw firm roots."[50] For Hitler, however, national resurgence following defeat was predicated on the restoration of material strength at home, for only once Germany "restored [its] national strength" would the German people have the confidence to "face the outside world." Only at that point would the German people be able to experience the pride felt only by those who "know the greatness of [their] nation."

States seeking to reassert themselves on the world stage can therefore be stymied both physically and psychologically by the effects of material and political decline following a humiliating event. Decline can exacerbate the threats to self-concept already engendered by the humiliating event itself as well as the existing doubts about the state's ability to successfully pursue its interests.

States that have experienced repeated or extreme humiliation will also be more likely to respond with increased avoidance and passivity in the years following the vent.[51] States for whom material and political decline do not accompany humiliation should be expected to respond immediately to humiliating events with more assertive status-seeking acts. Similarly, those states that manage to reestablish political stability and place military and economic indicators along an upward trajectory will, in turn, restore some sense of collective efficacy and esteem that primes them to reemerge as assertive forces in international affairs. To be clear, domestic recovery alone cannot completely assuage self-doubt or a sense of national humiliation. It represents only the first stage in the movement toward more positive identity within the state. The second stage occurs when the humiliated state successfully returns to the world stage to demonstrate to itself and others that it is worthy of high status.

It is important to note that while elements of domestic recovery essentially precede international assertions of capabilities and status, it is also possible for strong leaders to shape collective beliefs about the efficacy of the state using rhetorical devices aimed at arousing anger and outrage toward the state or states deemed responsible for national humiliation. "Humiliation entrepreneurs" like Hitler can deliberately activate and manipulate feelings of national humiliation to coalesce and mobilize citizens to engage in aggressive actions against one's humiliator. Humiliating international events indeed provide perfect fodder for leaders to generate a stronger sense of national identity and national competence in the face of unjust and belittling others. Yet, I argue, even these strong leaders will be constrained by beliefs about the ability of the state to act successfully and by the desire to avoid repeated humiliating events. The legitimacy of such leaders is perhaps predicated on successful assertions of will on the world stage to an even higher degree than that of other leaders.

The prediction that humiliated states will wait to engage in more aggressive assertions of their status until they have sufficiently recovered their material wherewithal highlights another important feature of national humiliation's effects. Contrary to the common view that emotionality fosters irrationality and reactivity, humiliation does not necessarily lead to haste. Humiliated states often pursue cautious, deliberate, and rational foreign policies in their efforts to shape social perception. They prioritize foreign policy success and seek to avoid further blows to status and esteem. On the face of it, this prediction seems to go against the prediction of prospect theory that states in the realm of status loss act in haste and with greater acceptance of risk. The definition of humiliation illustrates why there is little contradiction. Humiliation involves a perception of injustice. Humiliated states are loath to accept that they are in the realm of status loss but will instead adopt caution to ensure that they do not end up there through repeated failure. One failure on the world stage can be written off as a fluke, whereas multiple failures rapidly start to substantiate a pattern of inefficacy with the increasing potential to undermine social perceptions of the state and decrease the group's ability to plausibly blame others for perceived unjust threats to their status. Humiliated states will vie to reaffirm their status, but only once they believe they can accomplish success.

Such success on the international stage is essential if humiliated states are to bolster the sense of efficacy and authority they so desire. This is not to say that we should expect all attempts at the reassertion of status using force to end in victory or all strategies aimed at diplomatic opposition to successfully obstruct others' policies. It is to say that humiliated states will prioritize victory and success more than non-humiliated states, as they seek to avoid at all costs to avoid confirming others' suspicions of their decline. This leads to an additional observable implication of the theory:

> H3: *States that have recently experienced a humiliating event will be more likely to achieve favorable outcomes within subsequent aggressive actions than will states that have not recently experienced a humiliating event.*

The need for success in the aftermath of humiliating events will trump even the most successful national recovery efforts. Even those states that manage to reestablish political stability and recover from material losses will refrain from risking further humiliation. Those states that never suffered material losses in the first place will be similarly constrained by the desire to convincingly demonstrate the abilities and intentions of the state in ways that bolster collective esteem.

To ensure that they will be able to succeed in their subsequent attempts to further bolster their esteem and image on the world stage, humiliated states will be willing to wait, largely avoiding international dealings while focusing efforts on internal rebuilding. As stated, rebuilding often involves a massive and time-consuming restructuring of institutions. Such was the case in post-war Russia after the country's substantial losses during the Crimean War. In 1857, Tsar Alexander II wrote to a friend of the "absolute need to diminish, at any cost, our expenses and even restrain our military operations for a year or two" because of the deplorable effects the war had had on Russian finances.[52] Future war, the tsar wrote, was inevitable if Russia was to regain its status, but success in the war would require adequate preparation. Until then, the tsar announced, Russia would "wait for [its] time to come."[53] During its period of retrenchment, the size of the Russian military was cut in half and the country's financial and educational systems underwent massive modernization programs seen to best enable Russia to catch up with the industrial capacity of its European rivals.

As we will see, the caution and patience evidenced by the tsar broadly characterize the behavior of humiliated states. The strategy of patient retrenchment following humiliating events has been shown to provide the best path to what it is that humiliated states seek—renewed status. MacDonald and Parent show that states that temporarily retrench following defeat are far more likely to eventually regain their military capabilities and status than are those states that go down fighting.[54] States that fail to shore up their capabilities before reentering the world stage are far less likely to ever return to their original position.

The discussion so far has focused on recovery as a feature that distinguishes humiliated states that engage in the most aggressive actions. But at what type of target will these aggressive actions be aimed? I argue that the status of the humiliated state will influence whether the state targets the state responsible for its humiliation or goes after third-party states. Models of conflict have repeatedly shown that states are most likely to fight states with whom they share a border. Great powers, however, have typically been defined as those states that can project power far beyond their borders. Humiliated lower status states possess fewer means by which to mollify the corrosive sense of inferiority and to channel the empowering sense of other-directed outrage engendered by humiliating events. By definition, then, we should expect humiliated great powers to target their aggression against third-party states with greater frequency than humiliated lower status states. By targeting third parties, humiliated great powers can demonstrate the efficacy of the state in ways that bolster collective confidence. The targeting of weaker, third-party states is perhaps more likely to achieve success, enabling great powers to accomplish this fundamental goal of re-instilling a sense of efficacy and authority.

This is not to imply that humiliated great powers will never engage in revenge. The likelihood that they do so, however, will depend on another important determinant of state responses to humiliation—the state's capabilities, primarily military in nature, relative to the capabilities of the state deemed responsible for its humiliation. High status states that are thought to have an extremely large military advantage against a humiliator will be far more likely to engage in revenge than will states with moderate or lesser advantages. This logic gives rise to the following prediction:

> H4: *Humiliated great powers that do not have a significant power advantage vis-à-vis their humiliator will be more likely to engage in demonstrations of power against weaker, third-party states than humiliated great powers that possess equal or greater strength than their humiliator.*

By extension, we should expect humiliated great powers to target weaker states on average than non-humiliated great powers who may are less likely to prioritize success within a dispute.

A few additional factors further condition our expectations of how exactly states are likely to behave in the period following a humiliating event. First, though we have defined a general condition for the increased assertiveness of humiliated states, we should also expect a sense of proportionality to constrain aggressive responses to humiliating events. Smaller instances of disrespect or failure pose less threat to the status of the state and therefore pose weaker emotional and instrumental challenges. Acts of disrespect in which states ignore the rights or requests of others are, for instance, unlikely to generate demands for military revenge, unless they are seen to be part of a more systematic effort to humiliate the state.

Second, though international failure and one's disrespectful treatment by others both engender a sense of humiliation, we should expect the precise source of humiliation to play some role in shaping how the state will respond. The humiliating loss of homeland territory, for instance, will induce self-doubt that will best be overcome through the forceful acquisition of territory. The significant self-doubt instilled by military failure is likely to be alleviated only through subsequent success on the battlefield. States will best be able to overcome the self-doubt associated with the denial of expected rights or privileges by successfully engaging in the exact behavior that other states have attempted to prohibit. States who are denied recognition of what they believe is their right to acquire symbols of high status will best demonstrate their efficacy in the face of this status threat through the acquisition of said symbols. In short, we should expect the following:

> H5: States are more likely to respond to humiliating events by engaging in assertive actions related to the nature of their humiliation and self-doubt rather than by selecting a completely distinct assertive act.

As predicted above, states will be unlikely to engage in this sort of historical reenactment or fulfillment until they are highly confident in their ability to succeed the second time around. They will remain cautious, attempting to retake lost territory only when they are certain they can do so successfully. In the meantime, they may seek to demonstrate their efficacy through similar, but less aggressive or less destabilizing means.

The Systemic Effects of Status Seeking

This chapter has so far focused on how humiliating events affect states that have recently experienced a humiliating event. These effects do not occur in isolation. Status-seeking acts engendered by humiliating events can have broad and systematic effects on the behavior of other states that may not have been originally involved in the original humiliation. Because status is a constant sum good, strategies aimed at increasing the status of one state can lead to a decline in the status and influence of others. Status assertions by one state can increase the incentives of others to match these status investments even when such investments come at a cost to their immediate interests. Such patterns of investment can develop into international races for status in which added status is assigned to the state which acquires the highest amount of the good. The degree to which a participant in an international race values the good that serves as the focal point of the race depends on the amount the participant perceives that others value the good and not on the inherent value that the state itself assigns the good.

Not all cases of status investment, however, spawn an international race for status. Under what conditions are they most likely to occur? First, it is important to note that because status is rooted in social perception and second-order beliefs, states need not experience an actual decline in their status to believe that reciprocal investments in status are necessary to avoid demotion. They need only perceive that others perceive the status hierarchy to be in flux because of others' status investments.

Second, while status competitions are the constant sum, all investments do not increase a state's incentive to invest in its status by an equal amount. Whether the status investments of humiliated states lead others to match those investments depends on the relative status of the investing state. A state has little incentive to match another state's investment unless the state is convinced that the investment could result in its demotion. Such a challenge is unlikely to come from those with significantly less status but instead from states with proximate but slightly lower status. The closer an investing state's position within the social hierarchy, the more incentive a state will have to match its investment.

Third, the likelihood that a state will join a competition for status also increases with the number of other participants in the competition as the state becomes increasingly fearful of being left behind and demoted out of the great power club. Fourth, a successful challenge depends on the creation of common knowledge that the objective of the bid is to increase the investing state's status. This requires not only that each individual state perceives the investment as a bid for status but also that these states perceive that other states also believe this to be true. What represents high status depends on the way in which members of a social grouping define admirable characteristics. It is this element of social construction that differentiates status from other common motivations in international politics

Finally, not all types of status investments threaten to equally challenge the status of others. Perceptions of status threat may be especially pronounced in the case of material strategies aimed at demonstrating that a state has sufficient capabilities and wherewithal to obtain symbols associated with high status. Such material practices are unique in that they are often highly public, and because success and failure in the attempt to obtain symbols of status can be clearly distinguished.[55] The acquisition of new colonies by a humiliated state, for instance, is highly visible to all. States often match investments in these material practices for fear that, if they do not, public acquisitions by others will shape common knowledge in a way that erodes their social position.

International races for status are not rare or peripheral to international affairs. As we will see, the Scramble for Africa, an event that oversaw the conquest or annexation of over 95 percent of the African continent, was an international race for status. Britain, Germany, Italy, and France conquered vast swathes of African territory despite acknowledging the costs of acquiring and maintaining African colonies. They did so in an effort to acquire the prestige associated with being able to easily conquer and hold land abroad. As the Scramble wore on, the pace of conquest became feverish, as conquests by one country spurred further conquests by others. The competition became less about gaining prestige through single acts of territorial occupation and more about gaining the status associated with possessing the largest amount of African territory.

We will also see that the dramatic buildup of strategic arsenals during the middle of the Cold War at the end of the 1960s was in part an international race for status. Both the United States and the Soviet Union recognized the limited utility of adding weapons to their already substantial arsenals while continuing to pursue strategic parity with the other despite the costs. The Soviets originally engaged in a buildup of their arsenal to match the status of the United States following the Cuban Missile Crisis. The United States responded not because it found inherent value in acquiring additional weapons, but because its leaders perceived that the Soviets and other states believed that the state with the largest arsenal had the highest status. The degree of concern the United States applied to matching Soviet arsenal sizes was driven not by U.S. military interests but by beliefs about what competitors perceived to be of interest.

Distinctions from Alternative Models of Conflict

This chapter has laid out specific behavioral implications of humiliating events. The theory predicts that although national humiliation is not deterministic in its effects, it does result in an overall increase in the probability that states engage in status-seeking acts, many of which include the use of aggression or actions that threaten to destabilize the international system. The greater the level of recovery within the state, the more assertive the state will be in its attempts to shore up its status. The relative capabilities of the state vis-à-vis the humiliator determine the state's likely target in any acts of post-humiliation aggression. On the face of it, such predictions seem to coincide with those of standard realist and rationalist theories of state behavior. Closer examination, however, reveals that the behavioral predictions generated by the theory of humiliation above differ in important ways from previous models.

First, in contrast to realist theories, the model predicts that leaders of humiliated states will prioritize the desire to affect social perception, both within and outside of the state, over their immediate and long-term material and strategic objectives. Each of the foreign policy actions described above—strategies of diplomatic opposition, the acquisition of status symbols, and the use of force abroad—can serve rationalist or realist objectives aimed at augmenting the security and material resources of the state. Such acts do not, however, always do so. The use of force against third-party states, for instance, can come at the expense of more immediate security goals against rival competitors. I argue that humiliated states will often be willing to pay such costs in their quest to reestablish their social position in the eyes of others and to restore collective confidence in the abilities of the state.

Second, realist models are generally unclear about how we should expect states to behave in the wake of international failures like defeat. These models would expect defeated states to maintain a commitment to the material and security objectives they failed to accomplish within the first unsuccessful conflict. In many cases, revanchism would offer the best or only path to meeting those failed security objectives, as would be the case with the desire to occupy territory with unique strategic importance. In other cases, it may be possible for states to achieve their objectives through the targeting of weaker, third-party states if these target states offer the same material resources and advantages as the state responsible for the original humiliation. In general, however, realist theory gives us little reason to expect states to systematically engage in third-party aggression or to expect states to engage in this aggression when it comes at a broader cost to the security of the state.

This alludes to other important unique behavioral predictions of the model above. The model predicts that humiliated states will generally prize success more than non-humiliated states and that this desire for favorable outcomes will lead them to target states with fewer relative capabilities than would non-humiliated states. The tenets of realism provide little in the way of explanation of these particular behaviors, which fit squarely into a theoretical framework in which state actions are aimed at building confidence within the state.

Third, offensive realism predicts that states will become more aggressive as their relative military capabilities increase unless they achieve hegemony.[56] Similarly, power transition theory predicts that rising states will be more likely to engage in aggression as their relative capabilities grow vis-à-vis the dominant state.[57] But the historical record clearly indicates that not all rising states engage in aggressive acts. Moreover, those that have sufficient capabilities do not always engage in aggression to the same degree or in the same ways. Past humiliating events help explain significant variation in the levels of aggression exhibited by rising states. Humiliating events provide strong motivation for aggressive acts, even long into the future, as states seek to reestablish their confidence and their standing. Increased capabilities merely endow humiliated states with sufficient confidence that they are prepared to successfully reassert themselves on the world stage.

Finally, the theory above predicts that the timing and nature of state actions following humiliating events will significantly depend on the material capabilities of the state relative to its prior capabilities and much less so on the changing nature of the state's relative capabilities vis-à-vis other states. Material and political recovery within the state augments the likelihood of state success in subsequent conflicts while bolstering confidence and morale. Accruing a material and military advantage over others can serve as a source of enhanced confidence, but this factor is not overriding. National recovery can prime humiliated states to act assertively even if others' capabilities also simultaneously increase, rendering the balance of power largely unchanged. Conversely, the nature of humiliation implies that state confidence can decline even when the state's material capacities remain largely unchanged. The collective doubt that formed within the United States following the country's retreat from Vietnam or after the Iran Hostage Crisis serves as evidence of this fact. Thus, confidence is linked less to the absolute material capacities of the state than it is to perceptions of how a state's current capacities compare with those it possessed in the recent past.

Distinctions from Previous Theories of Humiliation and Status

The theoretical framework of national humiliation presented in this and the last chapter differs from prior discussions of international humiliation in several key ways. First, prior accounts of humiliation at the international level have largely focused on the denial of the rights of individuals within other states rather than on the denial of states' rights and privileges.[58] While acknowledging the significant and lasting impact that the denial of individual-level rights can have, this book focuses more on the humiliation that arises when the status of the state that one identifies with is threatened. Second, these accounts focus on humiliation arising from the acts of others and exclude the failure to perform in the ways they and others expect as a powerful source of humiliation. Public failure, however, calls the status of the state into question in similar ways to public acts of disrespect. Both events can trigger deep self-doubt, a key distinguishing feature of humiliation, as well as the strong desire to blame others for one's unfortunate fate. Finally, existing discussions have assumed a degree of intentionality in the actions of the actor inflicting humiliation.[59] Within the model above, intention is not always necessary. Though negative intention can exacerbate a sense of humiliation, actors whose rights and privileges are somehow ignored will often be inclined to attribute negative intention even when it does not exist.[60]

The model of humiliation within this book also expands on and differs from existing models of status in important ways. First, the model offers unique predictions about when exactly status will matter most to states. Models of status inconsistency predict that status concerns will be triggered when a state receives less influence than its relative material capabilities would merit.[61] The model of humiliation presented above suggests that the amount of influence a humiliated state expects to hold is often uncoupled from the state's underlying relative capabilities. Humiliating events arouse a sense of injustice and a resulting reluctance to internalize any potential fault of the state. States are reluctant to adopt lowered status expectations, even in the face of international failure and a decline in relative capabilities.[62] States will be reluctant to adopt lowered status expectations, even in the face of international failure and a decline in relative capabilities, and will often only do so after repeated humiliations. Meanwhile, in the period following a humiliating event, significant inconsistency often arises between the influence the state expects to hold, determined to a large degree by its past influence and the influence that others believe it deserves, determined by the state's recent performance on the international stage.[63]

Others have argued that status concerns are most likely to be salient during periods of power transition when the distribution of power is ambiguous.[64] The model above suggests that while it is possible that instances of humiliation and disrespect more likely occur during shifts in relative capabilities, states also experience humiliation and disrespect when the distribution of capabilities is relatively stable and unambiguous. Because of the difficulty of objectively measuring how one's characteristics rank relative to others, states obtain estimates of their status through the amount of consideration they receive from others. Instances of disrespect allow for such estimates and therefore serve as triggers for status seeking whether the underlying distribution of forces shifts or not.

Social identity theory (SIT) provides the foundation for several additional theories of status in the international system.[65] SIT predicts that actors will be more likely to engage in status-seeking strategies when the achievements and qualities of their group compare unfavorably with those of salient reference groups. The model presented here predicts, by contrast, that the mere perception of inferiority is a less potent motivator than the feeling that one's status has intentionally been degraded by others or that one's inferiority is completely undeserved.[66]

Second, others have remarked on the international effects of disrespect and humiliation, but their emphasis has been on the outrage humiliating events produce. Larson and Shevchenko, for instance, make an argument rooted in SIT that the denial of others' status can have emotional repercussions that lead to offensive actions aimed at restoring the state's status.[67] Within their model, anger and vengefulness, and not the need to overcome self-doubt, are the motivating emotions. The omission of collective self-doubt is not insignificant. Although anger may lead specifically to acts of vengeance against those seen to be responsible for one's status decline, states seeking to restore their own sense of efficacy may respond to status decline by engaging in several different assertive measures, not solely revenge. This broadened conception of humiliation enables us to better understand the full range of humiliation's effects.

Finally, this book's model presents precise predictions about the strategies that states afflicted by status concerns will pursue. SIT offers the general prediction that states will engage in competitive strategies, in which states attempt to outdo others along existing dimensions of status criteria when they perceive the borders between status groups to be "impermeable."[68] Existing theories rooted in SIT do not provide conditions under which status-motivated states will be more likely to use force in their quest for improved self-image.[69] Nor do they provide predictions about who exactly will serve as the target of that aggression.

This chapter has addressed two primary questions related to national humiliation: 1) Why do humiliating events alter state behavior? and 2) how should we expect states to respond to humiliating events? Humiliated states are motivated to engage in assertive status-seeking acts by the desire to eradicate self-doubt and restore the image of the state in the eyes of others. States that manage to recover their political and material wherewithal in the aftermath of humiliating events are the most likely to engage in risky and aggressive status-seeking strategies, which may be aimed at humiliator states, but which are often targeted at those who were uninvolved in the original humiliation. Such strategies can set off international competitions for status as states vie to ensure that public perception of the state's relative status does not erode.

Humiliation has the potential to linger over long time periods. In extremely rare cases, national humiliation lasts over generations. For it to do so, humiliation must be repeated, or past humiliations must be incorporated into the historical and political narrative of the state, as is the case with China's Century of Humiliation or Bolivia's contemporary anti-Chilenismo narratives stemming from the state's loss to Chile in the War of the Pacific.[70] In many other cases, states find ways to reestablish their sense of authority. In yet others, states that experience repeated humiliating events eventually assume responsibility for the decline in their status, rather than direct their outrage about status decline at others, and as a result downgrade their status expectations.

Significant theoretical questions about the role of humiliation in international relations remain. This chapter has largely treated the state as a unitary actor. International behavior is the product of individual decision making and domestic political incentives. The next chapter investigates the validity of the unitary actor assumption as it applies to the effects of humiliation and the pursuit of international status. Through the analysis of variation within domestic perceptions of and preferred reactions to humiliating events, we can make predictions about the staying power of national humiliation.

3

NATIONAL HUMILIATION AT THE INDIVIDUAL LEVEL

What does it mean to speak of the emotional condition of a state? And even if we accept that emotional consensus can arise in response to events affecting a state, why are we to assume that this shared emotional reaction will have a substantive effect on the foreign policy of the state? This chapter examines national humiliation as a group-based emotion in light of recent research in social psychology and draws connections between these findings and the foreign policy of states. The chapter presents the first empirical support for the book's theory of humiliation. Through a set of survey experiments, I show that national humiliation is both similar to and different from national anger and national shame ways and that a variety of instances international failure and disrespect can evoke a sense of national humiliation, even within individuals who have not personally experienced the humiliating event. The results demonstrate the extent to which individual-level reactions to these events vary while also showing that significant consensus in reaction exists among those who strongly identify with the state. Strong identifiers respond to humiliating events involving the United States by increasing support for policies that assert the status and rights of the state through material practices and the projection of power abroad.

The experimental analysis presented in this chapter includes explicit tests of alternative explanations for why humiliating events generate increased support for assertive actions. Although results show a clear relationship between heightened emotions and increased support for assertive actions, it is also possible that humiliating events motivate aggression because these events raise concerns about the security of the state. Failure in the past may provoke increased challenges to security in the future, and aggressive actions may be thought to ward off such challenges. It is also possible that such events illicit primarily instrumental concerns about the declining influence of the state. The results show that these security and instrumental implications are significantly overshadowed by emotional motivations for increased aggression after humiliating events.

Group-Based Emotions and National Humiliation

Few people would deny what psychologists have repeatedly shown—that a sense of humiliation can have a profound impact on individual behavior. But how do we understand the humiliation of a state? Many scholars believe that citizens within a state agree that national security is an imperative simply because survival is ultimately at stake. However, they may question that uniformity in public opinion exists about the importance of status, the causes of national humiliation, or the appropriate responses to national humiliation. As Stein puts it, "Groups ... do not feel or think; individuals do."[1] States consist of individual citizens, after all, and individuals each possess their own idiosyncratic beliefs, political preferences, and emotional reactions to their social world. How could we possibly assume then that a large national collective would coalesce around a shared emotional reaction to an international event?

Research in social psychology has provided a strong foundation on which to build theories of national emotion. Extensive observational and experimental research has demonstrated that emotional responses are not solely aroused by events immediately affecting an individual but also by events that instead affect a member of a group with which the individual identifies or the group as a whole.[2] These shared emotional responses to events affecting one's group can be distinguished from individual-level reactions to the same event even among group members who did not experience the event first hand.[3] Individuals who identify with a particular social group are more likely to interpret events involving the group in similar ways and are more likely to feel similar emotions in response to their shared interpretation.[4] Preferred group behavior is tied more to these group-level emotions than it is to individual emotive states.[5]

Significant events affecting one's group will not always garner an identical emotional reaction within the group. One has only to look to divergent reactions within the United States to the 9/11 attacks for evidence of this variation. Some Americans reported anger as a primary response, whereas others reported experiencing a deeper sense of sadness.[6] We do know, however, that because individual self-esteem is, in part, a product of the perceived identity of one's group, individuals are prone to strong emotional reactions in response to status-threatening events. That this is so is perhaps no surprise if one is to consider the centrality of status hierarchies to social life. Biologists have demonstrated that social hierarchy has deep physiological and evolutionary roots, existing not only among humans but also within a wide range of animal species, including apes, baboons, chickens, ants, and fish.[7] Actors at the top of social hierarchies typically experience heightened levels of pleasurable serotonin, which decrease if they are demoted.[8] Alternatively, status threat and unstable social hierarchies increase cortisol levels and negatively affect cardiovascular pathology, autonomic, endocrine, and immune systems in humans.[9]

Social hierarchies are likely so pervasive among animal species because they provide a more efficient and less costly alternative to incessant conflict.[10] Rather than allowing for direct conflict to decide which actor will have influence over a particular decision, social hierarchies rely on a willingness of lower status actors to defer to those who possess distinctive amounts of valued characteristics.[11] Meanwhile, those actors at the top of the hierarchy receive greater social and material rewards. Stable social hierarchies also help groups function more efficiently in that they resolve coordination problems and reward competence in skills that a group finds beneficial and admirable.[12]

Despite the potentially severe physiological and social implications of humiliation, social psychologists have only begun to probe the nature and impact of group-based humiliation through experimental analysis. Research has shown that members of groups confronting a humiliating threat to their status are more likely to adhere to dogmatic belief structures.[13] They are more likely to derogate and discriminate against both members of the out-group deemed responsible for the status threat as well as lower status out-groups.[14] This rise in out-group differentiation and derogation equates more generally to an increase in nationalism at the state level with its associated destabilizing effects on international relations.[15] Threats to status also engender higher levels of identification with one's threatened group as well as higher levels of in-group favoritism.[16]

Within existing studies, the two contrasting action tendencies associated with humiliation and described in the last chapter are apparent. Group-based humiliation, in some instances, has been associated with an increase in the likelihood that an individual will engage in collective action aimed at the defense of the threatened group.[17] In other instances, the humiliation of one's group conversely triggers inertial effects in which support for violent and vengeful acts by members of one's group declines.[18] What explains these contrasting action tendencies among humiliated actors? As already suggested, the answer is likely dependent on perceptions of blame and on perceptions of efficacy.[19] Those states that place greater blame on themselves for their failure or disrespect will be more likely to adopt the avoidant tendencies associated with shame.[20] Avoidance becomes more likely as actors experience repeated instances of status threat over time, and, as a result, it becomes more difficult to not internalize some degree of responsibility for one's inferior position.[21] Those states that place blame on others but feel completely impotent in the face of the international failure or disrespect will also be more likely to withdraw from international assertions of status. Those states that maintain a minimum degree of confidence will be sufficiently emboldened to assert themselves on the world stage in an attempt to fully overcome their sense of self-doubt.[22]

How Does National Humiliation Shape Foreign Policy?

The evidence presented below demonstrates that average levels of support for assertive foreign policy actions are higher within populations primed to feel humiliated on behalf of their state. Even if we accept that certain international events elicit group-based humiliation among citizens of the state, which increases support for aggression, we must explain how this sense of national humiliation within a large segment of the populace is likely to have a measurable effect on foreign policy decision making by state elites. Group-based humiliation is likely to affect foreign policy in three non-exclusive ways.

The first mechanism occurs solely at the elite level. As stated, the degree to which an individual experiences a group-based emotion is highly contingent on the degree to which that individual identifies with the group.[23] Strong identifiers are also more likely to perceive a threat to their in-group and to possess bias against an out-group than are those who identify less strongly.[24] We can safely assume that national identity is particularly if not uniquely salient among those politicians who make key foreign policy decisions on the country's behalf. While individuals often have numerous overlapping and perhaps competing identities, the idea that decision makers identify with the state "is generally a given."[25] Moreover, defeat and failure of the group have been shown to increase group cohesion and identification, especially among those group members who feel personally responsible for group decisions, as would obviously be true of a country's decision-making elite.[26] Thus, the emotional effect of threats to national identity will likely be just as strong, if not stronger, among leaders of the country as the average degree of emotional response within the population.

The two other intertwined mechanisms by which individual emotional responses to events affecting their state translate into shifts in foreign policy involve the interaction between elite actions and public opinion. First, the type of leader selected by a humiliated, outraged populace may be significantly different from leaders selected within non-aggrieved states. In their quest to feel empowered again and to slough off their sense of helplessness, citizens of humiliated states may on average be more likely to select strong, charismatic leaders who draw strong distinctions between "us" and conspiratorial "others" and who promise to restore the status and strength of the humiliated state through whatever means necessary.[27]

Second, the gap between public opinion, and foreign policy can be narrowed by the expectation of leaders that they will pay high political costs if they do not carry out the will of the people. Elites can have strong domestic incentives to follow the will of the people when making foreign policy decisions.[28] Thus, leaders of humiliated states may feel pressed to engage in more assertive policies aimed at renewing the confidence of the people for fear that if they do not, they will confront electoral costs or threats to the regime's legitimacy.

Elites can also play a role in activating national humiliation narratives that might, in turn, dictate the public's foreign policy preferences. Leaders of states that have experienced humiliating international events may have an incentive to deliberately manipulate the feelings aroused by these events to gain domestic support and legitimacy.[29] The outrage such leaders cultivate can then constrain their ability to engage in cooperative diplomacy, thereby increasing the likelihood that the state engages in conflict. Having activated the emotionality of the public, these leaders will have a relatively clear assessment of the electoral incentives and constraints they have either inadvertently or intentionally created for themselves.

Leaders who seek aggressive policies may have the greatest incentive to evoke humiliating events while also promising to restore national pride. Such leaders, as a result of successful emotional priming of the public, may experience fewer electoral and domestic constraints when attempting to launch aggressive policies.[30] Propaganda campaigns presenting international events as inhumane and humiliating can also be used, as Hitler rightly predicted, to "arouse national sentiment to the highest pitch" and to transform feelings of indignation into a "spirit of dauntless resistance," leading the people to join in the common cry: "To arms again!"[31] Because the anger an individual feels on behalf of his group is directly proportional to the individual's willingness to engage in costly collective action, leaders of states with higher levels of group-based anger may also be able to assemble large standing armies more easily.[32]

Though leaders may both strongly identify with the emotional reaction of the populace and play a role in shaping it does not necessarily mean that leaders and their publics will always advocate for the exact same policy responses to humiliating events. The previous chapter described a number of potential assertive responses leaders could choose to engage in an effort to restore state status following a humiliating event. In some cases, the preferred response of leaders and the public may diverge. An angered populace, unconstrained by concerns about capabilities and the likelihood of success, is likely to focus its attention on revenge at all costs against the state responsible for the state's humiliation. Leaders who confront material realities and deem revenge too risky must still manage the instrumental and emotional implications of status threats. Aggressive action against third-party states or material practices aimed at influencing the perceptions of other states also promise to boost the self-esteem of the state and to demonstrate state intentions to maintain or to augment their status. Humiliated states will seek to engage in policies that make them look influential, powerful, and successful on the world stage. This need for success and positive self-identity can serve to moderate policies based in unchecked emotionality.[33]

National Humiliation: An Experimental Approach

The survey experiments described below enable us to empirically address the following questions: What types of events elicit national humiliation? To what extent do emotional, instrumental, and security motivations drive these shifts in foreign policy preferences? And, finally, how much variation exists within individual perceptions of national humiliation and within responses to humiliating international events and what are the sources of that variation? The results of experiments presented here allow us to assess the degree to which we can, as Stein has put it, "attribute to the collective what is an embodied individual experience."[34] An experimental approach enables us not only to isolate the potential causal impact of humiliating events on foreign policy attitudes but also to parse the underlying causal mechanisms motivating aggressive behavior following a humiliating event.

How then do we manipulate a sense of humiliation at the national level among individual subjects? The survey design used in this research relies on experimental techniques used by social psychologists in the study of humiliation at both the individual and group level. At the individual level, researchers have frequently relied on self-recall and report, a process in which subjects are asked to write for an extended period of time about a scenario, often professional in nature, in which they felt humiliated.[35] The extensive reflection required during this process allows emotional reactions to be more deeply activated at the physiological level.

Social psychologists have also engaged in numerous experimental techniques to test the effects of status threat and humiliation at the group level, both by manipulating the status of artificial groups in a laboratory as well as the degree of status threat to real-life groups with which subjects identify.[36] Researchers have utilized methods of both self-comparison and intergroup-comparisons as seen through the eyes of others. In a series of experiments, Russell Spears and his colleagues, for instance, manipulated a sense of inferiority within college majors both through a process of self-comparison, in which students within psychology, art, or physics were asked to compare their group to the other two along with eight traits relating to intelligence or creativity.[37] In another study, researchers provided students with favorable and unfavorable intergroup comparisons of the education majors as made by "average Dutch citizens." Other studies have elicited particular group responses by relying on historical events involving one's group. Ginges and Atran, for instance, primed a sense of group humiliation among Palestinians by reminding subjects of particularly humiliating aspects of the Israeli occupation.[38] Yet other studies have generated novel scenarios depicting the humiliation of one's group. For example, Branscombe and Wann manipulated status threat by showing U.S. and Soviet subjects a video of either a U.S. or a Soviet boxer winning a boxing match and then assessing in-group bias and out-group derogation.[39]

To assess the impact of national humiliation on foreign policy attitudes, a variety of these methods were incorporated into the survey experiments discussed below.[40] The surveys employed a process of self-report following descriptions of recent historical events involving the United States and a salient out-group, as well as intergroup comparisons by outside, third-party observers in order to manipulate a sense of national humiliation among U.S. subjects.

Researchers have noted the potential difficulty in studying the effects of humiliation and status threat within high status groups like the United States in that members of these groups may be more inclined to express confidence in their group and less inclined to admit a feeling of status threat.[41] It is possible, as Branscombe and Wann argue, that humiliating events involving high status groups are more surprising and may receive more attention and assume greater salience than would events favoring high status groups.[42] At the time the experiments were conducted, Americans were a relatively unconfident bunch—polls showed that Americans possessed the lowest levels of confidence in the status trajectory of the US on record.[43] Confidence levels in U.S. institutions were also at all-time lows, suggesting that Americans may possess less restraint in acknowledging potential weaknesses of their group than do other high status groups.

Expectations

The survey experiments presented here induce a sense of national humiliation by priming individual subjects with scenarios involving either the intentional disrespect of the United States or the failure of the United States to meet the expectations associated with its preeminent status. The theoretical framework in this book provides the four following predictions: 1) The rate of support for assertive foreign policy actions will be higher within groups primed to feel humiliation in response to an international event. 2) Support for assertive policies will extend to acts directed against third-party states as well as toward the state responsible for the humiliating event. 3) Increased support for assertive actions will be motivated significantly by the emotional solace that assertive actions offer after humiliating events. 4) Individual variation within emotional responses to international events will depend on perceptions of the efficacy of the state and on who is to blame for the international failure or disrespect.

Figure 3.1 depicts this last behavioral prediction—those subjects who blame the United States for a status-threatening event will be more likely to support avoidance and withdrawal. The same will be true of subjects reporting outrage toward other states and perceptions of the United States and its institutions as highly ineffective. Those subjects who feel outrage toward others and who view the United States to be highly effective will be more likely to report higher levels of anger than humiliation.[44]

Prior work on group identification has suggested that the more one identifies with the group, the more likely they will be to perceive a threat to the group, to show in-group bias and to discriminate against an out-group. I hypothesize that those who report stronger identification with the United States will report higher levels of humiliation when primed by a humiliating event than will weaker identifiers. Strong identifiers will also be more likely to perceive the United States as effective on the world stage and will therefore be more likely to experience anger

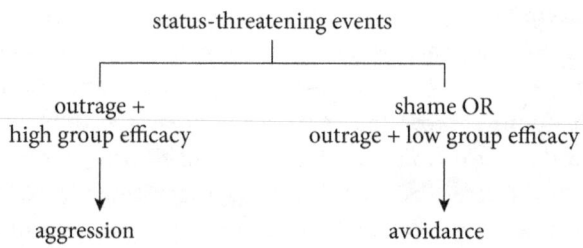

FIGURE 3.1 Behavioral predictions

following a humiliating event than to experience shame. Lower levels of identification may, conversely, be associated with higher levels of shame and greater support for passivity.

Experimental Design

Two surveys were fielded in July 2016 in the United States. The first was administered on 1,177 American subjects using Amazon's MTurk.[45] The second was administered by Survey Sampling International on a representative sample of 2,682 Americans. The demographic breakdown, described in the Appendix, was largely similar between the two subject pools. In both studies, subjects were first informed that they would be taking a short two-part survey in which they would be asked about their foreign policy preferences.[46] They were then asked a standard battery of three questions aimed at assessing the degree to which they identify with the United States. Subjects were then randomly assigned to either the control group or evenly assigned to one of four different treatment groups. The subjects within the treatment groups each read about one relatively recent event involving the United States. These events were chosen based on the criteria offered in Chapter 1 about the sorts of international events that are likely to be perceived as threatening the status of the state. Multiple events were used to prime subjects to ensure internal validity and to ensure that ingrained reaction to some particular historical event or rival to the United States were not driving reactions.

Two of the four scenarios described instances in which the United States definitively and infamously failed to achieve its foreign policy goals on the world stage. The first scenario involving a failed U.S. endeavor centered on the failed mission to rescue hostages from Iran in 1979. The paragraph read,

> On April 24, 1980, the U.S. military attempted to free fifty-two U.S. hostages held for six months in the U.S. embassy in Tehran. The operation was aborted before it really began when two helicopters suffered mechanical difficulties and got caught in the sand. Seven U.S. aircraft were also destroyed in the desert. The operation came to symbolize the U.S.' failure on the world stage. The U.S. press dubbed it the "The Debacle in the Desert" and 71 percent of U.S. citizens polled perceived the operation to have been handled incorrectly. As one European leader said of the event at the time, "In Iran, the United States suffered a very public defeat on the world stage." One U.S. general agreed, declaring the event to be the "greatest humiliation of the United States since Vietnam."

The second failure scenario focused on the costly failure of the U.S. military to successfully train more than five Syrian soldiers to combat ISIS. The format and information included in the two scenarios were held constant to the degree possible. It stated,

> In 2013, the U.S. military announced its plan to train Syrian troops to fight ISIS. The plan was to be the showcase of U.S. efforts in the war-torn country. The goal was to train 5,000 troops by the end of 2015. By October 2015, the program had spent half a billion dollars but had managed to train only four Syrian soldiers. Following the closure of the program, Vladimir Putin of Russia mocked the lack of progress by the United States, saying that the money would have been far better off in Russian hands. He subsequently committed Russian planes and soldiers to the fight in Syria. As one European leader has said of the failed U.S. program, "The United States suffered a very public failure on the world stage. It was unable to exert its influence in a convincing way." One U.S. general agreed, declaring that the failed efforts to be a source of international embarrassment.

The remaining two scenarios involved recent historical events in which the rights and privileges of the United States were intentionally ignored by one of two salient out-groups, either Russia or China. These treatments focused on actual actions taken by the Russians and Chinese in 2015. The scenario involving Russia read:

> Last year, Russia engaged in acts taken by many to be disrespectful of the U.S. international rights and interests. For instance, though Russia had no acknowledged legal claim to the Arctic Circle, it repeatedly sought to deny the United States its right to navigate international Arctic waters. Russian submarines were also detected within the U.S. restricted territorial waters. The Pentagon indicated that the submarines posed no threat—they were likely sent to spy on the U.S. Navy. Finally, Russia sent numerous planes to fly through Californian and Alaskan airspace last year on the symbolic date of July Fourth. As one European leader stated of Russia's actions, "Russia repeatedly disrespected the United States, attempting to deny its rights as a sovereign state and its privileges as a great power."

The scenario involving China, presented in the Appendix, described a set of similar acts in which China denied the United States its rights and privileges as a great power.

After reviewing one of the four scenarios, respondents in the treatment groups were asked to spend a few minutes thinking and writing about how these events might have affected the image of the United States in the eyes of others. They were then asked about the degree to which they believe the events humiliated or disrespected the United States and to state on a scale from 1 to 7 the degree to which they felt the following emotions: humiliation, anger, shame, fear, indifference, embarrassment, and helplessness. Those respondents who indicated they felt some degree of anger were then asked to think for a moment of the source of their anger and then to state in two separate questions how much of their anger was directed toward a) the U.S. government and how much of their anger was directed toward b) other countries. Respondents were asked to what degree they perceived the United States to be at fault for the described events and about whether they believe the United States is treated fairly by others.

Subjects were then told they would begin the second part of the survey in which they would provide opinions about possible changes in U.S. foreign policy. They were asked about six different potential foreign policy shifts. For example, subjects were asked about the degree to which they would support the United States to lead an international mission to Mars or an international mission to defeat ISIS in Syria if the odds of success were higher than 65 percent. They were asked about their support for ensuring that the United States maintained the largest and most advanced nuclear arsenal in the world. Four questions were also included that described aggressive or non-cooperative actions that could be taken against Russia, China, and Iran. These questions and a complete copy of

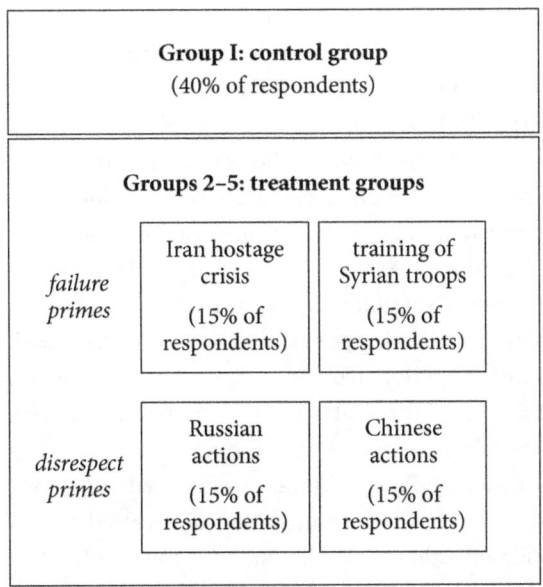

FIGURE 3.2 Experimental conditions

the survey are included in an online appendix.[47] Half of the respondents were asked before the historical primes three efficacy questions aimed at gauging the degree to which they perceive the United States and its military institutions to be effective at achieving their aims. The other half was asked the same questions toward the end of the survey.

The set of questions presented to those subjects within the control group, which accounted for roughly 40 percent of respondents in both surveys, was identical to that in the treatment groups but for two differences. In lieu of reading about a historical event, control subjects were asked to spend a few minutes writing about their day. They were asked to report about their emotional state and then to spend a few minutes thinking about "the conduct of U.S. foreign policy and the treatment of the United States by other countries." Like the treatment groups, they were then asked to describe how the degree to which they felt angry, ashamed, embarrassed, scared, and indifferent when doing so. Those who expressed any degree of anger were then asked about the source of their anger just as in the questions presented to treatment groups described above. They were then asked about their degree of support for the six foreign policy actions listed above. Finally, control subjects were presented with the questions aimed at assessing perceptions of group efficacy.

The design of the survey for the representative population was identical in all ways to the MTurk survey, but for the addition of the three questions presented after subjects responded to the foreign policy questions. Respondents in the treatment groups were asked to think again about the events described within their primes. All groups, including the controls, were then asked to express the extent to which they agreed with the following three statements: "If the United States fails to assert itself on the world stage, it will lose international influence;" "If the United States fails to assert itself on the world stage, it will face greater threats to its security;" and finally "It feels good when the United States successfully asserts itself on the world stage." These three questions were included to determine the degree to which three possible mediators—a desire for influence, security concerns, and a desire for psychological well-being—might explain the relationship between a national humiliation and a shift in underlying foreign policy attitudes.

The primary dependent variables used in the analysis below are composite variables, which account for the degree to which respondents showed support for the set of assertive foreign policy changes. Four of these policies—intervention against ISIS, patrolling the Taiwan Strait with U.S. aircraft carriers, planting a U.S. flag in Russian-claimed territory in the Arctic, and providing additional support for anti-Russian soldiers in Ukraine—involved either direct or indirect aggression. Reneging on the Iran nuclear deal involved a less cooperative stance. The last policy, investing in the first manned mission to Mars, involved a material practice likely to be seen as a marker of international status. Questions about these policies were answered on a 7-point scale from "Strongly agree" to "'Strongly disagree." Respondents were given the option of answering "Don't agree or disagree."' These answers were excluded from the analysis. Binary variables were then created that were coded as 1 if respondents reported any degree of support for one of these individual policies and 0 if subjects reported any level of opposition to the policy. A composite variable, *Support for Assertive Policies*, was then created in which support for the six individual policies was totaled. A second variable, *Support for Aggressive Policies*, totals support for the four policies involving explicit or indirect aggression.

Results

The results presented in this section are based on the SSI data but include only those that were replicated within both the MTurk and the representative surveys.

Figure 3.3 shows the different levels of support for all six assertive policies, distinguishing between respondents receiving one of the two scenarios describing

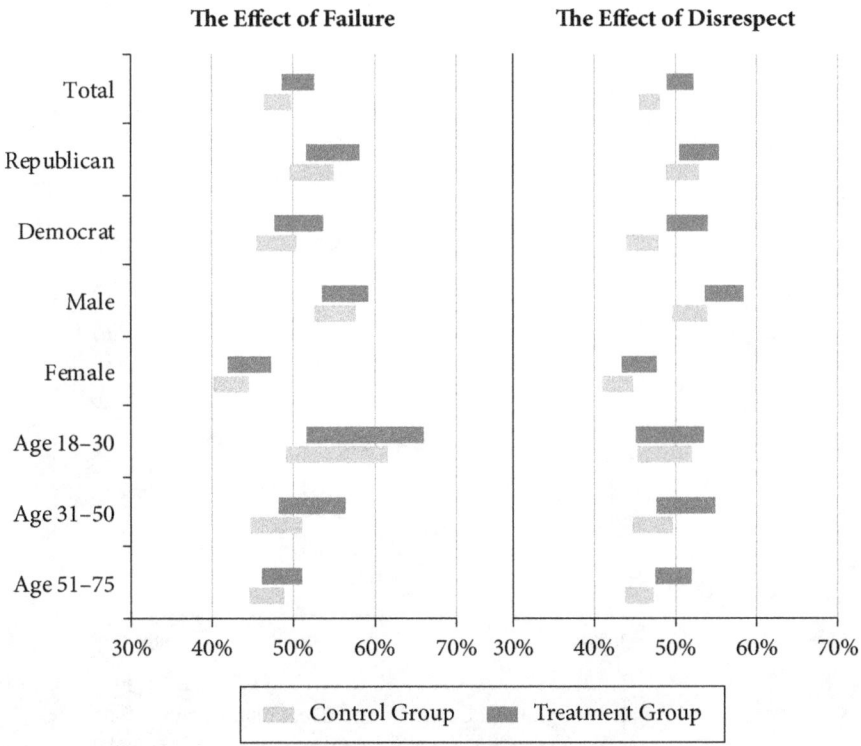

FIGURE 3.3 Support for assertive foreign policies

public and unexpected failure of the United States and those receiving one of the two scenarios describing disrespectful treatment by others. The white bars indicate the 95 percent confidence intervals that surround support for aggressive policies among respondents who read one of the four randomly assigned scenarios describing a status-threatening event involving the United States. The gray bars indicate the estimated levels of support for the aggressive policies within the control group that was not reminded of a recent humiliation. The figure shows similar increases in support for assertive policies, though this increase is more substantial among those reading about acts that disrespect the rights of the United States.[48]

Figure 3.4 presents the average level of support for those policies that involved the use of force within the total population and then broken down demographically. As the figure shows, support for aggressive policies increases within the total population by about 4 percent. Among Democrat subjects, exposure to a humiliating scenario involving the United States increased support for aggression by about 7 percent, raising support to roughly the same level among the generally more aggressive Republican respondents. The treatment also generated

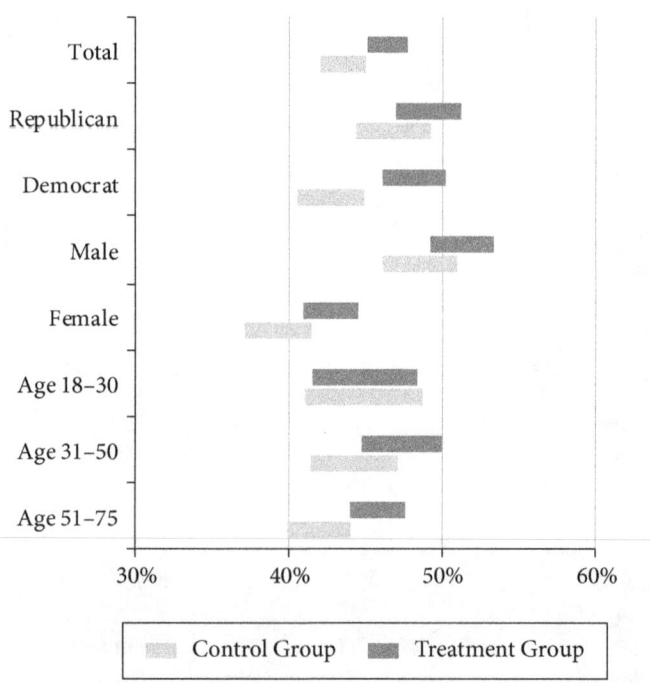

FIGURE 3.4 The effect of treatments on support for aggression

significant differences within the population of fifty-one to seventy-five-year-olds and women, who supported aggressive acts to a far lesser degree than men.

The results obtained when we look at levels of support for individual foreign policies are largely as expected. Disrespectful acts by another country increase support for aggressive or non-cooperative policies against that state. Support for a U.S. military presence in the Taiwan Strait, for instance, is 11 percent higher amongst respondents who read about disrespectful acts by China directed at the United States than those in the control group.[49] Support for planting the U.S. flag in the Arctic seabed, an act that respondents were told Russia had tried to forbid, is 10 percent higher among those reading of Russian disrespect than those in the control group. Perhaps more surprising is support for competitive and aggressive actions that do not directly or indirectly involve the state responsible for the threat to one's status is also higher among those who receive treatment of either type. For example, support for U.S. military presence in the Taiwan Strait was 7 percent higher among those reading about acts of Russian disrespect than it was among those in the control group. Support for planting the Arctic flag was 5 percent higher among those reading of Chinese disrespect than it was among those in the control group. Increased levels of support for aggressive and competitive policies were not directed only at one's humiliator. Rather, underlying support for aggression increases across the board and involves actions directed at third-party states.

What Motivates Increased Support for Assertive Policies?

Although we have shown that exposure to the historical scenarios increases support for assertive foreign policy actions, we have yet to establish the mechanism explaining this increased support. The particular historical scenarios used in this analysis were selected because they include the types of events that Chapter 1 predicted would induce a sense of national humiliation. It is possible that the instrumental or security implications of these events, and not the psychological effects, motivate respondents. Those confronting the loss of status may fear the subsequent loss of influence that a decline in status often implies and may, therefore, be willing to pay short-term costs in order to engage in acts that befit a state of their desired status in hopes of bolstering their image in the eyes of others and maintaining their existing influence. It is also possible that threats to national status engender fear for the state's security and that the state now will confront more direct challenges by rivals. In such cases, aggressive acts following humiliation would be intended to demonstrate one's strength to potential rivals.[50] Finally, it is possible that the historical events motivate support for assertiveness not because of national humiliation but through other potential emotional channels such as anger.

Strong evidence exists that emotions and the desire for psychological solace are strong drivers for heightened support for assertiveness. Three mediating variables aimed at capturing the three non-exclusive mechanisms were measured directly from survey responses. Respondents were asked the degree to which it "feels good" when the United States asserts itself on the world stage. They were also asked two separate questions about the degree to which failure for the United States to assert itself on the world stage leads to "greater security threats" for the country and to a "loss of international influence." A structural equation model was used to assess the relative degree to which emotional, instrumental, and security concerns mediate the relationship between the treatments and attitude toward foreign policy.[51] These results are presented in Figure 3.5.

In all cases, exposure to the historical scenarios is associated with increased levels of the mediating variables when compared to the responses of the control group. These increases are reflected in the coefficients along the paths on the left between the treatment and the mediators. The figure shows that the increase is largest for the variable, which captures the emotional rationale for assertive actions. The figure also depicts a significant and positive relationship between the emotional rationale and the security rationale and increased support for aggression. No significant relationship is reported between the instrumental rationale and aggression. The indirect effects for each pathway are listed on the right-hand side of the figure. The indirect effect of humiliation through emotional rationale is .0475. The indirect effect of humiliation through security threat is .0150, roughly one-third of the size of the effect of emotional rationale. This is strong evidence in support of the notion that increases in support for aggression are

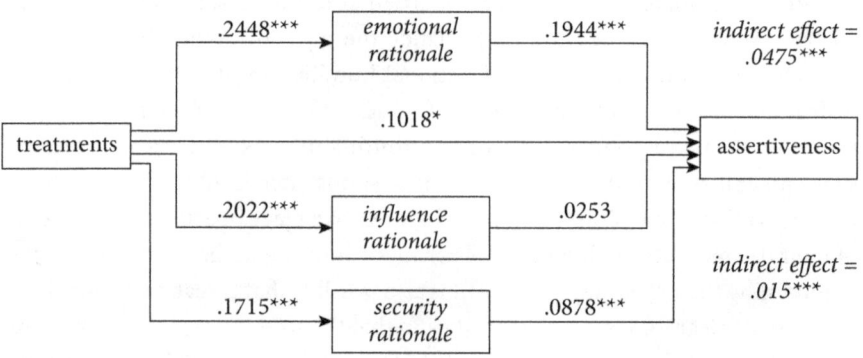

FIGURE 3.5 Motivations for assertiveness

higher among those exposed to the treatment scenarios largely because subjects are motivated to alleviate the negative consequences of humiliation rather than by a desire to shore up the security or influence of the state.

How do we know that humiliation is the primary emotional driver of this reaction? Within all treatment groups, the reported levels of humiliation, anger, and shame were higher on average than within control groups.[52] A structural equation model similar to that described above was conducted to assess the relative degree to which these emotions mediated support for assertiveness. Figure 3.6 illustrates the results of this analysis. The treatments produced the largest increase in reported levels of humiliation, with lower reported levels of anger and shame. Anger had the highest direct effect on support for assertive policies. This is as would be expected given that anger is distinguished from humiliation by a sense of efficacy. Reported humiliation also has significant and positive effects on assertiveness while shame is not associated with an increase in assertiveness, which is also as we would expect given the predictions in Figure 3.1. The indirect effect of the treatments via reported humiliation as a mediator is larger than that of the treatments via reported anger.

As further testament to the role that humiliation played in eliciting greater support for assertive responses, support for aggression was 18 percent ($p < .05$) higher among respondents who indicated that the historical scenario they read about humiliated the United States a "great deal" versus those who indicated that the scenario did not humiliate the country at all. Support for aggression was 26 percent ($p < .01$) higher among those who perceived that the victor country within the scenario had disrespected the United States a great deal versus those who did not perceive the treatment by others to be disrespectful. This increase was 11 percent ($p < .05$) among those within the "failure" groups.

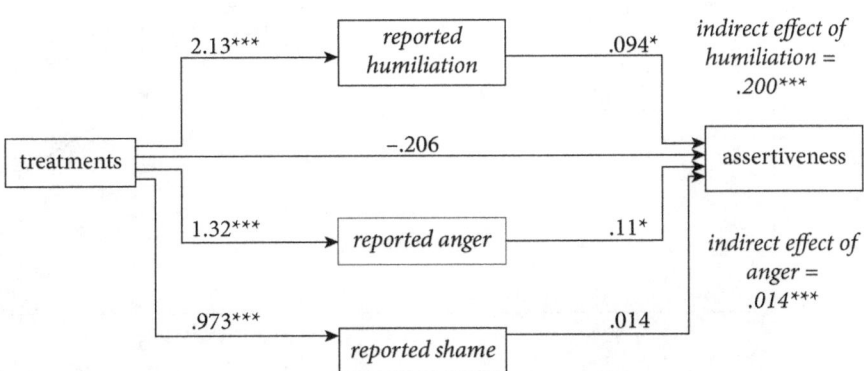

FIGURE 3.6 Emotional motivations for assertiveness

CHAPTER THREE

What Are the Sources of Variation in Individual Responses?

The results so far have assessed the average effect of the treatment primes on support for assertive policies as well as the relationship between the treatments, individual emotions and foreign policy attitudes. It is likely, however, that not all individuals responded to the historical scenarios in the same ways. This section examines the key conditions that give rise to humiliation rather than anger or shame and shows that, in keeping with the finding of others, perceptions of efficacy and perceptions of blame in part dictate primary emotional responses to status-threatening international events.

I first created a binary variable *Outrage*, which was coded 1 if subjects who received the treatment reported "quite a bit" or "a great deal" of anger at other states for the instance of U.S. failure or disrespect described within the treatment.

To assess the relationship between efficacy and outrage, I interacted *Outrage* with *Efficacy*, the measure of perceived efficacy of the United States and its military institutions. I then assessed the relationship of this interacted variable with a binary outcome variable, *Humiliation-Anger*, coded 1 if the subject reported higher levels of humiliation than anger and 0 if the reverse was true.[53] I then conducted a logit analysis to assess the relationship between perceived efficacy among those feeling outraged and primary emotional response reported. Figure 3.7 shows that as

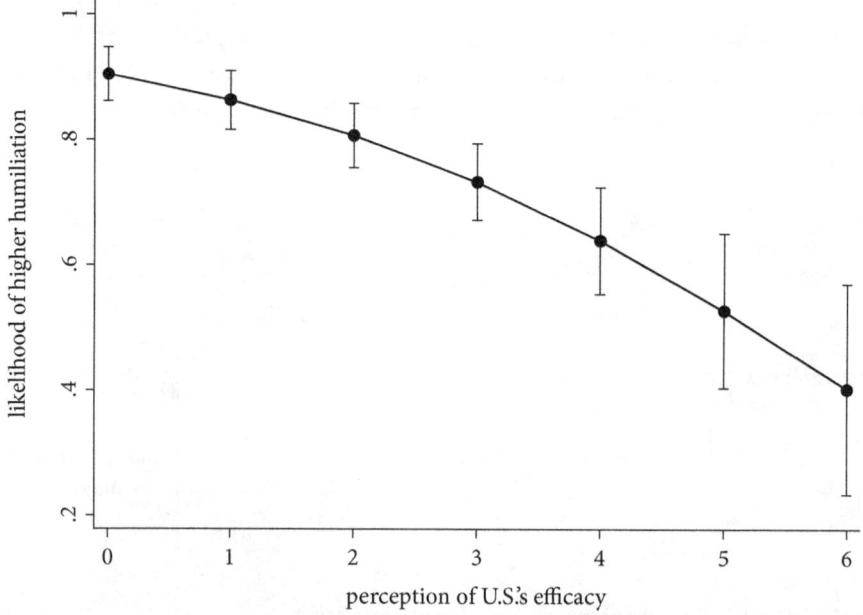

FIGURE 3.7 The relationship between efficacy and humiliation

perceptions of efficacy increase among those who have high levels of other-directed outrage, subjects become more likely to report higher levels of anger than humiliation and vice versa.[54]

To assess the distinctions between humiliation and shame as primary emotions, I created a binary variable, *Humiliation-Shame*, coded 1 if the treatment subject reported a higher level of humiliation than shame and a 0 if the reverse was true.[55] Using logit analysis, I examined the relationship between the variable *US at Fault*, which is measured on a 7-point scale with 7 meaning that the United States was completely at fault for the international events described in the treatments. The results of the model show that the likelihood of experiencing more humiliation than shame was 27 percent ($p < .001$) higher among those who did not believe that the United States was in any way at fault compared to those who believed that the United States was completely at fault.

One final mediation analysis was conducted to assess the action tendencies generated by differing perceptions of fault. Two potential mediating variables—"anger at others" and "group-based fault"—were chosen because they best capture the primary distinction between anger and shame—other-directed outrage versus feelings that an outcome was deserved.[56] Although I have hypothesized that both the disrespect and international failure primes will increase overall levels of support for aggression, it is likely that the two types of primes engender different proportions of other-directed outrage and shame. The acts of disrespect described in the primes, in that they involve relatively low levels of subjugation and discrimination, should arguably be expected to elicit lower amounts of shame and perceptions of U.S. guilt than the primes describing the failure of the United States on the world stage. International failure should similarly elicit lower levels of other-directed outrage than does disrespect. I focus here on the effects of the two treatments involving U.S. failure.

The path diagram and results of the model assessing the effects of the international failure primes on aggression are presented in Figure 3.8. Again, we see a significant and positive impact of the treatments on the two mediators—other-directed anger and group-based fault. We also see a positive relationship between other-directed anger and support for aggression. Unlike the previous model, however, the results show the predicted significant negative relationship between the group-based fault and support for aggression. An increase in the belief that the United States was at fault corresponds with a decrease in support for aggression compared with those in the control group. No significant statistical relationship between failure primes and aggression is reported. The indirect effects of international failure are reported on the right-hand side of the figure. The indirect effect of failure via other-directed outrage is positive and significant at .1317. The indirect effect of failure through the group-based fault is negative and, at -.045, significantly smaller than that of anger.

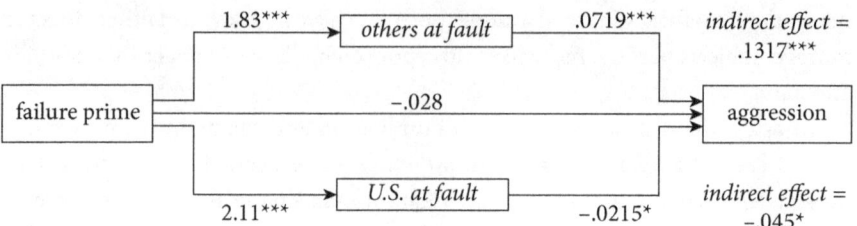

FIGURE 3.8 The dual effects of failure primes

Finally, I assessed the correlation between group identity and the intensity of group-based emotional responses. The probability that a respondent reported more anger at others than at the United States was 69 percent higher ($p < .05$) among those who indicated, prior to receiving treatment, that they agreed or strongly agreed that they saw themselves as and were pleased to be Americans. Those who strongly identified with the United States (those who scored 18 and up on a 24-point measure of identification) reported levels of humiliation that were 10 percent ($p < .001$) higher than those who only moderately identified with the United States (those with scores between 12 and 18). Increasing group identification was also strongly correlated with higher levels of anger and shame and with significantly lower levels of indifference within treatment groups.

The results also show that group identification, perceptions of group efficacy, levels of other-directed outrage, support for aggression, and outcomes affecting one's group are all correlated and difficult to disentangle. Strong identifiers are more likely to perceive their group to be effective and to feel other-directed outrage toward events negatively affecting their group. At the same time, events that negatively affect one's group can lead to decreases in-group identification among low and middle identifiers and in their subsequent perceptions of the efficacy of the group.[57] Though respondents in the surveys described above were asked about group identification prior to reading about potential national humiliation, these prior perceptions were obviously dependent on views of prior historical, possibly humiliating, events that involved the state. Thus, we cannot say which might have come first—a sense of shame of the United States in response to status-threatening events or a lower-than-average perception of U.S. military effectiveness.

The analyses in this chapter have provided significant support for numerous theoretical arguments presented in Chapters 1 and 2. This chapter has shown that: 1) Instances of international failure and international disrespect can have similar effects on foreign policy attitudes. 2) Status-threatening events increase the average individual levels of support for aggressive and assertive policies. 3) Increased support extends not only to aggressive acts directed at the state responsible for the threat to one's status but to third-party states not involved in the original status-threatening event as well. 4) Increased support for aggression among those primed with status-threatening events is motivated in large part by the emotional solace that aggression promises to provide. 5) Concerns about security to a lesser degree also mediate post-humiliation attitudes toward aggression.

These results provide a plausible explanation of how individual reactions to events affecting their state may translate into actual shifts toward a more assertive foreign policy. Individual citizens are likely to be emotionally affected by events that threaten the status of their state and will be more likely to support assertive acts in the hope that such actions will provide emotional relief. Elites, as citizens who perhaps most closely identify with the state, will also likely suffer negative emotional repercussions from humiliating events and may be more likely to advocate aggressive policies. These same elites can also frame historical events in ways that elicit a sense of national humiliation. When they combine this humiliation narrative with a message of domestic resurgence and strength, these same leaders can activate nationalist anger that can then be used to garner support for aggressive and assertive actions on the world stage.

4
THE CROSS-NATIONAL CONSEQUENCES OF HUMILIATING INTERNATIONAL EVENTS

Humiliating international events on average increase individual support for assertive foreign policy actions, including acts of aggression aimed at third parties. But do these shifts in individual attitudes translate into changes in the foreign policies of states that have experienced such events? This chapter provides strong evidence that they do. It examines the relationship between two potentially humiliating events—defeat in conflict and involuntary territorial loss—and levels of subsequent aggression and hostility. The analysis shows that states that have recently experienced these two types of events behave differently than those that have not. States that have experienced recent defeat, for instance, are 42 percent more likely to initiate conflict in the ten years after a defeat than states that have not recently been defeated. The analysis also demonstrates that not all defeats or territorial losses affect states in the same way. Rather, those instances of defeat predicted in Chapter 1 to be deeply humiliating are indeed associated with higher levels of subsequent aggression.

The statistical analysis presented here enables the examination of other key theoretical predictions discussed in Chapter 2, which relate to the roles that the degree of material recovery, the relative capability of the victor state, and the state's status play in shaping how and when states respond to humiliating events. In keeping with predictions, we will see that great powers behave differently than non-great powers do in the years after defeat. We will also see that rather than engaging in aggressive actions to make up for lost capabilities, defeated states are far more likely to wait until they have recovered their lost material capacities before initiating aggression. For some states, this process can take years.

Humiliation is subjective. Those who identify with the state are likely to perceive the same types of events to undeservedly challenge the status of their state. The analysis in this chapter focuses on the effects of two types of international failure that I have hypothesized will be likely sources of national humiliation. This focus on international failure, as opposed to international disrespect, is largely a function of data availability, as it would be difficult to collect the universe of cases in which states fail to acknowledge the rights and privileges of other states. Defeat in conflict and involuntary territorial loss are often perceived by statesmen, historians, elites, and the masses as sources of deep national humiliation. Because, like unexpected international failures, acts of intentional disrespect sow national self-doubt as well as other-directed outrage, we can expect them to engender similar responses to those described below.

For ease of reading, only general variable descriptions and intuitive tables illustrating the substantive results are presented within the analysis below. Detailed discussions of the empirical models, including model specifications and coefficient tables, are presented in the endnotes and in the Appendix.

The Effects of Defeat

In Chapter 2, I discussed that the likelihood of conflict initiation would be higher for recently defeated states than states that have not recently experienced defeat. I argued that defeat, on average, poses what is perceived to be an undeserved threat to the status of the state. This threat elicits the two prominent characteristics of national humiliation: outrage directed at the victor and intense self-doubt stemming from the state's inability to prevent such undeserved threats to its social standing. The desires to overcome intense helplessness and to right wrongs lead defeated states to engage in assertive international behaviors such as diplomatic opposition or the use of force abroad.

Are Defeated States More Likely to Initiate Disputes?

Here I explore the validity of this proposed relationship between past defeat and future conflict behaviors using logistic regression analysis of cross-national data. The analysis utilizes data on conflict initiation and war outcomes from the Correlates of War 4.2 and the Dyadic Militarized Interstate Disputes (MID) 3.1 datasets spanning 1816 to 2007.[1] Defeat is defined as any instance in which a state yielded in war after fighting if the opponent fought to victory.[2] Conflict initiation is defined as any instance in which a state is the first to either threaten, display, or use force against an opponent.[3] In order to capture the effect of defeat over extended periods following defeat, dichotomous variables, *Defeat in the Last 10 Years* and *Defeat in the Last 20 Years*, were constructed which are defined as 1 if the state has experienced a defeat against any state in the last ten- or twenty-year periods.[4] These periods were chosen because humiliation can persist over extended periods of time and because it can take states many years to recover capabilities lost associated with defeat.

In addition to assessing the effect of defeat, the analysis also investigates the effects of victory and stalemate in war over a ten- and twenty-year period. *Victory in the Last 10 Years* is coded 1 in the last year of a dispute if a state fights to victory or if its opponent yields after fighting and if it does not also experience defeat within that same period. *Stalemate in the Last 10 Years* is coded 1 in the last year of a conflict if neither state accomplishes objectives held at the outset of the war and if the state does not experience defeat within the decade. If defeat and victory work in the hypothesized way, we should expect victory to have little effect on the conflict behavior of states—victory will not undermine status so the state will have little need to assert its status expectations in the future through acts of aggression. The effects of stalemate on a state's status are less clear. It is possible that stalemates could pose a threat to the status of a stronger state fighting a weaker state. Like backing down, however, fighting to a stalemate may be seen to provide more insight about the resolve of the state rather than the state's capabilities.[5]

Figure 4.1 illustrates the substantive results of this analysis.[6] Within the figure, we see that the predicted probability of conflict initiation is 42 percent higher

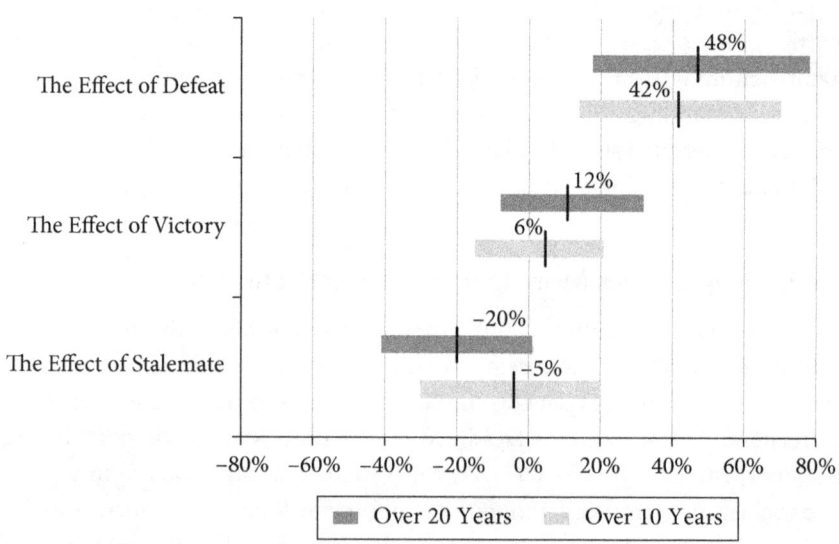

FIGURE 4.1 The effect of war outcome on the probability of conflict initiation

among states defeated within the last ten years than it is among those states that have not recently been defeated and 48 percent higher among those states that have been defeated in the last twenty years than those states that have not.[7] As predicted, this relationship stands in contrast to that between past victory or stalemate and the likelihood of conflict initiation. While recent victory is associated with a 6 percent increase in conflict initiation in the ten following years, this effect cannot confidently be distinguished from zero. The initiation behavior of states that have experienced stalemate in the last ten years also cannot be confidently distinguished from the conflict propensity of states that have not experienced stalemate in the last ten years. Over twenty years, however, states that experienced stalemate are significantly less likely to initiate conflict than states that have not.[8]

Are Defeated States More Hostile in Subsequent Disputes?

We have seen that defeated great powers are more likely to initiate conflicts than states that have not recently been defeated. So far, we know little about the nature of these disputes. It is possible that defeated states simply engage in more threats of force, rather than the actual use of force, than do non-defeated states in the period after defeat. Figure 4.2 illustrates the percentage of disputes initiated by defeated and non-defeated states within the twenty years following defeat which involve the threat of force, the display of force, the use of force, and, finally, all-out war. The two bars at the top of the figure show the percentages for all states and the two at the bottom address great powers only.

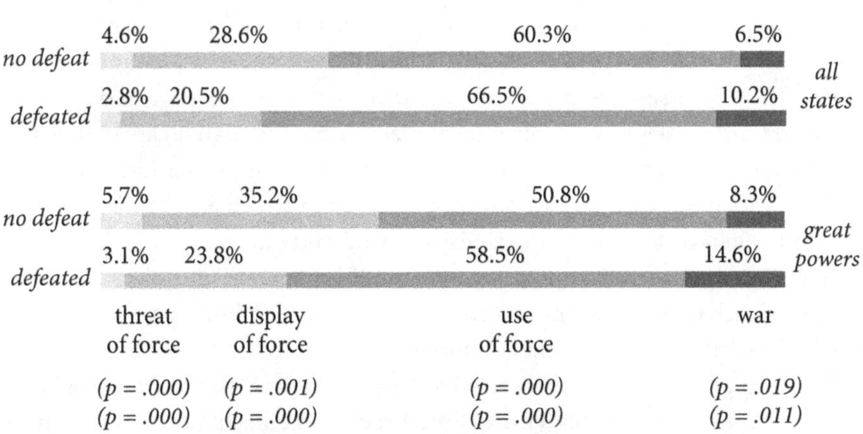

	threat of force	display of force	use of force	war	
no defeat	4.6%	28.6%	60.3%	6.5%	all states
defeated	2.8%	20.5%	66.5%	10.2%	
no defeat	5.7%	35.2%	50.8%	8.3%	great powers
defeated	3.1%	23.8%	58.5%	14.6%	
	(p = .000)	(p = .001)	(p = .000)	(p = .019)	
	(p = .000)	(p = .000)	(p = .000)	(p = .011)	

FIGURE 4.2 Hostility levels of initiated conflicts. The top p-values refer to the difference of means tests for conflict by all state. The bottom p-values refer to the difference of means tests for conflict behavior by great powers behavior.

The figure demonstrates that not only are defeated states more likely to initiate more conflicts than non-defeated states, but the conflicts they initiate are more aggressive in nature. For instance, 6.5 percent of disputes initiated by non-defeated states involve all-out war, but this rate increases to 10.2 percent among defeated states. Among great powers, the rate of war initiation is over 6 percent higher for defeated states. More generally, the probability that a defeated great power uses force, even when a conflict does not escalate to war, is 14 percent higher than it is among non-defeated great powers. Thus, defeat's effects are not explained by a mere increase in aggressive rhetoric of threats. Defeat correlates with substantively and statistically significant increases in the degree of aggression in the international system.

The pattern of aggression presented in Figure 4.2 bears out within logit analysis aimed at predicting the probability that states will not only initiate a dispute but will use force within subsequent disputes.[9] When including a dependent variable measuring the use of force within the model used to estimate dispute initiation above, we find that defeat in war in the last ten years was associated with a 30 percent increase in the likelihood of subsequent use of force and a 51 percent increase in the subsequent twenty years.[10] Neither victory nor stalemate in the last ten or twenty years is associated with any significant change in the likelihood that a state engages in the use force.

What Kinds of States Do Defeated States Target?

The results so far have assessed the relationship between defeat and aggression without specifying the target of that aggression. Defeated states may opt to initiate conflict against the state or states responsible for their recent defeat or may choose to target their aggression against third-party states that played no role in their defeat. To assess the predicted probability of acts of revenge and those of directed third parties when controlling for factors such as relative capabilities and regime type, the variable *Same Opponent* was included in the regression model.

This variable is defined as 1 within each dyad in which a state was defeated within the ten- or twenty-year periods afterward and otherwise as 0.

Figure 4.3 presents the changes in probabilities of conflict initiation against targets of each type in the ten- and twenty-year periods following defeat. The figure indicates that the probability of initiation against both types of targets is significantly higher in the twenty years following defeat than the baseline likelihood of conflict initiation among non-defeated states. The likelihood of targeting a state responsible for one's recent defeat is roughly 80 percent higher than the likelihood of conflict initiation among non-defeated powers. While most post-defeat aggression in the ten years following defeat can be characterized as acts

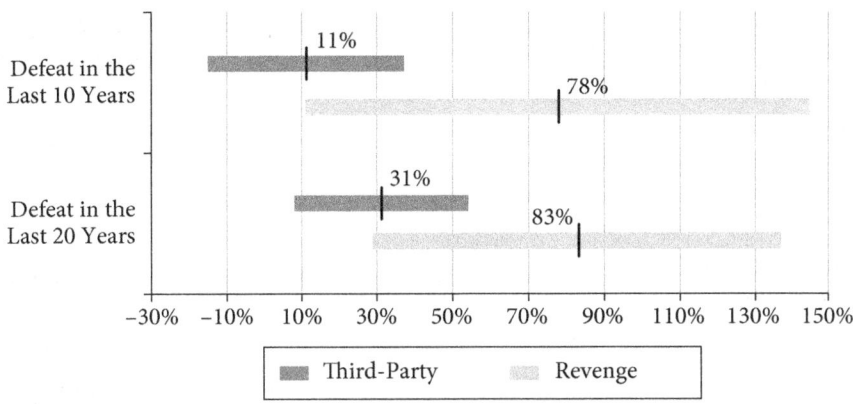

FIGURE 4.3 Probability of initiation by target type

of military revenge against any state which played a role in one's recent defeat, a significant proportion of the aggression comes at the expense of third-party states in the twenty years after a state is defeated.

As was discussed in Chapter 2, states with great power status would be more likely to target different types of states in the years following defeat than are non-great powers, largely because they are more capable of seeking status through the projection of power abroad than are minor powers. The ability to project military power abroad in pursuit of more globalized interests and to successfully maintain spheres of influence has long distinguished great powers from those states that lack the technological, military, organizational, or economic prowess to do so.[11]

By engaging in aggression against third parties, defeated states can restore their self-confidence while demonstrating to others that they maintain both the power and the intention to remain high international status. Acts of revenge may be more common for lower status states that possess fewer capabilities, both economic and military, to initiate aggression against third-party states.

Figure 4.4 provides an initial confirmation of this predicted pattern. The figure illustrates the targets that both great powers and lower status states choose in their acts of aggression in the ten- and twenty-year periods following defeat. We see that great powers experienced twenty-three instances of defeat over the roughly 180 years in question. Of the seventy acts of conflict initiation in the ten years following these defeats, only 5 or 7 percent, targeted a state responsible for the great power's defeat. Over a twenty-year period, only 12 percent of the instances of great power aggression are acts of a direct military revenge. As the figure shows, the target selection of lower-status states differs, split roughly 30/70 between revenge and third-party targets.[12]

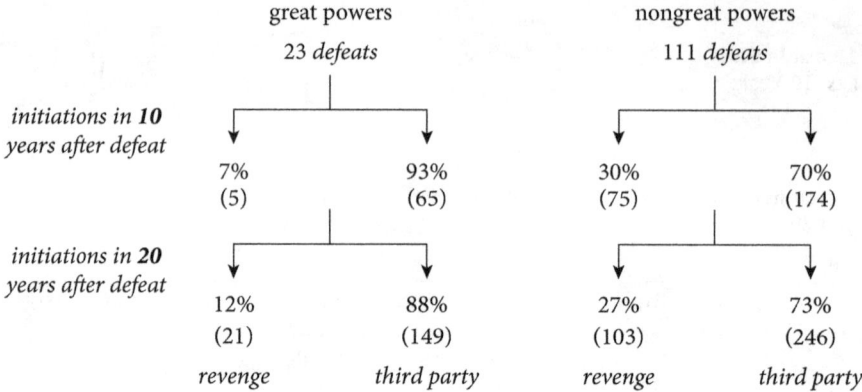

FIGURE 4.4 Targets of subsequent aggression as a percentage of total. Data is taken from the MID 4.2 dataset. The figure lists the number and percentage of disputes initiated by defeated great and non-great powers against states responsible for recent defeat and states that were not.

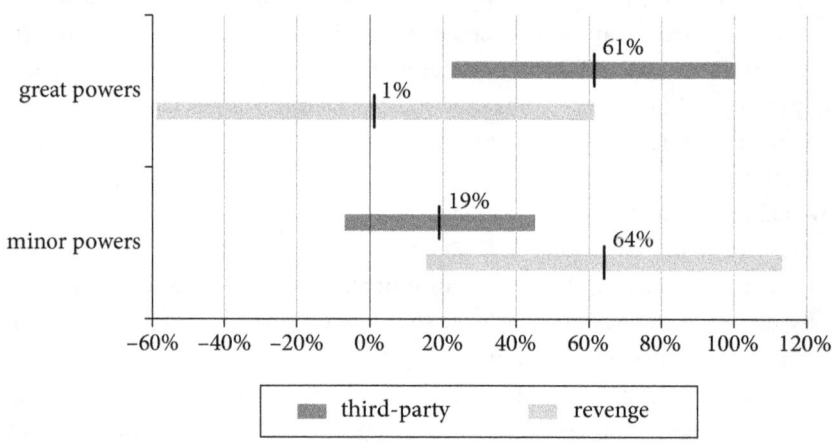

FIGURE 4.5 Effect of defeat on the probability of use of force

So far, the results have included acts of initiation that may involve only the threat or demonstration, but not the use of force. Ultimately, we would expect the most significant divergence between the behavior of great and minor powers to exist in the likelihood that they use force against third-party, often noncontiguous states. Figure 4.5 presents the substantive results of logit analysis comparing the conflict behavior of defeated and non-defeated major and minor powers. It shows how the likelihood that defeated major and minor powers use force against third-parties or 'humiliator' states within the twenty years after defeat compares with the baseline likelihood of the use of force among non-defeated states of similar status.[13]

The results in the figure provide further evidence that not all humiliated states behave alike. The figure illustrates that the patterns of targeting by great powers and lower status states in the twenty years following defeat are roughly reversed. Great power aggression in the twenty years after defeat comes primarily at the expense of third-party states not involved in the great power's original humiliation while increases in aggression by defeated minor powers come at the expense of states responsible for their recent defeat. The likelihood that defeated great powers initiate conflict against a third-party state within the twenty years after defeat is 61 percent higher than the baseline rate of conflict initiation by non-defeated great powers. The chance that defeated great powers target the state or states responsible for their defeat over the same period cannot be confidently distinguished from the baseline likelihood of conflict initiation among non-defeated great powers. The likelihood that non-great powers target the state responsible for their defeat is roughly 64 percent% higher than the baseline likelihood that non-defeated lower status states initiate conflict in the ten years after defeat. The evidence in support of increased targeting of third-party states by minor powers is far less strong.[14]

The theoretical framework in Chapter 2 provided an additional prediction about the conditions under which great powers are likely to pursue aggression. It argued that defeated great powers would be more likely to do so as their capabilities relative to their victor increased. Given the low rate at which defeated great powers pursue revenge in the ten and even twenty years following defeat, it is difficult to say with any certainty whether considerations about relative capabilities play a significant role in the considerations of humiliated great powers about target choice. It is true that the third-party states targeted by defeated great powers are on average weaker than the states humiliated great powers have targeted in acts of revenge, but the number of cases of great power revenge is too rare to distinguish these numbers with confidence.

How Does Material Recovery Affect Initiation?

With defeat often comes significant material and political decline. Humiliated states will wait to recover these lost capabilities before reasserting themselves on the world stage.[15] Humiliated states seek success on the world stage. Prior to reasserting their interests, they seek to regain confidence that the state will be able to successfully defend its interests on the world stage. Confidence and the likelihood of international success will be bolstered by the existence of sufficient domestic order and material growth. International failure often sows discord at home, engendering stark political divisions at best and revolution and violent civil unrest at worst, which forestalls the formation of coherent policy. The military, economic, and organizational capacity of the state is often affected by international failures in ways that then constrain the foreign policy options of the state. Humiliating events are often followed by periods of a military overhaul as the humiliated state attempts to rebuild its capacities to assert itself on the world stage.

This section assesses the effects of material recovery on the conflict propensity of defeated states. To assess this effect, the variables *Recovery in the 10 Years After Defeat* and *Recovery in the 20 Years After Defeat* are included into the relevant models described above in lieu of the binary *Defeated in War* variables. These variables measure the capabilities of the defeated state, as measured by the CINC score from the Correlates of War dataset, relative to the capabilities of the state three years prior to defeat. In other words, if defeat happens in time t, the variable in year $t+1$ is coded as $Capabilities_{t+1} / Capabilities_{t-3}$. The following year is coded as $Capabilities_{t+1} / Capabilities_{t-4}$, and so on. The capabilities of the state three years prior to defeat were chosen as a baseline against which to measure the overall material decline of the state because of the artificially high capability levels of states in the years building up to and during conflict.[16] The concept of material recovery is not dependent on maintaining levels of capabilities required to fight wars but on maintaining at least the peacetime capabilities that one views to be a partial basis to the particular international status of the defeated state. The variable is coded as 1 if the capabilities of the state in the ten and twenty years following defeat were the same as or higher than state capabilities in year $t-3$. The variables are respectively coded 0 during all years in which a state has not experienced defeat in the last ten- or twenty-year periods respectively and are continuous between values of 0 and 1 for all states that experienced defeat and subsequent material loss.[17]

The results of the model incorporating this measure of military recovery, reported in the Appendix, show support for the idea that, while defeated states are more likely in general to initiate conflict, the likelihood of initiation is significantly higher among defeated states that have fully recovered their resources than it is among defeated states that have not. The is particularly true for defeated great powers. Those that have fully recovered or never lost resources are, for instance, roughly 88 percent more likely to use force in the twenty years after defeat than defeated great powers that have not recovered the capabilities they possessed three years prior to the defeat. Fully recovered great powers are 40 percent ($p < .001$) more likely to use force than defeated states with only 90 percent of their pre-war capabilities and 97 percent ($p < .001$) more likely than those states possessing 80 percent of their pre-war capacity. Recovered non-great powers are no more likely to use force but are 9 percent more likely to initiate a dispute than lesser status states that have not fully returned to their pre-war levels.

The relationship between non-recovered defeated states and those states that have not recently been defeated is, however, more complex. The likelihood of the use of force among non-recovered defeated states is 37.8 percent ($p < .05$) higher than the likelihood among non-defeated states. Yet important differences exist in state behavior, depending on the level of capability depletion within the defeated state. Defeated great powers that possess less than 75 percent of their pre-war capabilities, for instance, are 40 percent ($p < .05$) less likely to use force and 79 percent ($p < .001$) less likely to go to war than non-defeated great powers. Defeated great powers that possess between 90 percent and 95 percent of their pre-war capabilities are 125 percent more likely to use force than non-defeated great powers.

Are Humiliated States More Likely to Achieve Favorable Outcomes?

A key prediction of Chapter 2 was that humiliated states would prioritize success on the world stage as they sought to renew collective esteem and the image of the state in the eyes of others. This prediction implies that defeated states will be more likely to achieve victory within subsequent disputes than states that have not recently experienced defeat and are involved in a dispute. The prediction also suggests that the difference in the odds of success between defeated and non-defeated states will be even higher within disputes that defeated states initiate. While defeated states may be forced into unwinnable battles by others, we would expect them to be more hesitant about picking fights they are not sure they can win than non-defeated states.[18]

Simple comparisons of the likelihood of victory within disputes by defeated and non-defeated states offer clear support for the proposition that humiliated states are more likely to prioritize success. In the ten years following defeat, defeated states achieve success are 37 percent ($p < .05$) more likely to achieve success in their disputes than non-defeated states.[19] Both defeated and non-defeated states are significantly more likely to succeed in disputes they initiate, but the rate of success among defeated states within these disputes is 76 percent ($p < .001$) higher than the percentage of disputes that end in success for non-defeated states.[20]

This pattern of heightened levels of success is not seen within the behavior of states that reached a stalemate within the previous war. Such states are 184 percent more likely to fail in subsequent disputes than states that have not recently fought to a stalemate. The likelihood of success among recently victorious states is 22 percent higher than those states that have not recently achieved victory, though this increase cannot confidently be distinguished from a null effect.

Are All Defeats Alike?

Certain defeats are likely to be perceived as more humiliating than others. Unexpected defeats in which a state is defeated by an opponent or opponents thought to have fewer material resources present a clearer threat to a state's image and are therefore more likely to arouse outrage and self-doubt. Similarly, loss in a war that one starts arguably poses a greater threat to the status of the state than loss in a war that is initiated by others. This may be because in starting the war, they convince others that they have committed their full military capabilities and resolve to the endeavor. We would therefore expect states that have experienced unexpected defeat or have lost wars they started to have a stronger incentive to engage in aggression after defeat in an effort to shore up the state's image in the eyes of its own citizens and in the eyes of other states.

To assess the differential effects of unexpected defeat, the variable *Unexpected Defeat* was incorporated into logistic models used to generate Figure 4.1. This variable measures the defeated state's military capabilities relative to the total capabilities of the state's opponents in conflict in the last ten years.[21] The results of this analysis indicate that as a state's ratio of dyadic capabilities with its victor increases, so does the likelihood that the defeated state will initiate conflict. The predicted probability of initiating a dispute is 97 percent higher ($p < .001$) among those states that lost to states with fewer capabilities than among states that lost to states of equal or greater size.

Although this finding is consistent both with the causes and effects of humiliation posited in this book, it is also possible that the finding could be explained by alternative explanations. One could imagine, for instance, that a state that has lost to a weaker opponent will be less likely to experience a decline in its capabilities because of the defeat. To account for this possibility, the variable *Capabilities after Loss* was included in the analysis. This variable accounts for a state's capabilities relative to the capabilities it possessed three years before it's defeat. The results of this analysis show that, counter to this alternative hypothesis, states are more likely to engage in aggression only after they have recovered their lost capabilities. This is strong evidence that post-humiliation aggression is not driven by a desire to make up for lost capabilities.

Figure 4.6 illustrates the predicted probabilities of conflict initiation associated with the degree of unexpected defeat.[22] The two graphs show the probability of conflict initiation as a function of the degree of unexpected defeat for two

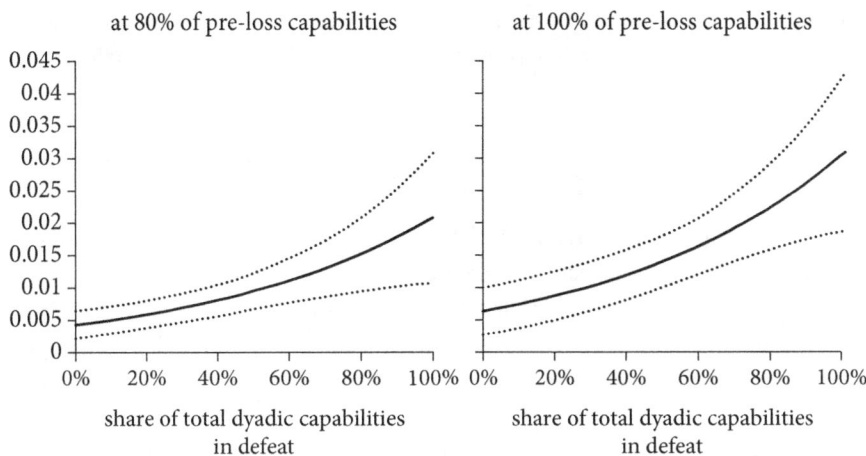

FIGURE 4.6 Effect of degree of humiliation on conflict initiation

types of states. The graph on the left illustrates the effects of degree of unexpected defeat among states that possess 80 percent of their pre-defeat capabilities. The graph on the right represents states that did not lose any capabilities because of their defeat. If those defeated states that lost to weaker powers are more likely to engage post-defeat aggression because they possess more capabilities, on average, to do so, we would expect to find no relationship between the share of capabilities in defeat and the probability of conflict initiation. Instead, we see that the pattern in both cases is the same, though the effect of greater humiliation is slightly more exaggerated among those states that lost to a weaker state and possessed equivalent capabilities to their pre-defeat levels.

To assess the effect of losing a war you started on the subsequent probability of conflict initiation, I used the variable *Originator in Defeat, Last Ten Years* as measured within the Correlates of War dataset, which is coded 1 if the state initiated a conflict and lost in the last ten years and 0 if it initiated a conflict and did not lose. This variable was first included within the model of conflict outcomes described in the first section but in lieu of the binary variable measuring all instances of defeat in the last ten years, not just those within wars that the defeated state originated. Predicted probabilities estimated using this model, reported in the Appendix, find that states that are defeated in wars they start are 50.8 percent (p <.05) more likely to initiate conflict than states that have not been defeated in wars they started. In a second analysis, I estimate the effect of this originator variable only within cases in which states had experienced defeat in the last ten years. This analysis, therefore, enables a comparison between the effects of defeat one originated and defeat that one did not. The predicted probability of conflict initiation is indeed 54.5 percent higher among those states that were defeated in wars they started than among those who were defeated in wars they did not ($p < .05$).

What Is the Effect on Diplomatic and Political Hostility?

In addition to predicting that humiliated states are more likely to engage in the use of military force against third parties and against the state responsible for one's humiliation, the framework in Chapter 2 highlighted several other potential behavioral effects of national humiliation, including increased diplomatic opposition. This section assesses the relationship of past conflict outcomes and new dependent variables drawn from Azar's COPDAB events data set which codes for international events, both cooperative and conflictual, from 1948 to 1978.[23] I rely on two primary measures of broader assertive foreign policy activity: *Diplomatic Hostility* and *Political Hostility*. Acts of diplomatic hostility include the imposition of economic sanctions or embargoes, the provision of sanctuary to opposition leaders or the blocking of communication between countries.[24] Acts of political hostility include support for opposition parties, the expulsion of military advisers, and attacks on diplomats or embassies. These variables were respectively coded 1 if a country engaged in any of these activities in a given year and 0 otherwise.

These variables were used as dependent variables within two additional sets of models. To ensure that these measures were not simply capturing the dispute data included within the models above, the analysis here excludes all cases of dispute within the Correlates of War dataset. The results of this analysis show that while victory and stalemate in the last ten years are not associated with and significant change in the likelihood of diplomatic hostility, defeat in the last ten years is associated with a 41 percent ($p < .001$) increase in the likelihood that a state engages in diplomatic hostility against third-party states not involved in the original defeat. The rate of diplomatic hostility against the state responsible for defeat cannot be distinguished from the baseline rate of diplomatic hostility among states that have not been recently defeated. Moreover, those states that were unexpectedly defeated are far more likely to engage in diplomatic hostility than are those that were defeated by states of equal or larger size. Stalemate in the past ten years also increased diplomatic hostility, though by only 22 percent ($p < .05$). Past victory is not associated with a significant change in diplomatic hostility.

Similarly, defeated states are 45 percent ($p < .05$) more likely to engage in acts of political hostility against third-party states than the baseline likelihood conflict initiation by non-defeated states. In this model, in contrast to that above, past victory is associated with a small significant increase in the likelihood of political hostility while stalemate in the last ten years is not associated with any significant changes in political hostility. Because of the truncated period of the dataset and because there are very few instances of great power defeat after 1945, we are not able to assess the differential behaviors between major powers and non-major powers in this analysis.

What Is the Effect of Repeated Defeats?

Finally, a single defeat can have dramatic consequences on a state's foreign policy. This is especially true of those states losing to a weaker state. But what should we expect of states that confront repeated losses within a short period of time? Although it is possible that repeated defeats exacerbate feelings of humiliation, leading to stronger subsequent assertions of the state's status, I have argued that numerous military defeats usually result within substantial material decline and the sometimes-permanent loss of confidence in the state. States that suffer repeated defeats often downgrade their status expectations, rendering them less likely to engage in status-bolstering actions. Figure 4.7 illustrates the predicted probability of conflict initiation as a function of the number of defeats

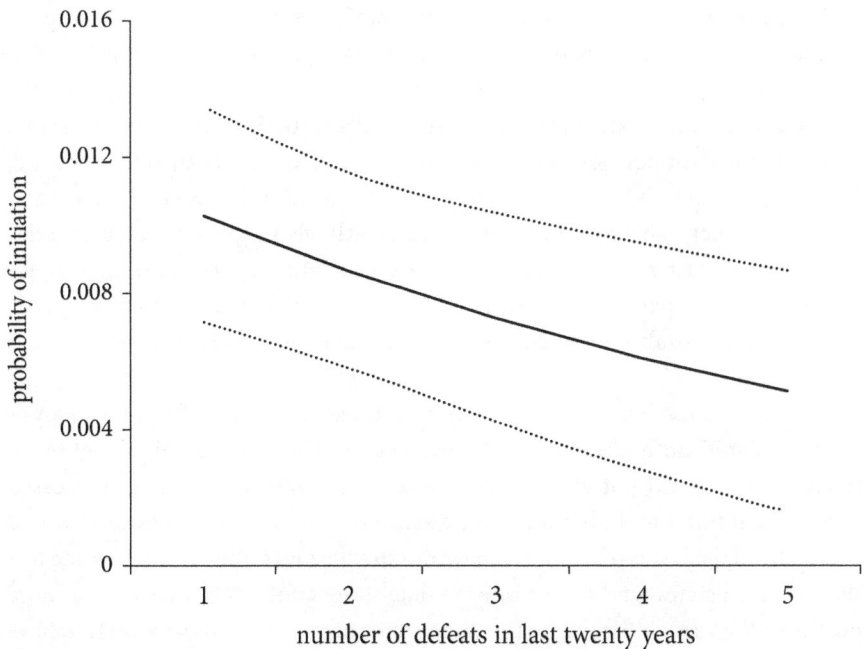

FIGURE 4.7 The effect of repeated defeat

experienced within twenty years. The highest number of defeats a state has experienced within the past ten years is five. The figure shows that the predicted probability of conflict initiation declines as the number of defeats increases. This suggests that as states lose repeatedly, they will be more likely to conclude that they are no longer deserving of or capable of successfully asserting high status.

An Examination of Alternative Hypotheses

We have seen that the relationship between past defeat and increases in future dispute initiation is robust to multiple forms of analysis. This finding is consistent with the theory of humiliation presented in this book, which outlines how states will behave in the years immediately following a humiliating event. There are, however, other possible explanations for this finding.

Hypothesis 1: The Relationship Can Be Explained by Heightened Levels of Activity

It is possible that some states in the system are simply more active than others. These particularly active states would be more likely to both experience defeat and initiate future aggression and could therefore explain the relationship we find above. Numerous facts, however, call into question the validity of this explanation. First, the analysis above includes a variable accounting for the recent activity of a state within the last five years. By including this measure, we can control for periods of particularly heightened activity by states. Second, if heightened activity were to explain the relationship between the past and present conflict behavior, then we would clearly also expect to see a correlation between past victory or past stalemate and future aggression. Instead, we find that neither past victory nor past stalemate is associated with any significant increases in subsequent conflict behavior over either a ten- or twenty-year period.

Third, the omission of the top 50 percent most active states from the analysis does not significantly alter the results presented in Figure 4.1. Finally, heightened levels of activity do not explain other important empirical findings discussed above, including the differential target selection by different types of defeated states, the higher rates of initiation by states that lost wars they started, or the fact that defeated states tend to not only initiate more conflicts but also to be more hostile in the years following defeat than states of the same status level that have not recently been defeated.

Hypothesis 2: Defeated States Are Motivated Solely by Failed Political Objectives

Just because we find a relationship between past defeat and future conflict does not ensure that national humiliation is driving this result. It is also possible that defeat is associated with failed political objectives, which then drive future conflict initiation. This hypothesis might explain the primary empirical relationship above if one assumes that victory is essential to achieving the key objectives that originally drove a losing state to war. The concept of failed objectives could also be extended to explain other empirical findings presented above. States that have failed to meet their objectives, for instance, may fight harder in subsequent rounds because they have engaged in strategic updating following defeat.[25] It also might explain why states that initiated the war they lost initiate subsequent conflict at higher rates if one assumes that initiation is a signal of commitment to objectives.

This hypothesis also does not explain other key findings discussed above. Political, strategic, and territorial objectives are often dyadic in nature—states seek concessions or policy changes from rivals. Although the results above are consistent with the idea that non-great powers are attempting to relitigate prior disputes with the same actor, the results for great powers do not fully fit within this framework. Great powers are more likely to target third-party states than they are to target their victor. Indeed, they are no more likely to target the state responsible for their defeat than are non-defeated great powers to engage in conflict initiation. It may be that, in some cases, great powers believe they can achieve their unmet political objectives by initiating conflict against some other state that was not involved in the original conflict, but it is not clear why this would be systematically so.

Further, one could argue that states that fight to a stalemate are also likely to be left with unachieved goals following conflict. We would expect states experiencing stalemate to also initiate conflict at higher rates than states that have not fought to a stalemate. Yet this is not the case. The rate of conflict initiation among states that were recently involved in stalemates is not significantly higher than the baseline probability of initiation among states that were not.

Finally, the hypothesis that failed objectives drive results does not explain why states defeated by weaker powers would engage in higher rates of subsequent initiation. One could argue that it is because such states would be less likely to experience military decline that would constrain the political ambitions of the state. Those that were defeated by weaker states are more likely to engage in aggression, regardless of whatever loss of material capabilities they may or may not have experienced (see Figure 4.5).

Hypothesis 3: Defeated States Are Motivated by a Concern for Their Security

As discussed in Chapter 3, humiliating events do not only threaten the status of the state. They may also signal a growing threat to the security of the state as well. Defeat in any form, but particularly unexpected defeat by a weaker power could have implications for a state's reputation either for behavioral tendencies, such as resolve, or for particular characteristics such as military strength.[26] As Weisiger and Yarhi-Milo note, one could draw multiple inferences from a state's defeat.[27] One might conclude that the defeated state lacked the necessary resolve to follow through and win or one might conclude that the state possessed sufficient resolve but insufficient fighting capacity. Or one could conclude that the state was deficient in both resolve and strength.[28] In both cases, a state confronting a reputation for lack of military strength or for irresoluteness would fear an increase in challenges by other states and would, therefore, have an incentive to proactively reestablish a reputation for strength and resolve through acts of aggression in an effort to appear less vulnerable and thereby to ward off potential challengers.

This hypothesis may explain the general increase in post-defeat aggression, but it does not explain the target selection of defeated states. Scholars contend that not all conflict encounters are equally salient in providing relevant information about a state's resolve or military strength.[29] Potential rival challengers will consider a target's past performance in encounters with similar states when forming opinions about the state's characteristics.[30] States seeking to proactively demonstrate resolve or strength to potential rivals, therefore, are able to send the most effective signal through conflict experiences with rivals of equal or larger strength. Military success in campaigns waged against weaker states fails to convey equivalent information about how the state would perform against an equally sized rival.[31]

Evidence that defeated states prefer weaker targets is found by interacting the variables for relative dyadic capability and recent defeat. Figure 4.8 illustrates the results of this analysis, showing the probability of conflict initiation among defeated states as a function of its military capabilities relative to those of their targets. As the figure shows, defeated states are more likely to target weaker states than they are states of equal or stronger size. The likelihood of dispute initiation increases significantly as the state becomes stronger than its target. If states were seeking to demonstrate their strength or resolve against equivalent or stronger states, we would expect to see either a negative correlation or no correlation between dyadic capabilities and past defeat. The reputation hypothesis as currently theorized, therefore, does not appear to provide a clear explanation for these findings.[32]

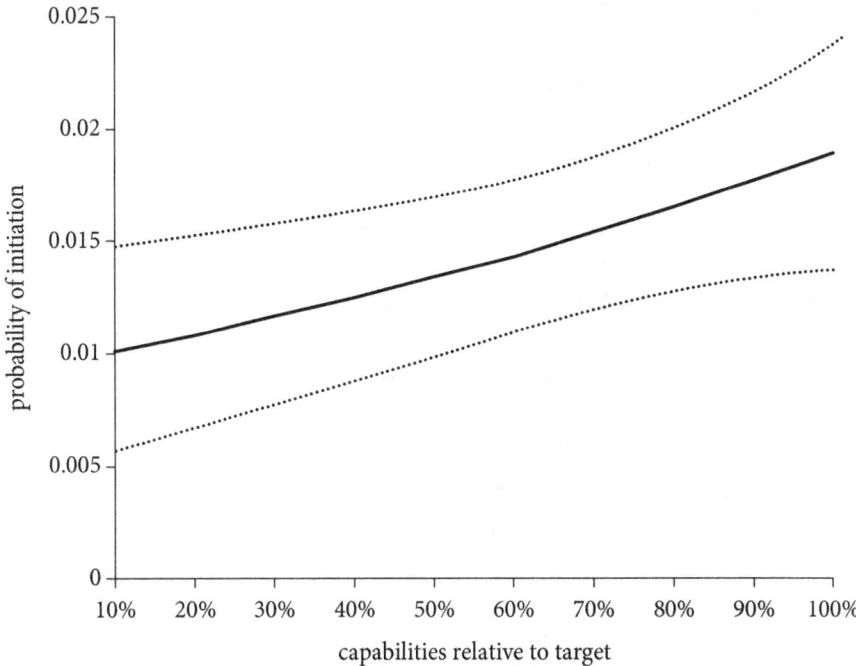

FIGURE 4.8 Relative capabilities of states targeted in post-defeat aggression

The theoretical framework presented in Chapter 2 explains the targeting of weaker states. Aggression against weaker, third-party states enables defeated great powers to diminish pervasive and painful feelings of inferiority and inefficacy while engaging in acts that have long defined their status. Such motivations do not necessitate that a defeated state takes on states of equivalent size to effectively signal its expected status. Aggression aimed at weaker states can also bolster confidence in the state by demonstrating both internally and externally that the state is able to behave as a high status state would. Given their aversion to repeated humiliating defeats, defeated states may indeed at first prefer weaker targets as they seek to re-establish themselves as playing an active role in world affairs.

Hypothesis 4: Defeated States Are Motivated by Material and Domestic Incentives

The impact of domestic, material, and strategic factors has not been explicitly tested within the empirical analysis above. It is certainly possible, if not likely, that states engaging in repeated acts of aggression are motivated by domestic factors such as a desire for the economic benefits of being in a war-time posture or the desire to reap the electoral rewards of nationalist policies. If war postures are on average financially, strategically, or electorally profitable, we would expect defeated, victorious, and stalemated states to have equal incentives to adopt them. We would not be able to distinguish the conflict behaviors of recently defeated states from those of victorious states or those states that had not recently been involved in the conflict. The results above indicate, however, that this is not the case. Past defeat correlates with future aggression while past victory and past stalemate do not and recently defeated states engage in higher rates of aggression than do non-defeated states.

In addition, the results above suggest that defeated states are not engaging in subsequent conflict in the hopes of making up for capabilities lost as a result of defeat. The findings show that rather than initiate conflict in order to recover, states wait to make up for their lost military capabilities prior to subsequently initiating conflict.

The Effects of Territorial Loss

In an additional test of predictions made in Chapters 1 and 2, this section explores the effects of another likely source of national humiliation—involuntary territorial loss—on state propensities for conflict. Involuntary territorial loss and defeat in war are obviously not completely distinct forms of national humiliation. Defeat is often accompanied by imposed territorial loss. The degree of overlap between the two potential sources of humiliation is not, however, extensive. Of the eighty-six instances of defeat between 1816 and 2000, roughly 20 percent resulted in territorial loss through conquest or annexation. According to an originally coded dataset on territorial losses and gains used in this analysis, based on data on territorial change from Tir et al., eighty-nine additional cases of involuntary territorial loss have not, however, followed total defeat in war.[33] These cases of territorial loss have resulted from the threat or use of force by a rival and the subsequent failure by the target state to fully engage in acts of war in defense of threatened territory. The analysis below assesses the effects of all instances of territorial loss, regardless of whether they accompanied defeat, though for purposes of robustness also confirms that the instances of defeat that conjoin territorial loss are not driving results.

The evidence presented here focuses on one specific response to involuntary territorial loss: aggressive territorial expansion. As suggested in Chapter 2, we would expect the likelihood that states pursue territorial expansion following a threat to status will depend on whether territory played a role in the initial instance of humiliation or disrespect. We can imagine that states that have been humiliated through the loss of territory would be more likely to respond by engaging in territorial aggression aimed at reacquiring lost domains, if they are able, or at taking territory elsewhere to signal their intentions of maintaining the expansive foreign policy of a high status state. Similarly, if a state's sphere of influence has been disrespected, the disrespected state will likely assert the right to claim territory, either disputed or otherwise, as would befit a state of its desired status.

The ability to defend one's territorial integrity and the ability to project power abroad in order to conquer and administer vast swathes of territory have both been crucial to legitimate claims to great power status for much of international history.[34] Support for the norm of territorial integrity by Western powers, and in particular by the United States, after World War II has rendered colonization and conquest more unacceptable forms of behavior for a majority of states within the international community.[35] Concurrently, technological development enabled the rise of new status symbols such as nuclear weapons, space missions, and aircraft carriers. Recent acts of territorial aggression by both the Russians and the Chinese in their previous spheres of influence, which appear to be motivated in large part by a desire to reassert status following humiliating and disrespectful treatment by the West, suggest that some states continue to view territorial expansion as an effective means of asserting great power status.[36]

The following analysis compares the effects of voluntary and involuntary territorial loss. Territory lost through involuntary means involving the threat or use of force can have lasting effects on the image and collective self-esteem of the state that can lead to similar effects as those of defeat. Territory lost through voluntary means such as mutual agreement and mutual secession should not, by contrast, challenge the status of the state. Contrary to standard realist thinking, states often willingly cede territory, as was the case with the Czech Republic and Slovakia in 1993 or Britain and Hong Kong in 1998. France, for instance, was not threatened with force when it decided to transfer its territories in Newfoundland to the British in 1904. Nor was China coerced when it willingly conceded numerous territorial tracts to both weaker and stronger neighbors in the post-war period.[37]

The loss of territory through voluntary and involuntary means on average generates similar strategic and material costs for the losing state. If states are guided primarily by material considerations, we would expect loss through both means to similarly alter the behavior of states. If states are instead motivated to act by concerns about their image, we would expect the involuntary and voluntary loss to differently affect state behavior. This prediction differs from that of prospect theory in that future changes in behavior depend not only on the fact of loss itself but also on the way the loss occurred.

As with defeat, we can assume that those states with high status to lose will be less likely to risk targeting the state responsible for its loss. Even if national narratives focus on the restoration of the lost territory, leaders of those states may recognize the impossibility of safely seeking their return until the state has sufficiently augmented its capabilities. In the meantime, those states with the capability to do so will likely seek territorial gains at the expense of, often weaker, third-party states. Even these actions, however, often come only after pre-loss capabilities have been restored, a process that can often take many years. By contrast, we should not expect that territory lost through voluntary means to significantly affect the likelihood that states will pursue conquest.

All models of the effects of territorial loss in this section rely on a fully recoded and expanded dataset of all instances of territorial change between 1816 to 2001. The territorial change dataset builds on the data collected by Tir and colleagues and includes sixty-five new cases and recodes all cases according to nine mechanisms of territorial change. This allows for clearer distinctions between voluntary changes achieved through mutual-agreement and involuntary cession of territory resulting from the threat or use of force.[38]

Are States That Lose Territory More Likely to Pursue Conquest?

To assess the effect of territorial loss on attempted territorial gains, four primary variables were used, in addition to numerous control variables described in the Appendix.[39] The first variable of interest, *Coercive Attempted Gain*, was defined as 1 if a state either acquired or attempted to acquire territory through coercive means involving the use or threat of use of force in that country year.[40] In total, there were 507 cases of successful or attempted coercive gains. To assess the long-term effects of coerced loss, the variables *Coerced Loss in the Last 10 Years* and *Coerced Loss in the Last 20 Years* were created, which were defined as 1 if the state had experienced a coerced loss as a result of conquest, annexation or a war of independence in the specified time period. The period of twenty years was selected because it best enabled a test of the theoretical framework above, which predicts that states will often delay their responses to humiliating events until they have recovered their capabilities and confidence following a territorial loss.[41]

Similarly, the variable *Voluntary Loss in the Last 20 Years* was coded 1 in the country year in which a state lost territory through mutual agreement or exchange or voluntary secession. Finally, the variable *Same Opponent* was coded 1 when a state had lost territory to the other state within the dyad within the last twenty years and 0 when the state had not experienced a loss to its dyad partner in that time frame.

Figure 4.9 presents the substantive results of this analysis.[42] The top of the figure shows the difference in the predicted probability of attempted territorial aggression between those states that have not lost territory in the last twenty years in an involuntary manner and those that have. Among all states, we see that this difference is both statistically and substantively significant. Those states that have lost territory in this way are 68 percent more likely to attempt future territorial aggression than states that have not. Within the top of the figure, we also see that this increase occurs among both great powers and non-great powers. By contrast, territorial loss through voluntary means, not depicted in the figure, is *not* correlated with any significant difference in the subsequent conflict behavior of states that have willingly given away territory.

Given the nature of the status threat, we would also assume that contiguous coerced losses would be more humiliating and thus more likely to increase the

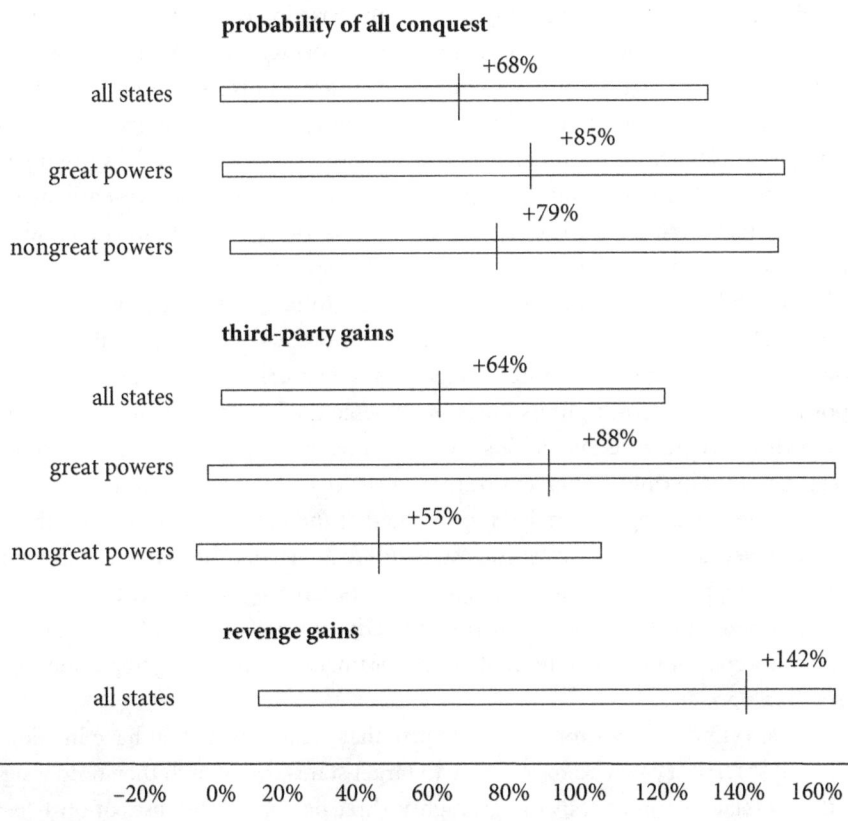

FIGURE 4.9 Effect of coerced loss in the last twenty years

probability of coercive attempted gains than would non-contiguous territorial losses. A variable was added to the dataset capturing whether the lost territory was directly contiguous to the state losing the territory. The states were contiguous if the territory was part of the country's homeland and if the territory was adjacent. The results confirmed the contiguity hypothesis, indicating that if the coerced loss was contiguous, the probability of a coercive attempted gain was 50.46 percent ($p < .05$) higher than following a non-contiguous coerced loss in territory.

What Kinds of Territory Do They Seek to Conquer?

The middle and bottom portions of Figure 4.9 specify the effects of involuntary loss on both gains directed at third-party states and those directed at the state responsible for their territorial loss. We see, similar to defeat, that much of the subsequent increase in territorial aggression following coerced loss comes at the expense of third-party states. Among great powers, the rate of aggression against third-party states is 88 percent higher than the baseline rate of territorial aggression among great powers that have not recently lost territory. A smaller increase in third-party gains may also exist among non-great powers, though we cannot say with similar levels of confidence. Finally, efforts to exact revenge against the state responsible for one's territorial loss increase dramatically in the subsequent twenty years. Among all states, the likelihood that states that have recently involuntarily lost territory pursue revanchist gains is 142 percent than the baseline likelihood that they target any other state in the system.

Though both types of states are more likely to target third-party states, further analysis shows that great powers are far more likely to pursue discontiguous, third-party gains following coerced losses than are non-great powers. Great powers targeted discontiguous states in 80 percent of their attempts at conquest following a coerced territorial loss whereas non-great powers targeted discontiguous states in only 34 percent of their post-loss attempts to gain territory. As further evidence, logistic analysis indicates that the predicted probability that a great power targets a discontiguous state following a coerced loss is 146 percent ($p < .05$) higher than it is for non-great powers. This significant difference provides support for the notion that the projection of power abroad distinguishes great powers from lesser states that are either unable or unwilling to pursue such expansive policies.

We also find strong support for the idea that great powers that have involuntarily lost territory will be more likely to target states over which they hold a significant relative military advantage. Eighty-three percent of the cases of post-loss territorial expansion by great powers occur within dramatically skewed dyads in which the gainer has at least 75 percent of the total dyadic capabilities. Great powers experiencing recent territorial loss attempted gains within dyads in which their relative military advantage is on average 8 percent (p < .05) higher than it is for non-humiliated great powers attempting territorial aggression.

Second, the analysis underscores the importance of success to reaffirmations of status following humiliating events. Humiliated great powers are 12.9 percent more likely to be successful in their subsequent acts of attempted gains than are non-humiliated states attempting to take territory. Finally, as further evidence that humiliated states direct subsequent aggression against less risky targets, states that have not recently lost territory are 131 percent more likely to attempt a territorial gain against a state involved in a defensive alliance than is a recently humiliated state.

What Is the Effect of Material Recovery on Attempted Conquest?

The evidence of the domestic effects of defeat described in this chapter corroborated Clausewitz's and Hitler's predictions: the feeling of powerlessness that follows humiliating events is often associated with avoidant tendencies. The desire to overcome the shame and powerlessness of the group can, however, intensify state efforts to rebuild, restructure, and revamp the capabilities and organizational capacity of the state. The reestablishment of the esteem and military capacity of the state can sometimes take decades.

Figure 4.10 indeed provides support for this mechanism within the domain of territorial losses and gains. The figure depicts the probability of conquest in each of the twenty years following a coerced territorial loss.[43] The black, curved line represents the probability of attempted gains against a third-party state by a major power over a twenty-year period following a coerced loss. The grey line shows the probability of an attempted coercive gain for a state that has not experienced a loss (.001), a probability that is equivalent in all years. The probability of a gain in the few years following a loss is roughly 1.75 times the average probability of a loss in that year without a loss.

This period is followed by a moderate decline in the probability of attempted gains from years 6 through 10 and then a significant leap in the probability between years 11 through 17 following a loss. In year 15, the estimated probability of an attempted gain is nearly four times the rate of gain when no coerced loss was experienced.

What explains this pattern of conquest over time? The high probability of gains in years 3 through 5 following a territorial loss suggests that a few states that have the ability to attempt gains against third parties do so relatively soon

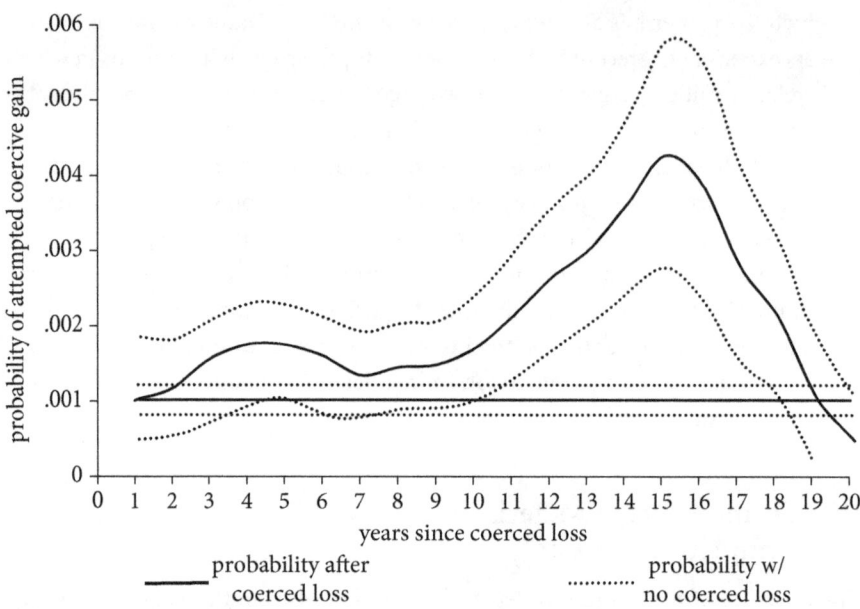

FIGURE 4.10 Third-party conquest in twenty years after coerced loss

after a loss. The decrease in probability after year 5 is possibly accounted for by a decrease in military capabilities among states that must rebuild prior to engaging in expansion again. As Figure 4.11 illustrates, the timing of the second peak of expansionary behavior closely corresponds with the average amount of time it takes great powers which have previously lost territory to recover their capabilities, excluding those states that lost more than 50 percent of their capabilities in conjunction with territorial loss. The figure shows that great powers experiencing a coerced territorial loss subsequently experience on average a 13 percent decline in their military capabilities; it takes these states on average about fourteen years before they return to within 95 percent of their pre-loss capabilities and roughly seventeen years to fully recover the level of capabilities they possessed prior to the territorial loss.[44]

Are Humiliated States Equally Likely to Seek Conquest in the Current Era?

As stated above, territorial conquest served to distinguish great powers for much of international history. The norm of territorial integrity that has arguably arisen since the end of World War II would indicate that conquest offers a less successful path to status recovery in the recent era. We would expect that states experiencing

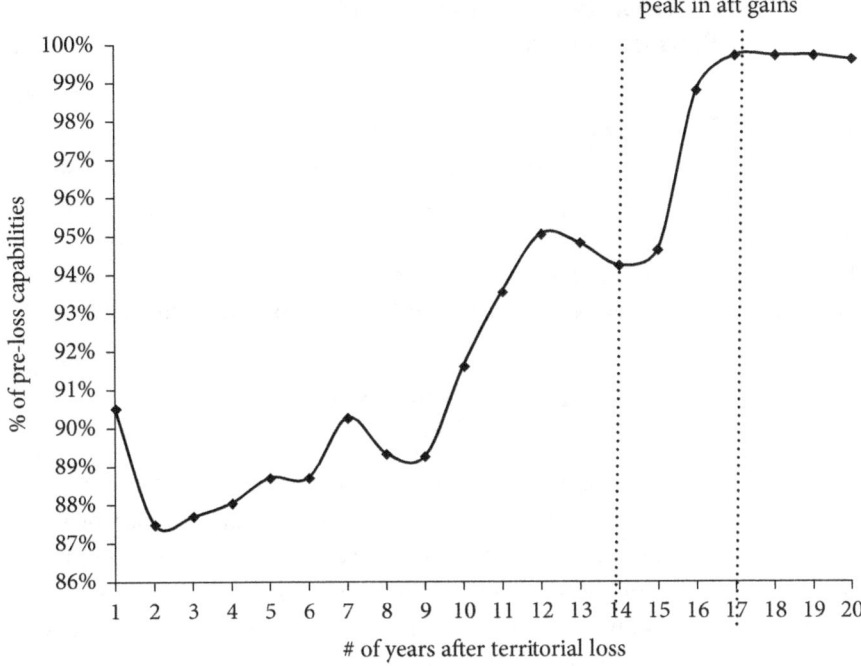

FIGURE 4.11 Average time to recover capabilities

a territorial loss in the post-1945 era would attempt conquest at a lower rate than in the pre-1945 era. Statistical analysis indeed reflects the importance of time. The baseline likelihood of a coerced loss pre-1946 is six times higher than it is after 1946. To test the impact of time, I included an interaction variable *Coerced Loss, Last 20 yrs. x Post-1945* within the model that generated Figure 4.8. The likelihood of a coercive attempted gain increased by 50 percent after a coerced loss before 1946; no significant correlation was found between losses and gains in the post-1945 era.

An Examination of Alternative Hypotheses

The findings above support this book's model of national humiliation. The involuntary loss of territory can arouse a deep sense of humiliation, leading those who identify with the state to seek to bolster both the collective esteem of the state as well as the image of the state in the eyes of others. It is again possible, however, that other factors might explain the relationship between involuntary territorial loss and attempted conquest.

Hypothesis 1: Great Powers Engage in Heightened Periods of Territorial Conflict

As with defeat, it is possible that some states are simply more likely to experience territorial change and to experience both defeat or territorial loss and aggression. The results presented here control, however, for a state's prior level of activity. Robustness tests presented in the Appendix provide further evidence that heightened activity is not driving results.[45] Moreover, omitting the top 50 percent of the most active states provides equivalent findings. These checks for robustness provide confidence that states at the high end of the activity spectrum are not driving the results.

Hypothesis 2: Leaders Pursue Conquest to Bolster Their Approval after Territorial Loss

Another possible explanation for the increases in subsequent aggression is that individual or leader prestige is the primary motivator of expansionary behavior rather than status considerations at the state level. First, acts of conquest might succeed at diverting public attention from economic or political unrest.[46] However, if this is true, we would expect leaders' incentives to engage in conquest to be driven by economic and political conditions within the state and not by last territorial losses the state has experienced.

Leader attempts at expansion might also stem from a desire to raise their popularity ratings in the years after an unpopular territorial loss or defeat. This would be especially true within democratic states. National defeat often leads to the overthrow of democratically elected leaders. In the case that aggression is motivated by leader prestige, we would also expect conflict initiation to occur within a relatively short time frame following a loss or defeat while a given leader remains in office. Given that a leader's tenure has been on average a little over four years over the past almost 200-year period, the result that a significant amount of territorial expansion comes more than a decade following an involuntary loss, calls into question the significance of leader prestige in motivating expansion after a loss. Examination of fifty randomly selected cases in which a coerced loss was followed by a coercive territorial gain found that the same leader was in place for both the loss and the gain in less than one-third of the cases.

Hypothesis 3: States Engage in Territorial Aggression to Regain a Reputation for Strength

Just like post-defeat aggression, territorial aggression following a territorial loss could be motivated by concerns about security and a desire to bolster the state's reputation for strength. As was true of the evidence involving defeat, however, the large majority of cases involve large powers responding to territorial loss by seizing territory from weaker non-rival states. Such acts of expansion, while involving direct coercion or the threat of coercion, likely do not require a display of strength on the part of the conqueror that would lead equally sized rivals to update their beliefs about the state's competitive abilities or their degree of resolve in battles against rivals. Instead, states engaged in acts of expansion against third-party non-rival states are likely attempting to signal to international observers their expectation that they should be considered among those with high status because they are both capable of doing something that only other significant powers can do easily and because they have sufficient influence to engage in international expansion without being constrained by groupings of other powers.

This is not to suggest that reputational and status motivations are orthogonal to each other. Indeed, this is not the case. Reputation and status concerns are often intertwined. A reputation for weakness generates concerns that a state's status may be in decline just as the declining status may signal to others that a state is likely to lack strength or resolve. This chapter has focused in part on the fact that states seeking primarily to signal their strength and those seeking to bolster their status are able to select from an overlapping set of policies intended to redress their concerns. If, in fact, states can signal resolve and strength through acts of aggression against far weaker states, then it is difficult to distinguish between reputational and status-driven post-defeat aggression. It is unclear, however, why such acts would force potential rivals to update their perceptions about how capable a state might be in direct conflict or about how willing they would be to pay costs in support of their interests against an equivalently sized or stronger state.

Hypothesis 4: States Seek Territory for Material or Strategic Reasons

A final set of considerations not considered within the analysis above was the features of the state targeted within subsequent acts of aggression. Certain territories may promise greater material benefits than others. While this may be true, it is not clear how the relative economic value of a piece of territory would explain the relationship between past losses and future attempted gains described above. This is especially true since we have seen that states appear to recoup any capabilities lost with the loss of territory prior to engaging in expansion. The omission of a variable describing the economic value of the territory is not, therefore, expected to bias the estimate of the effect of a past loss. The same can be said of the strategic value or the national and ethnic salience of a given territory. Although a state might desire a piece of territory for the strategic advantages it provides, there is no reason to think that this desire would be correlated with a past status-threatening loss and as a result would bias the relationship between a past involuntary territorial loss and the probability of future action. Moreover, while a state may desire to incorporate the territory of those who are ethnically similar, especially if they were once part of their state, this desire does not explain the increase in the targeting of third-party territories.

The findings presented in this chapter provide strong evidence that an important mechanism connecting past action with future conflict behaviors exists, which has been previously unaccounted for within the conflict literature. Defeated states and those that have lost territory through involuntary means are more prone to aggression in the subsequent years and decades than states that have not. The impact of these events is significant. States that have been defeated are 48 percent more likely to initiate a subsequent dispute and 51 percent more likely to use force in the twenty years following defeat than are those that have not recently experienced defeat. Great powers that have lost territory involuntarily in the last twenty years are 85 percent more likely to attempt conquest.

We have also found support for several other predictions laid out within the first two chapters. First, evidence supports the intuition and prediction that not all humiliations are alike. States that lose to weaker opponents are roughly six times more likely to initiate a subsequent dispute than states that have not recently been defeated.[47] States that lose contiguous territory are 50 percent more likely to engage in aggression than are those that lost territory abroad. These results hold even when controlling for the capability of the state relative to the systemic average and for the capabilities of that state relative to the capabilities it held prior to its loss.

Second, states are more likely to engage in subsequent aggression if they have recovered their lost capabilities. Those states that fail to recuperate lost capabilities shortly after a defeat or territorial loss are also less likely on average to initiate and escalate subsequent disputes. When states engage in extensive military reorganization and modernization projects following defeat, they will be less likely to behave aggressively during that time. Such states appear, however, to engage in higher rates of dispute initiation and hostility once their capabilities are ultimately restored. This process of recovery following a territorial loss on average takes more than a decade.

Third, we have seen that the status of the state correlates with what kind of state it targets in the aftermath of a humiliating event. The probability that states pursue aggression against the state responsible for their humiliation is higher in the second decade after the humiliating event than the baseline likelihood that any other state is targeted. Within the first decade after a defeat or territorial loss, however, great powers are more likely to target third-party states than they are to seek revenge. Defeated non-great powers, by contrast, are more likely to pursue revenge and are in fact less likely to initiate conflict against third-party states. The third-party states that great powers often target are far weaker than themselves. The major powers primarily responsible for aggression after defeat are far more likely to target states over which they hold roughly 50 percent more capabilities than they are to target equivalently sized rivals.

The findings in this chapter have underscored the importance of territorial change to the international status hierarchy. Involuntary territorial loss presents a humiliating threat to state status while its gain offers humiliated states a path toward status recovery. This point is illustrated in the forthcoming chapters and by numerous additional cases. For example, Russia's decision to acquire extensive amounts of territory in Central Asia in the mid-nineteenth century was motivated in large part by its humiliating loss of territory in the Crimean War and its desire to reassert its status vis-à-vis Britain.[48] Similarly, Stalin had not forgotten the "treacherous" and humiliating territorial loss of Sakhalin and the Kuril Islands during the Russo-Japanese War when he demanded their return forty years later at Yalta. As we will see in the next chapter, France's decision to conquer Tunisia in 1882, an act that was integral in the lead-up to the Scramble for Africa, was connected to the humiliating loss of Alsace and Lorraine ten years before.

5

SOOTHING WOUNDED VANITY

French and German Expansion
in Africa from 1882 to 1885

The evidence in Chapter 3 demonstrated that individual-level support for aggressive policies, both vengeful in nature and directed at third-party states, increases within states confronted with potentially humiliating international events. Chapter 4 provided evidence that these same mechanisms affect behavior at the national and cross-national level. This chapter and the next illustrate these dynamics within historical cases that vary across time and space.

Two international events played an essential role in generating the competitive dynamics of the Scramble for Africa during the 1880s. The first involves an instance of unexpected national failure. In 1871, France was defeated by Prussia in a war that it started, losing contiguous homeland territory in the process. As would be anticipated given the theory in this book, this unexpected, rapid defeat and loss of territory engendered a deep sense of both outrage and impotence throughout the country for years afterward. Rather than seeking revenge against a strong and ever-growing Germany, France pursued the more risk-averse strategy of rebuilding confidence and reasserting its great power status through the acquisition of colonial territory in Northern Africa, but only after it had restored political stability and recovered lost capabilities.

The second event involved the denial of great power privileges by a higher status state. The source of humiliation was different in nature but ultimately led to the same outcome—territorial conquest of a third-party state. In 1884, Germany perceived that Britain was attempting to enforce an unjust and intentional double standard aimed at highlighting German inferiority. Though they had little interest in acquiring colonies at this point, German leaders expected to be granted great power privileges including the right to imperial spheres of influence abroad. As the preceding chapters would lead us to expect, this perception of an intentional non-recognition of rights contributed to a deep sense of outrage within Germany along with a desire to assert the efficacy and rights of the state. Because Germany suffered no political or material decline during the event, German leaders were positioned to respond immediately by engaging in the very act they perceived British leaders had tried to prohibit—the taking of territory in South West Africa.

These acts of territorial conquest in Africa by France and Germany were consequential. They generated status and security concerns within Italy and Britain and led both states to adopt expansionary policies they likely would not have pursued otherwise. The initial acts of French and German expansion precipitated an escalatory and competitive investment dynamic with little material or strategic basis which eventually penetrated every corner of the African continent, eventually consuming the African continent over the following three decades and accounting for roughly 25 percent of all instances of territorial change between 1816 and 2010.[1]

To be clear, I do not offer a single explanation for all acts of territorial expansion during this time. To say that status concerns engendered by humiliating events shaped early decisions to expand is not to say that such concerns guided every instance of conquest throughout the Scramble for Africa or that leaders during this time were not guided by domestic, material, or strategic motivations. Rather, the evidence below demonstrates through the analysis of the immediate circumstances surrounding state decisions to adopt expansionary policies that without the impetus provided by humiliating events, the conquest of Africa, if it occurred at all, would likely have assumed a very different form.

A Brief Examination of Prominent Theories of the Scramble for Africa

Historians have described three grand theories of imperialism, which can generally be grouped under economic, strategic, and social motivations. Many early assessments, including those of Lenin and Hobson, focused on the value of colonies as new markets for the excess of goods and capital produced in developed, capitalist economies.[2] Later theorists, however, have noted how limited this economic argument is in explaining particular instances of colonial expansion. As A.J.P. Taylor points out, "the Economic analysis [of imperialism] breaks down in almost every case which has been examined in detail."[3] Others have noted that there was little about the need for new markets that necessitated annexation of territory.[4] Over the course of the nineteenth century, the British had come to adopt this view, arguing that protectorates were "unwelcome burdens" and embracing the notion that "trade, not territory" provided the means to the highest profits.[5] The costs of establishing protectorates represented an "unnecessary reduction in marginal profit."[6]

There is also little evidence to support the notion that imperialism was driven by capitalists' or the landed interests' needs for foreign outlets for their surplus capital. Langer notes that the most heightened periods of British colonial expansion coincided with a sharp decline in overseas investment of capital rather than with increased capital export.[7] The sad state of the balance sheets of the British East Africa Company and many of the German charter companies by the end of the 1880s also suggest that there was often little surplus capital to go around.[8] Some countries, like Italy and Portugal, experienced a shortage of capital, which led to a situation in which, according to Chamberlain, "far from capital fighting to get out, it was almost impossible to persuade it to go."[9]

Robinson and Gallagher offer the most prominent argument for the strategic rationale behind the Scramble for Africa. Refuting economic motivations, the authors cite British concerns that instability in Egypt would enable the French to steal a march on them, thereby giving France command of the Suez Canal as the primary British motivation for occupying Egypt in 1882.[10] The annexation of Egypt set off counter French annexations that then led to the British to reply in kind. However, as numerous scholars have argued, the evidence for British fears of French expansion simply does not hold up.[11] In addition to a lack of documentary evidence that the British feared loss of access to the Suez Canal prior to their ground invasion in June 1882, the British privately acknowledged months prior to their invasion that the French had no interest in taking part in a solo or joint effort to restore stability in Egypt.[12]

Finally, historians have argued that social conditions at home drove imperialism abroad. The argument is largely that colonies abroad would act as a "safety valve" for social unrest at home either through ensuring economic growth or by providing space for emigration. As British politician Cecil Rhodes saw it, new markets would provide work for citizens and keep money in their pockets, thereby reducing the likelihood of civil unrest. In Rhodes's words, "If you want to avoid civil war, you must be an imperialist." There is some evidence that Bismarck and French prime minister Jules Ferry both held this view. There is little evidence, however, of how such concerns relate to the timing of the intensification of the partition of Africa. Rhodes uttered these statements in 1895, long after massive segments of African territories had already been claimed. Instead, the initial attitude of the colonial states toward the partition was more one of gamesmanship than of essential struggle for the cohesion of the homeland.

These broad-sweeping explanations may provide some insight into the background conditions that gave way to colonization. Yet they often completely ignore the specific political context surrounding expansion and in so doing fail to explain anything about the timing or location of each instance of expansion or why the pace of expansion accelerated so rapidly once it began. Moreover, many of these explanations have often been based on imperial rhetoric "adduced as afterthoughts to justify territorial gains that had already taken place" as leaders attempted to sell skeptical publics with rational myths of colonial expansion even when the act of conquest originally lacked a material or strategic rationale.[13]

The First Stage of the Scramble for Africa, 1881–1885

Over the seven decades prior to the Scramble in Africa, European states had shown relatively little interest in establishing colonies in Africa. England, France, Portugal, and Spain had maintained small but gradually expanding footprints along the African coasts throughout the first half of the nineteenth century. However, gradual British and French expansion throughout this period had failed to generate any intense expansion or competition between rivals during that lengthy period. By 1881, France and Britain, the dominant powers of the time, held just under 10 percent of African territory, mostly in the northern and southernmost tips of the continent.[14]

This lack of interest was not for lack of experience in the region. Of this expansion occurring prior to 1881, 156,473 square kilometers, or 13 percent, were taken by the British around South Africa while 87 percent were taken by the French, primarily in Algeria over a period of forty years. In both cases, by 1880, the markets and the resources of Africa were of "almost negligible importance to the European economy."[15] Nevertheless, between 1881 and 1884, France, Germany, and Britain annexed approximately four times that amount. France acted first, annexing Tunisia in April 1881 and then territory in the Congo in November 1882. In both cases, French leaders were motivated to reassert French membership in the great power club by international events which they believed cast France's long-standing great power status into doubt. The relatively new German state, prompted by perceived British disrespect of its rights as an emerging power within the great power club, then decided to acquire its first colonies ever, taking land in South West in and East Africa between April and June 1884.

French Expansion in Tunisia, 1881

On April 28, 1881, 36,000 French troops arrived on the shores of Tunisia in what is considered to be the first act of expansion in the Scramble for Africa.[16] By May 8, French troops had acquired Tunis and the second largest city Bizerte and established a formal protectorate over Tunisia. For decades prior, the French had lacked any clear colonial calling or policy. Nevertheless, the French government, led by Jules Ferry and Léon Gambetta, opted to conquer over 116,000 square kilometers of Tunisian territory.

Though France and Britain had competed around the globe for international preeminence throughout the eighteenth century, their fates diverged in the nineteenth century. Britain prevailed as the paramount seafaring and colonial power throughout the century.[17] France, by contrast, had been defeated in the Napoleonic Wars and struggled in its attempts to found a Second French Empire in Mexico and Algeria.[18] In 1871, the country experienced its deepest humiliation yet: it's shocking defeat and the loss of 15,000 square kilometers in Alsace and Lorraine to a supposedly weaker confederation of German states, with Prussia at the helm.

The initial declaration of war by the French Parliament on July 19, 1870 had been greeted in Paris with delirium and the expectation of easy victory. Prime Minister Èmile Ollivier indicated that he was entering the war "with a light heart." French optimism did not last long. The failure of French leaders to recognize the shortcomings of France's military preparedness in the face of a larger, modernized Prussian force led to two of France's most historically humiliating battle defeats in less than two months—the Siege of Metz and the Battle of Sedan, where the French emperor Napoleon III was captured on the battlefield. The fall of the monarchy was followed by the rise of the Third Republic, which failed to negotiate an end to the war and instead persecuted the war for another five deadly months. The war ended on January 28, 1871 with Prussian soldiers symbolically parading down the Champs-Elysées and with Wilhelm I crowned German emperor in the Hall of Mirrors at the Palace of Versailles, acts that were taken with the express intent of humiliating the French.[19]

As is often the case, severe political instability followed this significantly humiliating national failure. The power vacuum that existed upon the withdrawal of the Prussians and the fall of the Second French Empire paved the way for the rise of the revolutionary Paris Commune, which ruled only from March to May 1871. France, and Paris in particular, descended into chaos as the national government and army were forced into retreat, the suppression of which eventually led to the killing of roughly 30,000 Frenchmen. Within a year, *l'année terrible*, the French had experienced the failure of not only the monarchy but also of the republic and had witnessed near-existential internal threats to the nation.[20]

The initial perceptions of the war within France were resoundingly homogeneous: the defeat and the loss of its provinces had inflicted humiliation on France. Upon the signing of the Treaty of Frankfurt in May 1871, which stripped France of Alsace and Lorraine, Prime Minister Gambetta correctly predicted that as a result of this "humiliating peace, revolution [would] break out in Paris."[21] French leaders perceived that the defeat threatened the first-rank status of France on the world stage, while the French public initially responded to the defeat with rage against the French army and government and then with outrage at Prussia and especially at Bismarck.[22] In the months that followed the defeat, attempts were made to commemorate French losses, especially in towns like Sedan that had become "tainted with memories of national humiliation."[23] But the French were nowhere near ready to turn humiliation into honor for French soldiers. France had experienced military defeat in its past, but this defeat had more significant repercussions on the image of France in its eyes and the eyes of others. Napoleon had lost after a long fight to a large coalition of powerful states. Napoleon III had been quickly defeated by a coalition of Prussia and a number of relatively tiny German states—states that France had expected and had been expected to defeat.[24] As Michael Howard notes, the blow to French self-esteem was particularly intense given that French leaders had announced the importance of victory to the status of the state when declaring war, but had then lost, thereby suffering a larger blow than they might have without such a declaration.[25]

The French were not alone in their perception that this defeat had threatened the status of their country. For the British prime minister Benjamin Disraeli, the defeat called into question France's very existence as a great European power. He commented privately in 1875 that he did "not see any prospect of the revival of France as a military puissance. She is more likely to be partitioned than to conquer Europe again."[26] Lord Salisbury remarked in 1871 that the "ceded [French] territory would be a constant memorial of humiliation."[27] Other international observers surmised as to how the humiliating loss would affect French behavior in the future. Austrian emperor Franz Joseph I questioned if Prussia was not actually losing by winning Alsace and Lorraine, predicting that "the occupation of those places would not exactly be peaceful and serene," and Tsar Alexander remarked that the defeat would "create an inexpungable hatred between these two peoples."[28] Bismarck himself almost engaged in a physical confrontation with Prussian field marshall Helmuth von Moltke over the nature of post-war settlement with France, with Bismarck arguing that an overly punitive treaty would add significantly to the depth of French humiliation and resentment and would eventually come back to bite Germany by permanently threatening peace on the European continent.[29]

French leaders almost immediately desired that France should work to re-establish its grandeur on the world stage, but it was clear that France was not politically, economically, militarily, or psychologically ready to do so. France would first have to undergo major institutional reforms which reshaped almost all major facets of French life. Even upon the collapse of the Paris Commune and the re-establishment of domestic order, French internal politics remained unstable, with both Monarchists and Republicans vying for power throughout the 1870s and with both sides blaming the other for France's unfortunate state of affairs.[30] Not until 1879, when the Monarchists were finally driven from government, did the Republicans firmly hold the reins of power.

Of all French institutions, the French Army, which had not won a single battle in the war, had been the most demoralized by the war.[31] In the years that followed, the Republican French government recognized the need to "devote all our energies" to a multi-year reform of the French army according to the Prussian model.[32] The eventual destruction of the Monarchist party in 1879 was credited to the success of these Republican-instituted military reforms. It was not until 1880, upon the completion of the military reforms, that Prime Minister Gambetta announced to the country that "France had recovered her full strength" and that it was time for France to "look forward with confidence to the future."[33]

It was not only France's material capabilities that were in need of post-war restoration. A mood of pessimism, shame, and self-criticism pervaded French society immediately following the war, with even French leaders acknowledging that "we must begin the new period with a spirit chastened by defeat."[34] Top religious leaders, who had obtained newfound power among a self-questioning public in the post-war period, told the people that Prussia would not have been vanquished by a nation "ten times stronger and richer than itself" if France had not merited the punishment.[35] That public demand played a role in the sentencing of General Francois Bizaine to death for his decision to surrender the fortress city of Metz, despite his four decades of distinguished service, indicates the extent to which the French people wanted someone to blame. For "if it had all been Bizaine's fault," then maybe "they had not really been defeated."[36] Along with questions about French responsibility for the defeat, were clear feelings of outrage combined with calls for an eventual resurgence. At his resignation from the National Assembly in March 1871, famous writer and statesmen Victor Hugo announced to cries of *Très bon, très bon* that "From tomorrow onward, France will have but one thought: to gather her strength; to instruct her children in righteous anger . . . so that the people and the army will be one . . . In a word, the nation will once more become the might, spirit and the sword. One day the nation will be ready and its revenge will be terrible."[37]

By 1880, French leaders perceived a renewed sense of confidence in the country's abilities, though they had not yet settled on exactly what shape France's immersion from its extended period of withdrawal would take. They sought the psychological satisfaction that would come with the successful reassertion of French status as a first ranked power within the international community.[38] Chamber member Joseph Chailley-Bert described it best: "We had been beaten in 1870. We had been demoted . . . from our position as the dominant power in Europe and almost master of the world to the status of a second-class power. We were dreaming of some event or effort through which we should later seek to recover our position as a first-class power."[39] Gambetta spoke of an "imminent justice" that would soon take place, telling a large crowd that it was time for those "who [had] seen France fall so low" to "raise her to her feet again and restore her to her rightful place in the world."[40] But how exactly would France go about reasserting her pre-eminent status on the world stage?

Certainly, the French public supported an act of revenge against Chancellor Bismarck and the newly crowned German emperor through which the lost French provinces would be regained. However, attempting to exact revenge against an ever-stronger Germany was risky. Another defeat would risk the solidification of France's decline in the eyes of others. In the face of unfavorable odds, French leaders privately reconciled themselves to the fact that revenge, if it were ever to come, would have to wait, even if they were reluctant to admit this publicly. Prime Minister Gambetta privately declared in 1876 that "Only madmen can think of regaining Alsace-Lorraine," also saying that "we must keep our heads."[41] He had also implored "let us not talk of *revanche*, let us gather our strength." Jules Ferry, on assuming the position of Prime Minister of France, emphasized one simple policy: forget revenge, which could lead to an even greater disaster, and focus on other less risky strategies of overcoming the humiliation of 1870.[42] For Ferry, and many other French leaders desiring a reassertion of French status on the world stage, the annexation of Tunisia offered the ideal means to do exactly that.[43]

Why did France focus its efforts to reassert its status on Tunisia? Territorial expansion abroad allowed France to remind the French people as well as the European community of the state's ability to project imperial power abroad, as befits a great power, and to demonstrate its strength as a seafaring nation.[44] The act of expansion also signaled France's intention to remain active in world affairs and to assert the rights it had long been afforded as a great power.[45] A failure to do so would equate to an implicit acceptance of a lesser position. As Prime Minister Ferry put it, "Should we steer French policy into a blind alley with our eyes transfixed on the Vosges Mountains, leaving everything to be done, managed, and decided on without us and around us? This would lead to the bankruptcy of our rights."[46] Finally, a successful act on the world stage would renew the pride and confidence of the French people. As Gambetta stated shortly before the invasion, "The most important thing for France right now is to break out of the narrow circle in which the timid of heart want to confine it. We must learn to take a deep breath, puff out our chest and, most important, march forward."[47]

Although the annexation of Tunisia came ten years following France's defeat, the subject of a French Tunisia did not first emerge in 1881. Rather, the idea was first planted in the minds of French leaders three years earlier at the Congress of Berlin. Although it is unclear who first proposed the idea, both Bismarck and Salisbury advocated a free hand for France in Tunisia at the 1878 meeting.[48] Both leaders recognized the building demand for resurgence and revenge on Germany among the French people. Bismarck attempted to divert 'the ambitions' of the French away from Germany by offering French foreign minister William Waddington the opportunity for territorial expansion along the shores of North Africa.[49]

That France's two most recent military rivals supported France's actions in Tunisia did not undermine France's primary motivation of re-establishing the collective confidence of the nation through the successful pursuit of its interests on the world stage. Both Bismarck and Salisbury had viewed it as inevitable that French humiliation would trigger a need for France to engage in a vigorous display in an effort to bolster its confidence and they merely sought to channel these aggressions away from the European continent where such ambitions could have been catastrophic. Bismarck also recognized that the acknowledgment by other great powers of France's right and expectation to project power abroad, typically the restricted purview of great powers, would serve to ameliorate perceptions of status threat, at least among the French elite. Expansion into Tunisia provided France with the social recognition it sought and which other great powers apparently believed it deserved.

France did not immediately send troops into Tunisia, however. While Waddington, who became the prime minister of France the following year, had immediately been attracted to the idea of a resurgent French Empire, he realized he first needed the support of the French public.[50] The French people, weary from the long fight in neighboring Algeria, became suspicious on hearing that expansion into Tunisia was being considered at the urging of Bismarck. Was he trying to distract them from a surprise attack? Was he trying to divert their attention from the stolen provinces?[51] Bismarck addressed these exact concerns quite directly to Saint-Vallier, the French ambassador to Berlin, disavowing the first possibility, but fully acceding to the second. He had no Machiavellian intentions, he claimed.

He did, however, want to distract France from the pain caused by that "hole in the Vosges," arguing that a "grand pays" like France deserved satisfaction for and distraction from her lost lands. Although he could not offer to return Alsace and Lorraine, he did believe that the conquest of Tunisia would, as he said it, help "soothe France's amour propre and satisfy its natural and legitimate need for expansion."[52]

In addition to his concern about the attitude of the French public, Waddington was concerned about how the Italian government would react to a French move on Tunisia. France had long been competing with Italy for influence in the territory.[53] On hearing rumors that France had been offered a free hand in Tunisia in 1878, Italy began a series of diplomatic moves intended to counter French influence there.[54] Prime minister Charles de Freycinet became particularly worried in 1879 when the Italian government paid more than four times the asking price for a Tunisian railway. Convinced by Thèodore Roustan, his man on the ground in Tunisia, that France could not allow a lesser-ranked Italy to enhance its status before France re-established its own, Freycinet prepared to send troops into Tunis.[55] French action in Tunisia stalled when Freycinet was replaced by Ferry on September 23, 1880.

At the time Ferry took office, neither Ferry, who would later become France's most ardent imperialist, nor Lèon Gambetta, the leader of the opposition, showed any interest in engaging in military action in Tunisia. Saint-Vallier had entreated Foreign Minister Saint-Hillaire on January 26, 1881, imploring: "Save our country from the new humiliation, the new 'amoindrissement' (lessening) that threatens us ... We have our backs to the wall and Europe is watching us to judge if we are still something; one act of firmness, or energetic will ... and we will resume our place in the good opinion of other nations."[56]

Failure to act, he added, would relegate France to the ranks of Spain.[57] Convinced by the plea, Saint-Hillaire approached Ferry who expressed concern about domestic and parliamentary opposition.[58] The decision to invade depended largely on the position of Gambetta, whose change of heart on the matter can be pinpointed to a conversation he had on March 23 with the director of Political Affairs in the Ministry of Foreign Affairs, Baron de Courcel. A career diplomat, Courcel had not taken an interest in commercial or financial matters. Instead, he was long interested in the need to protect French honor and standing in the world. According to his memoirs, Courcel pled his case for French expansion into Tunisia in his March 23 meeting Gambetta exactly along these lines.[59] Great power status was ephemeral, he argued; action in Tunisia would bring honor and pride to France and would stabilize France's international position. At no point in this pivotal conversation did Courcel mention commercial or financial motivations in Tunisia. Gambetta was said to have left the meeting a convert, later that week announcing that "In Africa, France will take the faltering first steps of the convalescent."[60]

After Gambetta pressed his followers into conversion, Ferry quickly came on board, requesting authorization to send troops immediately.[61] In the eyes of his domestic opponents, Ferry had played into the hands of Bismarck, had cost France the friendship of Italy, and had provoked the British.[62] His government was immediately overthrown. Despite the opposition of the masses, French statesmen believed that the acquisition of Tunisia would serve as a demonstration to the French people of the efficacy of the state while also re-establishing the image of France in the eyes of other nations. Gambetta wrote Ferry privately on the signing of the treaty with the Bey of Tunis that "there will be people everywhere who will not like it, but they will have to put up with it. France is becoming a Great Power again."[63] That France had retrieved her status as a first-ranked power by adopting a vigorous and expansive policy in Tunisia became a part of national rhetoric.[64]

Alternative Explanations for the French Occupation of Tunisia

Not only did the key discussions among French leaders that led to the invasion of Tunisia in April of 1881 contain remarkably little consideration of the material, strategic, or social benefits that Tunisia might provide, the annexation lacked logical rationales along these lines.[65] First, France had little reason to expect any material windfall. While El Dorado myths about Sudan were pervasive at the time, there were few such myths about Tunisia.[66] French experience in neighboring Algeria had not engendered dreams of profit or natural abundance. Rather, as one French explorer put it in 1870, the only thing of plenty in Algeria was the desert and the only thing "plentiful in the desert was air."[67] Moreover, by 1870, over 300,000 lives had been lost attempting to quell unrest in neighboring Algeria. While the different domestic and demographic features of Tunisia suggested that it would likely be easier to quell than had been Algeria, this did not alter expectations about the degree to which North African colonies would materially benefit the French state.

Moreover, little evidence exists that the French state engaged in expansion in Tunisia at the behest of French coalitions of colonialists or entrepreneurs with parochial interests. As Andrew and Kanya-Forstner describe, French business remained mostly indifferent to colonial expansion throughout the nineteenth century and clashed with the interests of the small and relatively inchoate colonial parties.[68] French entrepreneurs with significant interest in Tunisian markets did campaign for financial protections, but no evidence indicates that they had an interest in or campaigned for full occupation of the territory.[69] Even if special interests had petitioned French leaders for expansion, the near-unanimous opposition of the French public to colonial expansion and its suspicion that colonial enterprise benefited the few while costing the many made support for special interests in an election year extremely costly while providing little electoral advantage for French leaders.[70]

In addition, the annexation of Tunisia made little strategic sense for France. Most important, it did not serve France's primary security imperative, which was the maximization of its continental security.[71] Since France's shocking defeat in 1871, it had become isolated on the European continent while Germany had continued to grow in power. French strategic concerns would have been better served by consolidating French economic and military resources to shore up its defenses within Europe, rather than engaging in far-flung colonial exploits with few perceived material benefits, as many argued at the time.[72] To many French politicians, colonies were more than a mere distraction; they were a liability. As one prominent Bonapartist argued, colonies were "costly in peacetime and dangerous in wartime."[73] Conquest and colonial administration would dissipate the country's strength just when she was most concerned with her continental security.[74] France also did not expand out of a concern about relative gains or a desire to balance recent territorial gains by others. The annexation of Tunisia followed a period of relative calm among the European powers; no state had acquired African territory outside of South Africa in more than ten years.

Finally, French leaders were not swayed to expand into Tunisia by domestic considerations. Rather, the French masses initially viewed colonies as a luxurious and costly distraction, providing little commercial, economic, or strategic benefit.[75] As stated above, protests broke out in the street on word that Bismarck was in support of the move, and the government was quickly overthrown following the invasion.[76] As one newspaper described at the time, "There has never been an epoch nor a country more indifferent to distant adventures than the Third French Republic."[77]

The divergence between elite and public opinion on how to respond to French humiliation was great. The preferences of the French public, driven by an emotional desire for revenge long stoked by politicians vying for political office, were unconstrained by considerations of strategic viability or relative military advantage. French leaders clearly shared the public's emotional desire for revanche, and yet perceived the significant risks involved. Out of fear of domestic political repercussions, leaders were reluctant to advertise the relative impotence of the state. It was only after major political efforts by moderate Republicans that public support for colonial expansion was aroused. Leaders advertised the material and economic benefits of expansion and suggested that, while colonies could not serve as a replacement for Alsace and Lorraine, they could bolster national energy so that France would be able to take back the provinces when the time was right.[78]

French Expansion in the Congo, November 1882

In mid-1882, French leaders were generally satisfied with the statement made by their larger footprint on the North African shore; they had no plans for a sustained march through Africa. Another humiliating failure occurred, this time diplomatic in nature, that would lead France to fully adopt a forward expansionary policy in Africa, starting with an act of annexation in the Congo. The French government had explicitly declared its lack of interest in the Congo in 1880 when French explorer Pierre de Brazza had set off for the region. When de Brazza returned in 1881 with the signed treaty, Prime Minister Freycinet further indicated that it was a matter for the AIA, the charter company that had financed the trip, and not for the French government, which was officially not interested in the interior of Africa.[79] Nevertheless, on November 12, 1881, Charles Duclerc submitted for ratification an agreement signed by de Brazza and Makoko, chief of the Bateke, in which the chief promised to "cede his territory to France ... and his hereditary rights of supremacy."[80] This case of French expansion cannot be understood without considering the impact of the Egyptian Crisis, which had played out in the months prior, on French attitudes.[81]

In the late 1870s, the British and French had assumed direct control over Egyptian finances in an effort to protect the substantial financial investments of their citizens in the face of a series of Egyptian economic crises. In 1879, following the declaration of bankruptcy by the Egyptian khedive, Britain and France officially assumed Dual Control over Egypt. This gradual encroachment of Europeans in Egyptian affairs engendered an Egyptian national movement that targeted British and French bondholders in particular. Over the course of 1882, nationalist efforts to eradicate European influence and to oust Egypt's European-backed leader led to British and French reprisals and a cycle of escalating violence. Growing nationalist resistance to this foreign interference led to joint naval demonstrations off Alexandria on May 17, 1882, further exacerbating the furor when fifty Brits and Frenchmen were killed in protests. By mid-July, Prime Minister William Gladstone had become convinced that direct military intervention in the country was necessary.[82] While his true motivation for initiating an attack has been debated, we do know that Gladstone initially proposed a joint attack on nationalist forces by both Britain and France.[83] Freycinet supported quelling the dissent but wanted to avoid direct action in Egypt, fearing the backlash of public support at the mounting costs of the intervention. In lieu of an all-out invasion, Freycinet proposed a joint intervention to protect access to the Suez Canal. Even this more limited plan failed to win the support of the French Chamber, leading to Freycinet's resignation the following day on July 30, 1882. Many had not expected what happened in August when 40,000 British troops entered Egypt alone, quickly occupying Cairo and Alexandria and taking control of the Suez Canal. By October, the status quo in Egypt had been irreparably altered; Gladstone requested a renegotiation of the distribution of influence in the country, effectively omitting a role for France. The extended era of French influence in Egypt was officially over. British troops, however, would remain on the ground until 1936.[84]

The primary point of interest of this case for assessing the role of humiliation in the Scramble for Africa is less the British motivations for occupation than the impact that the event had on the French. France had considered itself as having rights in Egypt superior to those of the other European powers since the time of Napoleon.[85] Though the blame for French inaction lays solely with the French people and French Chamber, Egypt quickly became synonymous with an almost intolerable affront to French self-esteem and status.[86] The editors of the well-read *Journal des Debates* confessed their humiliation at the event and remarked that this reaction conformed "exactly with spirit of the chamber and of the country."[87] As evidence of the fact that past humiliation increases sensitivity to future status threats, the loss of Egypt was spoken of by some in the same sentence as the loss of Alsace-Lorraine, referred to as the "second disaster" with consequences almost as disastrous for France as the war of 1871.[88] As is often the case with national humiliation induced by failure to live up to expectations, the humiliated party looked for someone to blame. The likelihood that England had profited from French irresoluteness was indeed sufficient to stimulate throughout French society a strong sense of other-directed outrage at the British, though the British themselves had in no war directly intended the humiliation of the French.[89]

The humiliation wrought by France's failure to act in defense of its global interests, as is expected of great powers, engendered a renewed desire, this time among French leaders and the public, to assert French status on the world stage for fear that French status would otherwise be reduced to that of Italy or Spain.[90] Although French leaders had not initially planned to expand beyond Tunisia, the notion that further annexation in Africa could compensate France for any decline in status resulting from the Egyptian affair started to take root shortly after the British invasion.[91] Because France had experienced no material decline as a result of its humiliating withdrawal and because public demand for action had been quickly aroused, France wasted no time in reasserting itself on the world stage. A few weeks after Gladstone's October request to renegotiate the status quo in Egypt, the French government ratified de Brazza's treaty in an act of "patriotic grandeur."[92] King Leopold of Belgium recognized that this new instance of French humiliation would impact French colonial policy, informing Queen Victoria, "In Paris they are raging; they seek a twofold revenge, against the Germans and for the success of the British in Egypt. They want to expand in every direction. Tunis is not enough; they want the Niger and the Congo in Africa."[93] French inaction in Egypt had called into question the efficacy of the state as well as France's intentions to once again be a preeminent seafaring power with unmatched influence. Action in the Congo would serve to reiterate these intentions to both a domestic and an international audience while also offering a relatively risk-free path toward renewed national confidence.[94]

It is important to note that this move to ratify the annexation of the Congo in an effort to repair France's image and collective confidence was in all other ways rash. The government did so without at all examining the financial or international implications of the treaty. Not only were leaders not guided by material or strategic interests in ratifying the treaty, they knew virtually nothing about the whereabouts or the characteristics of the annexed lands. As Stengers puts it, "Never has a government submitted to parliamentary ratification a treaty of the reality and results of which it knew so little."[95] To date, the French government had also taken great care to not provoke the British in their quest for greater influence. Moreover, the British, up to this point, had expressed little to no interest in West Africa, a region its leaders had acknowledged as having little material or economic value. This convinced Duclerc that the annexation of the Congo provided a relatively less risky way for France to signal its intentions and ability to maintain its great power status.

Early German Expansion, 1884: Angra Pequeña, Togo and the Cameroons

Among European statesmen of the mid to late 19th century, there had been no more ardent anti-imperialist than Bismarck. In 1868, he had defended Prussian abstention from colonial expansion, saying: "The advantages which people expect from colonies for the commerce and industry of the mother country are mainly founded on illusions, for the expenditure very often exceeds the gain . . ., as is proved by the experience of England and France in their colonial policy."[96]

Bismarck had yet to change his tune by 1881, a year before France annexed Tunisia, stating "I don't like colonies at all. They are only good as supply posts."[97] He worried not only about a colonial drain on resources and the costs associated with administering them but was also about the drain on German military capabilities as colonies would require protection from powerful naval fleets which Germany did not at the time possess. Furthermore, Bismarck had serious misgivings about becoming more reliant on parliament or individual states and about increasing the tax burden or federal deficit in order to amass funds to support colonial initiatives.[98] He maintained his anti-colonial policy up until only a few months prior to Germany's first act of annexation in April 1884, turning down parochial requests for colonial establishment in South West Africa and East Africa as late as December 1883.[99] Between April and October of 1884, however, Bismarck claimed territory first at the South West African port of Angra Pequeña, current day Namibia, and then in Togo and the Cameroons.

What explains this dramatic change of heart? Given his persistent doubts about the utility of colonization, why ultimately did Bismarck decide to follow Britain, France, and Belgium into the colonizing fray? Historians have long debated the impetus for this shift in policy.[100] They have largely rooted their explanations in general economic, financial and social trends of the time, citing the desire for economic growth, the desire for a solution to overpopulation and domestic discontent, and finally the desire for electoral support from imperialist domestic interest groups.[101] As will be shown, each of these general explanations confronts serious challenges. Analysis of the statements surrounding Bismarck's shift in attitude indicates instead that his decision to annex was in direct reaction to Britain's disrespect of Germany's expected privileges. Britain's failure to recognize Germany's rights to annex territory abroad, a privilege it believed it was afforded by its status as a relatively new great power, angered the confident Bismarck, who believed that a failure to assert rights associated with great power status risked demotion of Germany's newfound status.

British Indifference, German Status, and African Colonies

Bismarck first received a request for the official "protection of the flag of the German Empire" from Herr Lüderitz, a factory owner in Angra Pequeña, in November 1882.[102] Bismarck felt it necessary, as he had in the past, to first inquire with the British who held territory in the vicinity before extending consular protections to German citizens in Africa, a testament to the extent that Bismarck above all had prioritized maintaining good relations with the British and respecting their interests abroad.[103] In February 1883, Bismarck wrote to notify London of Lüderitz's request, stating that Germany "would be happy to see England extend her efficacious protection to the German settlers in those regions" and adding that Germany "naturally reserved the right to grant protection herself if the settlements in question lay outside England's influence."[104] Bismarck's intention was to provide basic consular protections, but only in the case that the British were not willing to extend their own.[105] The British understood this inquiry to be very much in keeping with Bismarck's ardent anti-colonial stance.

Six months later, Bismarck had yet to receive any indication from the British as to their interests in the area. In September, he requested for the German embassy in London to make a "cautious inquiry" to the British with the intention of establishing British intentions toward the territory as well as the basis of any claim to the title of the land that the British might have had. He requested the ambassador inquire about provisions the British might make for the protection of German traders in the case that title was claimed.[106] The response was again slow in coming. On November 12, ten months after his initial inquiry, an increasingly impatient Bismarck again asked the British directly if they claimed sovereignty over the territory.[107] Only on November 17 did Bismarck receive an official British response. It stated that although the British had no interest in, title to, or intention to occupy Angra Pequeña, they would perceive "any claim to sovereignty or jurisdiction by a foreign power ... [to] infringe their legitimate rights."[108] This response left Bismarck surprised and outraged. The British were effectively declaring a "Munro [sic] doctrine for Africa,"[109] attempting to unfairly exclude the influence of all other powers from the continent regardless of whether Britain had an interest in or intention to occupy the territory or not.[110]

Setting aside his concerns about raising the ire of the British as well as his doubts about the advantages of imperialism, Bismarck responded in December with a strongly worded letter requesting that Britain provide a legitimate basis for its claim and citing an extensive list of the numerous British disavowals of their title to and interest in the area over the years.[111] On delivering Bismarck's response to the British, Count Münster, Germany's ambassador in London, felt the need to soften Bismarck's language, suffused as it was with impatience and annoyance. This inquiry, too, went unanswered for six months, leaving Bismarck outraged at the disregard of German interests and status and fuming in March that the British had handled the Angra Pequeña affair, "not only with indifference but with severity and deliberate injustice."[112] On April 24, 1884, without receiving any response to his strongly worded note, Bismarck ordered the German flag to be planted at the port and Germany took responsibility for the protection of the Angra Pequeña settlement.

Within a few months, Bismarck's hope that the British would extend sovereignty over the Angra Pequeña territory in order to protect German traders had morphed into outrage at Britain's unfair treatment and a desire to teach Britain a lesson that it could not ride roughshod over the interests of other European powers.[113] As a result, he proceeded to acquire not only Angra Pequeña but also territory within Togo and the Cameroons, failing to notify the British of the latter until after the fact.[114] Following these initial annexations, Bismarck felt it necessary to convey his annoyance at British high-handed behavior. Stating that Germany would not abide by the "arrogance and selfishness of the English forever," he wrote to Münster that "the Munro [sic] Doctrine, that monstrosity in International Law, was being applied in favor of England to the coast of Africa . . . This nave egoism is in itself an insult to our national feeling . . . The 'quod licet Jovi, etc.' cannot be applied to Germany."[115] Why was it that England forbade others from the right to colonize, a right which England practiced so actively, Bismarck wondered?[116] It was exactly this sense of a British double standard—the British belief that its elevated status somehow privileged it in ways which it was unwilling to grant to others—that prompted Bismarck's colonial turn. A failure to assert Germany's right to acquire colonies, a right Germany should be afforded because of its high status, in the face of such disrespect would threaten both Germany's self-image as well as its status over the long term. Bismarck declared as such to Münster: "London is not showing the consideration to our overseas trade to which it is entitled. If we fail to push our rights with energy, we shall risk, by letting them sink into oblivion, falling into a position inferior to England, and strengthening the unbounded arrogance shown by England and her Colonies in opposition to us . . . Seeing the want of consideration shown in British colonial policy, modesty on our part is out of place."[117] It was not simply the extension of British influence around the globe, but the fact that the British extended their influence without due consideration for those of near-equivalent status that motivated Bismarck to annex territory abroad, an act reserved for those with great power status.[118]

For its part, London was shocked on hearing of the German claims. The British had long taken Bismarck at his anti-colonial word and had not expected his change of heart regarding German colonies. They felt it necessary to apologize for the slight, with Granville claiming to have been guided by the belief in Bismarck's anti-colonialism when he deemed German colonial inquiries to be of secondary importance. Beyond a mere apology, the British focused on righting the wrong with a spirit of generosity. The British cabinet decided in mid-June that Bismarck, who they recognized was greatly irritated with the British Government because of Angra Pequeña, "was to have all he wanted."[119] In September 1884, Gladstone made clear his low regard for the quality of Germany's new colonies, stating: "The world contains other waste places in want of occupants which would reward plantation better than these. Great Britain is very far from grudging their annexation to Germany. Colonization is costly and troublesome work."[120]

Bismarck's lesson for the British was not finished.[121] Following months of conspiring with the French about how to confront unchecked British arrogance in Africa, Bismarck convened the Berlin Conference in November 1884, a gathering intended to address the "miniature scrambles" starting to multiply along the African coasts, but intended to have a far greater symbolic significance.[122]

For Bismarck, who had only entered the colonial game in the few months prior, there was no greater recognition of Germany's status as a great imperial power than British willingness to convene in Berlin in order to discuss African affairs.[123] In contrast to popular skepticism over French expansion in Tunisia, the attitude of the German people toward colonialism reversed almost as rapidly as had Bismarck's when news of Britain's failure to acknowledge Germany's interests came to light. The German press so actively reported anti-British news that an official at the British embassy in Berlin decried the relentless "campaign against England" being waged by the press. The official concluded that the campaign was motivated in part by jealousy and partly "that England [was] really the only great Power whom it has been thought safe to abuse."[124] Whatever the underlying cause among the press, stories of British disrespect engendered significant other-directed outrage at the British throughout German society as well as broad support for policies that defied perceived British attempts to constrain German influence and which demonstrated Germany's general efficacy and assertiveness.[125]

Nationalist sentiment in support of colonies likely also influenced Bismarck's decision to expand his colonial holdings beyond Angra Pequeña. Acknowledging the shifting popular attitude toward colonial expansion, the British ambassador to Germany Lord Ampthill noted in the spring of 1884 that "Bismarck's interest in the [colonial question] is increased by the prospect of a General Election this autumn in which the Opposition may raise the popular cry of 'Colonies for Germany.'"[126] In the summer, prior to the election, Ampthill declared that: "Bismarck had discovered an unexplored mine of popularity in starting a Colonial policy, which Public Opinion persuaded itself to be Anti-English . . . Bismarck is taking advantage of the national craze that England opposes Germany's colonial aspirations, as an election cry."[127] As time went on, the expansion of the German footprint in the world became an increasingly predominant electoral issue among the German public, with Bismarck citing in 1885 that "At present, public opinion in Germany sets such great store by colonial policy that the government's position in home affairs largely depends on its success. The smallest corner of New Guinea or West Africa, even if in actual fact completely worthless, is at present more important for our policy than the whole of Egypt and its future."[128]

Alternative Explanations for the First Stage of German Imperialism

As with discussions leading up to France's early acts of annexation in Africa, Bismarck's correspondence and recorded conversations regarding Germany's first acts of imperial expansion contained little reference to material, economic, or strategic calculations. Moreover, expansion into Angra Pequeña lacked a logical economic or strategic rationale. Bismarck had little reason to expect a great material reward in the region.[129] Numerous reports had circulated prior to annexation about the barren deserts of South West Africa, a place devoid of water but replete with restless natives.[130] Prior to official annexation, one German explorer reported back that the port was "inhospitable even for a penal colony."[131]

Another stated, "It is one of the least economic coasts on earth ... no tree, no bush, no leaf is to be seen, nothing but sand."[132] Furthermore, the British had held islands directly off the coast since 1867 but had not expressed the slightest interest in the region, attesting to the area's lack of obvious natural appeal. Even if there had been abundant material resources within the region, extracting them would have required a significant amount of infrastructural development, investments Bismarck was absolutely not willing to make. Even after official annexation, Bismarck's attitude toward the colonies remained one of "indifference," much to the dismay of the explorers and few settlers there, and official colonial policy was that the state would play as small a role as possible in colonial administration or protection.[133] Furthermore, he had little reason to believe that private investors would fill the need for capital given their reluctance to fund colonial exploits in the years before and long after annexation.[134]

It is also unlikely that Bismarck was substantially swayed by the possibility of generating economic growth through the acquisition of new markets or by an increase in German exports to South West Africa. The German economy had been hit hard by the economic crisis of 1873, a crisis caused by industrial overexpansion funded by war reparations paid by France following its loss in the Franco-Prussian War. Attention after the crisis shifted toward a need for larger markets to absorb German industrial goods.[135] The undeveloped, largely unpopulated area around Angra Pequeña offered no possibility of boosting the demand for such goods.[136] The substantial infrastructural investment would be required to create an industrial marketplace but, as mentioned, neither the government nor German capitalists were willing to front such investments.[137]

In keeping with more particularist explanations of expansion, domestic financial and trading groups did propagandize for German expansion overseas.[138] The vast majority of these groups were small in size and influence and generated little direct financial or commercial involvement in Africa prior to or after the formation of the colony.[139] Historically, Bismarck had had no problem keeping interest groups at bay. By assuming direct control over Angra Pequeña, Bismarck met the demands for protection by the traders at the Angra Pequeña post. As the case evidence suggests above, however, the protection of German trading interests there was more a side effect of Bismarck's primary aim of signaling German status to the British than it was a motivating aim in itself. This is also evidenced by the fact that Germany's colonial holdings extended beyond the terrain of the German trading posts.

Another oft-cited explanation for German expansion into Africa was growing social unrest due to the economic crisis and booming population and the resulting need to acquire territory for German settlement abroad.[140] Germany held too many people, the argument went, and expansion abroad could act as a "safety valve" to prevent disorder if domestic conditions became too difficult.[141] For many of the aforementioned reasons, however, emigration to the African colonies was not perceived as an attractive opportunity for settlement. Beleaguered by a lack of investment, the regions suffered from poor communication, insufficient resources, and the hostility of native populations. Few Germans ever emigrated to German colonies in Africa. By 1913, only 23,500 Germans lived within all of Germany's African holdings.[142]

Finally, Bismarck was not motivated by strategic rationale in his choice to annex African colonies. The locations of the colonies were determined far more by what territories were available at the time and by the position of German explorers on the ground than they were by any foresighted strategic calculations. Prior to annexation, Bismarck believed colonial adventures generated strategic weakness. The German empire, scattered in far-flung regions across the continent, lacked geographical unity and presented exactly the challenge to an effective defense that Bismarck had feared.

The Systemic Effects of National Humiliation

Italy was the next European state to adopt an aggressive colonial policy. Like France and Germany, Italy held aspirations of great power status. Throughout the process of Italian unification, Italian nationalists had harkened back to Italy's golden era, promising the restoration to Italy of the grandeur and preeminent status of the Roman Empire.[143] Italy was great once, they argued, and it could be again if it embraced a policy of *Italia irredenta* and exerted its influence around the Mediterranean Sea, or *mare nostrum*, as it was called. Italy was unusual in that it had a history as a preeminent power but now was seen as an emerging power vying for great power status. Such ambitions to greatness were delayed by Italy's relative lack of capabilities and influence. While Germany had come into being as a relatively strong state in the international system, Italy had entered the system as a relative weakling. Its navy outsized that of Germany, but its army was relatively weak and its economy stagnant. Moreover, Italian interests were frequently and openly disrespected within European affairs, its room to maneuver subject to the whim of the great owers. Referred to as "6th Wheel" and the "least of the great powers," Italy's claim to great power status during the late nineteenth century was tenuous at best.[144]

Italy in Africa, 1882–1885: The Mediterranean, Eritrea, and Ethiopia

The limited extent of Italy's influence among the European powers was demonstrated most clearly in the case of Tunisia. Italy had advocated for an independent Tunisia in which the large number of Italian immigrants there would be protected. Italy had not dreamed of acquiring Tunisia for its own. Resources were limited and it could not afford "the luxury of an Algeria."[145] That Salisbury and Bismarck had disregarded Italian interests in Tunisia, though their interests had been presented clearly, and that France had radically altered the status quo in North Africa without notifying the Italians—despite numerous promises to the contrary—proved to be humiliating to the Italians.[146] If there had been any illusions about where Italy stood in the international hierarchy, the "Tunisian bombshell," as it was called in the press, epitomized the low esteem in which Italy was held by the international community.[147] Because Italy lacked sufficient capabilities to convincingly assert its expected rights, it would have to do so in whatever affordable ways it could and with the tacit acceptance or support of the great powers, which was slow in coming.

Italy's failure to exert influence in Tunisia had a significant and long-lasting impact on Italian foreign policy. Italian leaders feared the incident would pose a grave threat to Italy's tenuous status as a great power, with Foreign Minister Carlo Nicolis, conte di Robilant noting to statesman Luigi Corti in 1878, shortly after it became clear that Italian interests in Tunisia would be ignored, that "abroad Italy does not exist: we are falling into the state of Spain."[148] To bolster Italian status, leaders pursued a Triple Alliance with Germany and Austria, the true benefit of which proved to be psychological rather than strategic or material.[149] Above all, inclusion in the alliance achieved a form of recognition, signaling to the international community that Italy was on par with other great powers and that it should be considered a full member of the European great power club.[150] Italian leaders had hopes that with this alliance, Italy would lose its status as the 6th Wheel.[151]

In the mid-1880s, it became clear that Italian leaders were considering shifting their attention away from cooperative status-seeking policies toward the more aggressive material practice of colonization. Throughout the 1870s and early 1880s, Italian leaders had maintained a generally negative attitude about colonies. This negativity had likely been driven in part by the material constraints confronting Italy but was also shaped by the belief that colonies were financially detrimental and came at the cost of nation and economy building at home.[152] In 1882, Prime Minister Pasquale Mancini privately decried the system of territorial colonies as "sterile and harmful . . . a source of weakness rather than of strength." He continued, "I fully believe that those nations which do not already have territorial colonies should not consider procuring them."[153] His reproach of colonial expansion persisted at least through May 1884 when he declared to the Italian Senate that it was dangerous for Italy to "launch out in expensive and perilous adventures in distant lands, to initiate what is called a colonial policy."[154] Peace, retrenchment, and reform would instead be the key to raising Italy's international status. By January 1885, Mancini was actively asserting Italy's need for colonial holdings not just in Tripolitania, but also in less competitive areas along the Red Sea and in the Sudan, Somalia, and Zanzibar.[155] The next month, Mancini ordered the occupation of Massawa in current-day Eritrea on the Red Sea. What had motivated his dramatic shift in attitude toward the colonies and toward the need to adopt such a costly material strategy for the assertion of Italian status?

Certainly, Italian perceptions about the material and strategic value of East Africa had not changed. The Italians had shown little interest in the East African coast until that time. Although they had acquired the small Eritrean port of Assab from an Italian steamship company in 1882, they had found the port inadequate for use and the region far too hot and arid for habitation.[156] Trade with the port represented a minuscule fraction of all Italian trade abroad. Strategically, the majority of Italian statesmen deemed the Red Sea colony to be a significant distraction from Italy's primary interests on the Mediterranean.[157]

Although historians have debated the cause of Bismarck's dramatic colonial conversion, they have agreed on the factors that lead to Mancini's change of heart.[158] The timing of the shift in attitude can be pinpointed almost exactly to the Berlin Conference in November 1884. It was at this conference that Germany announced itself as a serious colonial player on par with Britain and France, both through its colonial holdings as well as its leadership of the conference. When African colonization had been perceived as a game between just the British and French, the Italians had had little reason to act beyond the Mediterranean. Bismarck's dive into the African competition, however, profoundly affected Italian statesman who saw German actions as setting a new precedent that could and should be followed.[159] As one diplomat stated at the time, "Germany had acted; Italy must act."[160] Italy had received nothing at the Congress of Berlin in 1878, it had been humiliated in Tunisia, and it had failed to exert itself in Egypt in 1882.[161] These events had injured Italian self-esteem but had done little to alter the underlying international hierarchy of status with Britain and France at the helm.[162] Germany's imperial debut threatened to alter the status hierarchy fundamentally, relegating Italy to a lower status. If Italy was to ever acquire its "place in the sun," it would have to "abandon prudence" and engage in costly African expansion like the other European powers.¹⁶³ Francesco Crispi, prime minister in the 1890s and an ardent colonialist, advocated this position as well: if other powers were acquiring colonies in Africa, Italy should also acquire them in order to look more like a great power.¹⁶⁴ The Italian statesman Antonio Starabba, Marchese di Rudini also later admitted as such, acknowledging that Italy had sought colonies "in a spirit of imitation . . . for pure snobbism."¹⁶⁵

Though Italy's strategy of aping the great powers in an attempt to defend Italy's tenuous hold on great power status initially met with success, it rather quickly became clear that Italian goals to maintain a new Roman Empire abroad remained unmatched by the country's material capabilities. Because Italian leaders had been unsuccessful at establishing their interests along the Mediterranean, they turned toward East Africa, a far less competitive area, in hopes of success. With secret sanction by Britain, Italy managed to easily take the port of Massawa in modern-day Eritrea in 1885. Two years later, however, Italian soldiers confronted a massive uprising there and were convincingly defeated in the Battle of Dogali. It would take four years of military engagement for Italy to bring its coveted Ethiopia back in to the fold in 1889, though the colony would be lost again after an incredibly unexpected and humiliating defeat at the hands of Menelik II in 1896, a defeat that was followed by an extended period of significant retrenchment. The humiliation of this defeat would not, however, be forgotten.¹⁶⁶ Italian obsession over Ethiopia persisted into the 1930s, long after colonial adventures had become outdated, leading Mussolini to launch a new imperial project there aimed at reasserting Italy's great power status over three decades later.¹⁶⁷

The Reluctant Turn: Britain Adopts a Forward Policy, 1884

Britain was the last of the European powers to adopt a forward policy in Africa in late 1884, and even then, British leaders did so reluctantly. For most of the nineteenth century following the defeat of France in the Napoleonic Wars, Britain had been a satiated power whose primary ambition was to keep the peace.¹⁶⁸ Excepting its expansion in the South and its reluctant move into Egypt, Britain had opted against major expansion into Africa in the nineteenth century, despite its unrivaled ability to do so through most of the period. Rather, relying on its unchallenged status as the preeminent seafaring power, Britain had maintained influence informally all around the globe without having to take on the costs of conquest and occupation.

Beyond simply opting against expansion throughout the early 1880s, Britain had encouraged the expansion of potential rivals into Africa. Salisbury, for instance, had agreed with Bismarck to support French expansion into Tunisia. Gladstone, who maintained a strong distaste for imperialism throughout his terms in office, outwardly supported German expansion into South West Africa, looking with "satisfaction, sympathy and joy upon the extension of Germany in these desert places of the earth."[169] To Parliament, he declared, "If Germany is to become a colonizing power, all I say is 'God speed to her!'"[170] At this point, the early expansion of rivals had also done little to arouse either the jingoism of the British public or the press.[171] As late as March 1885, *The Times* referred to the early territories taken by the Germans in East Africa as "sterile sand holes" but noted that if the Germans were foolhardy enough to embark there, the English would offer a "hearty welcome to the development of the Teuton abroad."[172]

In December 1884, Gladstone wrote to Granville, "I would give Bismarck every satisfaction about his Colonial matters." Regarding further British expansion, he stated: "I see great objection to it; and generally considering what we have got I am against entering into scramble for the remainder." To Derby, he wrote, "Is it dignified, or is it required by any real interest, to make extensions of British authority without any view of occupying but simply to keep [the Germans] out?"[173] By late 1884, some British attitudes about the expansion of others were starting to change. Although Gladstone would always perceive there to be "something absurd in the scramble for colonies," he oversaw the first reluctant, half-hearted act of British expansion outside of South Africa in August 1884 with the formation of the Oil River Protectorate.[174] Only two years earlier, the British Foreign Office had declared of the region that "Such an extensive protectorate . . . would be a most serious addition to our burdens and responsibilities. The coast is pestilential; the natives numerous and unmanageable."[175] By 1884, Foreign Office secretary Percy Anderson believed that the French had adopted a policy in West Africa intended to directly antagonize the British, leaving the British with no choice but to counter the spread of French influence there. He noted that "Action [in West Africa] seems to be forced on us . . . Protectorates are unwelcome burdens, but in this case, it is . . . a question between British protectorates which would be unwelcome, and French protectorates which would be fatal."[176] Given how little financial, commercial or strategic interest the British had in the area, it is difficult to understand the severity of this reaction without recognizing the deep fear that Anderson, and later Salisbury, had that Britain's long-uncontested status as the preeminent seafaring imperial power was coming into question.[177] Anderson was optimistic in hoping that one assertive act now would ward off a French challenge and would prevent "an unseemly and dangerous race with the French."[178]

British leaders at that time were also growing increasingly concerned about the intentions of the "young and ambitious" Germany. It was becoming clear that

Germany's colonial incursions were not simply electoral stunts, as British leaders had at one time assumed.[179] Instead, by mid-1885, the British were beginning to sense that Germany was continuing its surreptitious assault on Britain's "Monroe policy in Africa," expanding in Togo and the Cameroons around the same time that the Oil Rivers Protectorate was being formed.[180] The value of the land being taken was not of chief concern. Rather, it was the feeling that Germany, like France, was intentionally disrespecting Britain's spheres of influence to challenge Britain's "effortless preponderance." As the possibility of a challenge to Britain's "comfortable position" of preeminence grew more pronounced with each French and German acquisition, the language of "expand or perish" became a prevalent symbol of British national self-doubt.[181] Britain had grown complacent in her ascendancy; some thought her "position [was] lost—irrevocably."[182]

Although they were collectively slow to respond, British leaders eventually realized that if Britain were to remain a preeminent power, they could not allow Britain to be "cheeked by Bismarck or anyone else."[183] Without a "positive and vigorous effort" to assert British rights as the preeminent power, Britain would be left behind, suffering the inevitable decline of an empire.[184] According to *The Times*, "With the colonies massed around us we can hold our own in the ranks of the world Powers . . . Without them we must sink to the position of a merely European kingdom, a position which for England entails slow but sure decay." British leaders agreed, with Chamberlain stating that a failure to expand further would "strike at the root cause of our great position."[185] By the end of 1885, Britain had acquired territory in Somalia, Botswana, and Niger and had increased its territorial holdings in South Africa. By the turn of the century, Britain—the once reluctant imperialist—possessed control over roughly one-quarter of the entire African continent.[186]

The Second Stage of the Scramble for Africa: The Pace Accelerates

By early 1885, events in Africa had started to take on "the character of a steeplechase," a transition prompted largely by Britain's decision to finally adopt a forward policy in Africa.[187] Despite that a significant number of existing colonies had proven to be economic failures,[188] European states that wanted to be perceived as great powers pursued colonial acquisitions throughout the remainder of the century with abandon. And each state appeared to do so for a remarkably consistent reason. As we saw above, the British feared that if they did not match others' colonial holdings in Africa that England would sink into slow decay as a lower ranked continental state. Foreign Minister, Ferry described French colonial policy in similar terms in July 1885: "We can see so many rivals increasing in stature around us . . . a policy of containment or abstention is nothing other than the broad road leading to decadence! France must put itself in a position where it can do what others are doing. If we do not, then we shall meet the fate which has overtaken other nations which played a great role on the world stage centuries ago but which today, for all their power and greatness past, are now third or fourth-rate powers."[189]

German views on colonies also converged to this perspective. By the end of the 1880s, Bismarck had returned to his disillusionment with African colonies, abandoning his colonial initiative almost as quickly as he had adopted it because the colonies had proven, as he had expected, to be financially burdensome without the promise of future reward.[190] Bismarck was removed from office in 1890 and with him went a moderate approach to German colonization.[191] As Sanderson notes, on Bismarck's departure, his "pragmatism gave way to an official conviction that Germany's future greatness depended on further expansion overseas . . . and therefore to pressure for repartition."[192] A failure to do so would relegate Germany to second if not third-tier status as more of a continental than an international power. Announcing in 1896 that "nothing must henceforth be settled in the world without the intervention of Germany and the German Emperor," the Kaiser indicated that African affairs would remain within Germany's purview for the foreseeable future.

Thus, the accelerating pace of territorial acquisition as the 1890s wore on was guided by an almost internal, "self-propelled momentum" in which state desires for more territory depended largely on the amount of territory states perceived others were taking or wanted to take rather than on any material or strategic value that states perceived the desired territory to hold.[193] Colonial expansion in Africa had become the mark of great seafaring powers, a great power club even higher within the status hierarchy than mere continental powers. Remaining a great imperial power necessitated "energetic vigor" aimed not only at imitating the policies of others but at matching their colonial acquisitions point by point. The Portuguese writer Eca de Quieroz describes the dynamic in this way: "Precisely what preoccupies us, what gratifies us, what consoles us, is to contemplate just the number of our possession; to point here and there on the map with the finger; to intone proudly 'we have eight, we have nine; we are a colonial power, we are a nation of seafarers.'"[194] What had started as an attempt by states to reassert their great power status following humiliating events ended as a competition motivated by jealousy and concerns that a state's membership within the club of great powers would be revoked if it did not at least match the material practices of relevant comparison states.[195]

By 1910, European powers had consumed most of the African continent. The entire process had taken less than twenty years.

This chapter has shown us that the effects of humiliating events on foreign policy do not exist around the margins. Rather, national humiliation led states to pursue sometimes costly policies of territorial conquest they likely would not have pursued otherwise that led to the conquest of almost an entire continent. Although the humiliation that France and Germany experienced was different in nature—with France humiliated by defeat and territorial loss and Germany flagrantly disrespected by the British—both instances of humiliation engendered public outrage as well as serious concerns about status demotion. The expansionary policies these states adopted in responses to humiliating events threatened the status and interests of other states and, in turn, led these other states to mimic the expansionary policies in an effort to maintain their international position.

Beyond these general points, the chapter provides support for the specific predictions of state behavior defined in this book. First, in none of the cases of humiliation described above did the humiliated great powers develop sufficient relative military advantage over its humiliator to render revenge a viable path toward renewed status and in none of them did the humiliated great powers engage in targeted acts of military revenge. *La revanche* was a popular subject in France for decades following its 1871 defeat. Yet French leaders, realizing the potential for even greater catastrophe, did not devise even an inchoate plan for military revenge against the Germans. Cognizant of the immense risks involved in such a strategy, they instead sought a far less risky competitive strategy through which they could signal France's great power expectations.

Following its humiliation in Egypt, France similarly targeted a weaker, third party in the Congo rather than attempt to seek compensation from Britain, whom many French came to perceive as the villain of the story. In the case of Germany, Bismarck did select a policy he perceived to go against British interests in response to perceived British disrespect. This approach could have risen to the level of diplomatic revenge, but Bismarck ultimately chose to use force, such as it was, against a far weaker, third-party state rather than against Britain itself, for such acts would have likely seemed disproportional and would have risked Germany's newfound claim to great power status.

Second, the exact timing of the status seeking, expansionary acts also supports the theoretical predictions. Rather than immediately returning to the world stage following its defeat, France rebuilt, restructured and reformed. International retrenchment allowed leaders to focus on the stabilization and restoration of

French capabilities and confidence. Only once these capabilities were perceived to be restored did French leaders actively begin their search for ways to demonstrate the renewed capacity and vigor of the French state. France was immediately ready to make claims in the Congo following its self-induced humiliation in Egypt both because events in Egypt had had no direct effect on French capabilities and because the French had recently experienced a boost in self-esteem following its success in Tunisia. The same was true of Germany following the diplomatic disregard of German interests by Britain. Because capabilities were not diminished by the humiliating event, the Germans were afflicted with less self-doubt than outrage and were prepared to respond immediately to British disrespect.

Third, numerous states chose colonial expansion because they viewed it to symbolize great power status. The overheated competition for colonies was a symbolic one in which considerations of material or strategic value held secondary weight at best. The acquisition and maintenance of colonies provided states the opportunity to demonstrate their ability and intention to assert their power abroad in a way that distinguished them from mere continental powers. Thus, we see that engaging in symbolic competitions over territorial expansion provides a way for humiliated states to signal that they want to be perceived as powerful without having to engage in costly direct competition with states of a similar size. France, in a move that undoubtedly changed few minds about its military capability relative to that of potential European rivals, handily acquired control of the bankrupt Tunisian government within less than two weeks. Similarly, Germany's initial act of imperialism involved little more than planting a flag at a remote, barren port. Rather, both states sought to signal their expectation of holding higher status by exercising the prerogatives associated with their desired status.

Finally, the cases in this chapter show that the public's desired response to humiliating events often overlaps with that of their leaders. However, cases exist in which public demands for revenge, rooted in outrage at the state seen to be responsible for the humiliation, cannot be met by strategic leaders. German leaders and the German public were all equally on board with actions intended to push back against a disrespectful British double standard. The risks involved were relatively few and the perception that the Germans would be able to get the upper hand through conquest in Britain's backyard in Africa was pervasive. French leaders, by contrast, recognized the potential political costs of not targeting Germany but recognized that another failure at the hands of the Germans would be far more costly, both in terms of French lives but also in the likelihood that it would permanently relegate France to less-than-great power status.

This is not to say that elites were somehow motivated less by the direct emotional and psychological components of humiliation and more by "rational" considerations about the instrumental consequences of humiliating events. As stated earlier, the psychological and instrumental effects of status enhancement are difficult to differentiate. Influence can be a good in itself, but can also be enjoyed because of the boost in self-perception and self-esteem that it typically provides. Thus, French leaders may have been as motivated as their public by the psychological desire to once again perceive themselves to be part of a high-status group. Masses, however, are free to demand ideals. Politicians attempting to achieve desired goals must confront material reality and its constraints.

6

"OUR HONEYMOON WITH THE U.S. CAME TO AN END"

Soviet Humiliation at the Height of the Cold War

The last chapter established the important role that humiliating events played in stimulating the symbolic competition for status on the African continent. This chapter shows that two humiliating international events played an equally significant role in stimulating conflict and competitive material practices within the second decade of the Cold War. The first instance involved the repeated breach by the United States of the Soviet Union's airspace in the late 1950s into 1960. The revelation that President Dwight Eisenhower had authorized these surveillance flyovers, in flagrant denial of the Soviet Union's basic rights as a sovereign state, engendered deep humiliation within the Soviet Union that had come to expect equal treatment to that of the United States. This revelation almost solely prompted a dramatic breach in U.S.-Soviet relations and gave way to a more assertive Soviet foreign policy and a rise in tension that persisted for years after the incident.

A sense of prolonged humiliation also seems to have followed Soviet failure in the Cuban Missile Crisis, an event that reinforced Soviet views that the United States perceived the Soviet Union to be inferior and unworthy of the privileges of superpower status. While it is difficult to say with certainty, given the few historical documents available for the period, the evidence suggests that this highly public failure led Soviet leaders to pursue numerical parity within the United States in the number of offensive strategic forces it possessed, leading to the largest buildup of offensive capabilities in history.

This chapter also examines the similarity in status dynamics during this period and the period of intense status competition at the end of the nineteenth century. Just as French and German status-seeking strategies in Africa challenged the status and interests of England and Italy, leading those states to engage in aggressive policies they likely would not have pursued otherwise, the Soviet Union's attempts to seek status through material practices befitting their desired superpower status presented a potential challenge to the status of the United States. To ensure that perceptions of U.S. position on the world stage were not undermined by Soviet actions, the Americans shifted their focus to numerical parity of strategic forces, not because of any underlying strategic value that parity offered, but because of the belief that relative arsenal size had come to symbolize relative international standing in the eyes of others.

In many important ways, therefore, the role of colonies as symbols of status in the late nineteenth and early twentieth century had, by the mid-twentieth century, been replaced by nuclear weapons and offensive strategic forces like intercontinental ballistic missiles. With the rise of the norm of territorial integrity, the maintenance of empires abroad no longer offered the clearest path to great power status. With the use of the first nuclear weapons in 1945, it quickly became clear that international status distinctions would be drawn in part along the nuclear dimension. Like the establishment of expansive colonial holdings, the development of large nuclear arsenals enabled states to demonstrate their relative technological, organizational, and financial capacities that distinguished them from lesser states.

The argument that weapons are acquired for the high status they symbolize and not for the military advantages they provide is not a new one. Scholars have clearly shown that status concerns played a key role in French, Indian, and Chinese decisions to go nuclear.[1] The evidence in this chapter shows that status concerns motivate states to not only acquire initial nuclear capabilities but also to pay costs for arsenals the size of which are not supported by obvious strategic rationales. Status-threatened states engage in such symbolic competitions over numerical supremacy because they believe the winner will acquire preeminent status and international distinction. As with the Scramble for Africa, competition over the size of these arsenals eventually came to be largely symbolic and was largely driven by concerns about how the size of arsenal affected one's image in the eyes of others.

Before presenting the detailed analysis of the effects of the U-2 and Cuban Missile crises, it is important to note that these two humiliating international events were chosen for analysis largely because of the significant role they played in shaping Soviet foreign policy. As other scholars have noted, these two events were certainly not the only times in which status concerns motivated Soviet behavior during the Cold War.[2] Soviet expectations about the rightful amount of influence and privilege the state should have in international affairs at the end of

World War II, for instance, were largely shaped by the state's role in the "world historical victory" against the Germans. Given the Soviets' large conventional advantages after the war, Soviet leaders expected to have influence equivalent to that of the United States over important post-war political events, including the occupation and future of Germany and Japan and the reconstruction of Europe. At the end of the war, the USSR declared that it now stood "in the ranks of the most authoritative of the world powers," declaring that issues of international importance could no longer be resolved without input from the USSR.[3]

Despite these expectations, the Soviets at times found themselves shut out of several key post-war decisions. That the substantial military capability demonstrated by the Soviets during the war had failed to translate into a proportional position within the hierarchy of influence after the war generated serious status concerns and a desire for recognition by the Americans that would plague the Soviets and render them particularly sensitive to slights to their status throughout the Cold War.[4] Although here I focus on the analysis of the early 1960s, a period chosen mainly because it enables further assessment of the validity of the book's theoretical predictions, the effects of national humiliation affected Soviet behavior throughout the Cold War as it sought to assert itself as "the other superpower."

The U-2 Incident and the Four Powers Summit

While post-war Soviet leaders had expected equality with the United States, the two countries confronted different material realities in the late 1940s. The Soviets had suffered the loss of roughly 18 percent of its population, on the battlefield or through disease, and the destruction of roughly one-quarter of its capital resources. The war was followed by severe drought and famine and the further decline of average life expectancy. In 1949, streets in major Soviet cities still lay in ruin.

The 1950s witnessed dramatic improvements in the USSR. Soviet economic recovery occurred at a rapid pace. Soviet steel production doubled from its 1940 levels. Improvements in quality of life were accompanied by a series of significant technical and military advances. In 1953, the Soviets tested their first hydrogen bomb, only four years after the United States. In 1957, the Soviets launched the first artificial satellite *Sputnik*, beating the United States into space. That same year the Soviets also claimed to successfully launch their first intercontinental ballistic missile, only one month after the first U.S. test ended in disaster. Moreover, the Soviet military continued to largely outnumber NATO troops stationed throughout Europe.

By the late 1950s, bolstered by Soviet recovery in the aftermath of the war, Soviet leaders had come to view these achievements as an even stronger foundation for expectations of Soviet equality with the United States. As the Soviet leader Nikita Khrushchev told U.S. diplomat Averill Harriman in 1959, "We developed the hydrogen bomb before the US. We have an intercontinental bomb while you have not. Perhaps this is the crucial symbol of our position." Khrushchev most succinctly described Soviet expectations at the time, arguing that "Where there are equal forces, there must also be equal rights and opportunities."[5]

In early 1960, the U.S.-Soviet relationship appeared to be on an upward trajectory. At the end of 1959, Khrushchev had enjoyed a successful twelve-day trip to the United States, during which the Soviets had been received with full honors and during which Khrushchev was pleased that Eisenhower had addressed him as "my friend."[6] On his return, he was "bursting with optimism and enthusiasm" because of the acts of public respect that the United States had shown the Soviets. He, in turn, expected tensions between the US and Soviet Union to ease, calling for "peaceful coexistence with United States" and praising Eisenhower personally, saying that "If only the President could serve another term, . . . our problems could be solved."[7] In the spirit of such optimism, Khrushchev had agreed to a summit, the first in five years, with the Western leaders. British Prime Minister Harold Macmillan, French President Charles de Gaulle, Eisenhower, and Khrushchev were all to meet in Paris for a three-day summit held between May 15 and May 18. The four leaders entered into the summit with varying expectations, but Khrushchev had indicated in December that a summit agreement on Berlin was "almost a sure thing" and that a nuclear test ban accord was also likely.

Although all parties did arrive in Paris on May 15, the summit did not truly come to fruition. In fact, it lasted all of three hours. Khrushchev, whose optimism even one month earlier had given Macmillan reason to believe that the world was "on the eve of a great leap forward,"[8] left the summit the following day, realizing that a dramatic and significant breach had taken place within U.S.-Soviet relations. Soviet policy toward the United States proceeded to take a dramatic turn in the months and even years after the failed summit. This shift became clear almost immediately, when Khrushchev, on his departure from Paris, made a symbolic stop in Berlin, foreshadowing the escalation of tensions that would soon take place over the German question. Khrushchev canceled Eisenhower's scheduled trip to the Soviet Union and refused to have any significant interaction with the once-praised Eisenhower for the remainder of Ike's presidency. This aggressive Soviet stance continued to plague relations through Khrushchev's meeting with Kennedy in Vienna the following year.[9] The cancellation of the summit left many pondering the counterfactual "if the two leaders had met, a great deal of what happened in the world might have been quite different."[10] Macmillan, who had worked toward a policy of détente for over two years, declared the day of the summit failure to be the "most tragic day of his life."[11]

There is little ambiguity about the events that led to this shift in Soviet policy. On May 1, exactly two weeks before the start of the summit, the Soviets engaged surface-to-air missiles to successfully shoot down a U.S. U-2 plane piloted by Gary Powers, an employee of the CIA charged with the photographic surveillance of intercontinental ballistic missile (ICBM) sites in central and northern Russia. Both Soviet and U.S. leaders agreed that this incident and the events surrounding it were ultimately responsible for scuttling the summit. Khrushchev personally told Eisenhower face to face as he was leaving the summit that if there had been no U-2 incident, the Soviet delegation "would have come here in friendship and in the best possible atmosphere."[12] Eisenhower shortly afterward told his aides that if the U-2 incident had not occurred, the summit could have greatly improved U.S.-Soviet relations. The event had significant implications on Cold War relations for years to come. It is, therefore, important to understand how and why it altered Soviet policy.

There is no doubt that Soviet leaders perceived Gary Powers's flyover to be humiliating. The Americans had knowingly disregarded Russia's international right to sovereign airspace in an act that was not only a flagrant violation of international law but also a "gross insult to the Soviet Union" that engendered significant outrage among Soviet leadership. But Powers's was only one in a long line of CIA surveillance missions through Soviet airspace. Such flights had been ongoing, with the knowledge of the Soviets, on and off since 1946, but even more actively since 1952. Every time a violation of airspace would occur, some even penetrating Moscow's airspace, the sense of impotence in the Soviet Union would grow. In response to the first few flyovers they learned of in the late 1940s, Soviet leaders had privately protested the U.S. policy. Once it became clear that the Americans had no intention of stopping the flyovers and that the Soviets lacked the technical capability to shoot the planes down, the Soviet leaders stopped protesting, largely to avoid the humiliation of doing so since the protests only served as an admission of their inferiority and inefficacy.[13]

Soviet leaders also perceived negative intention in these acts. As Soviet ambassador Anatoly Dobrynin described it, Khrushchev believed that the U.S. denial of Soviet sovereignty had been intended to humiliate the Soviet Union and to demonstrate to the whole world Soviet helplessness and the inability of Soviet leaders to protect their own borders.[14] Khrushchev's memoirs indicate that the Soviets were "sick and tired of being subjected to these indignities," which he thought were intended to "show up [Soviet] impotence." Khrushchev acknowledged that tremendous anger had built up in response to the incident that demanded an outlet, writing "we did not agree with the idea that a great power had the right to commit insult and injury even to small countries" and the Soviet Union was not a small country but indeed a great power with the largest territorial claims on earth.[15]

Thus, when the Soviets finally managed to successfully shoot down a U.S. plane, it was deemed a triumphant righting of wrongs. The assertion of Soviet rights in the face of the hypocritical U.S. policy would, Soviet leaders perceived, provide a much-needed boost of collective confidence among the Soviet elites who were aware of the flyovers. Reporting that he felt "extraordinarily pleased" on hearing that the plane had been shot down, Khrushchev declared that the Soviet Union wanted friendship with the United States but would "not tolerate humiliation." He reported feeling that he had not only avenged the Soviet Union but also that the act had restored the confidence of the Soviets, who would now not feel "impotent any longer."[16]

Khrushchev's desire to reassert the rights and status of the Soviet Union and to inflict further punishment on the Americans were not yet sated. He proceeded with an act of diplomatic revenge intended to pay the Americans back for Soviet humiliation.[17] The Soviets, despite their excitement, intentionally withheld any mention of either the plane or its pilot, waiting instead for the Americans to first concoct an explanation of events. On May 5, the Americans announced, assuming that the pilot of the lost U-2 had been killed, that a NASA plane had disappeared and that it was suspected that the pilot of the plane had fallen asleep at the helm, allowing the plane to veer from Turkey into Soviet airspace. Two days later, on May 7, Khrushchev announced that the plane had been shot down by Soviet forces, still giving no mention of the captured pilot. To this point, Khrushchev had wanted to believe that Eisenhower had not known about or sanctioned the flyover and instead believed that Secretary of State John Foster Dulles had likely conducted the flyover with the intention of torpedoing the summit. On May 10, the head of the United States House Committee on Appropriations announced that the U-2 flight had occurred not under the aegis of NASA but rather under the command of the CIA and that its intended purpose had been security-motivated surveillance of missile sites. The committee head suggested that knowledge of the flight existed within the highest echelons of the government. This did not yet dispel rumors that Eisenhower had not known about the flyover nor that the president had not been in full control of his government and military. On May 11, with the intention of fully discrediting such narratives, Eisenhower held a press conference to not only announce that he had known about but had indeed ordered the flyover. Most significant, he avowed that the United States would continue to engage in similar flyovers because it was in the country's security interests to do so.

Within his immediate response to this revelation, Khrushchev declared a willingness to cooperate with Eisenhower as long as the path forward did "no further harm to national dignity." He felt optimistic about a resolution of tensions, especially because it was his state, Russia, that had "suffered an injury to its national pride" that was proposing the resolution. Shortly before he departed for Paris, Khrushchev discussed specifics of Eisenhower's upcoming visit with his son, fully indicating that he still expected to host Eisenhower in Russia.[18] Khrushchev boarded the plane to Paris on May 14 with the Soviet delegation, expecting to at least meet with if not work out a tentative agreement with the Americans.

On the plane, however, Khrushchev and the rest of the Soviet delegation experienced a change of heart. Khrushchev had become "more and more convinced that [Soviet] pride and dignity would be damaged if we went ahead with the meeting as though nothing had happened. Our prestige would suffer, especially in the third world." The goal of the Soviet Union remained "peace and friendship" but the Soviets would not allow themselves "to be abused and degraded." Khrushchev decided, in agreement with his colleagues, that in order to make it clear that the Soviets were standing up to defend their honor, he would publicly demand that Eisenhower not only publicly apologize for "insulting our country" by invading its airspace but also retract his claim that the United States had the right to conduct such spy missions.[19] If Eisenhower refused Khrushchev's request, the summit would be off, and Eisenhower's Soviet visit would be canceled, for how, Khrushchev asked, "could we treat [Eisenhower] as a guest and show him around? . . . It would be humiliating and insulting. It would be demeaning to our country and its leadership."[20] After landing, Khrushchev met with de Gaulle and Macmillan, both of whom tried to temper his anger but also to make clear that the United States, as a preeminent power, would not be willing to make a public apology. Khrushchev declared, with his anger growing, that the Soviet Union was not a "second-rate country" and that it would not allow itself to be treated as such. He, therefore, fully intended to go through with the demand, despite the likelihood that the conference table that was to have united the parties would instead "crumble into dust." As expected, Eisenhower refused to make a public apology, though he was willing to do so privately, and with that, as Khrushchev put it, "our honeymoon with the U.S. came to an end."[21]

Alternative Explanations for the Shift in Soviet Policy

This book's theory of national humiliation offers a convincing explanation of the events and reactions described above. The sense of extreme national humiliation experienced by the Soviets in response to the public revelation that Eisenhower both knew about and would continue to sanction the infringement on Soviet airspace is, for instance, exactly as we would expect given the framework presented in Chapter 1. The massive discrepancy between Soviet leaders' superpower expectations and the disdainful public disregard of the Soviet Union's most basic rights indeed would lead us to predict a deep well of Soviet outrage. As predicted in Chapter 2, Soviet leaders in the aftermath sought to demonstrate and renew a sense of collective efficacy, undermined by repeated flyovers and the public revelation of what had been the Soviet Union's long-term inability to defend itself. Although we would not expect the Soviet Union to target the United States in its efforts to reassert itself, largely because of the risk of repeated public failure, the targeting of the U.S. spy plane was, quite unusually, risk free in that the Soviets need only announce their success once they had achieved it.[22]

Khrushchev's most direct and immediate responses to Eisenhower's public admission of his intention to continue disrespecting the Soviets were, as also might be predicted given the highly competitive and potentially escalatory strategic context of the time at the time, largely diplomatic in nature. Though Khrushchev had little expectation that his initial demand for a public apology would be met, this demand promised to re-instill Soviet esteem while also publicly highlighting the moral transgressions of the United States and demonstrating that the USSR would not permit infringement on its rights without penalty. This public demand was backed by a decision to break diplomatic ties with the United States and the reemergence of a generally more assertive Soviet foreign policy, precipitated not only by a desire to shape public opinion but also by a new and fundamental mistrust of the United States and its intentions following Eisenhower's announcement.

The memoirs of both Western and Soviet leaders written during this time largely agree that collective humiliation shaped the crucial events in the ways just described. Yet it remains possible that additional factors beyond collective humiliation played key roles in stimulating the important shift in Soviet policy. First, it is possible that the shift in Soviet policy was motivated by the security concerns or issues of uncertainty engendered by the U.S. flyover. Certainly, the United States was gathering information through such surveillance flights to gain a strategic advantage over the Soviet Union. However, the evidence refutes the idea that these concerns motivated the Soviet Union to adopt a more assertive stance when they did. First, the memoirs of the Soviet decision makers offer little to no mention of the security implications of the flyover, even though they had little reason not to mention them. Second, Powers' flyover did not represent a new strategic reality but was only one in a long line of demonstrations of Soviet strategic inferiority. The shift in Soviet policy occurred, although no real shift in underlying material and strategic factors had taken place.[23]

A similar logic applies in the refutation of the hypothesis that the U-2 incident generated increasing mistrust and uncertainty between the states, which then led to the dramatic policy shift. While humiliating events can engender mistrust between states, this mistrust clearly did not arise with the Gary Powers incident. Instead, the Soviets had long wondered about the seemingly two-faced policy of the Americans, expressing outward displays of trust and friendship while secretly, or not so secretly, invading Soviet airspace. Thus, the mistrust of the United States was in no way new. It is true that in the months between Khrushchev's visit to the United States and the May 1 incident, Eisenhower had decided, in an act of good faith, to halt the flyover program. His decision to renew the flyover only a few weeks before the summit could have renewed mistrust within the Soviets, ultimately leading to the policy shift. Mistrust of the Americans had not, however, prevented Soviet moves toward conciliation in the period leading up to and shortly after Khrushchev's visit to the United States when Khrushchev thought that the Americans were finally prepared to recognize Soviet status claims.

Third, there is the possibility that Khrushchev decided to tank the summit because of domestic political pressure forcing him to do so. As part of his policy of gradual détente in early 1960, Khrushchev had decided to shrink the size of Soviet conventional forces, instead shifting focus to missile development. This move certainly had its opponents within the Soviet military. There is certainly no reason to believe that officials holding these positions in any way influenced Khrushchev or the other Soviet decision makers. As Khrushchev's son, Sergei, points out, no top officials from the Ministry of Defense were in the Presidium of the Central Committee.[24] They had no direct influence on decision making. Moreover, Khrushchev's recollections of these events fail at every point to make reference to domestic political considerations, instead focusing almost exclusively on concerns about the need to assert the status expectations of the Soviet Union following such egregious disrespect by the United States.

Finally, it is possible that the shift in Soviet policy reflected more the personality of the Soviet leader than a desired response of the Soviet leadership more broadly. Khrushchev may have been particularly sensitive to issues of status and respect. As his son described him, Khrushchev was "constantly on alert to see if any disrespect was shown to our country."[25] Khrushchev's memoirs are rife with references to perceived humiliations and resulting concerns about the image of the Soviet Union on the world stage as well as to the outrage he and other Soviet leaders felt toward the United States because of these actions. Khrushchev appeared to perceive symbols of status everywhere and no symbolic detail seems to have escaped his notice. He reports in detail about how the Soviet delegation did not want to arrive too early or too late in Washington, D.C., for their planned arrival for fear that erring on either side would strike "a blow to our prestige."[26] He ensured that the length of the flight be carefully calculated. On their arrival at the summit in Paris, Khrushchev reported feeling more confident about the relative status of the USSR because now their delegation had arrived, like those from the West, in a four-engine plane rather than a two-engine plane they had at a previous summit.[27] It is certainly true that other Soviet leaders acknowledged their doubts about Khrushchev's ultimatum to the United States and blamed him for so severely souring relations with the latter. As we will see below, Khrushchev was in no way unique as a Soviet leader in his desire to protect the Soviet Union against humiliating treatment or in efforts to assert the rights and privileges of the Soviet Union in the face of disrespectful treatment by the United States.

In short, security and domestic concerns do not offer convincing explanations of the dramatic shift in Soviet policy described above. The Soviets had endured humiliating U.S. flyovers for years but had still been willing to move toward a more cooperative relationship in early 1960 in the hopes that cooperation would bring recognition of Soviet status claims. Two fundamental changes had occurred, then, prior to Khrushchev's ultimatum to Eisenhower. The first was that it had become clear that Eisenhower knew about and sanctioned the humiliating flyovers, leaving no doubt in Soviet eyes that the U.S. president viewed the Soviet Union to be inferior and unworthy of the rights of sovereign states. The second was that the flyovers had been made public as had the U.S. intention to continue flagrantly violating Soviet sovereignty. Soviet leaders had felt humiliated on behalf of their state when only they and U.S. decision makers had known about the flyovers, but the acts had not threatened to undermine the image of the state in the eyes of others. Now that the acts had been acknowledged publicly, Soviet leaders felt obligated to respond with an assertive gesture or else risk the further degradation of their country's status in the eyes of its people and in the eyes of others. This assertive gesture did not involve the use of force, except in direct defense of Soviet airspace, but instead a highly public act of diplomatic opposition against a much more capable foe.[28] This diplomatic breach would have significant implications on U.S.-Soviet Cold War relations throughout the 1960s.

The Placement of Soviet Missiles in Cuba, 1962

According to Khrushchev's son, the U-2 incident would radically affect the psychological climate of the Soviet Union for years to come.[29] Optimistic gestures were replaced with harsh calls for vengeance as Soviet foreign policy came to reflect the outrage induced by U.S. flagrant disregard of Soviet status. In the years following the incident and leading up to the Cuban Missile Crisis, Khrushchev became more belligerent, more suspicious of U.S. intentions and more sensitive to possible slights and double standards aimed at highlighting the inferior status of the Soviet Union.

Of the many double standards perceived by the Soviets, none were perhaps more consequential than the U.S. policy of unilaterally installing missiles in countries neighboring the Soviet Union while attempting to prohibit other great powers from pursuing this same privilege.[30] Khrushchev was incensed by the status implications of U.S. hypocritical policy and frequently decried the treatment both privately and publicly. Indeed, Soviet reaction to U.S. attempts at prohibition played out exactly as would be predicted in Chapter 2, with Soviet leaders opting to engage in the very act that the United States had attempted to prohibit. In his memoirs, Khrushchev directly related the perceived double standard of U.S. policy with his decision to ultimately place missiles in Cuba, stating: "The US had surrounded the Soviet Union with its military bases and placed its missiles all around our country. We knew that the United States had missile bases in Turkey and Italy, not to mention West Germany! . . . Couldn't we counter with the very same thing?"[31] As he saw it, the Soviet Union, in placing missiles near U.S. shores in an effort to protect its ally, was "doing nothing more than the U.S. itself had done. It was a matter of equal rights and equal opportunity." The clear expectation was that Soviet policy should be governed by the "same rules and limits as the Americans."[32]

This is not to say that humiliation in the face of this U.S. double standard was Khrushchev's primary motivation for placing missiles in Cuba. Khrushchev did not believe that the missiles would provide any significant strategic advantage in the global confrontation with the United States. He did believe, however, that defending the Cuban revolution was of grave importance to the maintenance of the Soviet Union's international stature.[33] He questioned, "What will happen if we lose Cuba? If would gravely diminish our stature throughout the world. They would reject us, claiming that for all our might, the Soviet Union hadn't been able to do anything for Cuba except to make empty protests to the U.N."[34] He eventually convinced himself that Soviet missiles in Cuba would "establish a tangible and effective deterrent" to any threats to the Cuban regime. It is impossible to know if Khrushchev would have justified the risks involved in putting missiles in Cuba to protect his Cuban ally if the justificatory cover of U.S. missiles in Turkey had not existed. It does seem that Khrushchev derived psychological pleasure from putting the United States "in the same position they had inflicted on the Soviets" by engaging in the Soviet's "moral and legal right" to place missiles so close to American borders without any warning.[35]

Strategic Parity in the Aftermath of the Cuban Missile Crisis, 1963–1969

Though Khrushchev had reasons both professionally and politically to publicly declare the Cuban Missile Crisis a victory because of the status recognition it had garnered for both the USSR and Cuba, other Soviet leaders, and international observers more broadly, did not perceive world events in this way, instead sensing Soviet humiliation resulting from Khrushchev's massive blunder.[36] Opposition to Khrushchev had existed for some time within the Politburo of the Communist Party of the Soviet Union, but it began to escalate steadily following the events of October 1962.[37] On October 12, 1964, while vacationing in Pitsunda, Khrushchev received a call from the head of the Supreme Soviet Leonid Brezhnev, his protégé, requesting his presence back in Moscow. On his arrival back in the capital, Khrushchev was informed by Brezhnev, KGB chairman Vladimir Semichastny and first deputy prime minister Alexander Shelepin that a vote of the Central Committee had taken place to remove Khrushchev from office.

Earlier that month, Politburo member Dmitry Poylanksy, who would become chairman of the Council of Ministers in 1965, delivered a special report to party leaders on Khrushchev's foreign policy mistakes. The report criticized Khrushchev for allowing the "humiliating inspections of our ships" by the U.S. military. It argued that the withdrawal of Soviet missiles had "damaged the international prestige" of the Soviet Union, the Communist Party, and Soviet armed forces while bolstering the stature of the United States.[38] Shelepin leveled many of the report's critiques during Khrushchev's last Politburo meeting on October 13, 1964, citing, among other things, Khrushchev's "erratic behavior," his overindulged comfort with risk, and his smug overconfidence that had recently brought the world to the brink of nuclear war. He cited Khrushchev's risky approach both in Suez in 1956 and in Cuba two years prior, arguing that one should be able to get the Americans to accept Soviet positions without "juggling with people's fate."[39] Brezhnev also accused Khrushchev of the "imprudent and indiscreet conduct of foreign affairs," while underlining "The Polyansky Report" in his personal notes from the meeting.[40]

How would the new Soviet leaders overcome the pervasive sense of national humiliation engendered by Soviet withdrawal in an international crisis that had gripped world attention? They opted to focus on substantially changing Soviet defense policy.

Although Khrushchev had been responsible for bringing the second generation of nuclear warheads and intercontinental delivery systems online in the late 1950s and early 1960s, he had not made strategic parity with the Americans a primary objective.[41] Khrushchev, reluctant to invest in defense at the expense of domestic economic growth, had focused instead on the ability to inflict equal pain on the Americans in a second-strike attack. Once mutual destruction was assured, he sought to avoid further costly weapons build-up that he perceived would lack fundamental strategic purpose. Brezhnev and colleagues, by contrast, called for domestic sacrifice to achieve numerical parity with the United States in the size of offensive strategic forces. Shifting significant resources from the domestic to the military front, he cited the need for "long, intensive, tenacious and disciplined work on a massive scale . . . to broadly strengthen Soviet conventional as well as nuclear capabilities."[42]

Thus, despite the fact that the United States and Soviet Union already possessed 320,000 megatons of explosive power, an average of one hundred tons per person on earth, and despite the fact that U.S. military spending was in steep decline, the new Soviet leaders opted to undertake the largest military buildup in history in an effort to match the size of the U.S. offensive strategic arsenal.[43] To achieve this goal, they increased military spending by almost 40 percent between 1964 and 1970, while focusing the most substantial increases in the development of intercontinental offensive strategic capabilities.[44] CIA estimates indicated that Soviet military spending on offensive capabilities increased from roughly $4.9 billion in 1964 to somewhere between $7 and $8 billion by 1967, where the budget would stay for the remainder of the decade.[45]

This substantial increase in spending enabled the Soviets to accomplish their goal of strategic parity within a remarkably short period of time, given how behind they were at the beginning of the decade. In 1965, the U.S. ICBM arsenal was roughly five times that of the Soviets. A sharp uptick in the pace of development in 1965 and 1966 led the Soviets to match the roughly 1,100 ICBMs in the U.S. arsenal by 1969 and to surpass it the following year.[46] As a testament to the intensity of the arms race at this point, the Soviets conducted eighty ICBM tests in 1966 alone.[47] And though Soviet SLBMs (submarine-launched ballistic missiles) were far slower coming on line than U.S. SLBMs, the Soviet arsenal had managed to eclipse that of the Americans by the early 1970s.[48]

This shift provokes some obvious questions. Why did Soviet leaders choose a policy of strategic parity and why did they adopt this policy when they did? While both the United States and Soviet Union recognized the necessity for a flexible and survivable strategic arsenal, there is nothing about survivability and flexibility that necessitated a concern about parity or essential equivalence in the size of strategic arsenals.[49] As Robert Jervis notes, prioritizing parity with one's opponent rarely makes sense in the strategic context: "One could be 'far ahead' of the other side and still not have enough to destroy the required targets; one could be way 'behind' and still have sufficient forces to knock out all the targets one would want to."[50] Indeed, the precise size of the Soviet ICBM force does not appear to have been predicated on any formal military doctrine, but was rather based on the size of the U.S. force more as a "symbolic numerical equivalent."[51]

It is difficult to answer these questions with complete confidence because of the relative dearth of available Soviet documents covering foreign policy decision making during the crucial years of 1964 and 1965 and because Brezhnev, who was largely responsible for defense policy at this time, recorded far fewer reflections on his experiences than his colleagues before and after. We can, however, draw some conclusions about Soviet motivations from the timing of events and from the statements of Soviet leaders once they had accomplished their objective of strategic parity in the early 1970s. The timing of the decision corresponded with the change in leadership which, as was stated above, related directly to the events of October 1962. The exact connection between the Cuban Missile Crisis and the subsequent decision to arm has not been definitively established. Yet it would be highly surprising if the event, which brought the two countries to the brink of nuclear war and then ended with an apparent Soviet retreat, did not have a significant influence on Soviet defense policy. Rather, the new Soviet leaders appear to have felt as Soviet foreign minister Vasily Kuznetsov did following the Cuban Missile Crisis when he emphatically declared that the United States "will never be able to do this to us again."[52] Evidence suggests that Soviet leaders perceived two primary reasons that a shift toward parity would ensure that the United States would never again force the Soviet Union to back down from its global interests.

First, the prevalent view among Soviet leaders was that nuclear weapons could not be used effectively as military instruments for coercive purposes, whereas the Soviets were less sure about how U.S. leaders perceived the utility of strategic weapons. Soviet leaders feared that the Americans did not share their belief that nuclear superiority did not provide any military advantage and feared that the Americans believed that superiority could be successfully exploited in a preemptive first strike. The Soviets in part translated the events of the Cuban Missile Crisis along these lines—the United States might have believed they could use their weapons to their advantage, leaving the Soviets in a vulnerable position.[53] A Soviet military leader later reported believing that the first strike by the United States had actually been possible from about 1953 to 1963.[54]

But it was not only the fear of actual use of the weapons that shaped Soviet behavior. Although it appears that U.S. thinking was little affected by its numerical advantage during the Cuban Missile Crisis, the Soviets drew the conclusion that U.S. strategic superiority had provided the country with negotiating leverage by enabling the Americans to take greater risks and ultimately prevail in the crisis. If indeed, the Americans believed in the utility of the weapons, even if they did not intend to necessarily use them, this was likely to increase American risk-seeking behavior, thereby raising the risk of accidental escalation or the possibility the United States would attempt to blackmail the Soviets. The Soviets appear to have concluded that they would not again allow such risks to result from relative Soviet weakness and thereby grew to focus on parity with the United States as a "reliable guarantee of peace."[55]

Second, Soviet leaders believed that strategic parity would translate into status equivalence with the United States. Like Khrushchev, Brezhnev and his colleagues viewed ending the perception of Soviet status inferiority, a perception continually reinforced by U.S. disrespect and double standards, to be a high priority.[56] Unlike Khrushchev, they did not believe the outcome of the Cuban Missile Crisis had accomplished that objective.[57] The Soviets had made their interests clear and had then backed down in the face of U.S. demands, threatening perceptions of Soviet status in the process. Brezhnev reported feeling deeply embarrassed by Khrushchev's reckless actions in Cuba.[58] Soviet lieutenant general Nikolai Detinov indicated that the outcome of the Cuban Missile Crisis was taken "very painfully" by Soviet leadership.

In Detinov's estimation, it had been the strategic imbalance between the United States and USSR that had forced the latter "to accept everything that the US dictated to it," causing "a painful effect on our country and our government."[59] As a result, he concluded, "all economic resources were mobilized afterward to solve this problem." Brezhnev and his colleagues similarly perceived that the United States had not respected Soviet interests in Cuba largely because the Soviets at that time did not have sufficient weapons to demand their respect.[60] In their perspective, Khrushchev had pursued a more Potemkin-like material strategy when trying to bolster support for Soviet claims to superpower status and the United Stated had seen through it. Khrushchev had, for instance, advertised what proved to be a non-existent missile gap. He had promoted the symbolic nature of Soviet technological breakthroughs like the hydrogen bomb but had opted not to sufficiently invest in the size of the Soviet arsenal to ensure that it matched that of the United States. They would adopt a less risky, and hopefully more successful, strategy of status assertion involving a policy of "speak softly while you are getting a big stick."[61]

The strong expectation that numerical parity would resolve Soviet status concerns by "psychologically" convincing the Americans of Soviet equivalence was made perhaps the most clear by U.S. reflections about Soviet intentions once parity had been achieved and the Soviets were finally prepared to discuss arms control at the SALT I accords in 1971.[62] President Richard Nixon reflected in his memoirs on the degree to which the Soviets had craved "to be respected as equals."[63] National Security Advisor Henry Kissinger similarly remarked that equality seemed "to mean a great deal to Brezhnev," noting that it had been "central" to the Soviet bargaining position.[64] The U.S. State Department concluded that Moscow's primary objective in demanding parity was "to enhance the prestige of the bloc by presenting an image of a powerful and monolithic bloc ... which is at least equal ... and which must be dealt with on equal terms."[65]

The Soviet belief that strategic parity would finally put an end to U.S. disrespect of Soviet interests was further evidenced by the nature of the demands Soviet leaders made during the negotiations. Inclusion of "the principle of equality and equal security, respect for other's interests and the peaceful settlement of differences" within the Basic Principles of Mutual Relations to be signed by the two parties was deemed absolutely essential to Soviet leaders.[66] Kissinger noted that recognition of equality seemed even more important to Soviet leaders than the precise military terms of the SALT I accords, remarking that the Soviets were "addicted to declarations of principle" and inferring that the Soviets saw in them "some acknowledgement of equality." He pondered that perhaps there was "something in Russian history that leads them to value ritual ... and visible symbols."[67]

Why had the Soviets chosen a policy of strategic parity as their strategy to overcoming persistent inferiority? The perception that material capabilities should equate with the state's international standing was not new in Soviet thinking but rather was at the heart of Soviet status expectations coming out of World War II. Khrushchev had clearly expected that equal force would lead to equal status with the United States. He continued by stating, "Today it is acknowledged in the West that the forces of the Soviet Union ... are not inferior to the forces of the Western powers ... Yet our partners ... nevertheless want to dominate in international agencies and impose their will."[68] He clearly suspected that Americans perceived strategic capabilities to be the primary basis of U.S. superpower status and expected U.S. leaders to share this view, as shown when he directly challenged Kennedy in 1962, asking "How then does the admission of our equal military capabilities tally with such unequal relations between our great states? They cannot be made to tally in any way."[69]

That the Americans had continued to treat the Soviet Union as inferior even after mutual destruction had largely been assured suggested to Khrushchev's successors that the Americans would only inevitably accept Soviet demands for status equality if the Soviets possessed equivalent material symbols of their superpower status. Beyond mere symbolic recognition the Soviets expected the rights and privileges associated with superpower status, including all privileges the United States allowed for itself, and to have an equal voice in world affairs.[70] The Minister of Foreign Affairs Andrei Gromyko declared as such in 1971, when he said that there was now "no question of any significance which can be decided without the Soviet Union, or in opposition to her."[71]

The act of negotiation itself was seen as an indication of the success of the Soviet strategy. Soviet leaders credited strategic parity with convincing the Americans to finally negotiate with the Soviet Union as an equal partner, a fact that in and of itself publicly symbolized the Soviet Union's superpower status.[72] It was the perception that parity had succeeded in forcing the Americans to deal with the Soviets on the basis of equality that ultimately paved the way for détente.[73] Because parity had led to the formalization of the Soviet Union's status as a superpower, Soviet leaders could adopt a more accommodating and open attitude toward the West. The mutual recognition inherent within a joint policy of détente would, Brezhnev thought, offer the best way to "broaden the position of the Soviet Union in the world."[74] The policy of parity had been so successful at overcoming the consistent implication of inferiority by Western actions that it was deemed to be "one of the greatest achievements of the whole postwar period."[75] For Soviet leaders, parity represented "an unprecedented advance over the inferiority which had characterized the last two-thirds of a century of Soviet rule."[76]

Alternative Explanations for the Arms Buildup

The new Soviet leadership responded to the national humiliation engendered by Khrushchev's public international failure as would be expected, given the framework presented in Chapter 2. They seem to have prioritized, above all else, a successful strategy through which they could build esteem and the USSR's image in the eyes of others. Given the highly competitive atmosphere over spheres of influence during the Cold War, a status-assertion strategy involving the highly public use of force against the United States or any third-party state would have risked repeated international failure at best and catastrophic escalation at worst. Thus, the Soviets engaged in a material strategy aimed at asserting their rightful equivalence with the United States. The Soviets believed that the number of strategic arms held by a state symbolized, to both the Americans and other international observers, the state's position within the international hierarchy. The Soviets' strategy of vying for strategic parity was relatively risk averse in that the Soviets perceived they would be able to accomplish the task and because they believed that the United States would be forced to acknowledge Soviet equality on the establishment of strategic parity, thereby bolstering Soviet esteem while reducing the chances of repeated humiliation.

One might question why the Soviets chose a status-assertion strategy whose rewards would be so long and coming rather than adopting a strategy that would more immediately bolster the Soviet's claim to superpower status. Soviet leaders clearly knew that increasing their offensive strategic forces nearly five-fold would require time. Brezhnev and his colleagues were, however, relatively risk averse and insecure in the making of Soviet foreign policy early on. They wanted, above all, to ensure that the Soviet Union would not again be humiliated on the world stage and therefore sought recognition of the Soviet Union's superpower status. Given that the Soviet Union matched the United States in most other material capacities, the Soviet leaders became convinced that the absence of strategic parity was the primary factor enabling the United States to ignore Soviet status demands.

Though the evidence in the case fits well within the humiliation framework, it remains possible that alternative hypotheses might better explain events[77] One possible explanation for the arms buildup of the late 1960s is that the new Soviet leaders, unlike Khrushchev, believed they could use strategic superiority to fight and win a nuclear war. The conclusion of some U.S. analysts at the time was that the Soviet arming policy was predicated on the belief that they could achieve victory by taking out all U.S. Minutemen missiles with the Soviet ICBMs. If, the thinking went, the Soviets, after they concluded that war was inevitable, could destroy the U.S. land-based missiles in a timely fashion, then the United States would be forced to negotiate on Soviet terms for fear that U.S. cities would be targeted next. Certainly there were some in the Soviet military who focused on preparing for victory. Yet this perspective does not appear to have been shared by those in the Soviet Politburo who recognized the immense risk involved in such a plan.[78] For, as Brezhnev noted, there was little point to attacking the Minutemen missiles when so many other weapons would survive such an attack.[79] The United States would maintain survivable warheads on undetectable submarines and in bombers that could be used to retaliate against the Soviet Union, a response that most Soviet leaders deemed to be inevitable.

This belief reflected a more general one among Soviet leaders that a nuclear war could not be won, regardless of which side had the first-strike advantage.[80] As Marc Trachtenberg notes, Brezhnev was not a gambling man. It was thus unlikely that a perceived strategic utility of parity or superiority motivated Soviet arming decisions during this period. Rather, as Jonathan Hines concludes from a series of interviews with senior Soviet officials, "Forces were developed and deployed in the context of the arms race not necessarily on the basis of any compelling analysis or intention to achieve a force advantage that would enable the Soviets to launch a surprise preemptive attack."[81] While Soviet officials might have recognized the need, for purposes of morale and ideology, to advertise the belief that they could win a nuclear war, a nuclear victory was, as one Soviet official described it, a "theoretical" concept.[82]

There is also the possibility that bureaucratic or domestic factors were primarily responsible for shaping Soviet defense policy during this time. This is a primary conclusion of Hines and Shull, who argue that the quantity of Soviet weapons was conditioned by internal dynamics while qualitative advances were made in response to technological advances by the United States. The argument—that massive production was itself the "underlying and driving force that justified the existence of the massive force"—is predicated on the idea that the need of the defense-industrial establishment to maintain stability and continuity was allowed to substantially shape defense policy.[83] In order for this to be true, one or both of the following scenarios would have to be true. First, it is possible that Brezhnev for one reason or another was particularly sensitive to the needs of the defense industry. Indeed, it seems likely that he had developed a strong knowledge of and relationships with the industry while working on defense policy under Khrushchev. This does not explain, however, Brezhnev's persistent focus on equality with the United States or his perception that strategy parity would offer the most reliable way to finally assert the Soviet Union's rightful place in the world. Thus, while Brezhnev may have actively supported the defense-industrial complex, the resulting arms buildup also clearly served other Soviet objectives.

Second, even if Brezhnev's allegiance to the defense industry did not facilitate the arms buildup, it is possible that Brezhnev's personality and the resulting diffuse organizational structure of the Soviet government under his leadership allowed for assertive military officials to assume control of decisions about force size. According to Hines and Shull, Soviet officials described Brezhnev as "incompetent, indecisive, self-indulgent and lazy." Based on this argument, the massive Soviet arms buildup was not the product of any coherent, overarching policy or doctrine but was the result of a mindless, wandering bureaucratic process in which willful Soviet military officials were able to push their agendas in a government with no hand on the rudder. It is indeed reported that there were, at one point in the mid-1970s, twelve different Soviet ICBM development programs running simultaneously and that internal rivalries appear to have been responsible for much of this competitive redundancy.[84]

It also appears that inconsistencies existed between the stated Soviet defense strategy and the force structure developed in its support. Descriptions by Soviet officials of Brezhnev as a non-existent leader focus almost primarily, however, on the mid-1970s and beyond, a period during which Brezhnev was presumed to be incapacitated from mental illness.[85] The argument is less likely to apply to the years immediately following Brezhnev's instrumental role in the coup when decisions to match the ICBM arsenal of the United States were taken. While policy making was undoubtedly less streamlined under the collective leadership of Brezhnev and colleagues, it seems that Brezhnev was aware of the tradeoff between dramatic defense production increases and domestic production, as was signaled in his public speeches in the mid-1960s. Thus, it seems highly unlikely that the Soviets somehow stumbled into a situation of parity with the United States without the formal recognition and acceptance of top Soviet leaders.

The U.S. Response to Strategic Parity

This section demonstrates that, just as Soviet leaders had come to view strategic parity as a symbolic path toward status equality with the United States, U.S. leaders came to make decisions about the size of their strategic arsenal and delivery systems based on the perceived threat to U.S. status that the Soviet status investments presented. In that both countries pursued quantities of material items not for the strategic or military benefits these items conferred, but because they thought others believed numerical superiority was a mark of higher status, the competitive dynamics of the arms race during this period were similar to those during the latter stage of the Scramble for Africa.

While the Soviets spent the latter half of the 1960s and early 1970s focused on achieving strategic parity, the United States maintained much lower levels of defense spending than it had in the late 1950s. The United States had maintained an economic, political, and strategic advantage over the Soviet Union for much of the 1950s and early 1960s.[86] During this time, U.S. leaders had worried on occasion about the Soviet Union catching up militarily. Kennedy, for example, feared convergence with the Soviet Union during the supposed missile gap. His concerns about parity, however, did not stem from the security implications of parity so much as they did from the possible social implications of parity. If relative force size symbolized relative status, then, as Kennedy acknowledged, relative decline of the United States could not be allowed to continue without risking an increase in American irrelevance. Once concerns about the missile gap proved to be unfounded and the military became convinced of the ability to survive and flexibly respond to a Soviet strike, many U.S. military and political officials came to view the competition for strategic superiority as a costly endeavor with diminishing returns.[87]

Nevertheless, the fact that the Soviets achieved strategic parity forced U.S. leaders to turn their focus to the relative numerical balance of strategic forces. The U.S. leaders responsible for negotiating the SALT I accords had been willing to codify existing and growing strategic asymmetries with the Soviet Union. The agreement allowed for a Soviet stockpile of 1,618 ICBMs to the Americans' 1,054 and acknowledged the rapid Soviet development of SLBMs by allowing the Soviets an eventual SLBM stockpile of 950 and the Americans a stockpile of 710, suggesting how little of a security threat the Americans perceived inferiority in strategic delivery systems to be.[88] The public nature of the accords, however, created common knowledge throughout the international community about the existing balance of forces, the status of which had previously not been well-known. It also brought the asymmetries to the attention of U.S. statesmen and leaders like Senator Henry Jackson who in 1972 successfully attached an amendment to the SALT I agreement calling for "the President to seek a future treaty that, inter alia, would not limit the United States to levels of intercontinental strategic forces inferior to the limits for the Soviet Union." The debates surrounding the call for strategic parity in all future arms control agreements with the Soviets, a call eventually codified in the Jackson Amendment in 1972, played a significant role in both shaping concerns about relative arsenal numbers and in making these concerns common knowledge to all spectators both at home and abroad.[89]

Thus, it was only after parity had been reached and inferiority institutionalized that American political attention turned more toward "equality" with the Soviet Union.[90] After 1972, the language of "equivalence" that had been used by advocates of the amendment during the debates found its way into reports to Congress made by subsequent secretaries of defense. In contrast to that of the Soviets the U.S. focus on parity would assume more of the characteristics of Khrushchev's Potemkin strategy. In one interesting and telling exchange, Secretary of Defense James Schlesinger reported to Congress in 1974 that "there must be *essential* equivalence between the strategic forces of the United States and the USSR."[91] The added emphasis here, and throughout much of Schlesinger's report on strategic parity, is on "essential" equivalence rather than on exact equivalence in each weapon type. When pressed by Congress to more precisely define what "essential" equivalence meant, Schlesinger stated that establishing "perceived equality" was the primary objective of the policy, rather than ensuring that the United States matched the Soviets one-to-one in all segments of the strategic arsenal. Schlesinger's successor Donald Rumsfeld similarly maintained in his 1977 Report to Congress that the United States should take all necessary "actions to create the necessary perception of equivalence."[92] Harold Brown, secretary of defense under President Carter, clarified that the concern about superiority was about *perceptions* and not about any security threat that Soviet superiority might pose, stating that "Insistence on essential equivalence guards against any danger that the Soviets might be seen as superior—*even if the perception is not technically justified.*"[93]

But whose perceptions were the Americans worried about? On the one hand, U.S. leaders were concerned about how the Soviets perceived nuclear superiority. Though they had little direct knowledge about Soviet perceptions, U.S. leaders could draw tentative conclusions from Soviet actions and statements to others. Caspar Weinberger concluded from the fact that the Soviet investment in strategic forces had been two to three times the size of the U.S. investment that the Soviet leadership "did not share the judgement that additional capabilities are pointless."[94] Schlesinger's 1975 Congressional Report indicated that although while U.S. analysts were not exactly sure how the Soviets perceived the importance of superiority, they could conclude from rapid Soviet arming that the Soviet leadership did perceive some value in it. Schlesinger also noted that this belief was bolstered by the fact that the Soviets had touted their strategic superiority to leaders of other states, suggesting to U.S. leaders that the Soviets at least believed that superiority would provide some diplomatic advantage.[95] U.S. leaders also feared that the Soviets would potentially behave more aggressively if Soviet leaders believed that superiority did provide a political or military advantage.

As Luttwak notes, however, it was not Soviet perceptions that most preoccupied U.S. leaders.[96] According to Schlesinger, it was important that equivalence was perceived "not only by the Soviet Union, but by *third audiences* as well."[97] U.S. leaders and analysts were of the belief that leaders of other countries, not just allied or rival countries, and "informed public opinion the world over" paid attention to which state had more strategic weapons.[98] Schlesinger believed that "many leaders" kept note of and reacted to numerical comparisons of the number of warheads, mega-tonnage, and relative force size, and suggested that "to the degree that we wish to influence the perception of others, we must take appropriate steps (by their lights) in the design of the strategic forces."[99] The emphasis Schlesinger placed on the importance of managing perceptions suggests that he must have believed he was taking the "appropriate steps" to do so within his force and budget requests he annually made of Congress.

Above all, managing these perceptions was deemed important because, the Americans believed, perceptions of superiority were tied directly to estimations of status and influence in the international system. "More" was generally regarded as implying greater "power," and the nature of this power was typically political. Again, Secretary of Defense Schlesinger's statements provide insight into the U.S. thinking on the matter. He indicated that equality was important for symbolic purposes "in large part because the offensive strategic forces for us have come to be seen by many, however regrettably, as important to the status and stature of a major power."[100] One Arms Control and Disarmament agent described the situation in a similar fashion, stating that observer states were "trying to estimate the power relationship in part based on things like relative nuclear forces" because they "want to be sure they pick the winner" and because they believe that other states would also be using relative nuclear forces as a measure of who the winner should be.[101] U.S. leaders also suspected that the desire to achieve a particular stature in the eyes of others was more important to the Soviets than was balancing security threats. This belief is made clear by a former joint chief's comment about U.S. military leaders' efforts to achieve parity: "I think they are wise enough to know that there's no threat . . . There's a prestige item associated with this, where the Soviets want to be considered, image wise, as being an equal with the US."[102]

Enhanced status was not only prized in and of itself. Its importance also resided in the relationship between international position and international influence. U.S. leaders, in particular, feared that third-party countries and allies would defer less to the United States if it was perceived that the United States was being eclipsed in any important way by the Soviet Union. As a result, U.S. leaders were hoping to manage perceptions of the country's relative position so that "the world—the third world particularly, and everybody else, even our own allies—perceive that the Soviets are inferior to us and that they, as a result, become 'more likely to acquiesce to us.'"[103] Leaders believed that obtaining such acquiescence from third parties provided political influence which indirectly provided the best path to security within a nuclear context. Admiral Stansfield Turner suggested as such with his comment that "Whatever we do, it must not only correct the actual imbalance of (nuclear) capability; it must also correct the perception of imbalance . . . Changing the world's perception that we are falling behind the Soviet Union is as important as not falling behind in fact."[104] As this quote suggests, the pursuit of security was seen as best accomplished more indirectly through the pursuit of greater status rather than through the pursuit of actual strength.[105]

The argument that status concerns motivated the U.S. focus on strategic parity does not imply that U.S. officials were not also concerned about demonstrating resolve to the U.S. allies. As Schlesinger stated in the 1975 report to Congress, "Friends may believe that willingness on our part to accept less than equality indicates a lack of resolve to uphold our end of the competition and a certain deficiency in staying power."[106] Yet even buildup motivated by a desire to convey resolve was rooted in perceptions of perceptions rather than within any nuclear reality. While matching the arms of the Soviet Union could be in part a costly signal to allies that the United States was willing to do whatever necessary to protect itself and its allies, much of the added strategic force provided no additional ability for the United States to do so. While Schlesinger and his successors did highlight to some extent their concerns about properly managing the perceptions of allies, the greater number of references to the perceptions of third parties and the world more generally about the strategic balance indicates that resolve was not the primary driver behind the desire to keep up with the Soviet Union's arsenal buildup.

Finally, while numerous leaders of the U.S. military in the 1970s and 1980s emphasized the importance of strategic parity, this does not tell us the extent to which these concerns impacted the size of U.S. strategic arsenals. Given that "perceptions" of parity were deemed more important than actual parity, leaders might have engaged in maneuvers, much as Khrushchev did in the 1960s, to draw attention to highly visible elements of U.S. superiority while ignoring those areas where the United States had fallen behind or while failing to engage in actual weapons buildup. Instead of focusing on buildup to match the Soviet numbers, the Americans focused their efforts on arms reduction and freezing the total strategic delivery forces of both sides at an equal number. While SALT I had institutionalized asymmetries in arsenal sizes in 1972, the United States worked hard to repair that asymmetry by negotiating an overall reduction in strategic force sizes, getting the Soviets to agree to an aggregate strategic delivery arsenal of 2,400 in SALT II seven years later.[107] That the two sides agreed on a single, easily digestible and highly visible number to institutionalize the two sides strategic parity rather than on an agreement that focused on ensuring actual military balance of the number of ICBMs, SLBMs, and heavy bombers indicates the priority placed on managing the perceptions of others and on controlling the costs of any future competition aimed at shaping these perceptions.[108]

In short, just as England reluctantly adopted a focus on its relative territorial holdings in Africa for fear that a failure to do so would affect its international stature, the United States became focused on the relative size of its strategic arsenal largely for the same reason. As was the case with Britain, the United States, as the dominant state in the system, was initially reluctant to proactively pursue a strategy aimed at status-maintenance, instead waiting until it became clear that observer states might be using the balance of forces as an important symbolic measure of international standing. Indeed, the United States turned its focus to equivalence only after it had allowed the Soviets to catch and even surpass U.S. stockpiles of some strategic weapons, long after the weapons could have presented a security threat. A military logic for strategic balancing fails to explain these inconsistencies or the focus on the relative number rather than on the absolute number of survivable warheads and delivery devices.[109] Rather, the shift in U.S. emphasis toward "equivalence" was rooted in a desire to manage the perceptions of the Soviets, U.S. allies, and most important, the international system more generally about which state was deserving of more status, and subsequently, more deference. U.S. policy regarding the balance of forces came to be guided far less by first-order U.S. concerns than by concerns about second-order beliefs and the creation of an international narrative about relative decline of the United States.

This chapter has examined two additional cases in which humiliating events motivated significant shifts in foreign policy involving actions aimed at asserting the status of the humiliated state. The U-2 incident effectively comprised several different sources of Soviet humiliation. First, the Soviets were sensitive to additional slights coming off of years of disrespect by the United States of their right to sovereign air space, a right bestowed to all states by international law. Soviet failure to defend the country's air space, as would be expected of a state of its desired status, engendered significant self-doubt about the efficacy of the state. Though the Soviets experienced a confidence-bolstering victory when they finally shot down the U-2 in 1960, the sense of humiliation was only exacerbated by Eisenhower's public recognition of this repeated disrespect and by the public statement of his intentions to further disregard Soviet rights.

The Cuban Missile Crisis was also related to several sources of Soviet humiliation. The first humiliating element of the crisis related to the Americans' attempt to apply a double standard to the Soviet Union, forbidding the placement of missiles in Cuba while the Americans had surrounded Soviet territory with missiles of its own. Most significant, the crisis of October 1962 came to represent the failure of the Soviet Union to assert its interests on the world stage, a failure that, while not entirely unexpected given the power asymmetries between the United States and USSR that existed at the time, followed public statements by Khrushchev of the Soviet's rights to place missiles on the island. Perhaps no single policy failure short of defeat has been so publicized on the world stage.

Soviet reactions in both cases were relatively risk averse. Given the likelihood of repeated failure against the United States, the use of force against the Soviets' humiliator did not offer a viable path toward the recovery of national confidence and status. Overcoming humiliation through intervention in the affairs of third-party states also risked military reaction by American leaders focused on checking the expansion of Soviet influence around the globe. Soviet leaders pursued material and diplomatic strategies that promised to successfully augment the esteem and status of the USSR. Though Soviet leaders displayed a relative risk aversion in their response to national humiliation, the strategies they selected had significant implications for the stability of world affairs.

The case of strategic arms buildup in the late 1960s, for instance, provides further evidence of the important ways that the status-seeking behavior of humiliated states can generate symbols of international status which are then sought by other states seeking to maintain their relative position. The United States became focused on numerical equivalence with the Soviet Union because U.S. leaders wanted to demonstrate both the intention and the ability to maintain the high status of the state. They became convinced that strategic arms served, in the eyes of others, to "identify the state's estimate of its relative standing in the world."[110] The case, therefore, demonstrates the power of second-order beliefs in shaping status-driven behavior. The United States did not believe the size of nuclear arsenals passed the point of mutually assured destruction mattered militarily, but they did become convinced that the Soviets and third-party states believed nuclear superiority to be a symbol of status, just as empire had been in a prior era. The Soviets also pursued a large strategic arsenal because they believed that the United States likely perceived such capabilities to define superpower status. Both states, in selecting a defense policy, relied at least equally if not more so on their second-order beliefs about what other states in the international system viewed to symbolize status than they did on their own strategic assessments about the security implications of asymmetric stockpiles. U.S. leaders were often willing to allow concerns about social perceptions of the state to trump sound strategic logic, as evidenced by CSIS executive director Ray Cline's belief that a growing and innovative arsenal would "be perceived as more powerful than one which is static—even if the latter still retains an advantage in purely technical terms."[111]

Conclusion

THE ATTENUATION AND PREVENTION OF NATIONAL HUMILIATION

> **A public humiliated by military defeat is easily enchanted by myths.**
> —Yegor Gaidar

Humiliating international events shape how states react to each other, increasing the likelihood of mistrust, animosity, and intractable conflict. They motivate states to engage in more assertive actions with the intention of restoring collective esteem and status, even at the expense of the state's material and strategic interests. Humiliating international events are arguably frequent within international affairs. But it is those events in which a large disparity between expectations and reality are revealed that promise to most significantly affect state behavior. States that are expected to behave like great powers but that are rapidly defeated by far weaker states or states that expect to be treated as great powers but are denied basic rights associated with sovereign statehood are most likely to internalize particularly malignant and affecting forms of national humiliation.

Efforts to bolster national confidence following such events can significantly destabilize the international system, dramatically increasing the propensity for aggression among other states, and the likelihood of international status competitions aimed at shaping public perception of states' relative social standing. The effects of the two primary status competitions of the nineteenth and twentieth centuries—the Scramble for Africa and the latter half of the arms race during the Cold War—are long-standing and significant. In the decades after World War II, roughly fifty newly independent African countries entered the international system after decades of colonial rule which continue to shape domestic politics within Africa as well as the international distribution of political and economic influence. The strategic delivery systems amassed by the Soviet Union during the late 1960s—which enabled the Soviet Union to threaten any point on earth with nuclear destruction—continue to serve as a primary basis for Russian claims to great power status in the contemporary era. Competitions over status, guided by a desire to accumulate symbols of status often at material and strategic cost, can clearly have significant material and strategic implications over the long run.

This book has focused on the effects of humiliation at the national level. There is ample evidence, however, that the described relationship between group-based humiliation and aggression extends beyond the level of the state. Prime Minister of Malaysia Mahathir Mohamed described a palpable sense of humiliation in the Muslim world in 2003: "We are all being humiliated . . . The whole Muslim community [is] treated with contempt and dishonour. . . . Our only reaction is to become more and more angry."[1] In his first statement after the 9/11 attacks, Osama bin Laden directly related the eighty years of "humiliation and degradation" suffered by the Islamic nation at the hands of the West with the September 11 attacks on U.S. targets, declaring that "What America is tasting now is something insignificant compared to what we have tasted."[2] In a February 2003 speech, shortly before the U.S. invasion of Iraq, bin Laden dated the psychological "wounds" of the Muslim world back to acts of colonial occupation in the nineteenth century and to the Sykes-Picot Agreement of 1916, which "dissect[ed] the Islamic world into fragments."[3] The poet and official propagandist for the Islamic State, Ahlam al-Nasr, wrote that finally with ISIS's 2014 victory in Mosul, "the land of glory has shed its humiliation and defeat and put on the raiment of splendor."[4]

We also have little reason to believe that the predicted effects of humiliation witnessed in the historical cases discussed in this book are in any way unique. One need only look to contemporary foreign policy in China and Russia for further evidence of national humiliation's considerable effects. Contemporary China has internalized a sense of national humiliation into its national narrative to perhaps a greater extent than any other state, past or present.[5] National Humiliation Day is commemorated annually on the anniversary of the Japanese invasion in 1937, a key event in China's self-proclaimed Century of Humiliation during which China's long reign as the unchallenged hegemon of East Asia ended. The Century of Humiliation began with China's unexpected defeat by Western powers in the Opium Wars of 1839 and 1861 and continued with defeat by Japan, China's longtime vassal, in 1895 and 1937.[6] Within the span of roughly fifty years, China, once the largest empire in the world, contracted into a near vassal state in which others dictated its laws, controlled its ports and extracted its material resources. The empire was forcefully dismantled, stripped of Hong Kong, Formosa, the Korean and Liaodong peninsulas, and territories farther afield.

The injustice of this precipitous decline over one hundred years ago, as embodied in the dramatically reduced footprint of the Chinese state, remains central to narratives of Chinese national identity. National posters depict particularly humiliating events—the burning of the once-glorious Yuanming Yuan Palace by the British, the forced signing of unequal treaties with Japan and the West, and the complete subjugation of the Chinese people by the Japanese in the Nanjing Massacre.[7] Collections of maps illustrating the extent of lost territories are released annually.[8] The pervasiveness of this narrative of humiliation at the hands of the West and Japan has fostered a culture in which over two-thirds of Chinese citizens cite China's status on the world stage as among their top three priorities, above the economic development of the state.[9]

Chinese foreign policy has seemingly been shaped by this national humiliation narrative in ways that this book would lead us to expect. Humiliation has served as a filter through which the behavior of others is understood. Bill Clinton and his NATO allies, for instance, declared the NATO bombing of the Chinese embassy in Belgrade in 1999 accidental; yet *People's Daily* directly related past to present, stating "This is 1999, not 1899 . . . This is not the age when the Western powers plundered the [Chinese] imperial palace at will, destroyed the Old Summer Palace and seized Hong Kong and Macao . . . The Chinese people are not to be bullied, and China's sovereignty and dignity are not to be violated."[10] In the days after the bombing, Chinese President Jiang Zemin demanded a public apology from the United States while hundreds of thousands of Chinese gathered in state-supported protests, surrounding the U.S. embassy in Beijing, trapping employees inside for days, and firebombing a U.S. consul's house in Chengdu.

For decades, Chinese leaders have looked forward "to the day when [China] could recover its rightful place in the sun—a yearning reinforced by past memories of both greatness and humiliation," while also acknowledging that further material recovery and reorganization would be required before China would be truly ready to assert its greatness again.[11] Recent extraordinary rates of economic growth have enabled China to increase its share of global GDP from 4 percent in 1960 to roughly 20 percent in 2020, almost matching the 25 percent share of GDP Chinese empire held at its peak in the late 1700s.[12] Recovery has been accompanied by the precise sort of acts this book would lead us to expect, given the territorial losses that have long symbolized China's humiliation and decline. The state has engaged in acts of territorial expansion and, at times, aggression, often aimed at recovery of lost lands. China has forcefully claimed the Daioyu Islands in the face of Japanese counter claims. The Chinese Navy is attempting to control territorial waters within the Nine Dash Line, extending into the South China Seas and far beyond China's legal territorial waters into areas once possessed by the Chinese empire at its height. China's unwavering commitment to the return of Taiwan is also logically rooted within the island's role as a symbol of China's undeserved treatment at the hands of the Japanese.[13] Chiang Kai-Shek seemingly foreshadowed contemporary Chinese policy in 1943 when he declared that "not until all territories have been recovered can we relax our effort to wipe out this humiliation."[14] The effort to reunite the nation, by force if necessary, is seemingly motivated, therefore, not by material profit, but by the desire to eradicate memories of past humiliations and to restore "symbolic recognition, acceptance and respect."[15]

National humiliation has arguably shaped contemporary Russian foreign policy objectives in similarly dramatic ways. Commentators and scholars have extensively noted the persistence and effects of Russian humiliation as have U.S. statesmen charged with Russia affairs.[16] The large disparity between Russian expectations of continued great power status and equality with the United States after 1991 and the U.S. treatment of Russia as defeated and inferior has been said to have "unleashed a kind of Weimar syndrome in Russia, a great nation whose dignity and interests were trampled."[17] The Soviet Union's precipitous and unexpected demise and the extreme domestic disorder and hardship that followed within Russia were viewed by many Russians not as a failure of their state and leaders but as an injustice perpetrated by the Americans. This perception was fostered by Western claims that the West had "won" the Cold War.[18] Russia's requests for integration with the West were rejected on the belittling basis that Russian efforts to imitate the political and economic institutions of the West were insufficient.[19] Western leaders failed to consult Russian leaders, still longing to feel indispensable on the world stage, on matters within their backyard, including the expansion of NATO into Eastern Europe and the bombing of Russia's Serbian allies in 1999.[20] As Richard Haass, director of Policy Planning at the State Department under Secretary of State Colin Powell, admitted in hindsight, the United States in the post-Soviet era had "neglected the Aretha Franklin principle with Russia—we did not give them enough respect."[21]

Like China, Russian self-doubt and outrage fueled by others' disrespect of the state's expected rights and privileges were exacerbated by massive territorial loss. The dismantling of the vast Soviet empire was significant in scope, leaving Russia with the smallest footprint it has held since the reign of Peter the Great.[22] The impact of this territorial loss has been likened to phantom limb syndrome in that the pain of the loss has continued to be felt long after the fact.[23]

For Russia, the decade immediately following these extensive losses was consumed with the restoration of political and economic stability and the massive reorganization of domestic institutions. By 1998, Russian GDP remained at two-third of what it had been in 1991. Only by the mid-2000s did Russian economic indicators return to their pre-1991 levels, bolstered by soaring oil and gas prices.[24] It was around this point, according to Boris Yeltsin's Minister of Finance Yegor Gaidar, that Russian policy shifted away from domestic recovery and toward the active reassertion of Russian great power status. As Gaidar notes, "We had assumed that overcoming the recession and beginning economic growth . . . would allow people to replace the dreams of empire restoration with the prosaic cares of personal well-being. We were mistaken . . . When economic security is growing . . . and you see that life has changed but is returning to stability, you can come home and watch a Soviet film where we always win . . . and then talk about how enemies have destroyed a great country and we'll still show them who's best."[25]

In the decade since recovery, Russia has behaved quite as we would expect, given the nature of its humiliation. It has sought opportunities to bolster collective confidence through successful demonstrations of Russian capabilities and great power intentions on the world stage. The first act of Russian reassertion was the war in Georgia in 2008 when the Russian military came to the aid of pro-Russian separatists in the South Ossetia region.[26] In 2014, Putin managed to correct what he had described as an "outrageous historical injustice" when Russian troops successfully annexed the Crimean Peninsula.[27] At the time of Russia's military intervention in Eastern Ukraine later the same year, Putin decried the "winners" of the Cold War who had failed to consult Russia on Ukraine's admission to the European Union and who generally "want to bend the world to their will."[28] "Nobody wanted to listen to us," he said. "We don't want some sort of empire. We simply want . . . for our position to be respected." He concluded, "It is impossible to keep humiliating one's partners forever in such a way. That kind of relationship breaks down."

The following year, Russia deployed its largest fleet of ships since the Cold War off the coast of Syria as Russian cruise missiles hit Russian-labeled terrorist groups. In projecting power abroad in Syria, Putin has been able to project an image of Russia as an integral actor in world affairs while further demonstrating that the country possesses the distinctive capabilities required of great powers. Although there may be clear strategic advantages to maintaining influence in the Middle East, it seems that Russian actions are also bolstered by a desire to overcome a long-standing sense of inferiority. As one member of the Russian parliament put it when asked what Russia was fighting for in Syria, "For Yugoslavia! For Libya! For Syria! For everything you have done these past twenty years!"[29]

One might argue that China and Russia are behaving as standard realist models of conflict would lead us to expect. As both states have acquired a larger share of capabilities, they have engaged in acts of territorial aggression, arguably increasing their influence and security. Yet certain key elements of the cases above do not hew to this traditional story.

First, while Russia and China, and others before them, may have sought to expand their influence abroad, they have often done so in ways that undermine their material and strategic interests. The costs incurred through such actions have been apparent not only in hindsight but were clear to the leaders at the time. France and Germany chose, for instance, to augment their colonial holdings in Africa despite the recognition decades earlier that colonies on average had proven to be unprofitable. Russian leaders opted to annex Crimea and intervene in Eastern Ukraine, though with some expectation that this first forceful act would be met with broad economic sanctions, leading to the stark devaluation of the ruble, and an increased NATO presence along Russia's border.

It is possible that even status assertions that prove costly in the near term may have instrumental benefits in the future if the state's heightened status is a path toward greater influence. One could argue, for instance, that by pushing back against Britain's unilateral policy in west Africa, Bismarck was best serving the long-term material interests of Germany by signaling that the state would not allow its interests to be trampled on, even when those interests proved costly to Germany. But, as we have seen, assertive acts taken by states in the wake of humiliating events often fail to raise the profile of the state in the eyes of others or to augment the state's influence. Though Russia may have recently garnered greater influence over states within its sphere of influence, it has arguably done so at the cost of broader global influence. Regardless, Russian aggression has seemingly served to accomplish the primary objective of humiliated states—it has boosted collective esteem at home. Public trust and confidence in Vladimir Putin and in the Russian government have remained roughly twenty points higher than it had been in the days leading up to the Crimean annexation in 2014, despite the collapse of the ruble, the departure of foreign direct investment, and a significant jump in the Russian poverty rate.

Second, without the incorporation of humiliation and its effects, it is difficult to understand the pervasive mistrust that characterizes certain international relationships. If states are motivated solely by security concerns, they would presumably be suspicious of all others, and especially of those with the greatest ability to hurt them. One could argue that this was the case with Chinese interpretations of the embassy bombing by the United States. The Chinese assumed the worst of the United States, its most powerful competitor. Yet this explanation fails to truly explain the seemingly disproportionate reaction of the Chinese people who stormed into the streets, engaging in widespread violence and demanding that Clinton be charged with war crimes. According to President Hu Jintao, the protests "fully reflect the Chinese people's great fury . . . and the Chinese people's strong patriotism."[30] It is hard to imagine the strength of this response within a state that was not fighting off a persistent sense of impotence and inferiority inflicted by past events—within a state that felt it had little to prove to itself or to others. Such states would be less likely to interpret others' behavior as intentional disrespect or the attempted enforcement of their inferiority. These states would also be less likely to end up in volatile, escalatory crises catalyzed by unwavering distrust.

This perpetual mistrust fosters intractable and long-standing rivalries between states that are hard to understand if one looks only at the distribution of power. As we saw in Chapter 5, enmity persisted between France and Germany from 1871 to the lead up to World War I. The hardened and unquestioned opposition between these European powers is not what one might have anticipated given the multipolar environment of the time in which the distribution of power was in flux and in which foes and friends should arguably have been more flexible. Similarly, foreign relations between Bolivia and Chile have been strained since Bolivia's defeat in the War of the Pacific in 1883. Bolivians have viewed Chile to be their primary rival, despite shifting power dynamics over the course of the last century. They have remained fixated on the return of their lost route to the sea just as France remained focused on the recovery Alsace and Lorraine. And they have been willing to pay costs to avoid cooperating with their archrival. Though a needed oil and gas pipeline to the sea would have run most directly and economically through Chile, the Bolivian people in 2002 protested this direct route, campaigning instead to send the pipeline hundreds of miles off a direct course—through Peru.

Third, these states' leaders have frequently employed the language of the humiliated. They convey anger at arrogant others who deny them equality and respect. They decry double standards aimed at highlighting and reinforcing their inferior position. "I don't like it when the US flaunts its superiority," Yeltsin said to Strobe Talbott in 1996, before stating his expectations for equal treatment and promising that Russia would rise again.[31] Ten years later, Putin similarly declared that Russia was not "some kind of auxiliary subject to take command of" and decried the purposeful attempt in the United States to create an image of Russia in which "[Russians] are a little bit savage still or they have just climbed down from the trees."[32] In 2004, Hu Jintao angrily accused Western forces of not having given up "the wild ambition of trying to subjugate [China]."[33] These statements are but few of many similar protestations uttered in strong emotional terms against perceived injustices made by Russian and Chinese officials in recent decades and often in conjunction with the announcement of particularly revisionist or uncooperative policies.

I have provided ample reason for us to understand such rhetoric as an honest presentation of the emotional state of leaders and their publics and as an important driver of the states' behavior toward others. Still, there will be those that counter that the use of such rhetoric is merely strategic and aimed at enhancing the bargaining position of the state, or that it is justificatory and offered only to defend non-cooperative policies ultimately driven by material self-interest. Those states that have far deeper wells of historical grievance to draw from are, however, more likely than states that have experienced few of the particularly humiliating events described in Chapter 1 to invoke the rhetoric of the aggrieved. The latter states would have little basis to credibly employ such emotional pleas. The higher the emotional salience of an issue among the people within one's state, the more credibly the state's leaders can commit to opposing all policies that undermine the state's position on that issue. Emotional salience cannot, however, simply be summoned at a whim. It must be founded, even if somewhat loosely, in an existing version of history broadly shared within the state.

Further, the invocation of humiliation rhetoric is not without its costs. Complaints about the treatment of the state as inferior may foster domestic support for oppositional policies against a seemingly unjust rival. These protestations when not uttered in conjunction with, for instance, the use of force can highlight features of the state that those existing within an anarchic world would arguably seek not to—namely, the relative weakness and potential impotence of the state in the face of others' threats. Blaming others for one's lack of influence would not seem to be a logical strategy within an anarchic world in which states are motivated solely by security concerns and a desire for survival.

Finally, in contrast to those who argue that state expectations of influence are rooted solely in their relative material advantage, the evidence presented throughout this book shows that the correlation between capabilities and expected influence is loose at best. As we have seen, neither France, nor Russia, China, or post–World War I Germany substantially downgraded their expectations of great power status or influence even in the face of events that led to significant declines in their material capabilities. In sharp contrast to realist predictions, we see that some states will become more assertive as they confront relative decline. Why would this be so? One answer lies in the nature of national humiliation itself. Humiliation involves a sense of outrage at the unjust actions of others. If an international outcome that leads to the degradation of one's status can be perceived as an injustice reflecting the negative intentions of others, then the humiliated state has little reason to lower its status expectation in keeping with its material capabilities. The humiliating event by definition is not perceived to represent one's true capabilities but instead is blamed on unfair treatment by others. That this is so offers a plausible explanation for why humiliation's effects are often so long-lived.

Although observers are more likely to base their estimations of a state's status on the relative material capabilities of the state, the status expectations of the humiliated state are more vestigial in nature, attuned more to the past than the material present. Disjunctures naturally arise between how humiliated states see themselves and how others perceive them. Observers expect humiliated states to update in accordance with their new reality while humiliated states instead seek to update their material reality in accordance with the high status expectations they maintain even in the face of decline.

With its focus on the importance of the past and on declining powers, this book has departed from the more traditional focus on emerging powers found within work on international status. Although emerging states no doubt encounter disjunctures between their rising material capabilities and the speed with which other states offer them the influence and deference they believe they deserve, I have shown that declining states are at least equally affected by status concerns. The disjuncture between material capabilities and attributed status that naturally emerges when states are rising is further complicated among humiliated states by the way that the past status of the state shapes its current status expectations. Properly gauging the status expectations of humiliated once-great powers in a way that enables status recognition often proves to be more difficult than assessing the status expectations of rising states.

The Diminution of National Humiliation

Many states have experienced humiliating events of one form or another at different points in their history. Clearly not all of these states continue to be shaped by humiliation's effects. Among all collective emotions, national humiliation has the potential to carry the farthest into the future. Individuals indeed need not live through humiliating international events to find them humiliating. Contemporary Chinese youth educated with the history of national humiliation are among the most willing to protest current Japanese actions and to actively commemorate the anniversaries of past Japanese atrocities. President of Serbia Slobodan Milosevic's invocation in 1989 of Serbian humiliation at the hands of the Ottomans 600 years earlier similarly attests to the lingering effects that national humiliation can have across generations. Moreover, past grievance increases perceptions of future grievance, making it very difficult for states to escape from reinforced narratives of humiliation at the hands of nefarious others. Yet not all previously humiliated states continue to bristle at past grievances. What factors affect whether humiliation endures or declines?

The more the expectations have been undermined through the disrespectful treatment of others or through national failure, the more deeply embedded the state's narrative of humiliation is likely to be and the harder it will be to shed. Beyond the initial extent of humiliation, the legitimacy of domestic regimes can also play a significant role in determining whether humiliation persists or dissipates. When the legitimacy and stability of domestic regimes go unquestioned, leaders have less incentive to invoke past grievances in an effort to mobilize public emotion and support. Indoctrination of a sense of past grievance can be used, however, by weakened leaders as a crutch on which to build public legitimacy and to foment opposition against potential competitors deemed unwilling to sufficiently defend the interests of the state. Although Chinese leaders may have continued to guard Chinese honor during the Cold War, past grievances at the hands of foreign powers were not a dominant cultural narrative during that time. National humiliation is now a central feature of China's worldview in large part because of the Communist Party's need for a new source of legitimacy after the fall of the Soviet Union. If Chinese leaders had not confronted these domestic imperatives in the 1990s, it is possible that younger generations of Chinese would not be able to so easily channel a sense of outrage toward Japan and that alternative narratives emphasizing cooperation could have evolved.

The historical record also provides insight into key factors that may facilitate humiliation's decline. On the one hand, it is possible that a sense of national humiliation can diminish as a state gives up its expectation of higher status. This is most likely to occur if the state experiences repeated instances of humiliation accompanied by substantial material decline. As stated, status expectations remain sticky in the face of international failure or disrespect largely because they can be considered a statistical improbability. Repeated failures, however, especially in conjunction with material decline and persistent domestic instability will eventually force states to update their status expectations. Spain's sudden and humiliating loss of its colonies during the Spanish-American War in 1898, for instance, generated substantial frustration and soul-searching within Spain.[34] This "year of Disaster," as the Spanish called it, was followed both by plans of regenerationism and modernization, though these plans were stymied by a crisis of legitimacy and by domestic political factions that would fester up to the eve of the Spanish Civil War.[35] Although historians identify 1898 as the end of Spain's centuries-long run as a great power, it is possible that economic and political recovery at home following the 1898 defeat could have transformed Spanish malaise and grievance into reassertions of Spain's rightful place in the world. As it was, the decline in political and material stability eventually forced a shift in the identity and idea of Spain as a high status state.

It is also possible that a state's status expectations following humiliation will be meaningfully recognized by other states in ways that mitigate the sense of national outrage and inferiority. Bismarck, for instance, understood following French defeat in 1871 that France would need a way to bolster its *amour de soi* as well as its esteem in the eyes of others. He conveyed this recognition through his support of France's annexation of Tunisia ten years later. While this act of recognition did not serve as a complete salve for the pain inflicted by the defeat on the French public, French leaders conveyed a sense that the annexation of Tunisia had indeed served its intended role—by successfully establishing France's return as a leader on the world stage. This feeling maintained only until France's self-inflicted humiliation in Egypt the following year.

The days of territorial compensations for past humiliations do appear, at least temporarily, to be over. States in the contemporary international system must find other ways to convey recognition of a humiliated state's status expectations. The act of recognition can assume many forms. First, states may shape their rhetoric in such a way as to convey sensitivity to the status concerns of others and to verbally acknowledge states' rights to respect and status. Such rhetorical devices may include the act of verbal or written apology which acknowledges the legitimacy of another's grievance and can serve to diminish both outrage and the sense of impotence that often drives the behavior of humiliated states. States may also seek to soothe the wounded vanity of humiliated states by providing them peaceful ways to assert their interests and thereby reestablish their sense of efficacy in world affairs.[36] States could be made to feel effective if they play significant leadership roles within organizations with broad international membership or if they are granted membership to exclusive international clubs to which membership is predicated on some distinctive capabilities or influence.

If, however, high status states circumvent these organizations and fail to use them as a forum for discussion and the sharing of opinions among equals, then membership for a humiliated state may only serve to augment its sense of humiliation. The inclusion of states within the decision-making process or within multilateral military actions may offer a more substantial path toward recognition.

Finally, it is also possible that states seeking to mollify the humiliation of other states may engage in a campaign of social creativity on their behalf in which they attempt to recognize negative attributes of the state as positive achievements within a different domain.[37] India gained status, for instance, through its leadership of non-aligned states and its opposition to colonialism during the Cold War.[38] By recognizing the value of others' traits that were previously conceived of as negative, states may channel humiliated parties desire to rebuild confidence away from aggressive acts toward more cooperative, or at least more benign, forms of status reassertion. At the crux of such campaigns remains, however, the recognition that the features of the humiliated states should be valued and respected by the international community.

The paths to recognizing the status concerns of other states may be clear enough. Yet the states capable of the most satisfying forms of recognition often fail to take them, giving way to potentially destabilizing forces in the international system. This is true for several reasons. On the one hand, other states often fail to recognize status assertive acts following humiliating events as what they are—bids to overcome a sense of inferiority. On the other, states often perceive assertive status-motivated acts as intentional power grabs and as security threats rather than as demands for social recognition or equality. This assignment of negative intentions to the humiliated state serves to further ostracize the humiliated state and to thereby exacerbate the state's sense of humiliation.

Even when status concerns are recognized for what they are, significant challenges often work against the recognition of humiliated states. States seeking to recognize the status expectations of others must balance the benefits of minimizing the possibility of aggressive acts by other states with the domestic and material costs of doing so. Although the grievances of disrespected states may be lessened by apologies by the victor state, such apologies are often not forthcoming. Political leaders may fear the domestic audience costs of appearing to back down in the face of demands by other states. If negative intentions have been assigned by domestic competitors to the humiliated state's acts of status assertion, it can be difficult for those in charge to appear sensitive or conciliatory to the social grievances that might instead motivate such assertive acts. A failure to drive a hardline with aggressive humiliated may give way to more hardline domestic actors.

Another significant obstacle to the successful recognition of humiliated state's expected status, however, rests on the zero-sum nature of status and influence. Status can be club-based, meaning that states may aspire to and be welcomed into the exclusive clubs like that of the great powers; however, the distribution of influence within those clubs largely exists within a closed system. Status recognition implies a certain degree of deference to the needs and interests of others. These interests may clearly come into conflict with one's own. Providing a humiliated state the recognition it desires can, therefore, come at a significant material and strategic costs. This is not to say that higher ranked states will always deny influence and status to others. As we saw, British leaders eventually supported German expansion into Africa just as German leaders urged France to expand its footprint there in the early 1880s. Bismarck, like the British, recognized the potential costs to Germany if France failed to find a way to soothe its amour propre. Thus, leaders may find the loss of their own status, incurred through the recognition of the humiliated state, to be less costly than a protracted, enduring rivalry.

An examination of U.S. policies in the post–World War II period illustrates the competing incentives involved in successfully recognizing the desired status of humiliated states. Both France and Italy emerged from World War II humiliated—by defeat and by their post-war reliance on the United States. Both states had failed to perform admirably during the war and both had suffered substantial material decline. The need within both countries for the restoration of collective self-confidence and for the reassertion of status was clear to U.S. officials at the time. A briefing book prepared by U.S. officials for President Franklin Roosevelt prior to the Yalta Conference in 1945 pointed out that the French were "unduly preoccupied, as result of the military defeat of 1940 . . . with questions of national prestige." As a testament to the enduring effects of past status, the briefing elaborated that French expectations of international status and influence in the post-war era were clearly "out of proportion to their present strength."[39]

U.S. leaders were acutely aware of the potential costs of not providing sufficient recognition of these countries' status ambitions. A failure to bolster the esteem of France and Italy through acts of recognition would potentially undermine U.S. efforts at decolonization.[40] Moreover, U.S. officials feared the potential domestic implications of a failure to treat France and Italy's status concerns with sufficient sensitivity. The failure to restore the self-confidence of these states through acts of recognition would leave room for the rise of domestic political movements promising to restore the strength and respect of the state through more radical or assertive means, potentially giving rise to aggressive military or communist dictatorships.[41]

Given these potential threats to U.S. interests, the country's officials deemed it necessary to "take full account of this psychological factor" and to respect France "on the basis of her potential power and influence rather than on the basis of her present strength."[42] Roosevelt promised to restore Italy's "honorable place in the world" and Truman stated that France should resume its "rightful and eminent place" in world affairs.[43] At the urging of the British, who recognized the need for the French to balance German interests on the continent, the United States agreed to France's inclusion on the UN Security Council and within the Allied Control Council and European Advisory Commission responsible for deciding the fate of post-war Germany. Eisenhower recognized the need to channel Italy's inferiority-fueled interests on the Mediterranean Sea into active participation within NATO. The United States worked to remove all punitive elements from Italy's armistice, going so far as to label the country a co-belligerent in the fight against Nazism.[44]

Finally, and perhaps most significant, the United States attempted to redefine the basis of status among European powers, strongly encouraging integration and interdependence as a path to influence and prominence in European affairs. Just as they had done within post-war Germany, U.S. leaders emphasized French and Italian integration and development as the most promising ways to ameliorate the sting of the severe humiliations they had experienced. As a co-partner with Germany, France would assume a leading role in European affairs. U.S. leaders hoped that Italy would be distracted from its status assertions in Trieste by having a key role within an integrated Europe.

The Americans, in this case, highly motivated by fears of Soviet expansionism, created policy intended to minimize the destabilizing effects of states weighed down by the "psychology of the vanquished." Their efforts often failed and often came with political and strategic costs. The Americans struggled at times to balance their desire to foster self-reliance in these states with the costs of genuinely taking their divergent interests into account. In some cases like the Suez Crisis of 1956, the Americans opted to flagrantly disrespect French, and British, interests rather than sacrifice their own strategic goals, an act which exacerbated French humiliation in ways that the Americans had been trying to prevent. The restoration of French self-confidence and self-reliance was also accompanied by strong pushes for the reorganization of power within NATO, a struggle that culminated in France's withdrawal from the organization in 1966. Rather than perceiving membership within exclusive international organizations as a path to enhanced status, French leaders came at times to perceive it as a constraint on the influence of their country in world affairs.[45]

Over time, both France and Italy gave up their expectations of playing a significant global role. Given the extent of military and material decline as well as political instability in both countries after the war, it was not surprising that neither country ever experienced a complete military revival, especially given the active role that the United States played in channeling their efforts toward more cooperative efforts. Italian leaders more or less recognized Italy's destiny as a "middle power" within a decade or so following defeat. For France, acceptance of decline would take longer. Even after its loss of Algeria, France's second prominent humiliation on the world stage within two decades, De Gaulle would assert the need for French independence, and essentially status, by withdrawing from NATO's command structure. The act was largely symbolic, however. The United States and France signed a secret agreement within the year which reestablished a French role in NATO's command structure in the case that hostilities broke out. This secret agreement was an implicit acknowledgment by French leaders, who were not yet willing to convey it publicly, that France would not be able to compete for social standing within the top international tier.

U.S. leaders before and after the end of the war were similarly motivated to minimize the effects of humiliating defeat and occupation on Japan. Prior to the end of World War II, U.S. secretary of war Henry L. Stimson recognized the long-term benefits of doing so. Though Stimson sought to make the most "profound psychological impression" on the Japanese with the detonation of the first nuclear bomb, he avoided bombing Kyoto, the cultural and intellectual center of Japan, primarily because of the humiliation that such a wanton act would engender. The "long-term bitterness" that would ensue, he thought, would render postwar reconciliation between the United States and Japan impossible.[46]

The war had, nevertheless, brought massive destruction on the defeated state. At the time of the Japanese surrender in 1945, the extent of the country's utter devastation became clear.[47] Sixty-five percent of Tokyo had been flattened. Thirty percent of Japan's urban populations were homeless. As General Douglas MacArthur rather insensitively put it in a post-surrender press conference, Japan had fallen to the status of a "fourth-rate nation," an assessment that was "guaranteed to tear asunder the vital organs" of the Japanese and their leaders.[48] The U.S. refusal to recognize Japanese status expectations in the 1930s had, after all, invoked the great emotion that John Dower perceives as the ultimate reason the Japanese went to war with the West. If Japan had failed to push back in East Asia, Prime Minister Tojo Hideki had declared, it would have been relegated to "second-rate" if not "third-rate" status.[49] Post-war Japanese leaders mounted a campaign of "national penitence" to account for "mistakes of the government, the bureaucrats and the people" leading up to and during the war. Any sense of guilt and shame the Japanese people might have taken on, however, was at least at first supplanted by the outrage they felt at their own leaders, an outrage so strong that many Japanese came to view the Americans as their liberators.

U.S. officials confronted a similar choice in their policy toward a defeated Japan as they did in their post-war policy toward Germany in 1919. They could choose the punitive strategy imposed on Germany at Versailles, replete with stringent reparations and its suggestion of guilt and inferiority. MacArthur, however, set the course early on within the negotiation of the post-war treaty, rejecting early "imperialistic" drafts, which failed to sufficiently avoid "punitive or arbitrary" provisions.[50] John Foster Dulles, tasked with negotiating the post-war treaty with Japan, had attended the fated 1919 peace conference in Versailles and had apparently learned from the experience. He pursued a treaty with Japan based on minimal restrictions and on no reparations to make way for the peaceful economic development of the state.[51] Such an approach was, in his mind, the only way to minimize the possibility of Japanese alienation at the hands of the West.

This more peaceful approach, focused on integration and the support of economic revitalization as a path to self-confidence and status, was at first a tough sell with a public bent on punishment. For Dulles and his colleagues, however, the potential long-term costs of abandoning a humiliated Japan were clear. The potential for future conflict would be high if a resentful and humiliated Japan became economically, and eventually militarily, resurgent. U.S. officials also feared that a humiliated and insecure Japan would turn to the Soviet Union for financial assistance and a path to restore self-esteem. Thus, they selected a strategy of integration through the restructuring of Japan's political and economic institutions. While Japanese discipline and initiative were inevitably required for the country's remarkable recovery, U.S. support and investments contributed to the development of a stable and prosperous democratic state that would contribute to the post-war international order.

One can, finally, compare these cases with that of U.S. policy toward Russia in the wake of the collapse of the Soviet Union. In Secretary of State Madeleine Albright's ex post facto view, the United States had "worked hard at treating Russia with respect" as the country adjusted to its new political and economic reality in the 1990s.[52] Yet, U.S. efforts fell dramatically short, allowing a sense of alienation and resentment toward the West to fester within the country, giving rise to a policy of aggression aimed at reasserting Russian great power status. Rather than employing rhetoric aimed at conveying sensitivity toward Russia's plight and position, Western leaders used the nonchalant and sermonizing tone of a victor comfortable that its foe had been permanently vanquished. Western institutions provided funds in the post-war period, but these were largely for the purpose of stabilization rather than redevelopment and always came with significant strings attached which highlighted Russia's submissive role.

Why did U.S. officials fail to properly address Russia's status concerns engendered by the fall of its empire? There are numerous possible explanations for why this may have been so. On the one hand, unlike in the European cases, it seems that U.S. leaders did not fully internalize the severity of Russian humiliation after the collapse. Visual evidence of the humiliation of France, Italy, Germany, and Japan abounded in the post-war era. It was impossible to deny how far those countries had fallen from their pre-war heights. The impact of the Soviet Union on Russians was less stark. Russia had, of course, lost an empire. The Americans, however, viewed the collapse of the Soviet Union as a positive and inevitable result of the implementation of communism while failing to recognize that many Russians explained the fall in a very different way. Moreover, U.S. leaders at the time attended more to Russia's significant material decline as a basis for the country's rightful place in the world and less to Russia's own self-estimations which entailed disproportionate expectations as to the say and influence that Russia would have in the post–Cold War era.

Even if U.S. officials had possessed a clear understanding of Russian expectations, they had far fewer near-term incentives to adopt a proactive and intentional policy aimed at status recognition than they had in the post–World War II era. U.S. leaders in the post–Cold War world did not confront a larger threat which might have required Russian cooperation. Within the new unipolar, pre–9/11 world, U.S. officials saw little cause for integrated efforts to confront new international challenges. As efforts against terrorism grew in the 2000s, Russia argued for cooperation with the United States. Even then U.S. officials failed to perceive at least one long-term benefit that working with Russia might have provided—the reduction of Russian outrage as the country came to feel like an important and valued player in world affairs. Just as it had during the Cold War, U.S. policy instead continued to focus on the implementation of Western institutions and norms as a bar for equality. The inability or disinterest of Russia to fully implement Western institutions has since served as a continual wedge in Russia-U.S. relations. Short of the more thorough political and cultural change that complete and utter military defeat or revolution facilitates, this incompatibility is likely to remain unresolved regardless of the assertive actions Russia adopts in an effort to garner more status.

In hindsight, it seems surprising that U.S. officials after World War II had the long-term vision to prepare for the possibility of a resurgent Germany and Japan, again possibly one day able to sow international discord, while U.S. in the post–Cold War period appear to have not considered the potential costs of a resurgent and angry Russia. Japan and Germany had been politically, economically, materially, and culturally decimated. Yet post-war planning acknowledged the need for them to feel secure and un-aggrieved with their place in the world for fear that eventual military and economic resurgence could transform their humiliation into outrage and aggression. Similar long-term vision was not applied to post–Cold War Russia. Russia's nuclear arsenal and technological know-how had remained largely intact. The country confronted political and financial instability, and yet it was also clear that the country possessed significant oil wealth which might one day fund its comeback. Perhaps U.S. officials believed that by the time Russian recovered its confidence, the pacifying effects of democracy and capitalism would have kicked in, anesthetizing the Russians from their painful past. As it stands, the relentless yet incomplete push for Western values and norms has only exacerbated Russian perceptions of an aggravating double standard.

The Prevention of Humiliation

What steps can best be taken, then, to effectively minimize the likelihood that one's acts result in the humiliation of other states? It is impossible to fully prevent national humiliation. There will be times the material and strategic interests of states will render them unwilling or unable to compromise over issues deemed essential to the status expectations of another state. The numerous cases of national humiliation discussed within this book suggest, however, that certain policies aimed at the prevention and rectification of humiliation are likely to enhance international stability. On the one hand, states should strive to avoid suggestions of inferiority in both their rhetoric and their diplomatic practice. When President Barack Obama downplayed Russia's international role in March 2014, labeling the country a mere "regional power" acting "not out of strength but out of weakness," he was speaking within the competitive spirit of a 2012 election in which Mitt Romney labeled Russia "America's biggest foe." Such comments provide domestic fodder for leaders like Vladimir Putin, who are driven in part by status threat. Obama's recognition two years later that Russia was "a large important country" that "has to be a part of the solution on the world stage" perhaps reflected a recognition of the aggravating and alienating effects that belittling comments can have.

Effort should also be maintained to avoid the codification of inferiority within formal and informal treaties and negotiations. Just as U.S. officials did in the post-war period, leaders should internalize the unintended consequences that punitive treaties and settlements often have. The formalization of inferiority provides ample grounds on which nationalist leaders can rise to power promising to fight back against the injustice. The post-war punishment of one's enemy is often motivated by a short-sighted desire for emotional solace. Such strategies fail to consider the long-term effects if one's enemy, subjugated and laid low, is ever able to rise again. They also fail to acknowledge the fact that the anger generated by a people's subjugation can be used as fuel for their resurgence. The case of post-war Japan should give us reason to doubt the necessity of punitive measures for achieving positive strategic outcomes.

Steps may also be taken to minimize the effects of a humiliation that has already taken place. A prerequisite to these steps is the recognition that others feel humiliated. Language decrying "unjust treatment," "second-tier status," "double standards," and "subjugation" provides insight into the potential collective psychology of a state. It is unlikely that such a sense of outrage will subside without recognition of its existence and legitimacy. Rhetorical efforts should be taken, therefore, to acknowledge a state's value and contribution as well as any potential hardships it may be facing. Humiliation may also be redressed by the inclusion of states within summits and international organizations where their voices and interests can be heard. More effectively, one imagines, states should seek opportunities for cooperative endeavors with humiliated states. Joint actions against terrorism shared initiatives toward nuclear disarmament—these projects could have played a more substantial role in mitigating Russian humiliation in the 1990s in that they could have conveyed U.S. respect for Russian capabilities as well as a sense of trust one typically reserves for equals.

As Bismarck's success in guiding France's need to restore its amour propre away from Germany and toward north African shores suggests, humiliation's aggressive effects can be channeled into pursuits which highlight the abilities and efficacy of the state. Strategies of social creativity aimed at establishing more peaceful bases of international status on which the humiliated state might excel promise to rectify national outrage and inferiority. U.S. efforts to channel European status concerns into a joint effort toward integration likely had a pacifying effect on European foreign policies. Humiliated states may also be encouraged to take the lead in multilateral peacekeeping efforts, in crisis negotiation efforts or in international economic governance. These efforts aim at conveying a perception of equality while also raising the international profile and confidence of the state. Such policies are likely to come with costs. As French confidence increased, so did French demands. Qualified statesmen must carefully balance these short-term irritants with the enormous effects that powerful and aggrieved states can have on world history.

This book has provided answers to many key questions about national humiliation and its effects. A thorough understanding of the way that national humiliation functions in world affairs would also involve knowledge of numerous other issues as well. Much more work remains to be done to establish the underlying micro-foundations of humiliation. Some variation in individual level responses to humiliation discussed in Chapter 3 remains unaccounted for. One might conceive of many factors that might influence how a person perceives and responds to humiliation at both the individual and national levels. It is likely that one's moral foundations help to explain variation in these perceptions. Those who value fairness would arguably be more likely to perceive events as potentially humiliating and to respond to them accordingly. This finding would correspond both with the findings of other scholars that individuals who identify as liberals are more likely to value fairness than conservatives and with the finding in Chapter 3 that humiliating events had the largest overall impact on those subjects who identified as democratic.[53]

In addition to developing a deeper understanding of the micro foundations of humiliation, it is also necessary to further assess the relationship between domestic political structures and the likelihood that leaders work to develop national narratives centered around past grievances. The evidence presented has focused on contemporary cases and shown a tentative relationship between threats to domestic legitimacy and the top-down fostering of such narratives. Is this relationship true for all regime types or more likely for unstable autocratic regimes? Also, are there certain domestic political structures that better enable the formation of competing national narratives not so centered on the past?

Finally, and perhaps most important, once such narratives of national humiliation have become pervasive within a state, are there domestic paths toward the disentangling of such narratives that do not involve wholesale domestic change or international recognition? Once aggrieved and angry, members of a humiliated group will tend to hunker down in an us-against-them posture that is hard to shake. Recent U.S. politics appear to bear witness to this phenomenon, as subsets of Americans claim humiliation at the hands of the country's elites. At the domestic level, one can imagine that such divisions could be overcome by significant international events that could create a more threatening "other" around which a new narrative and a new sense of domestic cohesion could form, thereby overriding internal divisions. At the international level, this would equate to the victor and victim allying against a state or coalition of states that presented a larger threat to state security and status.

A deeper knowledge of these important topics will, however, only serve to underscore one clear truth: national humiliation affects world affairs in crucial ways. It led to important periods of international competition within the nineteenth and twentieth centuries and will, in all likelihood, continue to do so in the future. Humiliation is a deep and innate human reaction to socially threatening situations. There is no reason to expect that this powerful emotional force will cease to play its important international role anytime soon. We should expect that even as the assertive strategies that humiliated states choose to engage in change over time, the general conditions of humiliation outlined in this book will apply. Humiliated states that have the means will be more likely to engage in assertive behaviors in an effort to secure their status than will non-humiliated states. In recognition of the past, we should expect these actions to have far-reaching international consequences.

Acknowledgments

I am incredibly grateful to advisers, friends, fellow graduate students, panelists, audience members, and anonymous reviewers along the way who have contributed their valuable time to read and respond to the ideas contained in this book. Its shape and contents have been dramatically improved through their suggestions. I would like to acknowledge, in particular, Marc Trachtenberg whose work on diplomatic history originally drew me to the study of international relations. Deborah Larson's research has paved the way for this book and for research at the intersection of psychology and international relations more generally. I appreciate the valuable comments she has provided on material throughout the book. Barry O'Neill has provided much needed support and levity along the way. I thank Barry also for helping me curtail my apparent overuse of the word "actually." Art Stein was my primary guide for the early years of this project. His influence on the final product is significant.

Thanks also to Chad Nelson, Dov Levin, Allan Dafoe, Elizabeth Saunders, Joseph Parent, Alexander Debs, Bruce Russett, Jiyoung Ko, Nuno Monteiro, Michael Desch, Paul MacDonald, Eugene Gholz, Rosemary Kelanic, Brian Rathbun, Tanisha Fazal, Jonathan Mercer, Jonathan Renshon, Marcus Holmes, Matthew Gottfried, William Wohlforth, Nick Anderson, Andrew Szarejko, among many others whom I have undoubtedly forgotten, who have read and commented on work that has become portions of the book.

Finally, to my sweetest Winston and my dearests Robert and Francesca: my gratitude for your enthusiasm, encouragement, wisdom, and simple existence is unbounded.

Appendix

Chapter 1

TABLE 1. Examples of Humiliating Defeats Measured by Relative Capabilities

DEFEATED STATE	VICTORIOUS STATE	YEAR	RELATIVE CAPABILITY OF DEFEATED STATE/S
Cyprus	Turkey	1974	0.016
Egypt	United Kingdom	1882	0.018
Iran	United Kingdom	1857	0.0204
Paraguay	Brazil	1870	0.021
Thailand	France	1893	0.024
Denmark	Prussia, Austria-Hungary	1864	0.0306
Cambodia	Vietnam	1979	0.051
Spain	United States	1898	0.079
Greece	Turkey	1897	0.079
Mexico	United States	1848	0.09
Pakistan	India	1971	0.139
Turkey	Russia	1878	0.169
Russia	Turkey, United Kingdom, France, Italy	1856	0.178
Argentina	Brazil	1852	0.1934
China	Japan, United States, France, United Kingdom	1900	0.203
Argentina	Brazil	1852	0.224
Ecuador	Columbia	1863	0.235
India	China	1962	0.321
Austria–Hungary	Italy, Prussia, Mecklenburg	1866	0.3313
Bulgaria	Germany, Turkey, Romania, Yugoslavia	1913	0.333
Uganda	Tanzania	1979	0.347
Austria–Hungary	Italy, France	1859	0.35
Turkey	Italy	1911	0.351
Russia	China	1900	0.476
Guatemala	El Salvador	1885	0.517
China	France	1885	0.614
China	Japan	1933	0.716
Italy	Ethiopia	1936	0.741
Bolivia	Paraguay	1935	0.75
Russia	Japan	1905	0.7707
Russia	Poland	1920	0.791
Arab States	Israel	1967	0.867
China	Japan	1895	0.829
France	Mexico	1867	0.954
United States	Vietnam	1973	0.965

Chapter 3

—Survey Demographics

The MTurk sample was 49.7% female and 50.3% male and was an average age of 61 years of age. The SSI sample included 52.9% men and 47.1% women with an average age of 56 years old. The political affiliations of the two groups did differ somewhat. Filters were included in the MTurk study to ensure that an equal number of republicans, democrats and independents were included in the sample. The subject pool therefore contained roughly 1/3 Republicans, 1/3 Democrats, and 1/3 Independents, 48% of whom indicated that they leaned democratic in their political preferences and 52% saying they tended to be more right-leaning in their views. Within the SSI study, 58% reported to hold left-leaning political views and 42% reported holding right-leaning political views.

—Additional Historical Prime

Last year, China engaged in acts taken by many to be disrespectful of the United States' international interests and rights. For instance, China created an alternative to the World Bank, inviting many of America's European and Asian allies to join, but excluding the United States. Though China had no acknowledged claims to the South China Sea, it sought to block US freedom of navigation through international waters. It claimed a number of uninhabited islands from which it attempted to block naval access to American ships. Chinese submarines tracked the USS Ronald Reagan off the coast of Japan. The submarine posed no threat, but was likely sent to spy on the US Navy. Chinese planes came dangerously close to downing an American plane when they engaged in an 'unsafe interception' of a US aircraft traveling in international airspace. As one European leader stated of China's actions, "China repeatedly disrespected the US, attempting to deny its rights as a sovereign state and its privileges as a great power."

Chapter 4

Part I: The Effects of Defeat

The Dyadic MID 3.1 dataset recodes a number of conflict outcomes in ways that differ from the MID 2.0 dataset. After critically examining the changes focuses on war outcomes, I chose to restore three key data points back to their coding within the previous dataset for which the basis of the change was unclear and seemingly unfounded. First, the 1988 war between Iraq and Iran was coded as ending in a stalemate within the prior data but has been updated to reflect a victory for Iraq and a defeat for Iran. While Iranian leaders ultimately felt compelled to accept a ceasefire under Soviet and American pressure, Iraq failed to accomplish any of the objectives that motivated the conflict, including establishment of control over the Shatt al-Arab waterway. I therefore retain the original coding for this outcome.

Second, the Chaco War fought between Bolivia and Paraguay in 1935 is coded as ending in a stalemate, and yet Paraguay had come to control most of the disputed territories by the war's end. The war was understood as a victory within Paraguay, greatly increasing national territory and "working wonders for national pride."[1] Thus, I retain the original coding of a Paraguayan victory and a Bolivian defeat.

Finally, the Sino-Indian War, ending in 1962, is currently coded as a stalemate. The Chinese did declare a unilateral ceasefire, but only after establishing the Aksai Chin territory it sought at the outset of the dispute. Following the war, India accepted the new de facto border as the new line of control. Thus, I code the conflict as ending in a victory for China and a defeat for India.

These coding changes to not significantly alter the results relating to the effects of defeat and stalemate reported within the book.

Sections 1 and 2: Are Defeated States More Likely to Initiate Conflict? Are They More Hostile When They Do?

Logit models were used to estimate all models of dispute initiation and the unit of analysis utilized in each set of models is the politically relevant, directed dyad-year. In all models, the standard errors are clustered by directed dyad.

The following explanatory and control variables were also included within the models used to generate the predicted probabilities in Figure 1:

- *Defeated in War Last 10 Years*: coded as one if the state has experienced a defeat against any state in the last ten-years period and otherwise as zero.
- *Victory in War Last 10 Years*: coded to capture whether a state has been victorious in war in the last ten years and the country did not experience defeat within that time.
- *Stalemate in War Last 10 Years*: coded as 1 if the state has experienced a stalemate in war against any state in the last ten years and the country did not experience defeat within that time.
- *Defeated in War Last 20 Years*: coded as one if the state has experienced a defeat against any state in the last twenty-years period and otherwise as zero.

- *Victory in War Last 20 Years*: coded to capture whether a state has been victorious in war in the last twenty years and the country did not experience defeat within that time.
- *Stalemate in War Last 20 Years*: coded as 1 if the state has experienced a stalemate in war against any state in the last twenty years and the country did not experience defeat within that time.
- *Relative Capabilities*: To assess the relative strength of a state's target, this variable is included. The variable measures the natural log of the state's share of the dyadic capabilities as represented by the state's CINC score in the Correlates of War National Military Capabilities data set.
- *Alliance*: Coded as 1 if the states within a dyad possessed a defensive or offensive alliance or a neutrality pact and 0 otherwise.
- *Recent Activity Level*: States involved in many disputes would be more likely to both be defeated and to initiate conflict. In such a case, any relationship found between past defeat and future aggression could be spurious. Thus, in keeping with Weisiger and Yarhi-Milo (2015), I include control variables accounting for a state's recent level of activity. The variables are equal to the total number of MIDs in which the state was involved in the prior five-year period.
- *Joint Democracy*: To control for the likelihood that conflict is less likely within democratic dyads, I include a dichotomous measure of joint democracy, which relies on the Polity IV data set. The dyad is coded as democratic if both states possess a Polity score of 6 or higher and 0 otherwise.
- *Contiguity*: The variable is coded 1 if the states within the dyad are touching or are separated by a land or river border.
- *Temporal Dependence Variables*: To account for temporal dependence between observations of conflict initiation, a count variable was included which codes the number of years between instances of initiation by a state within a given dyad. The cubic polynomials of *Peace Years x 2* and *Peace Years x 3* are also included in these models. In models assessing the likelihood of the use of force, these variables code the number of years since the state used force within the dyad. Relevant polynomials are also included within those models.

The coefficient table for models used to generate the substantive predictions in Figure 1 in Chapter 4 is presented in Table 2. The models examine the relationship between past conflict outcomes and conflict initiation as well as the likelihood states fight in wars. The coefficients in Models 1–4 on the left represent the relationship between defeat, victory and stalemate in the last ten and twenty-year periods and the probability that a state initiates conflict with another state. Models 5 and 6 on the right illustrate the relationship between war outcomes

TABLE 2. Models of Conflict Initiation and War

		DV: DISPUTE INITIATION			DV: USE OF FORCE	
VARIABLES	MODEL 1	MODEL 2	MODEL 3	MODEL 4	MODEL 5	MODEL 6
Defeat, Last 10 Years	.326** (.10)	.222* (.09)		0197* (.10)	.265** (.09)	
Victory, Last 10 Years	.092 (.09)	.063 (.08)		.128 (.08)	−.052 (.09)	
Stalemate, Last 10 Years	.065 (.14)	−.061 (.13)		−.032	−.118 (.15)	
Defeat, Last 20 Years			.375*** (.07)			.419*** (.08)
Victory, Last 20 Years			.121 (.08)			.044 (.08)
Stalemate, Last 20 Years			−.229 (.13)			−.328* (.13)
Relative Capabilities	.096*** (.02)	.099*** (.02)	.095*** (.02)	.136*** (.02)	.043* (.02)	.041* (.02)
Joint Democracy	−1.23*** (.16)	−1.13*** (.15)	−1.13*** (.15)	−1.07*** (.16)	−1.41*** (.17)	−1.42*** (.00)
Activity Level	.048*** (.00)	.042*** (.00)	.043*** (.00)	.046*** (.00)	.037*** (.01)	.038*** (.00)
Contiguity	1.31*** (.09)	.994*** (.08)	.987*** (.08)	1.11*** (.09)	1.12*** (.08)	1.10*** (.08)
Alliance	−.026 (.12)	.082 (.10)	.071 (.10)	.100 (.11)	−.021 (.12)	−.031 (.12)
Peace Years		−.105*** (.01)	−.105*** (.01)	−.105*** (.01)	−.128*** (.01)	−.128*** (.00)
Peace Years x2		.001*** (.00)	.001*** (.00)	.001*** (.00)	.002*** (.00)	.001*** (.00)
Peace Years x3		−.000*** (.00)	−.000*** (.00)	−.000*** (.00)	−.000*** (.00)	−.000*** (.00)
	N = 142,528	142,538	142,528	137,440	142,528	142,528

*p < .05, **p <. 01, ***p < .001

and the likelihood that the state uses force within the following ten or twenty-year period. Models 1–3 show that defeat in the last ten and twenty-year period is significantly associated with an increase conflict initiation while victory and stalemate in those periods are not significantly correlated with any changes in subsequent conflict behavior. For purposes of robustness, Model 4 analyzes the same models, excluding the war years of 1915 to 1918 and 1940 to 1945. This was done to ensure that possible awkward codings of war outcomes following the world wars were not driving results. The results of this model show that defeat in the last ten years remains positively associated with conflict initiation while victory and stalemate are not associated with significant changes in conflict initiation. The variables measuring relative capabilities, joint democracy, contiguity and the past conflict behavior of the state in these models relate to conflict initiation as we would expect. States are more likely to target weaker, contiguous states. Conflict in the recent past leads us to expect a state to engage in more conflict in the future. Democratic states are significantly less likely to engage in conflict.

Models 5 and 6 show that changes in post-defeat behavior are not limited to mere threats to use of force, but in fact extend to the actual use of force. No significant relationship is found between recent victory or stalemate and the subsequence likelihood that states use force within a dispute.

Finally, for purposes of robustness, additional models were run which excluded each one of the major powers. The results were robust to these state-specific omissions.

Within-Country Analysis:

> To ensure that differences in states' underlying propensity for conflict are not ultimately driving the initial results reported above, a second statistical approach was employed that compares the average likelihood of conflict initiation by states in the periods before and after defeat.[2] The key variables of defeat and initiation were coded as defined above. Table 1 shows the change in probability of initiation in the ten and twenty-year periods following defeat when compared to the same period prior to defeat. The table illustrates changes in three types of conflict initiation over the period 1816 to 2010 for all states and for great powers only. The coding of the first variable *All Initiation* captures the effect of defeat on all types of initiation, including disputes initiated against a state responsible for one's recent defeat. States often experience numerous disputes with the same opponent in the years leading up to war.

To avoid over counting, I did not include these instances of initiation in the years leading up to the war or during war. To ensure that the sometimes-awkward coding of wartime dispute initiation was not driving the results, the same analysis was conducted omitting the periods of world war, 1914–1918 and 1939–1945. Finally, the third variable, *Third-Party Initiation*, compares instances of dispute initiation against states that were in no way responsible for the state's defeat. This analysis, therefore, assesses the relative probability of initiation against third-party states only.

TABLE 3. Changes in Conflict Initiation in Period after Defeat

		ALL STATES	GREAT POWERS
OVER 10 YEARS	All Initiation	+ 28% (p = .03)	+ 28% (p = .06)
	Excluding World Wars	+ 17% (p = .013)	—
	Third-Party Initiation	—	+ 25% (p = .09)
OVER 20 YEARS	All Initiations	+ 24% (p = .02)	+ 46% (p = .002)
	Excluding World Wars	+ 17% (p = .07)	+ 26% (p = .07)
	Third-Party Initiation	—	+ 38% (p = .01)

As the table shows, the probability of conflict initiation amongst all states is 28% higher in the ten-year period following defeat than in the ten-year period prior to defeat and 24% higher in the twenty-year period following defeat when compared to the twenty years before defeat.[3] We can also see some key differences in the behavior of great powers. In the ten years after defeat, great powers are 25% more likely to initiate disputes with such targets. In the twenty-year period after defeat, they are 38% more likely to initiate disputes against third-party states. No such significant increase occurs, however, when looking at the total population of states.

Section 3: What Kinds of States Do Defeated States Target?

The results depicted in Figure 3 in Chapter 4 were derived from the same models of defeat as in Table 1 above, but with the inclusion of the dichotomous variable, *Same Opponent*, to assess whether defeated states are more likely to target some states over others. This variable is coded 1 if the state has been defeated by the other state within the dyad within the last ten or twenty years and as 0 otherwise. All states that played a role in the state's defeat are included within the coding. Models in Table 4 in this appendix were used to generate the predicted probabilities within Figures 3 and 5 within Chapter 4.

Models 1 and 2 analyze the likelihood of conflict initiation by defeated states when including the additional variable accounting for the state's target. The results show that the majority of conflict initiation in the ten years following defeat comes at the expense of a recent victor. Within twenty years after defeat,

TABLE 4. Targets of Conflict Initiation and Use of Force

	DV DISPUTE INITIATION				DV USE OF FORCE			
VARIABLE	MODEL 1	MODEL 2	MODEL 3	MODEL 4	MODEL 5 MAJOR POWERS	MODEL 6 MINOR POWERS	MODEL 7 MAJOR POWERS	MODEL 8 MINOR STATES
Defeat, Last 10 Years	.123 (.10)		.147 (.11)		-.140 (.17)	.135 (.12)		
Same Opponent, Last 10 Years	.591*** (.19)		.529* (.23)		-.835 (.87)	.434 (.23)		
Defeat, Last 20 Years		.279** (.08)		.330*** (.08)			.478*** (.12)	.177 (.11)
Same Opponent, Last 20 Years		.612*** (.15)		.505** (.17)			.019 (.33)	.491** (.18)
Relative Capabilities	.105*** (.02)	.103*** (.02)	.039* (.02)	.033 (.02)	-1.30*** (.13)	.234*** (.03)	1.31 (.13)	.228*** (.03)
Joint Democracy	-1.13*** (.15)	-1.12*** (.15)	-1.40*** (.16)	-1.39*** (.16)	-1.68*** (.25)	-1.29*** (.20)	-1.69*** (.25)	-1.28*** (.20)
Activity Level	.042*** (.00)	.042*** (.00)	.036*** (.00)	.037*** (.00)	.046*** (.00)	.044*** (.00)	.046*** (.00)	.045*** (.00)
Contiguity	.974*** (.08)	.964*** (.08)	1.12*** (.08)	1.11*** (.08)	.741*** (.16)	.459*** (.11)	.705*** (.16)	.468*** (.11)
Alliance	.041 (.10)	.034 (.10)	-.011 (.12)	-.016 (.12)	.038 (.22)	-.064 (.14)	.052 (.22)	-.065 (.14)
Peace Years	-.104*** (.00)	-.105*** (.01)	-.126*** (.01)	-.127*** (.01)	-.101*** (.01)	-.137*** (.01)	-.101*** (.00)	.002*** (.00)
Peace Years x2	.001*** (.00)	.001*** (.00)	.001*** (.00)	.001*** (.00)	.001*** (.00)	.002*** (.00)	.001*** (.00)	.002*** (.00)
Peace Years x3	-.000*** (.00)	-.000*** (.00)	-.000*** (.00)	-.000*** (.00)	-.000*** (.00)	-.000*** (.00)	-.000*** (.00)	-.000** (.00)
	N = 142,538	N = 142,538	N = 142,538	N = 142,538	60,546	81,982	60,546	81,982

*p < .05, **p < .01, ***p < .001

the likelihood of conflict initiation against recent victors as well as third-party states is higher than the baseline probability of conflict initiation among non-defeated states. All other variables correlate with dispute initiation as we would expect within these models. Models 3 through 8 examine the likelihood that states use force in subsequent disputes following defeat by all states as well as by subgroups of major and minor powers. Models 3 and 4 shows that the pattern witnessed in Models 1 and 2 extends not only to dispute initiation but to the actual use of force against both victor and third-party states.

Models 5 through 8 conduct the same analysis but on truncated datasets including only great powers or non-great powers. The models illustrate that different patterns exist for states of different status. While Model 5 shows that the likelihood of the use of force is no higher among defeated great powers in the ten years after defeat than among non-defeated great powers, Model 7 shows that the likelihood of targeting third-party states is indeed higher than the great power baseline probability of the use of force. The same is not true of the likelihood of using force against one's recent opponent and victor. Models 6 and 8 show that this pattern is reversed for states with minor power status, which are more likely to use force against their recent opponent in the twenty years following defeat. The likelihood of using force against third-party states is no higher than the baseline likelihood among non-defeated minor powers.

These results are robust to ordered logit analysis assessing the relationship between past defeat, target type and an ordinal dependent variable measuring the level of hostility reached by a state within disputes. This data is taken directly from the variable measuring hostility levels in the MID 4.2 dataset.

Section 4: How Does Material Recovery Affect Initiation?

Not all states are prepared militarily or politically to reengage on the world stage immediately following defeat. Some states lose significant capabilities because of and in the years following defeat. To assess the effect material recovery, the variables *Recovery After Defeat, 10 Years* and *Recovery After Defeat, 20 Years* were created, as described in Chapter 4, and included as the primary independent variable in the core models from Table 1 above. Table 3 illustrates the effects of recovery in the ten and twenty-year periods following defeat. The table shows that the likelihood that states engage in post defeat aggression against the state responsible for their defeat increases significantly as the recovery variable increases. Models 1 through 4 examine the effect of the level of material recovery on the likelihood that states initiate conflict in the ten and twenty years following defeat. Models 1 and 2 use the primary recovery variable described in the manuscript. For purposes of robustness, Models 3 and 4 examine an alternate coding in which a state's level of recovery is compared with its material capabilities in the year before its defeat rather than compared with three years prior to the defeat. Finally, Model 7 examines the relationship between recovery and the likelihood a state uses force.

These models all find a positive relationship between level of recovery over twenty years after defeat and the likelihood of initiation and the use of force, meaning that as the state recovers relative to its past capabilities, it is more likely to act in aggressive ways. This finding undermines an alternative hypothesis which would predict that defeated states engage in aggression to make up for any material losses they experienced as a result of defeat. These findings also extend to both sub-groups of major and minor powers.

The dichotomous variables *Recovered* and *Recovered20* were also created and were coded 1 if the state's capabilities were restored and 0 otherwise. As stated in Chapter 4, defeated great powers that have fully recovered or never lost resources are roughly 88% more likely to use force in the twenty years after defeat than defeated great powers that have not recovered the capabilities they possessed three years prior to the defeat. This predicted probability was calculated by incorporating these dichotomous variables into Model 2 in Table 2 above, but running the model only on defeated great powers.

Section 5: Are All Defeats Alike?

This section examines the effects of varying two different features of defeat: the degree to which defeat was unexpected and who initiated the conflict which a state lost. To assess the degree to which a defeat was unexpected, and therefore more likely to be humiliating, a variable was coded which measures the state's capabilities, as represented by its CINC score in the Correlates of War National Military Capabilities data set, relative to the total capabilities of all opponents the state confronted in the war. Including the capabilities of a state's allies fighting on its side within this relative measurement did not significantly affect the findings reported below. The variable *Unexpected Defeat* lists this measure of a state's capability relative to that of the victor if the state lost in war in the last ten years and otherwise is coded as zero. If a state has lost more than one war in the prior ten-year period, the most unexpected defeat, the one in which it possessed the most capabilities relative to its opponent, is included as the measure over the subsequent ten years. This variable was included in the primary models in lieu of the binary defeat variables.

To assess other plausible explanations for the relationship between the variable as coded and increased levels of subsequent conflict, the analysis also includes the variable *Capabilities*, which is a monadic measure of the state's capabilities. This variable is included to account for the possibility that states of higher capability would be more likely to initiate disputes.

Models 5, 6 and 8 in Table 3 present the coefficients describing the relationship between the degree of humiliation and both probability of initiation and the use of force once involved in a dispute. These three models were each run only on states that had been defeated within the last ten years. To account for the alternative possibility that states defeated by weaker powers would be less likely to lose material capabilities and would be more likely to initiate conflict, Models 6 and 8 were run only on those states that had been defeated and had recovered all capabilities.

The relationship in each model is strongly significant and positive. As a state's ratio of dyadic capabilities with its victor increases, so does the likelihood that the defeated state will initiate conflict and use force. This is true of both states that failed to recover their capabilities and those that never lost capabilities or that managed to recover them. The models show that these results hold even when controlling for states' level of capability and the recent activity of the state.

Chapter 1 also hypothesized that states which lose a war they themselves originated will be more humiliated than if they lose a war they did not start. This may be because in starting the war, a state signals that they expect to ultimately win the war. Loss in that war could therefore have even larger status implications. To assess the differential impact of losing a war one started, the variable *Defeat in Originated War, Last 10 Years.* was coded as 1 if the state had lost a war it had originated in the last ten years and 0 otherwise. This variable was included within the primary model assessing the effect of conflict outcomes. The results of this model are shown in Model 1 in Table 4.

The first model shows that defeat in a war one originated is associated with a significant increase in conflict initiation in the ten years that follow when compared with states that did not recently lose a war they started. The second model compares the effect of defeat in war generally with the effect of defeat in a war one originated. This model also includes the variable it Same Opponent to assess the target of subsequent initiation. Model 2 assesses the likelihood of initiation following defeat in war one originated compared with the effect of defeat in wars that a state did not originate. This is estimated by looking only at cases in which *Defeated in War, Last 10 Yrs.* is coded as 1. The results show that states are far more likely to initiate conflict after defeat one originated than in defeat one did not. Models 3 and 4 estimate this same model on subsets of the data that include only potential great power initiators or potential non-great power initiators. We see that, as in earlier models, great powers that lose a war they started are more likely to target third party states than they are to engage in revenge and then are other great powers that have recently been defeated in war they did not start.

TABLE 5. The Effects of Recovery and Unexpected Defeats

VARIABLE	DV DISPUTE INITIATION				DV USE OF FORCE			
	MODEL 1 T-3	MODEL 2 T-3	MODEL 3 T-1	MODEL 4 T-1	MODEL 5	MODEL 6 RECOVERED	MODEL 7	MODEL 8 RECOVERED
Recovery, Last 10 Years	.246*		.189				.263*	
	(.10)		(.10)				(.11)	
Recovery, Last 20 Years		.414***		.406***				
		(.09)		(.08)				
Unexpected Defeat, Last 10 Years					.756**	1.03**		1.20*
					(.29)	(.44)		(.47)
Relative Capabilities	.103***	.088***	.104***	.089***	-.348***	.334*	.038*	.272*
	(.02)	(.02)	(.02)	(.02)	(.06)	(.10)	(.13)	(.11)
Capabilities					5.76***	5.21***		-7.29*
					(1.48)	(2.17)		(2.99)
Joint Democracy	-1.13***	-1.14***	-1.13***	-1.12***	-.777	-.637	-1.41***	-2.03***
	(.00)	(.16)	(.15)	(.16)	(.43)	(.59)	(.17)	(.94)
Activity Level	.042***	-.027***	.041***	.042***	.088***	.075*	.036***	.015
	(.00)	(.00)	(.00)	(.00)	(.02)	(.03)	(.00)	(.03)
Contiguity	.986***	1.00***	.987***	.985***	2.58***	3.01***	1.13***	.451
	(.08)	(.08)	(.08)	(.08)	(.20)	(.31)	(.08)	(.30)
Alliance	.036	.014	.037	.025	.373	.529	-.017	-.719
	(.10)	(.10)	(.10)	(.10)	(.26)	(.34)	(.12)	(.33)
Peace Years	-.105***	-.107***	-.105***	-.105***	-.160***	-.157***	-.128***	-.174***
	(.01)	(.01)	(.00)	(.00)	(.02)	(.03)	(.01)	(.04)
Peace Years x2	.001***	.001***	.001***	.001***	.003***	.003***	.002***	.004***
	(.00)	(.00)	(.00)	(.00)	(.00)	(.00)	(.00)	(.00)
Peace Years x3	-.000***	-.000***	-.000***	-.000***	-.000***	-.000***	-.000***	-.000**
	(.00)	(.00)	(.00)	(.00)	(.00)	(.00)	(.00)	(.00)

*p < .05, **p < .01, ***p < .001   N = 142,528 for all models

TABLE 6. Model of Conflict Initiation, Originated War

VARIABLES	MODEL 1	MODEL 2	MAJOR POWERS	NON-MAJOR POWERS
Defeated in Originated War, Last 10 Years	.416** (.14)	.530* (.24)	.592* (.29)	.001 (.5)
Victory in Last 10 Years	−.096 (.09)			
Stalemate in Last 10 Years	.066 (.16)			
Same opponent, Last 10 Years		1.99*** (.52)	.088 (.67)	1.98*** (.39)
Relative Capabilities	.153 (.14)	.630 (.49)	−2.18** (.41)	3.30*** (.66)
Alliance	.432*** (.11)	.729** (.25)	.712* (.32)	−.200 (.43)
Joint Democracy	−.616*** (.11)	−1.15*** (.28)	−1.24** (.41)	−.706* (.35)
Activity Level in L10Y	.027*** (.01)	.032*** (.01)	.051*** (.00)	.096*** (.02)
	N = 158,169	10,462	6,377	4,085

*p < .05, **p < .01, ***p < .001

Conversely, non-great powers that lose wars they start are more likely to engage in revenge than to target third party states and than are non-great powers that lose in wars they did not start.

Section 6: What is the Effect on Diplomatic and Political Hostility?

Events in the COPDAB dataset are coded based on a 15-point international scale ranging from highly cooperative actions (voluntary unification) to highly conflictual actions (extensive war). In between are numerous lower level actions which are unlikely to be included within the Correlates of War dataset and which provide a broader measure of a state's general level of activity and assertiveness within the international system.

The analysis relies on two primary dependent variables. *Diplomatic Hostility* is coded 1 if a state has engaged in actions of diplomatic or economic hostility which include imposing boycotts, imposing economic sanctions, hindering movement on land, waterways, or in the air, embargoing goods, refusing mutual trade rights, closing borders and blocking free communication, manipulating trade or currency to cause economic problems, halting aid, granting sanctuary to opposition leaders, mobilizing hostile demonstrations against target country, refusing to support foreign military allies and refusing visas to other nationals or restricting movement in country. *Political Hostility* is coded 1 if a state engages in acts such as inciting riots or rebellions (training or financial aid for rebellions) in other countries, encouraging guerilla activities against target country, limited and sporadic terrorist actions, kidnapping or torturing foreign citizens or prisoners of war;, giving sanctuary to terrorists, breaking diplomatic relations, attacking diplomats or embassies, expelling military advisors, and nationalizing companies without compensation.

Table 7 illustrates the relationship between these two dependent variables and past conflict outcomes, including defeat, victory and stalemate. These models were estimated on all data that was not coded as a dispute within the MID dataset to ensure that the analysis was explaining a separate set of less aggressive disputes. The first two columns assesses the likelihood of that a state engages in diplomatic hostility. The first column shows that states that have been defeated in the last ten years are significantly more likely to engage in such acts while states that have experienced victory in the last ten years are no more likely to do so than states

TABLE 7. Models of Diplomatic and Political History

	DIPLOMATIC HOSTILITY		POLITICAL HOSTILITY	
VARIABLES	MODEL 1	MODEL 2	MODEL 3	MODEL 4
Defeated in Last 10 Years	.380*** (.10)		.396**	
Same Opponent	.729 (.39)	.864* (.34)	.821 (.43)	.991** (.38)
Unexpected Defeat		.672*** (.13)		.612** (.18)
Victory in Last 10 Years	.025 (.08)	.045 (.08)	.284* (.14)	.297* (.13)
Stalemate in Last 10 Years	.223* (.09)	.226* (.09)	−.262 (.15)	−.267 (.15)
Relative Capabilities	.861*** (.12)	−.834*** (.13)	−1.23*** (.19)	−1.22*** (.19)
Alliance	−.057** (.08)	−.065 (.08)	−.000 (.12)	−.003 (.12)
Joint Democracy	.165*** (.07)	.146* (.08)	−.392*** (.11)	−.404*** (.11)
Activity Level in L10Y	.023*** (.00)	.020*** (.01)	.016* (.00)	.014* (.01)
	N = 22,512	22,512	22,512	22,512

*p < .05, **p < .01, ***p < .001

that have not experienced victory. Those that have experienced stalemate in the last ten years are more likely to engage in such acts, though to a lesser degree than those who have been defeated. The predicted probability of diplomatic hostility following defeat is 38% higher (p = .001) than it is for non-defeated states while the increase is 17% (p = .055). for those states experiencing recent stalemate. The second column show the correlation between degree of unexpected defeat and diplomatic hostility. We see that the more unexpected the defeat, the more likely states are to engage in diplomatic hostility. Models 3 and 4 use *Political Hostility* as the dependent variable. We see that very similar relationships exist between past defeat and political hostility—the likelihood of the latter increases amongst those that have recently been defeated and is higher amongst those states that lost to weaker opponents. Unlike in Models 1 and 2, however, recent stalemate is not associated with any increase in political hostility while recent victory is. Again, however, the impact of victory is lower than the impact of recent defeat. The predicted probability of political hostility is 43% higher amongst those experiencing recent defeat and 30% higher amongst those experiencing recent victory.

Alternative Hypotheses: Defeated States are Motivated by Security Concerns

What are the characteristics of the most likely targets of defeated states? Summary statistics indicate the following: defeated states are not likely to be any weaker than the average state in the system. Rather, defeated states on average possess 9% higher capabilities than do non-defeated states. Nevertheless, defeated states select targets of aggression which are substantially weaker than do states initiating conflict which have not recently been defeated. Non-defeated states initiate disputes within dyads in which they hold on average 55% of the dyadic capabilities. States which have been defeated, however, initiate disputes within dyads in which they hold on average 62% of the dyadic capabilities. These values can be confidently distinguished with a two-tailed t-test at the $p < .05$ level. This suggests that defeated states are systematically selecting far weaker targets than are non-defeated states.

Part II. The Effects of Territorial Loss

Territorial Change Data

The original Goertz and Diehl dataset or territorial change described in Tir, et al. (1998) contained 826 cases of territorial change for the period through 1996 and coded instances of change as resulting from one of six types of mechanisms: conquest, annexation, cession, secession, mandated territories, or unification. This dataset included only instances of territorial change in which the acquired territory was actually occupied. It therefore omitted numerous cases of imperial expansion in which states planted flags but did not send occupiers. For my purposes, it was not important to distinguish between occupied territory and non-occupied territory since the simple act of claiming the land may provide the best means to heightened status. I therefore added 65 cases of territorial change in which a state claimed but did not occupy territory, the majority of which took place in Africa. The recoded dataset therefore contained 891 total cases of territorial change.

I recoded each of these 891 cases according to nine procedural mechanisms: conquest, annexation, mutual exchange, voluntary secession, unification, wars of independence, arbitration, mandated territories, and decolonization. More information on these categories can be found at joslynbarnhart.com. The largest benefit of this recoding is that it enabled clear distinction between territorial change achieved through compensation or mutual-agreement and cession of territory that took place through conquest or annexation. Within the original dataset, all instances in which a piece of, rather than the whole, territory is passed from one state to another is coded as "cession" of territory. It was important for my purposes to distinguish between exchanges in which coercion played a role and those where it didn't.[4] A list of sample cases is provided in Figure 4.9.

Of the territorial losses by state actors, 382 occurred through either conquest, annexation or which resulted from wars of independence and 224 occurred through voluntary secession or mutual-agreement. Cases of territorial change occurring through unification, decolonization, arbitration and international mandate were dropped for the sake of analysis. Cases of unification were not included in the analysis because such cases can be considered instances of state death for the states incorporated into the larger state. Acts of unification were voluntary. Cases of decolonization in the 1960s and 70s were coded separately from successful secession achieved through wars of independence. Many can therefore be considered voluntary acts of territorial cession. The decolonizing states however experienced a great deal of international pressure to decolonize at this time—these states may have been humiliated by this fact, as was France in its act of giving up its colonies. Arbitration and mandate may also humiliate a state, but it is unreasonable to make systematic assumptions about their effect on the powers involved.

It is important to note that both the original and the updated territorial change dataset omit instances of wartime conquest in which the territory does not remain in changed hands following the end of conflict. If war-time conquest is formalized in a post-war treaty, the case is coded as conquest. The original dataset includes some instances of territorial loss that occurred just prior to the eruption of world wars, the response to which would be difficult to capture since it likely occurred during wartime and would not be included in the dataset. To account for these irregularities, all losses which occurred during the periods 1914–1919 and 1939–1945 were dropped. All cases of territorial change which resulted in state death were also dropped due to the inability of the deceased state to respond with gains of its own.

The territorial change data also included 263 instances of territorial loss by entities that were not listed as states in the State System Membership data at the time of the territorial change. Given the intent of this project to assess the impact territorial loss has on the future behavior of states, these instances of territorial change at the expense of non-state actors were not included as cases of loss but only cases of gains by the acquiring state actors.[5] The majority of these cases of loss by non-state actors occurred during the process of colonizing Africa. Inclusion of losses by these non-state actors would skew results of statistical analysis since the vast majority of these entities lacked state resources and the ability to respond to loss with subsequent gains of their own. Of these 245 remaining cases of loss, 105 occurred through involuntary means and 140 through voluntary means.

Additionally, territorial gains made during the first year of a state's life and any year that the state is reborn after a period of state death were not included in the dataset, leaving 574 remaining cases of territorial gain in the dataset. These cases were omitted because they did not allow for the testing of the hypotheses that gains are made at higher rates following losses. The vast majority of these gains are also associated with the process of unification.

Finally, the dyadic form of the data was used to control for revenge gains within the same dyad and because it enables testing the relevance of relative capability within the dyad to territorial acquisitions. Politically-relevant dyads were used because we were interested in dyads in which expansion was plausible. It appears implausible, for instance, that the Bahamas would choose to expand in Iraq.

Section 1: Are States that Lose Territory More Likely to Pursue Conquest?

The predicted probabilities in Figure 9 were derived from Model 3 in Table 8. The model includes both the three primary independent variables of interest—coerced territorial loss in the last twenty years, voluntary territorial loss in the last twenty years, and a variable accounting for revanchist attempts to regain lost territory. The model also includes variables accounting for a state's share of dyadic capabilities, the variable *Relative Capability After Loss* which, as described above, measures the capabilities of the state relative to its capabilities prior to the territorial loss. The model also includes numerous variables to account for the recent activity of the state, including *Coercive Attempted Gain in Prior 10 Yrs.* and

Coercive Attempted Gain in Prior 11–20 Yrs. which are count variables of a state's own attempted gains during those periods, and *Total Gains in My Region in Prior 10 Yrs* and *Total Gains in My Region in Prior 11–20 Yrs*, which account for the state's gains within its own region.

The model also includes *Total Systemic Gains in Prior 5 Yrs*, a count variable measuring the total number of recent territorial changes within the international system. Finally, the model includes the *Joint Democracy* variable coded 1 if both states are democracies and 0 otherwise as well as the variable *Border* which accounts for whether the targeted territory involves a border shared between the two countries. The coefficients for various models including these variables are presented as Models 1–3 in Table 8. These results show both the significant correlation between past coerced loss and future aggression against third-party states as well as a lack of significant correlation between future conquest and voluntary loss. We also see in these models that the rate of aggression against the state responsible for one's recent territorial loss is higher than the likelihood that any other state in the system would be targeted. Importantly, these results are robust even when accounting for recent activity in the system by the state and others.

TABLE 8. A Sample List of Involuntary Territorial Losses

COUNTRY	TERRITORY LOST	LOST TO	IN YEAR	ENTITY GAINED	IN YEAR
Austria-Hungary	Lombardy	Italy	1859	Denmark	1864
China	Kazakhstan	Russia	1871	Vietnam	1881
France	Alsace-Lorraine	Germany	1871	Cochinchina	1874
				Tunisia	1881
India	Kashmir	Pakistan	1949	China	1950
Italy	Ethiopia	Ethiopia	1896	China	1901
				Turkey	1905
Italy	Somalia	Somalia	1905	Albania	1914
Netherlands	Indonesia	Britain	1819	Papua New Guinea	1828
Russia	Danubian Princ.	Austria-Hungary	1854	Caucasus	1858, 1859
				Japan	1861
Russia	Vilna	Poland	1921	Japan	1925
				Afghanistan	1926
Spain	Suba, Philippines	United States	1898	Morocco	1907, 1908
Turkey	Merv	Turkey	1884	Greece	1897
Turkey	Libya, Dodecanese Ils	Italy	1912	Iran	1916
Britain	Equatorial Guinea	Spain	1843	South Africa	1847
Britain	Oregon	United States	1843	Brunei	1847
				Myanmar	1852
Britain	Sudan	Sudan	1884	Botswana	1885

TABLE 9. Influence of Coercive Loss on Attempted Territorial Gains

				FIXED EFFECTS MODELS		
VARIABLES	MODEL 1	MODEL 2	MODEL 3	MODEL 4	MODEL 5	MODEL 6
Coerced Territorial Loss in Prior 20 Yrs	.925*** (.20)	.870*** (.21)	.489* (.21)	.468** (.17)	.546** (.18)	.478* (.19)
Voluntary Territorial Loss in Prior 20 Yrs	.097 (.22)	.078 (.23)	−.185 (.24)	−.195 (.17)	−.199 (.17)	−.177 (.17)
Revanchist Gain?		.851** (.31)	.844* (.33)		−.226 (.34)	−.187 (.35)
Relative Capability After Loss	3.35*** (.86)	4.25*** (.85)	3.79** (1.19)	3.86*** (.96)	4.99*** (1.28)	4.24** (1.44)
Dyadic Relative Capability	1.31*** (.26)	1.37*** (.27)	.759** (.26)	1.79** (.75)	1.84* (.76)	1.38 (.77)
Total Gains in My Region in Prior 10 Yrs	.038*** (.01)	.038** (.00)	.029*** (.00)	.034*** (.00)	.034*** (.00)	.023*** (.00)
Total Gains in My Region in Prior 11–20 Yrs	−.006 (.05)	.007 (.05)	−.054 (.06)	.015** (.00)	.015** (.00)	.012* (.00)
Totally Systemic Gains in Prior 5 Yrs	.052 (.09)	.042 (.09)	.005 (.09)	.002 (.01)	.002 (.01)	−.000 (.00)
Coercive Attempted Gain in Prior 10 Yrs			1.09*** (.15)			.921*** (.14)
Coercive Attempted Gain in Prior 11–20 Yrs			.572* (.22)			.199 (.15)
Joint Democracy			−1.65*** (.37)			−1.87*** (.44)
Backed Down in Last MID			−.091 (.22)			.155 (.25)
Border			4.75*** (.49)			3.82*** (.45)

*** = Coefficients significant at the .000 level. N = 174,874
Robust standard errors, clustered by dyad, in parentheses.

Models 1–3 were also run using fixed effects for each directed dyad. This approach analyzes the effect of coerced loss only within those dyads that have experienced a coerced loss. The results of these tests are presented in Models 4–6. The variable coerced loss in the past twenty years is significantly correlated with attempted gains in each of the three models. This includes those controlling for revanchist motivations and for one's own past activity. Again, voluntary loss does not significantly correlate with future aggression. Further analysis illustrates that the odds of attempting a gain if you have experienced a coerced loss are roughly 1.54 times those if you have not. Additionally, the odds of targeting the state responsible for one's original humiliating loss are not significantly higher than the baseline odds of territorial aggression amongst non-humiliated states.

As with defeat above, a one-sample t-test was also performed to assess whether the probability of attempted gains was higher in the twenty years following a coerced loss than it was in the twenty years leading up to the coerced loss. To isolate the effect of coerced loss, cases of coerced loss were dropped if they occurred within the twenty-year period following a prior loss. Cases were also dropped if either the twenty-year period before or after the loss corresponded with either major world war. This was done to ensure an equivalent number of country year observations before and after losses. The data was reduced to 35 separate country-year observations. Analysis showed that while the probability of gains was 18.9% higher in the period following a loss, this probability could not confidently be distinguished from rates of gains before the loss ($p = .16$). The same test was then performed on great powers using ten observations with non-overlapping time periods. The two-sample t-test of great power observations indicates that the rate of attempted gains is 48% higher in the period following a loss than in the period before the loss. This difference can be distinguished at .05 level ($p = .01$). Cases of revenge were then removed from the data, leaving 7 observations. The rate of attempted gains against third parties was 43% higher in the period following a coerced loss ($p = .02$).

Alternative Hypotheses: Heightened Activity Explains Territorial Aggression

To be confident in the significance of the relationship between past losses and future gains, we must eliminate the possibility that the relationship is merely an artifact of heightened levels of territorial change in the system or one's region. Within the primary models in the manuscript, five control variables were included in Model 3 above which accounted for levels of activity prior to an attempted gain. The relationship between past losses and future gains holds even when controlling for this past activity in the system.

The robustness of results was also assessed by excluding cases based on prior levels of activity. Model 3 above was run excluding all cases in which states had engaged in territorial aggression within the ten years prior to an attempted gain. Though not presented here, analysis shows that coerced loss significantly correlates with attempted gains even within these truncated datasets which exclude states with past activity.

Finally, several placebo tests were run which aimed at ensuring that coerced loss in the present does not predict territorial gains in the past, as we would expect it to if periods of heightened activity were explaining the results. These tests assessed the relationship between coerced or voluntary loss in the present with three different sets of dependent variables lagged over various time periods in the past. The lagged dependent variables were chosen because we would expect the associations of these outcomes with coerced loss in the present to be zero. In all models that were analyzed, the explanatory and control variables were the same as those used within Model 3 within the manuscript with one exception. The models exclude the variable measuring a state's capabilities after a territorial loss because we have no reason to believe that recovery in the present would predict past activity. Inclusion of this variable does not, however, significantly alter the results.

Results of this analysis illustrate the following patterns. Coerced loss in the present does not predict one's gains over any period assessed within the last twenty years. In two cases, that of gains over the last fifteen years and gains sixteen to twenty years ago, coerced loss actually predicts significant declines in past activity. These results stand in contrast to those predicting future activity. Coerced loss in the present is positively and significantly correlated with gains over all measured time periods in the future, including gains over the next 5 years.

The cumulative results of these robustness tests provide sufficient evidence that the relationship between coerced loss and future territorial aggression cannot be fully explained by systemic activity. Those states which have not recently engaged in territorial aggression either in the last ten years or in the ten years prior to losing territory engage in significantly higher levels of territorial aggression after coerced loss.

Notes

INTRODUCTION

1. Hitler 1939, 463, 513.
2. Shirer 1991, 742.
3. Quoted in Kennedy 1953, 71.
4. Quoted in Moisi, 68.
5. Comment made to Andrew Kuchin's during a meeting with Medvedev at the Valdai Conference in September 2008. Cited in Georgie Anne Geyer, "Russia Is First to Test New President," *Chicago Tribune,* November 14, 2008.
6. Transcript available on the Kremlin's website at http://en.kremlin.ru/events/president/news/46860.
7. Statman 2000; Hartling and Luchetta 1999, 264.
8. Levy 1983.
9. Otten and Jonas 2014; Coleman, Goldman, and Kugler 2009.
10. Galtung 1964; Volgy and Mayhall 1995; Renshon 2015.
11. Callahan 2004, 203.
12. Larson and Shevchenko (2010) is an exception. They examine three reactions to status threat: creativity, imitation, and competition.
13. Clare and Danilovic 2010; Weisiger and Yarhi-Milo 2015.
14. Mercer 2014.
15. Small, Lerner, and Fischhoff 2006.
16. Aday 2010.
17. As Mercer (2014, 518) notes, "Social emotion is not an abstraction. It is easy to produce, to manipulate, and to measure in the lab."
18. Larson and Shevchenko 2014.
19. Renshon 2015; Wallace 1971.

1. NATIONAL FAILURE AND INTERNATIONAL DISREGARD

1. Combs et al. 2010; Hartling and Luchetta 1999.
2. Fernández, Saguy, and Halperin 2015; Torres and Bergner 2012.
3. Coleman, Kugler, and Goldman 2007; Lacey 2011.
4. Scheepers and Ellemers 2005; Gruenewald, Kemeny, and Aziz 2006; Siegrist 1984; Kemeny 2009.
5. A common proposition is that humiliation results only from intentional acts. See Lindner 2002, xiv; Wolf 2011.
6. Dafoe, Renshon, and Huth 2014 Clunan 2009; Larson and Shevchenko 2010, 2014; Lebow 2008; Markey 1999; Nayar and Paul 2003; Paul, Larson, and Wohlforth 2014; Renshon 2015; Volgy et al. 2011; Wohlforth 2009; Zarakol 2011.
7. O'Neill (2006) argues that humiliation differs from honor and reputation because it resides in beliefs about others' beliefs.
8. Dafoe et al. 2014.
9. Leask 2013.

10. Volgy et al. 2011. A state may hold status as a member of a group, for example, the club of great powers, or within relevant status hierarchies, be they international or community specific. Renshon 2016.

11. Wohlforth 2014, 136.

12. Both sets of expectations are normative constructs that are subject to change. The nature of changing symbols of status will be discussed in Chapter 2.

13. Van Evera 1994, 32.

14. Both sets of expectations are normative constructs that are subject to change. The nature of changing symbols of status will be discussed in Chapter 2.

15. Katzenstein 1996; Ringmar 1996. On role theory, see Harnisch, Frank, and Maull 2011; Thies and Breuning 2012.

16. In 1939, for instance, Stalin expressed humiliation on behalf of the Soviet people when France and Britain sent low-ranking diplomats to the Soviet Union to negotiate. Ringmar (2002, 126–127) argues that the Soviet alliance with Germany might not have come to pass if Stalin's desire for great power recognition had not been denied by the Allied powers. Stalin perceived an additional slight in the fact that the British and French arrived by boat rather than a plane and as a result were significantly delayed.

17. These privileges are largely based on the current and historical behavior of states of a given status.

18. Honneth 1996. For more on the relationship between recognition and status, see Lindemann and Ringmar 2015 and Daase et al. 2015.

19. Wolf 2011, 106; Fikenscher, Jaschob, and Wolf 2015.

20. Clunan 2009, 28. On how identities form at the national level, see, for example, Hopf 1998, 2002; Neumann 2016.

21. Wendt (1994) and Mitzen (2006) argue that identity formation is dependent on recognition by other states. I agree with Wolf (2011) that states can form assessments of their own identity without recognition by others.

22. Clunan 2009; Zarakol 2011; Freedman 2015; Albert 1977; Zell and Alicke 2009.

23. Clunan 2009, ch.2 2.

24. Clunan 2009, 24–27.

25. Clunan (2009, 28) offers an in-depth discussion of how national images become institutionalized as a collective national identity. See also Clunan 2009, 47–52 and 82–86.

26. This estimate was calculated using the Correlates of War Dataset on National Military Capabilities.

27. Al-Ansari quoted in Fattah and Fierke 2009, 77. Moisi 2009.

28. Khashan 1997. Roughly 1,000,000 Arabs in occupied territories were placed under Israeli control.

29. Oren 2003, 3–6.

30. John McNaughton to Robert McNamara. March 1965. *The Pentagon Papers*, Gravel Edition, Volume 3.

31. Simons 1997.

32. Simons 1997, 25.

33. Half a decade later, Reagan entered office with the recognition of the lingering effects of the loss in Vietnam on U.S. collective consciousness and foreign policy. More than a decade after that, presidential candidate Bill Clinton also acknowledged the psychological syndrome induced by Vietnam was still in effect.

34. Trotter 2000, 21.

35. Trotter 2000 13, 20; Edwards 2008.

36. This analysis includes all history journals accessed through JSTOR.

37. These groups were formed using the Correlates of War data on National Military Capabilities. The cases used for this analysis are presented in Table 1 in the Appendix.

38. It is possible that leader statements do not provide a completely accurate measure of national humiliation, though leaders have little reason to suggest the state has experienced humiliation when it has not.

39. I rely on the Correlates of War coding of initiation in a war for this analysis.

40. $p < .01$.

41. $p = .11$.

42. Gary Sick, a member of the National Security Council at the time noted the persistent image of U.S. weakness and a policy of caution that produced failure and "repeated humiliation." See Sick 1985.

43. Brzezinski 1985.

44. Boutros-Ghali 1999.

45. Girard 2004; Fraser and Murray 2002. As David Halberstam (2001) notes, "rarely had the United States looked so impotent, its mighty military driven away from a banana republic by a pip-squeak dictator and hired mob."

46. Bowles notes on NSC Meeting, April 22, 1961, *Foreign Relations of the United States, X, Cuba, 1961–1962*, 313–314.

47. Ferguson 2015, 502.

48. As will be discussed, post-war treatment can humiliate even when defeat does not.

49. Wolf (2011, 128) notes that a state may be disrespected if its physical integrity, social importance, ideas and values, achievements, or effort are ignored or disregarded by others.

50. Chwe 2013; O'Neill 2001; Saurette 2006.

51. The costs of denying others' their rights and privileges, as we will see, can be high, coming in the form of mistrust and potential long-standing rivalry.

52. President Woodrow Wilson presciently forewarned his European allies of the negative long-term implications of imposing a postwar settlement on the vanquished. Such a peace, he predicted, would "leave a sting, a resentment, a bitter memory upon which terms of peace would rest, not permanently, but only as upon quicksand." Link, et al. 1985.

53. Lloyd George argued at Versailles for a "just peace," warning, "You may strip Germany of her colonies, reduce her armaments to a mere police force . . . if she feels that she has been unjustly treated . . . she will find means of exacting retribution from her conquerors." George 1938, 1:405. President Woodrow Wilson called for peace between equals, warning that if peace were forced on the loser, it would be "accepted in humiliation . . . and would leave a sting, a resentment, a bitter memory on which terms of peace would rest . . . but only as upon quicksand." Link, et al. 1985.

54. Tuminez 2000, 10; Feuchtwanger 1993; Smith and Brown 1989.

55. Smith and Brown 1989, 514.

56. Tan 2009, 17–18.

57. Tan 2009, 18.

58. Wang 2008, 60.

59. Paine 2005, 268.

60. Hitler 1939, 194.

61. Quoted in Tuminez 2000, 67.

62. Tuminez 2000; Sumner 1933; Clark 1942.

63. Quoted in Goldstein and Maurer 1994, 154.

64. Luo 1993.

65. Mee 1980; Neiberg 2015.

66. Neiberg 2015.

67. Leidner, Sheikh, and Ginges 2012.

68. Bushman and Baumeister 1998.

69. Callahan 2004, 202.

70. Jonas, Otten, and Doosje 2014.
71. Fischer (1999) shows that Spaniards are far more likely to attach importance to honor and social recognition than the Dutch. Nisbett and Cohen (1996) demonstrate the importance of honor and reputation within the Southern United States. Fontan (2006) assesses the role of honor in Iraq and resulting humiliation of the 2003 invasion. See also Pitt-Rivers 1966; Mosquera, Manstead, and Fischer 2000; Dafoe and Caughey 2016.
72. This concept is referenced for the first time in China in the fourth century B.C. See Hu 1944; Chang and Holt 1994; Ting-Toomey et al. 1991.
73. Hwang 1987; Macleod 2008.
74. Chang and Holt 1994.
75. Miller 1995, 10–11.
76. Bushman and Baumeister (1998) and Bushman et al. (2009) find that those individuals with high esteem are more likely to engage in aggression following an insult.
77. See Marr and Thau 2014.
78. Owens, Sutton, and Turner 2001.

2. WITHDRAWAL, OPPOSITION, AND AGGRESSION

Porter 1980, 86. Chamberlain made the comment in the first epigraph after the Boers successfully fought off a British raid in 1895. For more on this case, see Mercer 2017.
1. Lowenheim and Heimann 2008; Harkavy n.d.; Scheff 1994. Callahan (2004) is an exception.
2. Goldman and Coleman 2000; Bushman et al. 2009; Walker and Knauer 2011; Coleman et al. 2009; Hartling and Luchetta 1999.
3. Lacey 2011; De Rivera 2013; Barash and Lipton 2011.
4. Van Zomeren et al. 2004; Pagano and Huo 2007; Tausch et al. 2011.
5. Stollberg, Fritsche, and Bäcker 2015; Fritsche et al. 2013.
6. Quoted in Tuminez 2000, 67.
7. The instrumental benefits of status-seeking acts are a topic of ongoing debate. Renshon (2017) argues that aggression can lead to significant increases in the status of the state. Mercer (2017) argues that the pursuit of status through aggression or any other means rarely leads to increased deference by other states who have little desire to voluntarily bestow higher prestige on others. If states are reluctant to accord others' status voluntarily, then status hierarchies must be formed through a more coercive process. It is possible, then, that aggressive status-seeking actions garner state higher status because they demonstrate the state's intention of maintaining high status as well as the costs that others will pay for denying them that status.
8. Gollwitzer, Meder, and Schmitt 2011.
9. Dafoe, Renshon, and Huth 2014.
10. Huberman et al. (2004) show that individuals pursue high status as an emotional end in itself, independent of any material benefits high status might provide.
11. According to Margalit (2002) and Coleman et al. (2009), this fact distinguishes humiliation from other powerful emotions like anger and sadness. It is possible to recall events that engendered these emotions without again experiencing the emotions themselves.
12. Klein 1991.
13. Ginges and Atran 2008.
14. Schivelbusch 2003.
15. This pattern is not rare. Zarakol (2011) describes how Japan, Turkey, and Russia each engaged in the dramatic overhaul of domestic institutions hoping to better assimilate to Western norms and practices following their experiences with a humiliating defeat.

16. Hall (2011, 533) argues that emotional displays are often attempts at "impression management" aimed at shaping others' impressions of how you will behave. Tiedens (2001) shows individuals confer higher status on those who publicly display anger following a slight than those who respond with sadness.

17. Ohbuchi, Kameda, and Agarie 1989; Lind 2011.

18. Gries and Peng 2002. Apologies minimize the perceived superiority of the humiliator and raise the status of the victim.

19. Pipes 2009.

20. Larson and Shevchenko 2010; Lo 2002, 89–90.

21. Sivanathan and Pettit (2010) show that status goods have a reparative effect on the ego.

22. Sagan 1996; Kinsella and Chima 2001; O'Neill 2006. On aircraft carriers, see Gilady 2006. On dreadnoughts, see Murray 2010; Art 1973; Fikenscher, Jaschob, and Wolf 2015.

23. Maintaining a colonial empire demonstrates exclusivity because it relies on the distinctive military and organizational capacities needed to project and maintain power abroad.

24. Gilady 2006.

25. See also Volkan 1998; Lindner 2006; Coleman, Goldman, and Kugler 2009; Fontan 2006; Fattah and Fierke 2009; Lacey 2011.

26. Zarakol 2011; Duque, n.d.

27. Williams and DeSteno (2009) found that those subjects who engaged in verbal and non-verbal expressions of pride were more likely to assume leadership roles in groups and generally demonstrate greater motivation on difficult tasks.

28. Hitler 1939.

29. The German acquisition of its first colonies in 1884 put Bismarck in a position, for instance, to host the Berlin Conference attended by higher status imperial states.

30. Hetherington and Nelson 2003; Lai and Reiter 2005.

31. Quoted in Simons 1997, 23.

32. Reagan 1990, 45; Grow 2008, 157.

33. Barash and Lipton (2011) note that redirected aggression has been witnessed within cichlid fish, baboons, macaque monkeys, humans, and many other species.

34. Pedersen et al. 2008; Marcus-Newhall et al. 2000.

35. Barash and Lipton 2011, 33–35.

36. The projection of power abroad can provide an opportunity to highlight the technological and military prowess of the country. As one Russian commentator said of Russia's demonstration of power in Syria, "Our planes are beautiful and splendid. Our strikes are more precise and efficient than [America's.]" Quoted in "A Strategy of Spectacle" 2016, 21.

37. Research has also shown that non-verbal expressions of pride can lead others to perceive an actor as high status and can override significant signals that an actor possesses low status. Tiedens et al. 2000; Shariff and Tracy 2009; Martens et al. Shariff 2012; Cheng et al. 2010.

38. All states do not share the same set of norms. Western powers may advocate against the use of force while other states may continue to perceive the projection of power abroad as impressive and admirable.

39. Maria Lipman, the editor of *Counterpoint*, a Russian journal, notes that this may be the case of Russia's status-seeking acts of aggression. While such acts may not gain the admiration of the West, they provide a sense of confidence within the state itself.

40. Gilligan 1996; Walker and Knauer 2011, 18.

41. Wolf 2011.

42. Hoffman 2002, 376–377.

43. Leask 2013.

44. Kydd 2005.

45. Wolf 2011, 123.
46. Wang 2014.
47. Schivelbusch 2003.
48. Clausewitz 1956, 85.
49. Hitler 1939.
50. Hitler 1939
51. The Palestinian subjects in Ginges and Atran's 2008 study typically confronted repeated and sustained acts of humiliation, arguably eroding all sense of efficacy and leading them to increased passivity in the face of continued threat.
52. Quoted in Tuminez 2000, 69.
53. Quoted in Trager 2012, 252.
54. Macdonald and Parent 2011.
55. O'Neill 2006.
56. Mearsheimer 2003.
57. Distinctions between predictions of the humiliation model and more traditional models are further addressed in this book's Conclusion.
58. Lindner 2006; Saurette (2006) examines, for instance, the treatment of Iraqi prisoners at Abu Ghraib as a source of humiliation that can shape international relations.
59. The definition of humiliation in Lowenheim and Heimann (2008) is an exception. It is more similar to that offered here in that it does not assume intentionality but rather focuses on humiliating events that expose a party as weak and inferior, with obvious implications for the state's perceived status in the eyes of others.
60. Klein 1991.
61. Galtung 1964; Midlarsky 1975; Wallace 1971; East 1972; Volgy and Mayhall 1995. Renshon (2015) argues that inconsistency can relate to one's position in one of many status communities. Volgy et al. (2011), by contrast, argues that overachievers, or those states whose capabilities outpace their status, will more aggressively assert their status.
62. Clunan 2009; Mummendey and Simon 1989.
63. The residual effect of past status expectations creates behavioral predictions distinct from those of power transition theory, which suggests that expectations of influence remain in line with relative capabilities. Gilpin 1988; Organski 1980; Lemke 1997; Tammen et al. 2000.
64. Wohlforth 2009, 38–40.
65. Tajfel and Turner 1979; Abrams and Hogg 1988; Tajfel 2010. On SIT in international relations, see Larson 2010; Mercer 1995; Paul 2014.
66. Lacey 2011.
67. Larson and Shevchenko 2014.
68. Larson and Shevchenko 2010. Ward (2017) similarly argues status concerns arise when rising states hit a "glass ceiling" in the amount of status they are attributed. The permanent denial of privileges is not necessary for disrespect to affect state behavior. Moreover, status concerns do not arise only within rising states.
69. Lindemann 2010 does predict when non-recognition of identity will lead to war but does not relate this potential outcome to other options.
70. Van der Ree 2010; Farcau 2000.

3. NATIONAL HUMILIATION AT THE INDIVIDUAL LEVEL

1. Stein 2013; Mercer 2014; Ross 2006; Petersen 2002; Crawford 2014; Sasley 2011; Wendt 2004; Hutchison and Bleiker 2014, all posit an important role for group-based emotions in international relations and foreign policy decision making.
2. As Jonathan Mercer puts it, "Social emotion is not an abstraction. It is easy to produce, to manipulate, and to measure in the lab." See Baumeister 1991; Luhtanen and

Crocker 1992; Smith, Seger, and Mackie 2007; Abrams and Hogg 1988; Doosje et al. 1998; Kessler et al. 2010; Ellemers, Kortekaas, and Ouwerkerk 1999.

3. Kessler and Hollbach 2005; Smith 2014.
4. Leidner, Sheikh, and Ginges 2012; Mackie, Smith, and Ray 2008; Smith 1993.
5. Smith, Seger, and Mackie 2007; Seger, Smith, and Mackie 2009.
6. Small, Lerner, and Fischhoff 2006.
7. De Waal and Waal 1997; Barkow 1989; Sapolsky 1992; Angier 1991.
8. Edwards and Kravitz (1997) show that similar patterns in serotonin levels among dominant actors exist within vervet monkeys as well as college fraternities.
9. Siegrist 1984; Kemeny 2009; Gruenewald et al. 2006.
10. Thayer 2000, 134.
11. Stable hierarchies generate behavioral expectations as well as opportunities for status enhancement. In deferring, the low status actors may benefit from more intimate access to those with valued skills and knowledge. Henrich and Gil-White 2001; Pettit, Yong, and Spataro 2010.
12. Blau 1964; Loch et al. 2001; Ridgeway 1991; Willer 2009.
13. Abramo, Lundgren, and Bogart 1978.
14. Branscombe and Wann 1994; Cadinu and Reggiori 2002.
15. Mummendey et al. 1999.
16. Spears, Doosje, and Ellemers 1997; Ellemers, Kortekaas, and Ouwerkerk 1999.
17. Bar-Tal, Halperin, and De Rivera 2007; Van Zomeren et al. 2004; Stürmer and Simon 2009. Mackie et al. (2000) show that the level of group-based anger has been shown to predict the desire to attack a designated out-group.
18. Ginges and Atran 2008; Torres and Bergner 2012.
19. Leidner, Sheikh, and Ginges 2012; Fernández, Saguy, and Halperin 2015.
20. Shame can occur in private, but humiliation results from a public and visible event. The greater the visibility, the deeper the humiliation.
21. Leask 2013.
22. Mummendey et al. 1999. Fernández, Saguy, and Halperin (2015) show that humiliated and angry parties support aggressive responses to a similar degree, but that those reporting greater humiliation are significantly less willing to engage in the aggressive acts.
23. Spears, Doosje, and Ellemers 1997; Van Zomeren, Leach, and Spears 2010; McCoy and Major 2003; Smith, Seger, and Mackie 2007. Events, in turn, affect levels of group identification. Shepherd, Spears, and Manstead (2013) show that high status groups report lower levels of group identification when they feel shame about the group's actions and See also Kessler and Hollbach 2005.
24. Branscombe and Wann 1994; Cadinu and Reggiori 2002.
25. Wohlforth 2009, 26. Leaders can also perceive events as undeservedly threatening their own status. See Saurette 2006.
26. Turner et al. 1984.
27. Scheff (1994, 118) notes that leaders who are able to "decrease the shame level of a group . . . no matter how briefly or at what cost, will be perceived as charismatic."
28. Tomz, Weeks, and Yarhi-Milo (forthcoming) write that public opinion and elite foreign policy decision are brought into alignment through mechanisms labeled "selection" and "responsiveness."
29. Lindner 2002; Tooby, Cosmides, and Price 2006; Lopez, McDermott, and Petersen 2011.
30. Stein 2015.
31. Hitler 1939, 513–514.
32. Van Zomeren et al. 2004; Leach, Iyer, and Pedersen 2006.
33. Hall similarly (2011) argues that the decision by leaders to publicly express their emotions is a product of deliberate decision making.

34. Stein 2011.
35. Renshon 2015a; Pettit, Yong, and Spataro 2010.
36. Mullen, Brown, and Smith (1992) compare the salience of artificial and real-life group manipulation.
37. Spears, Doosje, and Ellemers 1997.
38. Ginges and Atran 2008.
39. Branscombe and Wann 1994.
40. Of the existing group-level experiments, none assess the impact of status threat on general foreign policy attitudes. Ginges and Atran (2008) have come the closest by asking the degree to which Palestinians supported acts of inter-group compromise.
41. Scheepers and Ellemers 2005.
42. Branscombe and Wann 1994.
43. http://www.gallup.com/poll/160046/americans-downbeat-state-prospects-future.aspx.
44. Leidner, Sheikh, and Ginges (2012) have hypothesized the general form of this relationship; however, its validity has yet to be confirmed.
45. Subjects were limited to those who had taken at least fifty Human Intelligence Tasks with a 95 percent acceptance rate.
46. In the MTurk study, subjects were then asked to provide their MTurk identification number to ensure that the survey was not taken multiple times by the same individuals.
47. Available at joslynbarnhart.com.
48. Variation within individual responses demonstrates that differences reported between the control and treatment groups are driven by national humiliation, anger, and shame and not simply by treatment groups being primed to consider world affairs. Below, we will see that respondents reporting higher levels of shame after reading the treatment, for instance, were no more likely to support aggression than respondents within the control group. Respondents exposed to U.S. failure and who perceived the United States to be ineffective were less likely to support aggressive behaviors than are those in the control group, a finding that could not be explained by the simple priming of foreign policy.
49. Each of the percentage differences described in this paragraph is statistically significant at the $p < .05$ level.
50. Clare and Danilovic (2010) argue that states that have backed down in the past will more likely initiate subsequent aggression in hopes of establishing a reputation for resolve.
51. Given that the dependent variable "support for aggression" is a count variable, poisson regression was used to model the relationship between the DV, IV, and the mediators. Linear regression was used to model the effects of the treatments on the mediators.
52. This was also true of reported levels of indifference, though the increase was only 13.9 percent higher within the treatment groups. By contrast, reported levels of humiliation were 112 percent higher and levels of anger were 77 percent higher. All of these differences are significant at the $p < .05$ level.
53. Those respondents who reported equal levels of both were not included in the analysis.
54. The observed range of responses spanned the 7-point scale, though with fewer data in the extreme tails.
55. Again, those respondents who reported equivalent levels of both were not included in the analysis.
56. Subjects did report their overall levels of anger, but for some this anger was directed at the United States. This self-directed anger is more similar to shame and guilt.
57. Spears, Doosje, and Ellemers 1997; Jetten, Postmes, and McAuliffe 2002; Doosje, Spears, and Ellemers 2002.

4. THE CROSS-NATIONAL CONSEQUENCES OF HUMILIATING INTERNATIONAL EVENTS

1. Singer 1988; Maoz 2019. Because the analysis must test hypotheses regarding the likelihood that states will initiate a dispute against a plausible rival—one with whom it has a diplomatic relationship, as opposed to third-party states—the unit of analysis utilized in each of the regression models is the politically relevant, directed dyad-year. In all models, the standard errors are clustered by directed dyad. More information about this data is presented in the Appendix.

2. This corresponds to a MID outcome of a victory for one's opponent or for the state yielding. To be coded as either victory or defeat, the hostility level of both states must reach 20 on the MID aggression scale. There are 241 cases of defeat, 235 cases of victory, and 82 cases of stalemate coded within the dataset.

3. This variable may not tell us which state most wants to alter the status quo. Rather, it is a measure of how likely states are to initiate aggression in response to demands from others or in support of their demands.

4. Analysis of the probability of initiation in each year following a defeat is presented in the Appendix.

5. Johnson and Tierney (2006) argue that assessments of victory and defeat by war participants are often subjective. Codings of war outcomes within the MID dataset are not solely dependent on the declared perceptions of those states involved in the conflict but on other measures of whether states made territorial gains or achieved political objectives.

6. Full descriptions of the models' variables and other summary statistics are presented in the Appendix, as well as in all coefficient tables (Tables 2–8).

7. These predicted probabilities were obtained using the *margins* command in Stata. All dichotomous variables, aside from those of primary interest, were set to 0. All continuous variables were set to their means.

8. Additional tests of robustness, including a within-country analysis, are presented in the Appendix.

9. The variable *Use of Force* is coded 1 in the first year of a dispute if the highest hostility level of the state within the dispute, as coded within the MID dataset, is a 4 or 5.

10. Both are significant at the $p < .001$ level. Ordered logit regression models, run using *Hostility Level*, as measured by the Militarized Interstate Disputes dataset, as the dependent variable, also confirm the correlations presented in Figure 4.2.

11. Levy 1983, 14; Wight 2002; Howard 1971; Buzan and Waever 2003. Volgy et al. (2011, ch. 1) note that those states that possess distinctive capabilities but do not demonstrate a willingness to act as a great power by projecting power abroad are usually not attributed great power status.

12. The difference in the rate of revenge between great powers and lower status states is significant at the $p < .001$ level.

13. These results were obtained by truncating the data to include only great powers or non-great powers within the population. This method ensures that findings for defeated non-great powers are not driven by the behavior of great powers, which engage in aggression at significantly higher rates.

14. A coefficient table listing these models and models examining the ten-year period is presented in Table 4 of the Appendix.

15. Researchers of humiliation at the individual level note that this is often the case. According to Barash and Lipton 2011, animals and individuals often delay aggressive responses to humiliation. See also Chapter 2 in this volume.

16. Alternative codings of this variable that used years *t-1 or t-5* did not significantly alter the reported results, as illustrated in the Appendix.

17. According to the data, the material loss did not accompany defeat in 61 of 134 cases. Among those states that suffered material loss, roughly 60 percent recovered those losses within ten years and roughly 72 percent within twenty years.

18. Other states may choose to preempt aggression by more threatening states rather than waiting for an opponent to gain the upper hand by starting a war. It is unclear, however, how measurement error of this kind would introduce any systematic bias correlating with the probability of conflict initiation.

19. "Success" here is coded 1 if the state achieves victory or if the other state or states yield in the dispute. This corresponds with MID outcome codings of 1 and 4. All disputes in which the outcome is coded as "unclear" (8) or missing (0) are removed from the analysis. By this coding, defeated states achieve success in 45 of their 617 (7%) disputes in the ten years after a defeat while non-defeated states achieve success in 243 of the 4,620 (4.7%) disputes they engage in. The large majority of disputes are coded as ending in a stalemate.

20. . The rate of success for defeated states in disputes they initiate is 15 percent. For non-defeated states, this rate is 8.4 percent.

21. Including the capabilities of a state's allies fighting on its side within this relative measurement did not significantly affect the findings reported below. If a state has lost more than one war in the prior ten-year period, the most unexpected defeat—the one in which it possessed the most capabilities relative to its opponent—is included as the measure over the subsequent ten years.

22. These estimated probabilities were generated using the core model described in the section titled "Are Defeated States More Hostile in Subsequent Disputes?", holding past victory, past backing down, joint democracy and disputes launched against the same opponent at 0. The capabilities of the state were held at .07, the mean capability for those states defeated in war.

23. For data and codebook, see Edward Azar, "Conflict and Peace Data Bank (COPDAB), 1948–1978," http://doi.org/10.3886/ICPSR07767.v4.

24. For more information, see Section 6 of the Appendix.

25. Leng (1983) argues that failure in one round of coercive bargaining will lead to tougher bargaining stances in future rounds.

26. While a reputation for resolve refers to others' perceptions of a state's willingness to pay costs to achieve its aims, a reputation for strength refers to others' perceptions about the military, technological, and organizational capacities of the state.

27. Weisiger and Yarhi-Milo 2015.

28. For this reason, Weisiger and Yarhi-Milo (2015) do not include past defeats and only focus on unambiguous cases of backing down—when states yield without fighting.

29. Clare and Danilovic 2010.

30. Crescenzi 2007.

31. Accordingly, Clare and Danilovic (2010) assess proactive reputation building by analyzing the impact of backing down on the likelihood that states initiate conflict against potential rivals of equal or nearly equal size.

32. Further information on the characteristics of targeted states is provided in the Appendix.

33. See Tir et al. 1998. The codebook for the recoded data on territorial change is available in the Appendix.

34. France's eighteenth-century "policy of prestige," for instance, mandated territorial expansion in North America for the sake of disputing British claims to naval superiority and announcing French grandeur to the world. Marshall 2005, ch. 1; Boyce 1999.

35. Zacher 2001; Fazal 2007.

36. Although all fifteen of the former Soviet states expressed support for territorial integrity following the collapse of the Soviet Union, their support can largely be attributed to pressure from the West. Zacher 2001, 222. See also the Conclusion in this volume.

37. Far from eroding China's status, these acts of voluntary cession have continued into more recent decades even as China's power and international status have continued to increase.

38. More information about this data, model specifications and variable coding is included in the Appendix.

39. The following section presents results on the impact of territorial loss within all politically relevant, directed-dyad years from 1816 to 2000.

40. Attempted coercive gains were coded from the Militarized Interstate Disputes dataset and were those in which the highest act of hostility listed for the country within a dispute was either the occupation of territory, even if temporary, or the threat to take territory and in which no subsequent transfer of territory took place.

41. As it is coded, the variable does not account for treaty settlements which stipulated the loss of territory but which were technically agreed to by both parties.

42. The analysis within the Appendix also assesses the effects on territorial aggression over a ten-year period.

43. This graph was estimated using Model 3 presented in the Appendix. It includes a count term for the twenty years following a loss along with the next three terms of its Taylor series.

44. The pace of attempted conquest following coerced territorial loss appears to differ from that of conflict initiation following defeat. Defeat is correlated with a shift in state behavior in the five to ten years immediately following the humiliating event, while the effects of territorial loss are obviously not so immediate. What accounts for this difference? Conflict initiation can range from the threat of force to its actual use, yet attempted conquest typically involves a significant commitment. Thus, we would expect for states to wait longer before attempting conquest while they recover lost capabilities.

45. As described in the Appendix, the reported results hold even when excluding cases in which a state attempted a territorial gain in the ten years before an attempted gain in time t. The results also hold when omitting data in which a state attempted a gain in the ten years prior to a coerced loss. Coerced loss in the present also does not significantly correlate with one's own gains or the gains of others in the past.

46. Tir 2010.

47. We would expect Germany and Japan, for instance, to have been relatively unlikely to initiate disputes following their defeats in World War II because both countries were ultimately defeated by coalitions much larger than themselves. Japan and Germany were significantly constrained in their abilities to pursue independent foreign policies in the decade after defeat. It is impossible that extended occupation following defeat explains the broader empirical patterns presented above since years in which states were occupied were not included in the analysis. Moreover, the variable for recent defeat was reset to 0 if a defeated state was occupied at any subsequent point.

48. Meyer and Brysac 2009.

5. SOOTHING WOUNDED VANITY

1. Other states participated but were far less active. Belgium engaged in one act of expansion, though a relatively large one of 2,344,858 square kilometers. Portugal during this time added 909,000 square kilometers. These figures are taken from Tir et al. (1998).

2. Hobson 1902; Lenin 1917.

3. Quoted in Hammond 1961, 79.

4. Robinson 1922.

5. British experience in the United States had called into question the need to annex territory. British trade with the former colonies increased significantly after secession. Robinson 1922, 160–168.

6. Sanderson 1974, 10; Chamberlain 1974, 40–44.
7. Langer 1935; Fieldhouse 1961; Platt 1968.
8. Chamberlain (1974) notes that the former was essentially bankrupt by 1890.
9. Chamberlain (1974), 40–44. Sanderson 1974.
10. Robinson and Gallagher 1965, ch. IV.
11. Schölch (1976), Sanderson (1974), and Galbraith and al-Sayyid-Marsot (1978), Cain and Hopkins (1993, 366–367), and Hopkins (1986) provide significant evidence to refute Robinson and Gallagher.
12. Schölch 1976, 775.
13. Mommsen 1982, 102; Fieldhouse 1973; Brunschwig 1966, 182–190.
14. Data taken from Tir et al. 1998.
15. By the mid-nineteenth century, Lord Melbourne noted that the loss of the British empire "might not be of material detriment to the interest of the mother country." Quoted in Reid 1906. British policymakers were also working towards devolution in parts of Australia, Canada, and South Africa.
16. Robinson and Gallagher (1965) argue the crisis in Egypt in 1882 prompted the Scramble. Chamberlain (1974); Newbury and Kanya-Forstner (1969) and Sanderson (1974) convincingly refute this argument.
17. Britain controlled roughly 8 million square miles with major colonial holdings in Canada, Australia, India, and South Africa in 1871.
18. Roberts 1963, 171. By 1870, France possessed territory in Algeria and Cochinchina.
19. Conklin, Fishman, and Zaretsky 2009, 31.
20. Varley 2008.
21. Schivelbusch 2003, 114.
22. Brunschwig 1960, 177.
23. Varley 2008, 68.
24. Schivelbusch 2003.
25. Howard 1990.
26. Letter from Disraeli to Lady Bradford in 1875. Quoted in Ganiage 1971, 43.
27. Quoted in Kennedy 1953, 71.
28. Quoted in Wawro 2005, 306, and 311.
29. Wawro 2005, 304–305. Wetzel 2003, 162.
30. Varley 2008, 65.
31. Schivelbusch 2003, 115.
32. It was perceived that Prussia won because of its superior organization, military education, and manpower. As a result, the French Army instituted five-year compulsory service and overhauled its military education program and organizational structure. Howard 1990.
33. Quoted in Carroll 1931, 78.
34. Quoted in Carroll 1931, 46.
35. Carroll 1931, 47.
36. Varley 2008, 120.
37. Quoted in Schivelbusch 2003, 127.
38. Brunschwig 1960, 55–58 and 176.
39. Quoted in Brunschwig 1960, 177.
40. Carroll 1931, 78.
41. Quoted in Amson 1994, 343; Schivelbusch 2003, 148.
42. Cooke 1973, 15–17.
43. Baumgart and Mast 1982, 56; Brunschwig 1971, 23–24; Carroll 1931, 84.
44. France did not perceive status to be gained only with expansion in Africa, but also in Asia from Saigon to Cochin China. Brunschwig 1966, 75–88.

45. As Gabriele Hanotaux, later minister of Foreign Affairs, put it, France engaged in Tunisia to prove its "savoir-faire et son energy." Quoted in Hanotaux 1903, 4:639.

46. Quoted in Hanotaux 1903, 79.

47. Quoted in Carroll 1931, 179.

48. For a relevant history of the events prior to and in Berlin, see Power 1944, 35–38.

49. Bismarck was also motivated by the fear that French enmity for the Germans would lead to a disastrous Franco-Russian alliance. Bismarck had a plan to satisfy the ambitions of each European power at the Congress by providing them territory equivalent to their perceived esteem. See Langer (1925, 59–60) and Roberts (1963). Waddington happily returned home with Tunisia in his pocket. He was nearly as delighted that France was again received at the tables of the great powers of Europe. Power 1944, 37.

50. Commission de publication des documents relatifs aux origines de la guerre de 1914 (1929; henceforth, DDF), Vol. III, Nos. 337 and 339.

51. Pakenham 1992, ch. 7; Wesseling and Pomerans 1996, 28.

52. DDF, Vol. III, Nos. 304 and 307. As noted in Baumgart and Mast (1982, 59–60), the practice of allowing an adversary to overcome the sting of defeat was common in the nineteenth century. In Bismarck's private correspondence, he emphasized the need to avoid a clash with France. Contrary to realist arguments, Bismarck was most concerned that another war would thoroughly annihilate France now that Germany was so much stronger.

53. The number of Italians in Tunisia was as high as 30,000 in 1880, while the number of French at the time was closer to 3,000. Villari 1930, 57–58.

54. Power 1944, 38–42.

55. DDF, Vol. III, No. 109.

56. DDF, Vol. III, No. 376.

57. Sanderson 1974, 9.

58. Ferry responded, "Action in Tunis in an election year, my dear Saint-Hilaire, do not think of it." Quoted in Hanotaux 1903, 4:650. Gambetta was far more interested in focusing on continental affairs. Power 1944, 48.

59. Hanotaux 1903, 4:650–652; Power 1944, 50; Ganiage and Hémery 1968, 74–76.

60. Quoted in Hyam 1964.

61. Years later, Ferry attested to the immense influence Courcel had in these affairs. Power 1944, 52. While raids of the Tunisian Kroumir tribes into Algeria were presented as the primary cause, the documents clearly attest that this was merely pretext for the intervention. Hyam 1964, 51.

62. Kelly 1955.

63. Quoted in Constant 1891, 182.

64. Brunschwig 1966, ch. 8–12.

65. Power (1944, 186–198) remarks that references to raw materials, to potential markets, or other economic factors were "conspicuously lacking from Ferry's creed."

66. Sanderson 1974, 12–13.

67. Roberts 1963, 177. French president Jules Grévy argued at the time that Tunisia was not worth 'un cigar à deux sous.' Quoted in Roberts 1963, 28. Tunisia in the 1870s was in bad financial straits. Twenty percent of the population perished in famines in 1867 and 1868. The government was bankrupt. Upon annexing the country, France assumed responsibility for Tunisia's mounting international debts. Wesseling and Pomerans 1996, 18.

68. Andrew and Kanya-Forstner 1976. As the authors note, pro-colonial coalitions did not become powerful in France until the turn of the century.

69. Wesseling and Pomerans 1996; Andrew and Kanya-Forstner 1976; Brunschwig 1966, 52–53. This included the two companies with the largest financial investments in Tunisia as well as the railway company which had received concessions to build in Tunisia.

While industrial production was increasing in France, industrialists did not expect to find a market in Tunisia. Power 1944, 197.

70. Power 1944, 27.

71. Burt (1956) argues that France confronted demographic disadvantages and could make up for them by acquiring Tunisian men to fight Germany. There is little evidence that France ever planned to incorporate or train Tunisian men within the French military. Louis 1971, 174–175.

72. Cooke 1973; Murphy 1968. Clemenceau, an ardent anti-colonialist, argued that expansion into Tunisia was a strategic mistake which would prove to be a "military liability for freedom of action on the continent." Quoted in Power 1944, 66.

73. Quoted in Power 1944, 57.

74. Ganiage 1971, 53; Brunschwig 1960, 77–80.

75. Ganiage 1971, 53.

76. Although French leaders had expressed belief in the "safety valve" function of colonies, the desire to stave off domestic unrest through expansion fails to explain why France expanded when it did. Civil unrest had existed for years. Wesseling and Pomerans 1996, 17–18.

77. Quoted in Townsend, Peake, and Langsam 1941.

78. Carroll 1931, 84–86.

79. Stengers 1971, 474.

80. In September 1882, de Brazza informed the Belgian foreign minister Walthère Frère-Orban that he was convinced that "neither the [French] government nor the Chambers would do anything [with regards to his treaty]." Stengers 1971. De Brazza's expeditions into the Congo coincided with those of Leopold II of Belgium, who cherished hopes of increasing Belgian prestige through colonial expansion. Leopold perceived colonies as "a means of giving us a more important place in the world." See Viaene 2008; Aldrich 1996, 54. According to Galbraith and al-Sayyid-Marsot (1978), Leopold wanted an empire anywhere he could find one. He even wanted land that others had abandoned.

81. On the Egyptian Crisis and British motivations, see Hopkins 1986; Sanderson 1965, ch. 1; Pakenham 1992, ch. 8; Wesseling and Pomerans 1996, 29–31.

82. DDF, Vol. III, No. 455.

83. DDF, Vol. III, No. 408.

84. The British foreign secretary Lord Granville claimed the conquest of Egypt had been "forced" on them and bemoaned that the British takeover of Egypt was "a nasty business, and we have been much out of luck." Quoted in Chamberlain 1974, 33.

85. Sanderson 1965, 114.

86. Girardet 1983; Stengers 1962; Sanderson (1965, 115). The French Chamber failed to support funding but also failed to acknowledge the inevitability of British involvement even if France did not participate.

87. Carroll 1931, 93.

88. Carroll 1931, 114–116. See Andrew (1968) for the impact of the loss of Egypt on Delcassé.

89. Carroll 1931, 94.

90. Stengers 1962; Baumgart and Mast 1982, 60.

91. Baumgart and Mast 1982, 59–62. For arguments in this vein, see the parliamentary debates on November 15, 1882 and December 12, 1882 in Nationale 1882. See also Chamberlain 1974 and Brunschwig 1960.

92. See Stengers 1971, 165. The French press publicized France's humiliation in Egypt and the need for France to assert itself elsewhere.

93. Quoted in Stengers 1971, 166.

94. This quest for renewed prestige in the Congo continued under Charles de Freycinet, who pressed the fact that enlarged French holdings in equatorial Africa would contribute significantly to the stature, glory, and prestige of France. Power 1944, 88–91.

95. Quoted in Power 1944, 475. See also Baumgart and Mast 1982, 62.

96. Quoted in Stoecker 1986, 17. See also Pflanze 1990.

97. Pflanze 1990, 114.

98. Henderson 1962, 10–12; Mommsen 1995, 76; Pflanze 1990, 122–123.

99. Turner 1967, 59–66.

100. Aydelotte 1937; Townsend 1922; Gifford et al. 1967; Taylor and Percivale 1967.

101. A.J.P. Taylor's controversial argument that Bismarck's expansion into Africa was aimed at angering the British to draw closer to the French had been refuted. Sanderson (1974) notes it is unclear why the Germans needed a quarrel with England to arrive at this outcome. Aydelotte 1937.

102. Recognizing the probability his request would be denied, Lüderitz downgraded his request to basic consular protections afforded all German citizens abroad in January 1883.

103. The British held only the guano-rich Walfisch islands off the coast.

104. Translated from the German in Turner 1967, 57–58. Many related German communiqués are in Aydelotte 1937, 32–39.

105. He continued throughout the months that followed to deny requests for anything more than consular protection even in African locales where German trading interests were directly and immediately threatened by the British.

106. Aydelotte 1937, 35.

107. Townsend 1922, 167.

108. Quoted in Pflanze 1990, 124.

109. Letter from Bismarck to Count Munster, May 25, 1884. Dugdale 1931.

110. This perception was augmented by the signing of the Anglo-Portuguese treaty of February 1884, which designated the mouth of the Congo River as Portuguese territory. Given Portugal's role as a British puppet, the treaty was perceived to be a veiled attempted by the British to expand their influence. This high handed behavior by the British was not limited to Africa. In January 1884, London rejected Bismarck's claims for a joint commission to address German claims to Fiji.

111. He had sent a similar inquiry to London in 1880, on the request of protection of missionaries in South West Africa, only to be told that London had no interest in the area and would not be able to extend such protections.

112. British denial of recognition was not, at this point, seen to be part of a broader scheme to maintain German inferiority. Britain's denial also remained in the rhetorical realm and therefore did not severely undermine perceptions of German efficacy within the state. For these reasons, Bismarck was undoubtedly motivated more by the outrage than a need to foster overcome collective self-doubt. It is possible, however, that self-doubt was aroused by this event that simply went unexpressed

113. Förster et al. 1988, 153; Turner 1967.

114. Bismarck may have deceived the British as to his true intentions, convincing them he was only extending consular protections so that the annexations would be a fait accompli. Turner 1967, 71.

115. Letters from Bismarck to Count Munster, May 25 and June 1, 1884. Dugdale 1931.

116. Aydelotte 1937, 72.

117. Letter from Bismarck to Count Münster, August 7, 1884. Dugdale 1931.

118. Förster et al. 1988. Bismarck's son, the only person who, according to Bismarck, possessed knowledge of all of his secrets, claimed that Bismarck had been motivated first and foremost by the need to check British arrogance. Collins 1969, 67:91.

119. Quoted in Aydelotte 1937, 97. Sir William Harcourt apologized profusely to Prince Herbert Bismarck on June 22, indicating that Germany could have all of Fiji and any land she might be interested in Africa. Aydelotte 1937, 99.

120. Hansard 1891, 978–979.

121. Murray (2010) shows this was the beginning of an era of German status assertions.

122. That the conference was intended as a lesson to the British was made clear by Bismarck's intention to declare an international rule that colonial land be occupied for the claim to be legitimate. Pogge von Strandmann 1988.

123. Robinson has described the conference as a "ritual drama signifying a change in seniority between sibling nations." Bismarck warned Britan that its hegemony overseas was over. Robinson 1988, 8–9. This was despite having fully supported British colonial expansion not a year earlier.

124. Quoted in Gifford, Louis, and Smith 1967, 24.

125. The German people were initially far more on the side of colonization than their brethren in France and England. This was in part because the French and British had embarked on extremely costly colonial missions in the past. Germans had yet to engage in colonial expeditions.

126. Ampthill to Granville, March 15, 1884. Quoted in Gifford, Louis, and Smith 1967, 319.

127. Quoted in Gifford, Louis, and Smith 1967, 7.

128. Quoted in Stoecker 1986, 34.

129. For quotes attesting to how little value Bismarck expected, see Brunschwig 1960, 75; Stoecker 1986, 16–20; Smith 1978, 27–34.

130. Pogge von Strandmann 1988, 107.

131. Quoted in Turner 1967, 60.

132. Another German explorer, on visiting the new protectorate, exclaimed: "What a terrible desert we have acquired." Quoted in Pflanze 1990, 134.

133. Bismarck wanted the state to play the smallest possible role in the maintenance of colonies. Pogge von Strandmann 1988, 106–107.

134. African investments were deemed highly risky and, with safer and more profitable investments closer to home and abroad on other continents, not worth the risk. Pogge von Strandmann 1988.

135. Hobsbawm 2010.

136. Pogge von Strandmann 1988, 106–107.

137. Famous German explorer Friedrich Fabri complained in 1885 of the inertia of "our financiers and capitalists" in colonial matters. Pogge von Strandmann 1988, 110.

138. Snyder (1991, 68–69, 99) argues that German expansion was far more likely to occur when German domestic politics was cartelized and run by groups of elites, from 1890 to 1918, or was dominated by a single dictator as it was in the 1930s and 1940s than it was under the unitary oligopoly of Bismarck.

139. As Smith (1978, 7–10) notes, the largest trading group advocating overseas expansion was facing bankruptcy at the time.

140. Mommsen 1995, ch. 5. The British thought Bismarck's colonial shift was prompted by the jingoistic demands of the German public. Bismarck's letters do convey a desire to take electoral advantage of growing nationalist sentiment. See Gifford, Louis, and Smith 1967, 24. It appears that Bismarck strategically released information about the arrogant British treatment of German interests to the German press to arouse such popular anti-British, pro-colonial sentiments. Aydelotte 1937; Chamberlain 1974, 56–59.

141. The population increased 25 percent to 50,000,000 between 1871 and 1890. Pflanze 1990, 116.

142. Förster, Mommsen, and Robinson 1988, 125.
143. Lowe and Marzari 2001, ch. 1.
144. Bosworth 1979. Bismarck wrote privately in 1880, "Italy is not a serious state; she should make painters, musicians, singers and dancers." Quoted in Bosworth 1979, 20.
145. Lowe and Marzari 2001, 8–20.
146. Langer 1925, 65–75.
147. Langer 1925, 70; Wesseling and Pomerans 1996.
148. In 1879, Robilant similarly noted, "We have lost every consideration in Europe." Quoted in Lowe and Marzari 2001, 8:20.
149. Italy would find little support from Bismarck in future colonial or European affairs, despite their alliance, eventually leading Italy to seek the support of Britain. Lowe and Marzari 2001, ch. 1.
150. Italian leaders vowed to counter any future extensions of French influence around the Mediterranean. Italian leaders were prepared to risk invasion and the ire of other European great powers to assert their expectation to be treated as a great power.
151. Lowe and Marzari 2001, 27.
152. Novati 1994.
153. December 7, 1881. Hess 1967, 154.
154. May 20, 1884. Lowe and Marzari 2001, 8:37.
155. Hess 1967, 157.
156. Foreign Minister Robilant later linked his initial disinterest in the port to the fact that it was "arid, deserted, of a rocky nature." Lowe and Marzari 2001, 8:58. The area around Assab is one of the hottest on earth.
157. For this reason, Mancini attempted to connect his actions in the Red Sea with Mediterranean security and attempted to convince skeptical Parliamentarians that "Red Sea is the key to the Mediterranean Sea." Novati 1994, 369.
158. Brogi 2006; Collins 1969; Hess 1967; Lowe and Marzari 2001; Sanderson 1974.
159. Hess 1967, 153.
160. Hess 1967.
161. Italy's unofficial colony in Egypt remained its largest, yet the British ignored Italian interests during the 1882 Egyptian Crisis. Roberts 1946.
162. Collins 1969, 67:111–114.
163. January 27, 1885. Quoted in Zaghi. See also Brogi 2006.
164. Sanderson 1974.
165. Quoted in Langer 1925, 281.
166. Bosworth 1979; Lowe and Marzari 2001. Count Giuseppi Mazari stated after the defeat, "I do not believe that history provides many examples of a country which has been ruined so completely and so shockingly as ours." Quoted in Lowe and Marzari 2001, 8:67.
167. Novati 1994.
168. Boyce 1999, 14–16. Since 1815, Britain had come to view colonies with "indifference tempered by uneasiness," as economic burdens.
169. This followed the confusion over Angra Pequeña. Quoted in Pakenham 1992, 215–216. He continued, "I would give Bismarck every satisfaction about his Colonial matters."
170. Quoted in Langer 1951, 308.
171. Uzoigwe 1974, ch. 3.
172. Quoted in Gifford et al. 1967, 4.
173. Aydelotte 1937, 164.
174. Derby to Granville, December 28, 1884. Granville Papers.
175. Quoted in Sanderson 1988, 209. Moreover, the British House of Commons had also voted in 1865 for Britain to give up any ports it had on the West African coast because of their cost. Uzoigwe 1974, chs. 4 and 5.

176. Quoted in Hyam 1999, 40.
177. Pakenham 1992, 197–199.
178. Quoted in Pakenham 1992.
179. Letter from Ampthill to Granville, March 8, 1884 in Knaplund 1944.
180. Lister to Salisbury, August 15, 1885. Quoted in Gifford et al. 1967. Carl Peters's rapid movements to enforce a policy of "effective occupation" in Zanzibar in 1885 also convinced the British of German intentions. Porter 1975, ch. 3; Sanderson 1974, 30–33.
181. Porter 1975, 117.
182. *The Pall Mall Gazette*, June 1885.
183. Quoted in Taylor and Percivale 1967, 71. Though it had long been clear that Germany had a larger population, more natural resources and greater potential industrial capacity than Britain, it was only once Germany became a colonial power that Britain became concerned about Germany as a threat to Britain's position.
184. Porter 1975, 82; Boyce 1999, 15; Robinson 1922, 180–190.
185. By 1890, Britain's transition to a self-conscious imperialistic power was complete. It became, as Porter has described, like a "cock-bird, blowing up his feathers to assert his dominance to rivals." Porter 1975, 119; Strauss 1971, 63–65.
186. Sanderson 1974, 28.
187. The first reference to events in Africa in terms of a collective competition was in January 1885 toward the end of the Berlin Conference. According to Ferry, "An irresistible movement drives the great European nations to conquer new territories. It is like a steeplechase moving headlong towards an unknown destination." Quoted in Baumgart and Mast (1982, 40); Brunschwig 1971.
188. In 1895, the output from the Belgian Congo made up for only 25 percent of colonial expenses. All German colonies were underwater or bankrupt. Brunschwig 1966, 170–175.
189. Brunschwig 1966, 80.
190. Pflanze 1990. In 1889, Bismarck went so far as to offer German South West Africa to Britain, stating "It was, he said, a burden and an expense, and he would like to saddle someone else with it." Quoted in Taylor 2011, 221.
191. Bismarck was replaced by Caprivi, who also acknowledged the limitations of colonies, stating that "it was commonly believed that once we came in possession of colonies, then purchased an atlas and coloured the continent of Africa blue, we would become a great people." Quoted in Baumgart and Mast 1982, 58.
192. Sanderson 1974, 40.
193. Gifford et al. 1967. The British view of the crisis over Morocco was: "Of course the Germans will ask for Mogador and I shall tell Lord L. that if they do we must at least have Tangier—of course it is all rot and it would not matter to us whether the Germans got Mogador or not but I'm going to say so all the same." Monger 1976, 189.
194. Quoted in Hammond 1961, 583.
195. Some came to view colonies as the key to great power survival itself, even though the underlying value of the African territory had not changed. Eventually, even Chamberlain became convinced that "imperialism was not only a form of survival. It was the *sole* policy for survival." Quoted in Thornton 1965, 88.

6. "OUR HONEYMOON WITH THE U.S. CAME TO AN END"

1. Sagan (1996) argues that France acquired a nuclear arsenal in an effort to restore the global grandeur France had lost during and after the war with the loss of its global empire. Kinsella and Chima 2001; Johnston 1995; Eyre and Suchman 1996.
2. Ringmar (2002) describes how the desire for recognition by the Soviets affected foreign policy shaped across the nineteenth century. Wohlforth (1993) argues that status

and the desire for influence were a primary driver of Soviet behavior, often more so than were concerns about possible military conflict.

3. Stated by Foreign Minister Vyacheslav Molotov in 1946. Quoted in Larson and Shevchenko (2001), which addresses more broadly ways that the Soviets' desire for status impacted their behavior.

4. As Wohlforth (1993, ch. 1) notes that ability to prevail in direct conflict did not correspond with actual political influence immediately after the fact calls into question realist assumptions that the nature of influence in the international system can be understood as a direct translation of absolute capabilities and resources. See also Wohlforth 1993, 129–133.

5. Wohlforth 1993, 158.
6. Khrushchev and Khrushchev 2007, 3:253.
7. Taubman 2003, 448.
8. Taubman 2003, 448.
9. Khrushchev 2000, 390.
10. Khrushchev 2000, 390, 389.
11. Taubman 2003, 464.
12. Taubman 2003, 464.
13. Taubman 2003, 462, 444, 443.
14. Dobrynin 1995, 41.
15. Khrushchev and Khrushchev 2007, 237–239, 245.
16. Khrushchev and Khrushchev 2007, 256, 238; Khrushchev 2000, 446.
17. Khrushchev 2000, 380. Fursenko and Naftali 1998, 290. Larson and Shevchenko (2014) also note that the humiliating impact of the flyovers led to an attempt to embarrass U.S. leaders on the world stage.
18. Khrushchev 2000, 200, 387.
19. Khrushchev 2000, 449, 388, 451–453.
20. Khrushchev and Khrushchev 2007, 3:245.
21. Khrushchev and Khrushchev 2007, 253.

22. All failed Soviet attempts to shoot down U.S. spy planes over the years had remained the private information of the Soviets and the Americans.

23. The knowledge that it was Eisenhower that sanctioned the flyovers would not have augmented any security threat since any significant information gleaned from these flyovers would logically have made it to his desk anyway.

24. See Khrushchev (2000, 383) for a broader refutation of this theory.
25. Khrushchev 2000.
26. Khrushchev 2000, 373.
27. Taubman 2003, 450.

28. That the United States had engaged in the act of war by flying the plane through Soviet airspace also significantly minimized the likelihood that the Americans would retaliate after its downing.

29. Khrushchev 2000, 390–392.
30. Garthoff 1985, 59.
31. Khrushchev and Khrushchev 2007, 3:325.
32. Khrushchev 1971, 1:496.
33. Khrushchev 2000, 489.
34. Khrushchev 2000, 493.

35. Khrushchev 2000, 489. Khrushchev and Khrushchev 2007, 3:336–337. As further evidence of the relationship between the U-2 incident and the Cuban Missile Crisis in Khrushchev's foreign policy considerations, Khrushchev reintroduces the discussion of the double standard of the Gary Powers incident within the middle of his discussion of the Cuban Missile Crisis in his memoirs.

36. Miokyan 2012, 494; Khrushchev 2000, 656; Fursenko and Naftali (1998, 504–506). Blight and Brenner 2006, 15.
37. Petroff 1988, 138.
38. The Polyansky Report on Khrushchev's Mistakes in Foreign Policy, October 1964. http://digitalarchive.wilsoncenter.org/document/115108.
39. Quoted in Fursenko and Naftali 1998, 537–540.
40. Quoted in Bacon and Sandle 2002, 90. See Zubok 2009, 390; Kaser and Brown 1977, 49.
41. Brezhnev served as minister of defense in 1963 at which time he may have played a role in calling for a significant increase in ICBMs. This would suggest that some portion of the delivery systems constructed during the late 1960s were potentially ordered before Khrushchev left office. Rhodes 2008, 94; Holloway 1984.
42. Quoted from a July 4, 1965 speech in Gelman 1984, 80. See also Rhodes 2008, 94.
43. See Kulski (1973, 30) on the first point and Rhodes (2008, 94) on the latter.
44. Catudal 1989, 60. The buildup also included conventional forces and the development of a blue water navy that would enable the Soviet Union to project its power abroad.
45. CIA Directorate of Intelligence, "Soviet Expenditures for Defense and Space Programs, 1962–1971," March 1971, 11.
46. CIA National Foreign Assessment Center, "A Comparison of Soviet and US Defense Activities, 1971–1980," October 1981, 7.
47. Zaloga 2014.
48. Freedman 2003, 330.
49. Kull 1988, 10.
50. Jervis 1989, 200.
51. Zaloga 2014.
52. Quoted in Bohlen and Phelps 1973, 495. See also Lambeth (1979) and Betts (1987).
53. As noted in Trachtenberg (1985), it was likely these considerations which prevented the Soviets from making war preparations during the crisis because Soviet forces were less numerous and therefore more vulnerable than U.S. weapons. Although American thinking and policy decisions do not appear to have been impacted by the country's strategic advantage, the Soviets translated particular aspects of U.S. policy and commentary as evidence of the U.S. belief that the state with more firepower would gain an advantage with a preemptive first strike.
54. Stated by Marshal Ogarkov, the chief of the General Staff from 1977 to 1984. See Nichols 1993, 122.
55. Trachtenberg 1985, 156–161.
56. Zubok 2009, 224.
57. Kennedy apparently recognized potentially harmful effects of national humiliation, stating: "You can't put another fellow in a position where he has no alternative except humiliation. This country cannot afford to be humiliated and neither can the Soviet Union. Like us, the Soviet Union has many countries which look to her for leadership and Khrushchev would be likely to do something desperate before he let himself be disgraced in their eyes." Kratochwil 1991, 50. Robert Kennedy similarly noted the efforts made not to humiliate the Soviet Union for fear that would lead to escalation.
58. Bacon and Sandle 2002, 90. Statesmen and historians have also concluded that Cuba caused Soviet humiliation. Robert Gates stated that "Humiliation in Cuba galvanized the Soviets into action." Quoted in Rhodes 2008, 94. See also Fursenko and Naftali (1998, 544) and Steele (1984, 39) for similar conclusions.
59. Quoted in Rhodes 2008, 94.
60. Kaser and Brown 1977, 49.
61. Kolkowicz 1971, 438.

62. See Garthoff (1985, 59) for a similar argument. See also Kull 1988, 262. President Lyndon Johnson had proposed to freeze strategic arms in 1964, but the Soviets rejected the proposal because it would have locked the Soviets into an inferior position. Holloway 1984.

63. Nixon 1978, 619.

64. The Americans focused on ways to convey parity at the first summit under Nixon. Kissinger 1979, 1141.

65. Quoted in Wohlforth 1993, 173.

66. Steele 1984, 20.

67. Quoted in Steele 1984, 56.

68. Quoted in Adomeit 1982, 251.

69. Quoted in Wohlforth 1993, 177–178.

70. Garthoff 1985, 62.

71. Quoted in Bacon and Sandle 2002, 91.

72. Edmonds 1983, 43; Bacon and Sandle 2002, 90.

73. Garthoff 1985, 40.

74. Quoted in Zubok 2009, 207.

75. Vikenty Matveyev, one of the Soviet Union's most experienced political commentators, went on to state that the Soviets cherished parity dearly. Quoted in Steele 1984, 55.

76. Garthoff 1985, 59.

77. Gray (1974) explores seven possible rationales for arms buildups, including deterrence, defense, diplomacy, domestic political advantage, domestic economic and industrial advantage, reputation or, as he at times refers to it, prestige, and technological advance.

78. Major General Rair Simonyan declared that "neither the addition of fresh consignments or armaments nor the increase of their destructive force can produce any substantial military advantage." Quoted in Kull 1988, 253.

79. Trachtenberg 2017, 17.

80. This finding was reported to the defense minister in 1968 by the leading research institute of missile technology which had modeled all possible scenarios and had concluded that the Soviet Union, whether it launched a first strike or a retaliatory strike, could not win a nuclear war. Hines and Shull 1995, 26.

81. Quoted in Trachtenberg (2017, 26) from John Hines et al. 1995.

82. Hines et al. 1995, 26.

83. Hines et al. 1995, 7, 13.

84. Hines et al. 1995, 28.

85. One official noted that the last time that Brezhnev effectively represented the Soviet Union "in working form" was in 1974. Hynes et al., 50.

86. Rosenberg (1983) addresses the causes of the massive U.S. strategic buildup from 1945 through the 1960s. Quester (2000) addresses why the United States did not use its nuclear monopoly to extract concessions from the Soviets during this time. See also Trachtenberg 1988.

87. McNamara 1964, 1967.

88. The Americans had been focused on the development of MIRVs (multiple independently targetable reentry vehicles), which allowed for the placement of several warheads within one missile. The United States also possessed a larger stockpile of nuclear warheads and an advantage in the number of manned bombers, though the bombers were becoming increasingly obsolete.

89. See Kull (1985) for more information on the Jackson Amendment and its impact on military thinking.

90. As noted in Kull (1985, 31), until the time of the Jackson amendment, traditional deterrence policy had recognized the importance of shaping the enemy's perceptions about retaliatory capabilities and intentions, but that afterward, perceptional priorities expanded at the expense of military reality.

91. Schlesinger 1974.
92. Rumsfeld 1978.
93. Brown 1978. Emphasis added.
94. *Annual Report to Congress Fiscal Year 1988*.
95. Schlesinger 1974.
96. Luttwak 1972, part II.
97. Schlesinger 1974. Emphasis added. The report expresses concerns about the general perceptions of other states in the international system about the status of the numerical balance.
98. Luttwak (1972) argues that nuclear weapons were "psychologically by far the most impressive of all instruments of power," which ensured that other states would certainly have a definite awareness of which side had more than the other.
99. Schlesinger 1974, 1975; Kull 1985. This belief that other states watched and attached importance to the count of strategic forces was echoed by many U.S. leaders and presented in the analysis below.
100. Schlesinger 1975; Luttwak 1972.
101. Quote taken from an interview with Arms Control and Disarmament Agency official. Kull 1988, 119. Such concerns about "picking the winner" have little to do with resolve or credibility of those in competition.
102. The quote is taken from a private interview in which the respondent was pressed to provide a rationale for American policy on strategic parity. Kull 1988, 229.
103. This quote was taken from an interview with a senior military official. Kull 1988, 117. It was thought, more generally, that third-party behavior would be impacted by their judgment about who was "doing the most to retain or acquire a relative advantage." Taken from an interview with a senior official from the Arms Control and Disarmament Agency. Kull 1988, 229.
104. Turner n.d. Caspar Weinberger also viewed "the political advantages of being seen as the superior strategic power" as "more real and more useful than the military advantages of in fact being superior in one measure or another." Quoted in Jervis 1989, 197.
105. Frank 1983, 399.
106. Schlesinger 1974.
107. SALT II was not submitted for ratification by Carter following the invasion of Afghanistan; however, Carter and Reagan complied with its tenets until 1986 when Reagan abandoned the agreement because of possible Soviet violations. See Newhouse and Newhouse (1989) on SALT accords.
108. The United States during this time also chose not to keep up with Soviet production of actual nuclear warheads, with the Soviet arsenal continuing to grow until 1986 and the US arsenal topping out in 1973. That the number of warheads was not a focus of the SAL talks suggests that attention was not drawn to the relative comparison and thus that the United States had less incentive to correct the imbalance. One can imagine that if more attention had been drawn to the warhead asymmetry, U.S. policy about warhead arsenals would have been different.
109. This focus on relative numbers extended to defense budgeting. In 1975, when a group of U.S. senators heard that the Soviets were spending twice as much as the United States, they made a push to simply match the Soviet budget. This was without knowing any details about the numbers or types of weapons the Soviets were developing, but only the bottom line number. Kull 1985, 34.
110. Gray 1974.
111. Quoted in Kull 1985, 33.

CONCLUSION

1. Speech at the 10th session of the Islamic Summit, October 22, 2003. Full transcript at https://www.smh.com.au/articles/2003/10/20/1066502121884.html.

2. Bin Laden had predicted in a statement five years prior that while Western powers would struggle to convince their soldiers to fight, the Islamic world would struggle to constrain its aggrieved youths to wait for their turn in the fight against the West.

3. Laden 2005, 19.

4. Creswell and Haykel n.d.

5. Peter Gries deems it "undeniable that in China the past lives in the present to a degree unmatched in most other countries." Wang 2008, 788; Chin 2005, 156; Kang 2008.

6. Scott 2008; Kaufman n.d.; Wand 2005; Callahan 2004; Luo 1993.

7. Scott 2008.

8. A map included in a state-published book titled *Maps of China's National Humiliation* characterizes China's territorial losses as follows: fifteen homeland territories, fifteen lost vassal states, four mandated territorial concessions, and fourteen maritime borders. One book from 1930 titled *The Geography of China's National Humiliation* estimated that China had lost roughly half of its territory from its peak. See Callahan 2009, 154–155.

9. Deng and Wang 2004, 52.

10. Quoted in Gries 2001, 32.

11. Swaine and Tellis 2000, 104.

12. This is according to the IMF World Economic Outlook Database, April 2018.

13. Shirk 2007, 186.

14. Quoted in Scott 2007, 12. As analysts have noted, China has found peaceful solutions to many of its disputed borders, but few of these resolutions involve territories robbed of China during the Century of Humiliation. See Fravel 2005.

15. Fravel 2005, 172.

16. Remnick 2014; Stent 2015; Forsberg et al. 2014; Larson and Shevchenko 2014; Simes 2007; Trenin 2006; Tsygankov 2008; Malinova 2014; among others. Richard Burt, arms negotiator for the United States, cites the "sense of humiliation and loss stemming from the end of the Cold War" as a major factor motivating Russian intransigence.

17. Karaganov 2014.

18. Lo 2002, 103; Stent 2015, 3.

19. Bill Clinton sensed the inevitable humiliation that such harsh demands would impose, remarking that "We keep telling ol' Boris, 'O.K., now, here's what you've got to do next,'" and continuing by equating additional Western demands to the application of more manure to Yeltsin's face. Quoted in Osnos et al. 2107, 46.

20. As Foreign Minister Andrei Kozyrev stated after the bombings, Moscow was not against the air raids per se, but was "against not being consulted." Quoted in Lo 2002, 105.

21. Quoted in Stent 2015, 75.

22. Sixty-five percent of Russians stated in 2006 that they believed that the demise of the USSR could have been avoided while 22 percent said it was inevitable. Shevtsova 2007, 50; Tuminez 2000, 185.

23. Gaidar 2010, xii.

24. Tsygankov 2008, 173–174.

25. Gaidar 2010, 50.

26. Samantha Power, among many others, assigned Russian motivations in Georgia as stemming from "brewing rage at [Russia's] lost grandeur." *Time*, August 13, 2008.

27. Lukyanov 2016, 34. Gessen 2014.

28. Transcript available on the Kremlin's website at http://en.kremlin.ru/events/president/news/46860.

29. Quoted in Yaffa n.d.

30. http://www.cnn.com/WORLD/asiapcf/9905/09/china.protests.02/.

31. Quoted in Osnos, Remnick, and Yaffa (2107, 46). For more quotes on Russian perceptions of humiliation during the 1990s, see Tuminez 2000, 185.

32. *Time*, "Person of the Year 2007—Putin Q&A: Full Transcript."

33. Quoted in Kaufman n.d.
34. Blinkhorn 1980.
35. Balfour 1995; Harrison and Hoyle 2000; Ortega 1980.
36. Studies have shown that humiliated actors are less inclined to pursue aggression when they are offered another mode of catharsis for the negative feelings associated with helplessness. Stürmer and Simon 2009.
37. Larson and Shevchenko 2010, 67.
38. Larson and Shevchenko 2010, 74.
39. Quoted in Brogi 2002, 31.
40. The Psychology Strategy Board in the United States perceived that France's desire to maintain its hold on Algeria was rooted not so much in "the potential benefit of overseas territories, but the liability of a patrimony of prestige which France cannot renounce without losing self-respect." Brogi 2002.
41. Brogi 2002, 15. See also Brogi 2006, 764.
42. Brogi 2002, 31.
43. Brogi 2002, 20. For examples of similar rhetoric, see Brogi 2002, ch. 1.
44. As Brogi (2002, 30) notes, the British wanted a five-year wait on any changes to the terms of Italian peace. U.S. officials, however, argued that it was not possible to keep Italy "deliberately in suspense as to whether her place [was] in the sun or in [the] shadow."
45. Brogi 2002.
46. Quoted in Bernstein 1995, 147.
47. For more on this, see Dower 2000, especially 41–44.
48. Dower 2000, 43–44.
49. Quoted in Dower 2000, 44.
50. Quoted in Finn 1992, 245.
51. Finn 1992, 252.
52. Quoted in Stent 2015, 38.
53. Graham, Haidt, and Nosek 2009.

APPENDIX

1. Chasteen 2001; Goldstein 1992.
2. To isolate the effect of a single case of defeat, cases were dropped if states had experienced another loss in the prior ten-year period. These cases were dropped because, as will be shown below, the probability of conflict initiation declines with each successive defeat within a ten-year timespan.
3. One-tailed t-tests were conducted to assess whether the difference in conflict activity before and after defeat was statistically significant. The p-values of this analysis are presented underneath the percentages.
4. My coding of voluntary changes also correlates highly with that of Kacowicz (1994) which lays out a theoretical description of peaceful territorial change. My coding differs in a few instances in which coercion or threat appeared to play a significant role in affecting the outcome, even if there the outcome did not immediately follow conflict.
5. Correlates of War Project. 2008. State System Membership List, v2008. Online, http://correlatesofwar.org.

References

"A Strategy of Spectacle." 2016. *The Economist*, March 19, 21.
Abramo, Joseph L., David C. Lundgren, and Dodd H. Bogart. 1978. "Status Threat and Group Dogmatism." *Human Relations* 31 (8). Sage Publications: 745–752.
Abrams, Dominic, and Michael A. Hogg. 1988. "Comments on the Motivational Status of Self-Esteem in Social Identity and Intergroup Discrimination." *European Journal of Social Psychology* 18 (4): 317–334.
Aday, Sean. 2010. "Leading the Charge: Media, Elites, and the Use of Emotion in Stimulating Rally Effects in Wartime." *Journal of Communication* 60 (3): 440–465.
Adomeit, H. 1982. *Soviet Risk-Taking and Crisis Behavior: A Theoretical and Empirical Analysis*. Allen & Unwin.
Albert, Stuart. 1977. "Temporal Comparison Theory." *Psychological Review* 84 (6). American Psychological Association: 485.
Aldrich, R. 1996. *Greater France: A History of French Overseas Expansion*. Palgrave Macmillan.
Amson, Daniel. 1994. *Gambetta, Ou, Le Rêve Brisé*. Editions Tallandier.
Andrew, C. 1968. *Théophile Delcassé and the Making of the Entente Cordiale: A Reappraisal of French Foreign Policy 1898–1905*. Macmillan.
Andrew, Christopher M., and Alexander Sydney Kanya-Forstner. 1971. "V. The French Colonial Party: Its Composition, Aims and Influence, 1885–1914." *The Historical Journal* 14 (1): 99–128.
Andrew, Christopher M., and A. S. Kanya-Forstner. 1976. "French Business and the French Colonialists." *The Historical Journal* 19 (4): 981–1000.
Angier, Natalie. 1991. "In Fish, Social Status Goes Right to the Brain." *New York Times*.
Annual Report to Congress Fiscal Year 1988. 1987. U.S. Department of Defense; GPO.
Art, Robert J. 1973. *The Influence of Foreign Policy on Seapower: New Weapons and Weltpolitik in Wilhelminian Germany*. Sage Publications.
Aydelotte, W. O. 1937. *Bismarck and British Colonial Policy, 1883–1885*. Philadelphia Press.
Bacon, Edwin, and Mark Sandle. 2002. *Brezhnev Reconsidered*, 203–217. Springer.
Balfour, Sebastian. 1995. "Riot, Regeneration and Reaction: Spain in the Aftermath of the 1898 Disaster." *The Historical Journal* 38 (2): 405–423.
Barash, David P., and Judith Eve Lipton. 2011. *Payback: Why We Retaliate, Redirect Aggression, and Take Revenge*. Oxford University Press.
Barkow, J. H. 1989. *Darwin, Sex, and Status*. University of Toronto Press.
Bar-Tal, Daniel, Eran Halperin, and Joseph De Rivera. 2007. "Collective Emotions in Conflict Situations: Societal Implications." *Journal of Social Issues* 63 (2): 441–460.
Baumeister, Roy F. 1991. *Meanings of Life*. Guilford Press.
Baumgart, Winfried, and Ben V. Mast. 1982. *Imperialism: The Idea and Reality of British and French Colonial Expansion, 1880–1914*. Oxford University Press.
Bernstein, Barton J. 1995. "The Atomic Bombings Reconsidered." *Foreign Affairs* 74 (1):135–152.
Betts, R. K. 1987. *Nuclear Blackmail and Nuclear Balance*. Brookings Institution Press.

Blau, Peter Michael. 1964. *Exchange and Power in Social Life*. Transaction Publishers.
Blight, James G., and Philip Brenner. 2006. *Sad and Luminous Days: Cuba's Struggle with the Superpowers after the Missile Crisis*. Rowman & Littlefield.
Blinkhorn, Martin. 1980. "Spain: The 'Spanish Problem' and the Imperial Myth." *Journal of Contemporary History* 15 (1): 5–25.
Bohlen, C. E., and R. H. Phelps. 1973. *Witness to History, 1929–1969*. Norton.
Bosworth, R. J. B. 1979. *Italy, the Least of the Great Powers: Italian Foreign Policy Before the First World War*. Cambridge University Press.
Boutros-Ghali, Boutros. 1999. *Unvanquished, a United Nations-United States Saga*. I.B. Tauris.
Boyce, D. G. 1999. *Decolonisation and the British Empire, 1775–1997*. Palgrave Macmillan.
Branscombe, Nyla R., and Daniel L. Wann. 1994. "Collective Self-Esteem Consequences of Outgroup Derogation When a Valued Social Identity Is on Trial." *European Journal of Social Psychology* 24 (6): 641–657.
Brogi, A. 2002. *A Question of Self-Esteem: The United States and the Cold War Choices in France and Italy, 1944–1958*. Praeger Publishers.
———. 2006. "Competing Missions: France, Italy, and the Rise of American Hegemony in the Mediterranean." *Diplomatic History* 30 (4): 741–770.
Brown, H. 1978. "Report of the Secretary of Defense to the Congress." Department of Defense, Washington, D.C.
Brunschwig, H. 1966. *French Colonialism, 1871–1914: Myths and Realities*. FA Praeger.
Brunschwig, Henri. 1960. *Mythes et Réalités de L'impérialisme Colonial Français 1871–1914*. A. Colin.
———. 1971. "Anglophobia and French African Policy." In *France and Britain in Africa*, edited by P. Gifford and W. R. Louis, 3–34. Yale University Press.
Brzezinski, Zbigniew. 1985. *Power and Principle*. Farrar, Straus and Giroux.
Bushman, Brad J., and Roy F. Baumeister. 1998. "Threatened Egotism, Narcissism, Self-Esteem, and Direct and Displaced Aggression: Does Self-Love or Self-Hate Lead to Violence?" *Journal of Personality and Social Psychology* 75 (1): 219.
Bushman, Brad J., Roy F. Baumeister, Sander Thomaes, Ehri Ryu, Sander Begeer, and Stephen G. West. 2009. "Looking Again, and Harder, for a Link between Low Self-Esteem and Aggression." *Journal of Personality* 77 (2): 427–446.
Buzan, Barry, and Ole Waever. 2003. *Regions and Powers: The Structure of International Security*. Vol. 91. Cambridge University Press.
Cadinu, Mara, and Cinzia Reggiori. 2002. "Discrimination of a Low-Status Outgroup: The Role of Ingroup Threat." *European Journal of Social Psychology* 32 (4): 501–515.
Cain, Peter J. 1999. *Empire and Imperialism: The Debate of the 1870s*. Thoemmes Press.
Cain, P. J., and A. G. Hopkins. 1993. *British Imperialism: Innovation and Expansion, 1688–1914*. Longman London.
Callahan, William A. 2004. "National Insecurities: Humiliation, Salvation, and Chinese Nationalism." *Alternatives: Global, Local, Political* 29 (2): 199–218.
———. 2006. "History, Identity, and Security: Producing and Consuming Nationalism in China." *Critical Asian Studies* 38 (2): 179–208.
———. 2009. "The Cartography of National Humiliation and the Emergence of China's Geobody." *Public Culture* 21 (1): 141–173.
Carroll, Eber Malcolm. 1931. *French Public Opinion and Foreign Affairs: 1870–1914*. Frank Cass.
Carter, D. B., and C. S. Signorino. 2010. "Back to the Future: Modeling Time Dependence in Binary Data." *Political Analysis* 18 (3): 271–292.

Catudal, Honoré Marc. 1989. *Soviet Nuclear Strategy from Stalin to Gorbachev: A Revolution in Soviet Military and Political Thinking.* Humanities Press.
Chamberlain, M. E. 1974. *The Scramble for Africa.* Longman.
Chang, Hui-Ching, and G. Richard Holt. 1994. "A Chinese Perspective on Face as Inter-Relational Concern." In *The Challenge of Facework: Cross-Cultural and Interpersonal Issues,* edited by Stella Ting-Toomey, 95–132. State University of New York Press.
Chasteen, John Chaler. 2001. *Born in Blood and Fire: A Concise History of Latin America.* Norton.
Cheng, Joey T., Jessica L. Tracy, and Joseph Henrich. 2010. "Pride, Personality, and the Evolutionary Foundations of Human Social Status." *Evolution and Human Behavior* 31 (5): 334–347.
Chin, Kin Wah and Leo Suryadinata. 2005. *Michael Leifer: Selected Works on Southeast Asia.* Institute of Southeast Asian Studies.
Chwe, M. S. Y. 2003. *Rational Ritual: Culture, Coordination, and Common Knowledge.* Princeton University Press.
Clare, Joe, and Vesna Danilovic. 2010. "Multiple Audiences and Reputation Building in International Conflicts." *Journal of Conflict Resolution* 54 (6): 860–882.
Clark, Chester W. 1942. "Prince Gorchakov and the Black Sea Question, 1866 a Russian Bomb That Did Not Explode." *The American Historical Review* 48 (1): 52–60.
Clausewitz, Carl von. 1956. *On War.* Jazzybee Verlag.
"Clinton Apologizes to China over Embassy Bombing." n.d. CNN.com, http://edition.cnn.com/WORLD/europe/9905/10/kosovo.china.02/.
Clunan, Anne L. 2009. *The Social Construction of Russia's Resurgence: Aspirations, Identity, and Security Interests.* Johns Hopkins University Press.
Coleman, Peter T., Jennifer S. Goldman, and Katharina Kugler. 2009. "Emotional Intractability: Gender, Anger, Aggression and Rumination in Conflict." *International Journal of Conflict Management* 20 (2): 113–131.
Coleman, Peter T., Katharina G. Kugler, and Jennifer S. Goldman. 2007. "The Privilege of Humiliation: The Effects of Social Roles and Norms on Immediate and Prolonged Aggression in Conflict." IACM 2007 Meetings Paper.
Collins, Robert O. 1969. *The Partition of Africa: Illusion or Necessity?* Vol. 67. John Wiley & Sons.
Combs, David J. Y., Gordon Campbell, Mark Jackson, and Richard H. Smith. 2010. "Exploring the Consequences of Humiliating a Moral Transgressor." *Basic and Applied Social Psychology* 32 (2): 128–143.
Commission de publication des documents relatifs aux origines de la guerre de 1914. 1929. *Documents diplomatiques français, 1ére série.* Paris.
Conklin, Alice L., Sarah Fishman, and Robert Zaretsky. 2009. *France and Its Empire Since 1870.* Oxford University Press.
Constant, Estournelles de. 1891. *La Politique Française En Tunisie.* Edited by Nourrit Paris E. Plon.
Cooke, James J. 1973. *New French Imperialism, 1880–1910: The Third Republic and Colonial Expansion.* David & Charles.
Crawford, Neta C. 2014. "Institutionalizing Passion in World Politics: Fear and Empathy." *International Theory* 6 (3): 535–557.
Crescenzi, Mark JC. 2007. "Reputation and Interstate Conflict." *American Journal of Political Science* 51 (2): 382–396.
Creswell, Robyn, and Bernard Haykel. n.d. "Battlelines: Want to Understand Jihadists, Read Their Poetry." *The New Yorker.*

Dafoe, Allan, Jonathan Renshon, and Paul Huth. 2014. "Reputation and Status as Motives for War." *Annual Review of Political Science* 17: 371–393.
Deng, Yong. 2008. *China's Struggle for Status: The Realignment of International Relations*. Cambridge University Press.
Deng, Yong, and Fei-Ling Wang. 2004. *China Rising: Power and Motivation in Chinese Foreign Policy*. Rowman & Littlefield.
De Rivera, Joseph. 2013. "Conflict over the Consequences of Humiliation." *Peace Review* 25 (2): 240–246.
De Waal, F., and F. B. M. Waal. 1997. *Good Natured: The Origins of Right and Wrong in Humans and Other Animals*. Harvard University Press.
Dobrynin, Anatoly. 1995. *In Confidence: Moscow's Ambassador to America's Six Cold War Presidents (1962–1986)*. Times Books.
Doosje, Bertjan, Nyla R. Branscombe, Russell Spears, and Antony S. R. Manstead. 1998. "Guilty by Association: When One's Group Has a Negative History." *Journal of Personality and Social Psychology* 75 (4): 872–886.
Doosje, Bertjan, Russell Spears, and Naomi Ellemers. 2002. "Social Identity as Both Cause and Effect: The Development of Group Identification in Response to Anticipated and Actual Changes in the Intergroup Status Hierarchy." *British Journal of Social Psychology* 41 (1): 57–76.
Dower, John W. 2000. *Embracing Defeat: Japan in the Wake of World War II*. WW Norton & Company.
Dugdale, E. T. S. 1931. *German Diplomatic Documents 1871–1914: Bismarck's Relations with England 1871–1890*. Vol. 1. Harper.
Duque, Marina. 2018. "Recognizing International Status: A Relational Approach" *International Studies Quarterly* 62 (1): 577–592.
East, Maurice A. 1972. "Status Discrepancy and Violence in the International System: An Empirical Analysis." In *The Analysis of International Politics: Essays in Honor of Harold and Margaret Sprout,* edited by James N. Rosenau, Vincent Davis, and Maurice A. East, 299–319. Free Press.
Edmonds, Robin. 1983. *Soviet Foreign Policy—the Brezhnev Years*. Oxford University Press.
Edwards, Robert. 2011. *The Winter War: Russia's Invasion of Finland, 1949–40*. Open Road Media.
Edwards, Donald H., and Edward A. Kravitz. 1997. "Serotonin, Social Status and Aggression." *Current Opinion in Neurobiology* 7 (6): 812–819.
Ellemers, Naomi, Paulien Kortekaas, and Jaap W Ouwerkerk. 1999. "Self-Categorisation, Commitment to the Group and Group Self-Esteem as Related but Distinct Aspects of Social Identity." *European Journal of Social Psychology* 29 (2–3): 371–389.
Eyre, D. P., and M. C. Suchman. 1996. "Status, Norms, and the Proliferation of Conventional Weapons: An Institutional Theory Approach." In *The Culture of National Security*, edited by Peter Katzenstein, 79–113. Columbia University Press.
Fattah, Khaled, and Karin M Fierke. 2009. "A Clash of Emotions: The Politics of Humiliation and Political Violence in the Middle East." *European Journal of International Relations* 15 (1): 67–93.
Fazal, Tanisha M. 2007. *State Death: The Politics and Geography of Conquest, Occupation, and Annexation*. Princeton University Press.
Ferguson, Niall. 2015. *Kissinger: 1923–1968: The Idealist*. Penguin.
Fernández, Saulo, Tamar Saguy, and Eran Halperin. 2015. "The Paradox of Humiliation: The Acceptance of an Unjust Devaluation of the Self." *Personality and Social Psychology Bulletin* 41 (7): 976–998.

Feuchtwanger, Edgar Joseph. 1993. *From Weimar to Hitler: Germany, 1918–33*. Springer.
Fieldhouse, D. K. 1961. "Imperialism: An Historiographical Revision." *The Economic History Review* 14 (2): 187–209.
———. 1973. *Economics and Empire, 1830–1914*. Cornell University Press.
Fikenscher, Sven-Eric, Lena Jaschob, and Reinhard Wolf. 2015. "Seeking Status Recognition through Military Symbols: German and Indian Armament Policies between Strategic Rationalizations and Prestige Motives." In *Recognition in International Relations: Rethinking a Political Concept in a Global Context*, edited by Christopher Daase, Caroline Fehl, Anna Geis, and Georgios Kolliarakis, 86–103. Springer.
Finn, Richard B. 1992. *Winners in Peace: MacArthur, Yoshida, and Postwar Japan*. University of California Press.
Fischer, Agneta H. 1999. "The Role of Honour-Related vs. Individualistic Values in Conceptualising Pride, Shame, and Anger: Spanish and Dutch Cultural Prototypes." *Cognition & Emotion* 13 (2): 149–179.
Fontan, Victoria. 2006. "Polarization between Occupier and Occupied in Post-Saddam Iraq: Colonial Humiliation and the Formation of Political Violence." *Terrorism and Political Violence* 18 (2): 217–238.
Forsberg, Tuomas, Regina Heller, and Reinhard Wolf. 2014. "Status and Emotions in Russian Foreign Policy." *Communist and Post-Communist Studies* 47 (3): 261–268.
Förster, Stig, Wolfgang Justin Mommsen, and Ronald Edward Robinson. 1988. *Bismarck, Europe and Africa: The Berlin Africa Conference 1884–1885 and the Onset of Partition*. Oxford University Press.
Frank, J. D. 1983. "Nuclear Arms and Prenuclear Leaders: Sociopsychological Aspects of the Nuclear Arms Race." *Political Psychology* 4 (2): 393–408.
Fraser, Thomas G., and Carl D. Murray. 2002. *America and the World Since 1945*. Palgrave Macmillan.
Fravel, M Taylor. 2005. "Regime Insecurity and International Cooperation: Explaining China's Compromises in Territorial Disputes." *International Security* 30 (2): 46–83.
Freedman, Joshua. 2016. "Status Insecurity and Temporality in World Politics." *European Journal of International Relations* 22 (4): 797–822.
———. 2105. "Status Insecurity and Temporality in World Politics." *European Journal of International Relations*, 22 (4): 797–822.
Freedman, Lawrence. 2003. *The Evolution of Nuclear Strategy*. Springer.
Fritsche, Immo, Eva Jonas, Catharina Ablasser, Magdalena Beyer, Johannes Kuban, Anna-Marie Manger, and Marlene Schultz. 2013. "The Power of We: Evidence for Group-Based Control." *Journal of Experimental Social Psychology* 49 (1): 19–32.
Fursenko, Aleksandr, and Timothy Naftali. 1998. *"One Hell of a Gamble": Khrushchev, Castro, and Kennedy, 1958–1964*. W.W. Norton & Company.
Gaidar, Yegor. 2010. *Collapse of an Empire: Lessons for Modern Russia*. Brookings Institution Press.
Galbraith, John S., and Afaf Lutfi al-Sayyid-Marsot. 1978. "The British Occupation of Egypt: Another View." *International Journal of Middle East Studies* 9 (4): 471–488.
Galtung, Johan. 1964. "A Structural Theory of Aggression." *Journal of Peace Research* 1 (2): 95–119.
Ganiage, Jean. 1971. "France, England and the Tunisian Affair." In *France and Britain in Africa*, edited by P. Gifford and W. R. Louis, 35–72. Yale University Press.

Ganiage, Jean, and Daniel Hémery. 1968. *L'Éxpansion Coloniale de La France Sous La Troisième Républque, 1871–1914*. Payot Paris.

Garthoff, Raymond L. 1985. *Détente and Confrontation: American-Soviet Relations from Nixon to Reagan*. Brookings Institution Press.

Gates, Robert M. 2014. "Putin's Challenge to the West." *The Wall Street Journal*.

Gelman, Harry. 1984. *The Brezhnev Politburo and the Decline of Detente*. Cornell University Press.

George, David Lloyd. 1938. *The Truth about the Peace Treaties*. Vol. 1. V. Gollancz.

Gessen, Masha. 2014. "Crimea Is Putin's Revenge." *Slate*. http://www.slate.com/articles/news_and_politics/foreigners/2014/03/putin_s_crimea_revenge_ever_since_the_u_s_bombed_kosovo_in_1999_putin_has.html.

Gifford, P., W. R. Louis, and A. Smith. 1967. *Britain and Germany in Africa: Imperial Rivalry and Colonial Rule: Imperial Rivalry and Colonial Rule*. Yale University Press.

Gilady, Lilach. 2017. *The Price of Prestige: Conspicuous Waste in International Relations*. University of Chicago Press.

Gilligan, James. 1996. *Violence: Our Deadly Epidemic and Its Causes*. G.P. Putnam.

Gilpin, R. 1981. *War and Change in World Politics*. Cambridge University Press.

Gilpin, Robert. 1988. "The Theory of Hegemonic War." *The Journal of Interdisciplinary History* 18 (4): 591–613.

Ginges, Jeremy A., and Scott Atran. 2008. "Humiliation and the Inertia Effect: Implications for Understanding Violence and Compromise in Intractable Intergroup Conflicts." *Journal of Cognition and Culture* 8 (3): 3–4.

Girard, Philippe. 2004. *Clinton in Haiti: The 1994 Us Invasion of Haiti*. Palgrave Macmillan.

Girardet, Raoul. 1983. *Le Nationalisme Français: Anthologie, 1871–1914*. Vol. 68. Seuil.

Goldman, Jennifer S., and Peter T. Coleman. 2000. "Intractable Conflict." Citeseer.

Goldstein, Erik, and John H. Maurer. 1994. *The Washington Conference, 1921–22: Naval Rivalry, East Asian Stability and the Road to Pearl Harbor*. Taylor & Francis.

Gollwitzer, Mario, Milena Meder, and Manfred Schmitt. 2011. "What Gives Victims Satisfaction When They Seek Revenge?" *European Journal of Social Psychology* 41 (3): 364–374.

Graham, Jesse, Jonathan Haidt, and Brian A. Nosek. 2009. "Liberals and Conservatives Rely on Different Sets of Moral Foundations." *Journal of Personality and Social Psychology* 96 (5): 1029–1046.

Gray, C. S. 1974. "The Urge to Compete: Rationales for Arms Racing." *World Politics* 26 (2). Cambridge University Press: 207–233.

Gries, Peter Hays. 2001. "Tears of Rage: Chinese Nationalist Reactions to the Belgrade Embassy Bombing." *The China Journal*, 25–43.

Gruenewald, Tara L., Margaret E Kemeny, and Najib Aziz. 2006. "Subjective Social Status Moderates Cortisol Responses to Social Threat." *Brain, Behavior, and Immunity* 20 (4): 410–419.

Halberstam, David. 2001. *War in a Time of Peace: Bush, Clinton, and the Generals*. Vol. 34. Simon & Schuster.

Hall, Todd H. 2011. "We Will Not Swallow This Bitter Fruit: Theorizing a Diplomacy of Anger." *Security Studies* 20 (4): 521–555.

———. 2015. *Emotional Diplomacy: Official Emotion on the International Stage*. Cornell University Press.

Hammond, R. J. 1961. "Economic Imperialism: Sidelights on a Stereotype." *The Journal of Economic History* 21 (4): 582–598.

Hanotaux, Gabriel. 1903. *Histoire de La France Contemporaine*. Vol. 4. Furne.

Hansard, Thomas Curson. 1891. *Parliamentary Debates. 3rd Series [1830–1891]*. T. C. Hansard.
Harkavy, R. E. n.d. "Defeat, National Humiliation, and the Revenge Motif in International Politics." *International Politics* 37 (3): 345–368.
Harnisch, Sebastian, Cornelia Frank, and Hanns W. Maull. 2011. *Role Theory in International Relations*. Taylor & Francis.
Harrison, Joseph, and Alan Hoyle. 2000. *Spain's 1898 Crisis: Regenerationism, Modernism, Postcolonialism*. Manchester University Press.
Hartling, Linda M., and Tracy Luchetta. 1999. "Humiliation: Assessing the Impact of Derision, Degradation, and Debasement." *Journal of Primary Prevention* 19 (4): 259–278.
Henderson, William Otto. 1962. *Studies in German Colonial History*. Frank Cass.
Henrich, J., and F. J. Gil-White. 2001. "The Evolution of Prestige: Freely Conferred Deference as a Mechanism for Enhancing the Benefits of Cultural Transmission." *Evolution and Human Behavior* 22 (3): 165–196.
Hess, Robert. 1967. "Germany and the Anglo-Italian Colonial Entente." In *Britain and Germany in Africa: Imperial Rivalry and Colonial Rule*, edited by P. Gifford, W. R. Louis, and A. Smith, 153–178. Yale University Press.
Hetherington, Marc J., and Michael Nelson. 2003. "Anatomy of a Rally Effect: George W. Bush and the War on Terrorism." *PS: Political Science & Politics* 36 (1): 37–42.
Hines, John G., Ellis M. Mishulovich, and John F. Shull. 1995. "Soviet Intentions 1965–1985, Volume I: An Analytic Comparison of U.S.-Soviet Assessments During the Cold War." BDM Federal, Inc. https://nsarchive2.gwu.edu//nukevault/ebb285/Vol%20II%20front%20matter.pdf.
Hitler, Adolf. 1939. *Mein Kampf: Complete and Unabridged, Fully Annotated*. Reynal & Hitchcock.
Hobsbawm, Eric. 2010. *Age of Empire 1875–1914*. Hachette UK.
Hobson, John Atkinson. 1902. *Imperialism: A Study*. J. Nisbet.
Hoffman, Aaron M. 2002. "A Conceptualization of Trust in International Relations." *European Journal of International Relations* 8 (3): 375–401.
Holloway, David. 1984. *The Soviet Union and the Arms Race*. Yale University Press.
Honneth, A. 1996. *The Struggle for Recognition: The Moral Grammar of Social Conflicts*. MIT Press.
Hopf, Ted. 1998. "The Promise of Constructivism in International Relations Theory." *International Security* 23 (1): 171–200.
———. 2002. *Social Construction of International Politics: Identities & Foreign Policies, Moscow, 1955 and 1999*. Cornell University Press.
Hopkins, A. G. 1986. "The Victorians and Africa: A Reconsideration of the Occupation of Egypt, 1882." *Journal of African History* 27 (2): 363–391.
Howard, M. 1990. *The Franco-Prussian War: The German Invasion of France, 1870–1871*. Psychology Press.
Howard, Michael Eliot. 1971. *Studies in War and Peace*. Viking Adult.
Hu, Hsien Chin. 1944. "The Chinese Concepts of 'Face'" *American Anthropologist* 46 (1): 45–64.
Huberman, Bernardo A., Christoph H. Loch, and Ayse Öncüler. 2004. "Status as a Valued Resource." *Social Psychology Quarterly* 67 (1). 103–114.
Hutchison, Emma, and Roland Bleiker. 2014. "Theorizing Emotions in World Politics." *International Theory* 6 (3): 491–514.
Hwang, Kwang-kuo. 1987. "Face and Favor: The Chinese Power Game." *American Journal of Sociology* 92 (4): 944–974.
Hyam, R. 1964. "The Partition of Africa." *The Historical Journal* 7 (1): 154–169.

———. 1999. "The Primacy of Geopolitics: The Dynamics of British Imperial Policy, 1763–1963." *The Journal of Imperial and Commonwealth History* 27 (2): 27–52.

Jervis, Robert. 1989. *The Logic of the Images in International Relations*. Columbia University Press.

Jetten, Jolanda, Tom Postmes, and Brendan J. McAuliffe. 2002. "'We're All Individuals': Group Norms of Individualism and Collectivism, Levels of Identification and Identity Threat." *European Journal of Social Psychology* 32 (2): 189–207.

Johnson, Dominic D. P., and Dominic Tierney. 2006. *Failing to Win: Perceptions of Victory and Defeat in International Politics*. Harvard University Press.

Johnston, A. I. 1995. "China's New 'Old Thinking': The Concept of Limited Deterrence." *International Security* 20 (3): 5–42.

Johnston, Alastair Iain. 2017. "Is Chinese Nationalism Rising?" *International Security* 41 (3): 7–43.

Jonas, Kai J., Marte Otten, and Bertjan Doosje. 2014. "Humiliation in Conflict: Underlying Processes and Effects on Human Thought and Behavior." In *Social Conflict within and between Groups*, edited by Carsten K. W. De Dreu, 51–68. Psychology Press.

Jones, Daniel M., Stuart A. Bremer, and J. David Singer. 1996. "Militarized Interstate Disputes, 1816–1992: Rationale, Coding Rules, and Empirical Patterns." *Conflict Management and Peace Science* 15 (2): 163–213.

Kang, David C. 2008. *China Rising: Peace, Power, and Order in East Asia*. Columbia University Press.

Karaganov, Sergey. 2014. "Europe and Russia: Preventing a New Cold War." *Russia in Global Affairs*.

Kaser, Michael, and Archie Brown. 1977. *Soviet Union Since the Fall of Khrushchev*. Springer.

Katzenstein, Peter J. 1996. *The Culture of National Security: Norms and Identity in World Politics*. Columbia University Press.

Kaufman, Alison A. n.d. "The 'Century of Humiliation' and China's National Narratives." Testimony before the U.S.-China Economic and Security Review Commission Hearing on "China's Narratives Regarding National Security Policy."

Kaufman, Alison Adcock. 2010. "The 'Century of Humiliation' Then and Now: Chinese Perceptions of the International Order." *Pacific Focus* 25 (1): 1–33.

Kelly, George H. 1955. *The Political Development of the French Overseas Empire*. Vol. 3. Stanford University Press.

Kemeny, Margaret E. 2009. "Psychobiological Responses to Social Threat: Evolution of a Psychological Model in Psychoneuroimmunology." *Brain, Behavior, and Immunity* 23 (1): 1–9.

Kennedy, A. L. 1953. *Salisbury, 1830–1903: Portrait of a Statesman*. J. Murray.

Kessler, Thomas, and Susan Hollbach. 2005. "Group-Based Emotions as Determinants of Ingroup Identification." *Journal of Experimental Social Psychology* 41 (6): 677–685.

Kessler, Thomas, Amélie Mummendey, Friedrich Funke, Rupert Brown, Jens Binder, Hanna Zagefka, Jacques-Philippe Leyens, Stéphanie Demoulin, and Annemie Maquil. 2010. "We All Live in Germany but . . . Ingroup Projection, Group-Based Emotions and Prejudice Against Immigrants." *European Journal of Social Psychology* 40 (6): 985–997.

Khashan, Hilal. 1997. "The New World Order and the Tempo of Militant Islam." *British Journal of Middle Eastern Studies* 24 (1): 5–24.

Khrushchev, Nikita Sergeevich. 1971. *Khrushchev Remembers*. Vol. 1. Little, Brown.

Khrushchev, Nikita Sergeevich, and Sergei Khrushchev. 2007. *Memoirs of Nikita Khrushchev*. Vol. 3. Pennsylvania State University Press.

Khrushchev, Sergei. 2000. *Nikita Khrushchev and the Creation of a Superpower.* Pennsylvania State University Press.

Kinsella, D., and J. S. Chima. 2001. "Symbols of Statehood: Military Industrialization and Public Discourse in India." *Review of International Studies* 27 (3): 353–373.

Kissinger, H. 1979. *White House Years.* Simon & Schuster.

Klein, Donald C. 1991. "The Humiliation Dynamic: An Overview." *Journal of Primary Prevention* 12 (2): 93–121.

Knaplund, P. 1944. *Letters from the Berlin Embassy, 1871–1874, 1880–1885.* U.S. Government Printing Office.

Kolkowicz, Roman. 1971. "Strategic Parity and Beyond: Soviet Perspectives." *World Politics* 23 (3): 431–451.

Kratochwil, Friedrich V. 1991. *Rules, Norms, and Decisions: On the Conditions of Practical and Legal Reasoning in International Relations and Domestic Affairs.* Vol. 2. Cambridge University Press.

Kull, S. 1985. "Nuclear Nonsense." *Foreign Policy* 58: 28–52.

——. 1988. *Minds at War: Nuclear Reality and the Inner Conflicts of Defense Policymakers.* Basic Books.

Kulski, Władysław Wszebór. 1973. *The Soviet Union in World Affairs: A Documented Analysis, 1964–1972.* Syracuse University Press.

Kydd, Andrew H. 2005. *Trust and Mistrust in International Relations.* Princeton University Press.

Lacey, David. 2011. "The Role of Humiliation in the Palestinian/Israeli Conflict in Gaza." *Psychology & Society* 4 (1): 76–92.

Laden, Osama Bin. 2005. *Messages to the World: The Statements of Osama Bin Laden.* Verso.

Lai, Brian, and Dan Reiter. 2005. "Rally 'Round the Union Jack': Public Opinion and the Use of Force in the United Kingdom, 1948–2001." *International Studies Quarterly* 49 (2): 255–272.

Lambeth, B. S. 1979. "The Political Potential of Soviet Equivalence." *International Security* 4 (2): 22–39.

Langer, William Leonard. 1951. *The Diplomacy of Imperialism: 1890–1902.* Knopf.

Langer, W. L. 1925. "The European Powers and the French Occupation of Tunis, 1878–1881, I." *The American Historical Review* 31 (1): 55–78.

——. 1935. "A Critique of Imperialism." *Foreign Affairs* 14: 102.

Larson, Deborah Welch, and Alexei Shevchenko. 2003. "Shortcut to Greatness: The New Thinking and the Revolution in Soviet Foreign Policy." *International Organization* 57 (1): 77–110.

——. 2014. "Russia Says No: Power, Status, and Emotions in Foreign Policy." *Communist and Post-Communist Studies* 47 (3–4): 269–279.

Larson, D., and A. Shevchenko. 2001. "Bringing Russia into the Club." In *The New Great Power Coalition: Toward a World Concert of Nations*, edited by R. N. Rosecrance, 311–326. Rowman & Littlefield.

Larson, D. W., and A. Shevchenko. 2010. "Status Seekers: Chinese and Russian Responses to Us Primacy." *International Security* 34 (4): 63–95.

Leach, Colin Wayne, Aarti Iyer, and Anne Pedersen. 2006. "Anger and Guilt About Ingroup Advantage Explain the Willingness for Political Action." *Personality and Social Psychology Bulletin* 32 (9): 1232–1245.

Leask, Phil. 2013. "Losing Trust in the World: Humiliation and Its Consequences." *Psychodynamic Practice* 19 (2): 129–142.

Lebow, R. N. 2008. *A Cultural Theory of International Relations.* Cambridge University Press.

Leidner, Bernhard, Hammad Sheikh, and Jeremy Ginges. 2012. "Affective Dimensions of Intergroup Humiliation." *PloS One* 7 (9): 46375.
Lemke, Douglas. 1997. "The Continuation of History: Power Transition Theory and the End of the Cold War." *Journal of Peace Research* 34 (1): 23–36.
Leng, R. J. 1983. "When Will They Ever Learn?" *Journal of Conflict Resolution* 27 (3): 379–419.
Lenin, V. I. 1917. *Imperialism: The Highest Stage of Capitalism*. Resistance Books.
Levy, Jack S. 1983. *War in the Modern Great Power System: 1495–1975*. University Press of Kentucky.
Lind, Jennifer. 2011. *Sorry States: Apologies in International Politics*. Cornell University Press.
Lindemann, Thomas. 2010. *Causes of War: The Struggle for Recognition*. ECPR Press.
Lindemann, Thomas, and Erik Ringmar. 2015. *International Politics of Recognition*. Routledge.
Lindner, E. 2006. *Making Enemies: Humiliation and International Conflict*. Praeger Security International.
Lindner, E. G. 2000. "The 'Framing Power' of International Organizations, and the Cost of Humiliation." Unpublished Manuscript.
Lindner, Evelin Gerda. 2002. "Healing the Cycles of Humiliation: How to Attend to the Emotional Aspects of 'Unsolvable' Conflicts and the Use of Humiliation Entrepreneurship." *Peace and Conflict: Journal of Peace Psychology* 8 (2): 125–138.
Link, Arthur, David W. Hirst and John E. Little. 1985. *The Papers of Woodrow Wilson* XL, 536. Princeton University Press.
Lo, Bobo. 2002. *Russian Foreign Policy in the Post-Soviet Era*. Palgrave Macmillan.
———. 2008. *Vladimir Putin and the Evolution of Russian Foreign Policy*. John Wiley & Sons.
Loch, C., M. Yaziji, and C. Langen. 2001. "The Fight for the Alpha Position: Channeling Status Competition in Organizations." *European Management Journal* 19 (1): 16–25.
Lopez, Anthony C., Rose McDermott, and Michael Bang Petersen. 2011. "States in Mind: Evolution, Coalitional Psychology, and International Politics." *International Security* 36 (2): 48–83.
Louis, William Roger. 1971. "The Berlin Congo Conference." In *France and Britain in Africa*, edited by P. Gifford and W. R. Louis, 167–220. Yale University Press.
Lowe, Cedric James, and Frank Marzari. 2001. *Italian Foreign Policy, 1870–1940*. Vol. 8. Taylor & Francis.
Lowenheim, O., and G. Heimann. 2008. "Revenge in International Politics." *Security Studies* 17 (4): 685–724.
Luhtanen, Riia, and Jennifer Crocker. 1992. "A Collective Self-Esteem Scale: Self-Evaluation of One's Social Identity." *Personality and Social Psychology Bulletin* 18 (3).: 302–318.
Lukyanov, Fyodor. 2016. "Putin's Foreign Policy." *Foreign Affairs*.
Luo, Zhitian. 1993. "National Humiliation and National Assertion: The Chines Response to the Twenty-One Demands." *Modern Asian Studies* 27 (2): 297–319.
Luttwak, Edward. 1972. *The Strategic Balance, 1972*. Library Press.
MacDonald, Paul K., and Joseph M. Parent. 2011. "Graceful Decline? The Surprising Success of Great Power Retrenchment." *International Security* 35 (4): 7–44.
Mackie, Diane M., Thierry Devos, and Eliot R. Smith. 2000. "Intergroup Emotions: Explaining Offensive Action Tendencies in an Intergroup Context." *Journal of Personality and Social Psychology* 79 (4): 602–616.

Mackie, Diane M., Eliot R Smith, and Devin G. Ray. 2008. "Intergroup Emotions and Intergroup Relations." *Social and Personality Psychology Compass* 2 (5): 1866–1880.
Macleod, Jenny. 2008. *Defeat and Memory: Cultural Histories of Military Defeat in the Modern Era*. Springer.
Malinova, Olga. 2014. "Obsession with Status and *Ressentiment*: Historical Backgrounds of the Russian Discursive Identity Construction." *Communist and Post-Communist Studies* 47 (3): 291–303.
Marcus-Newhall, Amy, William C. Pedersen, Mike Carlson, and Norman Miller. 2000. "Displaced Aggression Is Alive and Well: A Meta-Analytic Review." *Journal of Personality and Social Psychology* 78 (4): 678–689.
Margalit, Avishai. 1998. *The Decent Society*. Harvard University Press.
———. 2002. *The Ethics of Memory*. Harvard University Press.
Markey, D. 1999. "Prestige and the Origins of War: Returning to Realism's Roots." *Security Studies* 8 (4): 126–172.
Marr, Jennifer Carson, and Stefan Thau. 2014. "Falling from Great (and Not-so-Great) Heights: How Initial Status Position Influences Performance After Status Loss." *Academy of Management Journal* 57 (1): 223–248.
Marshall, P. J. 2005. *The Making and Unmaking of Empires: Britain, India, and America c. 1750–1783*. Oxford University Press.
Martens, Jason P., Jessica L. Tracy, and Azim F. Shariff. 2012. "Status Signals: Adaptive Benefits of Displaying and Observing the Nonverbal Expressions of Pride and Shame." *Cognition & Emotion* 26 (3): 390–406.
McCoy, Shannon K., and Brenda Major. 2003. "Group Identification Moderates Emotional Responses to Perceived Prejudice." *Personality and Social Psychology Bulletin* 29 (8): 1005–1017.
McNamara, Robert. 1964. "Fiscal Year 1964 Posture Statement." Department of Defense Appropriations for 1964, Hearings before the Subcommittee of the Committee on Appropriations, United States Senate, Eighty-Eight Congress.
———. 1967. "McNamara Statement Regarding Military Authorizations and Defense Appropriations for FY 1968 before the Senate Appropriations Committee." Hearings on Military Posture by the House Armed Services Committee.
Mearsheimer, J. J. 2003. *The Tragedy of Great Power Politics*. W.W. Norton & Company.
Mee, Charles L. 1980. *The End of Order, Versailles, 1919*. E.P. Dutton.
Mercer, J. 2005. "Rationality and Psychology in International Politics." *International Organization* 59 (1): 77–106.
Mercer, Jonathan. 2014. "Feeling Like a State: Social Emotion and Identity." *International Theory* 6 (3): 515–535.
———. 2017. "The Illusion of International Prestige." *International Security* 41 (4): 133–168.
Meyer, Karl E., and Shareen Blair Brysac. 2009. *Tournament of Shadows: The Great Game and the Race for Empire in Central Asia*. Basic Books.
Midlarsky, Manus I. 1975. *On War: Political Violence in the International System*. New York: Free Press.
Miller, Norman, William C. Pedersen, Mitchell Earleywine, and Vicki E. Pollock. 2003. "A Theoretical Model of Triggered Displaced Aggression." *Personality and Social Psychology Review* 7 (1): 75–97.
Miller, William Ian. 1995. *Humiliation: And Other Essays on Honor, Social Discomfort, and Violence*. Cornell University Press.

Miokyan, Sergo. 2012. *The Soviet Cuban Missile Crisis: Castron, Mikoyan, Kennedy, Khrushchev and the Missiles of November.* Stanford University Press.

Mitzen, Jennifer. 2006. "Ontological Security in World Politics: State Identity and the Security Dilemma." *European Journal of International Relations* 12 (3): 341–370.

Moïsi, D. 2010. *The Geopolitics of Emotion: How Cultures of Fear, Humiliation and Hope Are Reshaping the World.* Anchor Books.

Mommsen, W. J. 1982. *Theories of Imperialism.* University of Chicago Press.

———. 1995. *Imperial Germany 1867–1918: Politics, Culture, and Society in an Authoritarian State.* Arnold London.

Monger, G. W. 1976. *The End of Isolation: British Foreign Policy 1900–1907.* Greenwood Press.

Mosquera, Patricia M. Rodriguez, Antony S. R. Manstead, and Agneta H. Fischer. 2000. "The Role of Honor-Related Values in the Elicitation, Experience, and Communication of Pride, Shame, and Anger: Spain and the Netherlands Compared." *Personality and Social Psychology Bulletin* 26 (7): 833–844.

Mullen, Brian, Rupert Brown, and Colleen Smith. 1992. "Ingroup Bias as a Function of Salience, Relevance, and Status: An Integration." *European Journal of Social Psychology* 22 (2): 103–122.

Mummendey, Amelie, Thomas Kessler, Andreas Klink, and Rosemarie Mielke. 1999. "Strategies to Cope with Negative Social Identity: Predictions by Social Identity Theory and Relative Deprivation Theory." *Journal of Personality and Social Psychology* 76 (2): 229–245.

Mummendey, Amélie, and Bernd Simon. 1989. "Better or Different? III: The Impact of Importance of Comparison Dimension and Relative in-Group Size upon Intergroup Discrimination." *British Journal of Social Psychology* 28 (1): 1–16.

Murphy, Agnes. 1968. *The Ideology of French Imperialism, 1871–1881.* H. Fertig.

Murray, M. 2010. "Identity, Insecurity, and Great Power Politics: The Tragedy of German Naval Ambition Before the First World War." *Security Studies* 19 (4): 656–688.

Nationale, Assemblée. 1882. "Débats Parlementaires." *Journal Officiel de La République Française.*

"NATO Hits Chinese Embassy." n.d. BBC News. http://news.bbc.co.uk/2/hi/europe/338424.stm.

Nayar, Baldev Raj, and Thazha Varkey Paul. 2003. *India in the World Order: Searching for Major-Power Status.* Cambridge University Press.

Neiberg, Michael. 2015. *Potsdam: The End of World War II and the Remaking of Europe.* Basic Books.

Neumann, Iver B. 2016. *Russia and the Idea of Europe: A Study in Identity and International Relations.* Routledge.

Newbury, C. W., and A. S. Kanya-Forstner. 1969. "French Policy and the Origins of the Scramble for West Africa." *The Journal of African History* 10 (2): 253–276.

Newhouse, J., and J. Newhouse. 1989. *Cold Dawn: The Story of Salt.* Pergamon-Brassey's.

Nichols, Thomas M. 1993. *The Sacred Cause: Civil-Military Conflict over Soviet National Security, 1917–1992.* Cornell University Press.

Nisbett, Richard E., and Dov Cohen. 1996. *Culture of Honor: The Psychology of Violence in the South.* Westview Press.

Nixon, R. 1978. *The Memoirs of Richard Nixon.* Grosset & Dunlap.

"Not a Cold War, but a Cold Tiff." 2007. *The Economist*, February 2. https://www.economist.com/international/2007/02/15/not-a-cold-war-but-a-cold-tiff.

Novati, Giampaolo Calchi. 1994. "Italy in the Triangle of the Horn: Too Many Corners for a Half Power." *Journal of Modern African Studies* 32 (3): 369–385.
Ohbuchi, Ken-ichi, Masuyo Kameda, and Nariyuki Agarie. 1989. "Apology as Aggression Control: Its Role in Mediating Appraisal of and Response to Harm." *Journal of Personality and Social Psychology* 56 (2): 219–227.
O'Neill, B. 2006. "Nuclear Weapons and National Prestige." Unpublished Manuscript.
O'Neill, Barry. 2001. *Honors, Symbols and War*. University of Michigan Press.
Oren, Michael B. 2003. *Six Days of War: June 1967 and the Making of the Modern Middle East*. Presidio Press.
Organski, Jacek Kugler, A. F. K. 1980. *The War Ledger*. University of Chicago Press.
Ortega, José Varela. 1980. "Aftermath of Splendid Disaster: Spanish Politics before and after the Spanish American War of 1898." *Journal of Contemporary History* 15 (2): 317–344.
Osnos, Evan, David Remnick, and Joshua Yaffa. 2107. "Trump, Putin and the New Cold War." *The New Yorker*.
Otten, Marte, and Kai J. Jonas. 2014. "Humiliation as an Intense Emotional Experience: Evidence from the Electro-Encephalogram." *Social Neuroscience* 9 (1): 23–35.
Owens, David A., Robert I. Sutton, and M. E. Turner. 2001. "Status Contests in Meetings: Negotiating the Informal Order." *Groups at Work: Theory and Research* 14: 299–316.
Pagano, Sabrina J., and Yuen J. Huo. 2007. "The Role of Moral Emotions in Predicting Support for Political Actions in Post-War Iraq." *Political Psychology* 28 (2): 227–255.
Paine, Sarah CM. 2005. *The Sino-Japanese War of 1894–1895: Perceptions, Power, and Primacy*. Cambridge University Press.
Pakenham, Thomas. 1992. *Scramble for Africa, 1876–1912*. HarperCollins.
Paul, T. V., Deborah Welch Larson, and William C. Wohlforth. 2014. *Status in World Politics*. Cambridge University Press.
Paul, T. V., and M. Shankar. 2014. "'Status Accommodation through Institutional Means: India's Rise and Global Order." In *Status in World Politics*, edited by T. V. Paul, Deborah Welch Larson, and William C. Wohlforth, 165–191. Cambridge University Press.
Pedersen, William C., Brad J. Bushman, Eduardo A. Vasquez, and Norman Miller. 2008. "Kicking the (Barking) Dog Effect: The Moderating Role of Target Attributes on Triggered Displaced Aggression." *Personality and Social Psychology Bulletin* 34 (10): 1382–1395.
"Person of the Year 2007—Putin Q&A: Full Transcript." n.d. *Time Magazine*. http://content.time.com/time/specials/2007/personoftheyear/article/0,28804,1690753_1690757_1695787,00.html.
Petersen, Roger D. 2002. *Understanding Ethnic Violence: Fear, Hatred, and Resentment in Twentieth-Century Eastern Europe*. Cambridge University Press.
Petroff, Serge. 1988. *The Red Eminence: A Biography of Mikhail A. Suslov*. Kingston Press.
Pettit, Nathan C., Kevyn Yong, and Sandra E. Spataro. 2010. "Holding Your Place: Reactions to the Prospect of Status Gains and Losses." *Journal of Experimental Social Psychology* 46 (2): 396–401.
Pflanze, O. 1990. *Bismarck and the Development of Germany, vol. 3: The Period of Fortification, 1880–1898*. Princeton University Press.
Pipes, Richard. 2009. "Craving to Be a Great Power." *Moscow Times*, July 15.
Pitt-Rivers, Julian. 1965. "Honour and Social Status." In *Honour and Shame: The Values of Mediterranean Society*, edited by Peristiany, J. G., 21–77. Weidenfeld and Nicolson.

Platt, D. C. M. 1968. "Economic Factors in British Policy During the 'New Imperialism.'" *Past & Present*, no. 39: 120–138.

Pogge von Strandmann, Hartmut. 1988. "Consequences of the Foundation of the German Empire: Colonial Expansion and the Process of Political-Economic Rationalization." In *Bismarck, Europe and Africa. The Berlin Africa Conference and the Onset of Partition*, edited by Stig Förster, Wolfgang Justin Mommsen, and Ronald Edward Robinson, 105– 120. Oxford University Press.

Porter, Andrew N. 1980. *The Origins of the South African War: Joseph Chamberlain and the Diplomacy of Imperialism, 1895–99*. Manchester University Press.

Porter, B. 1975. *The Lion's Share: A Short History of British Imperialism, 1850–1970*. Longman.

Power, Thomas Francis. 1944. *Jules Ferry and the Renaissance of French Imperialism*. King's Crown Press.

Quester, G. H. 2000. *Nuclear Monopoly*. Transaction Publishing.

Remnick, David. 2014. "Watching the Eclipse." *The New Yorker*.

Renshon, Jonathan. 2015. "Losing Face and Sinking Costs: Experimental Evidence on the Judgment of Political and Military Leaders." *International Organization* 69 (3): 659–695.

———. 2016. "Status Deficits and War." *International Organization* 70 (3): 513–550.

———. 2017. *Fighting for Status: Hierarchy and Conflict in World Politics*. Princeton University Press.

Rhodes, Richard. 2008. *Arsenals of Folly: The Making of the Nuclear Arms Race*. Vintage Books.

Ridgeway, C. 1991. "The Social Construction of Status Value: Gender and Other Nominal Characteristics." *Social Forces* 70 (2): 367–386.

Ringmar, Erik. 1996. "On the Ontological Status of the State." *European Journal of International Relations* 2 (4): 439–466.

———. 2002. "The Recognition Game Soviet Russia Against the West." *Cooperation and Conflict* 37 (2): 115–136.

Roberts, Lucien E. 1946. "Italy and the Egyptian Question, 1878–1882." *The Journal of Modern History* 18 (4): 314–332.

Roberts, S. S. H. 1963. *The History of French Colonial Policy, 1870–1925*. F. Cass.

Robinson, Howard. 1922. *The Development of the British Empire*. Houghton Mifflin Company.

Robinson, R. E., and J. Gallagher. 1965. *Africa and the Victorians: The Official Mind of Imperialism*. Vol. 131. Macmillan.

Robinson, Ronald. 1988. "The Conference in Berlin and the Future in Africa, 1884–1885." In *Bismarck, Europe, and Africa: The Berlin Africa Conference 1884–1885 and the Onset of Partition*, edited by Stig Förster, Wolfgang Justin Mommsen, and Ronald Edward Robinson, 1–35. Oxford University Press.

Rosenberg, D. A. 1983. "The Origins of Overkill: Nuclear Weapons and American Strategy, 1945–1960." *International Security* 7 (4): 3–71.

Ross, A. A. G. 2006. "Coming in from the Cold: Constructivism and Emotions." *European Journal of International Relations* 12 (2): 197–222.

Ross, Robert S. 2009. "China's Naval Nationalism: Sources, Prospects, and the Us Response." *International Security* 34 (2): 46–81.

Rumsfeld, D. 1978. "Report of Secretary of Defense Donald H. Rumsfeld to the Congress on the FY 1978 Budget, FY 1979 Authorization Request and FY 1978–1982 Defense Programs."

"Russia's Lower House to Consider US Citizens' Blacklist." 2016. *Russia Today*.

Sagan, S. D. 1996. "Why Do States Build Nuclear Weapons?: Three Models in Search of a Bomb." *International Security* 21 (3): 54–86.

Sanderson, G. N. 1965. *England, Europe & the Upper Nile, 1882–1899: A Study in the Partition of Africa*. Edinburgh University Press.

———. 1974. "The European Partition of Africa: Coincidence or Conjuncture?" *The Journal of Imperial and Commonwealth History* 3 (1). Routledge: 1–54.

———. 1988. "British Informal Empire, Imperial Ambitions, Defensive Strategies and the Anglo-Portuguese Treaty of 1884." In *Bismarck, Europe, and Africa: The Berlin Africa Conference 1884–1885 and the Onset of Partition*, edited by Stig Förster, Wolfgang Justin Mommsen, and Ronald Edward Robinson, 173–198. Oxford University Press.

Sapolsky, Robert M. 1992. "Cortisol Concentrations and the Social Significance of Rank Instability Among Wild Baboons." *Psychoneuroendocrinology* 17 (6): 701–709.

Sasley, Brent E. 2011. "Theorizing States' Emotions." *International Studies Review* 13 (3): 452–476.

Saurette, P. 2006. "You Dissin Me? Humiliation and Post 9/11 Global Politics." *Review of International Studies* 32 (3): 495–522.

Scheepers, Daan, and Naomi Ellemers. 2005. "When the Pressure Is up: The Assessment of Social Identity Threat in Low and High Status Groups." *Journal of Experimental Social Psychology* 41 (2): 192–200.

Scheff, Thomas J. 1994. *Bloody Revenge: Emotions, Nationalism, and War*. Westview Press.

Schivelbusch, Wolfgang. 2003. *The Culture of Defeat: On National Trauma, Mourning, and Recovery*. Macmillan.

Schlesinger, J. R. 1974. "Annual Defense Department Report, FY 1975." Washington, D.C.: U.S. Government Printing Office, 1975.

———. 1975. "Annual Defense Department Report, FY 1976." Washington, D.C.: U.S. Government Printing Office 1976.

Schölch, A. 1976. "The 'Men on the Spot' and the English Occupation of Egypt in 1882." *Historical Journal* 19 (3): 773–785.

Scott, David. 2007. *China Stands Up: The PRC and the International System*. Routledge.

———. 2008a. *China and the International System, 1840–1949: Power, Presence, and Perceptions in a Century of Humiliation*. State University of New York Press.

———. 2008b. "India's Drive for a 'Blue Water' Navy." *Journal of Military and Strategic Studies* 10 (2): 1–42.

Seger, Charles R., Eliot R. Smith, and Diane M. Mackie. 2009. "Subtle Activation of a Social Categorization Triggers Group-Level Emotions." *Journal of Experimental Social Psychology* 45 (3): 460–467.

Shariff, Azim F., and Jessica L. Tracy. 2009. "Knowing Who's Boss: Implicit Perceptions of Status from the Nonverbal Expression of Pride." *Emotion* 9 (5): 631–639.

Shepherd, Lee, Russell Spears, and Antony S. R. Manstead. 2013. "'This Will Bring Shame on Our Nation': The Role of Anticipated Group-Based Emotions on Collective Action." *Journal of Experimental Social Psychology* 49 (1): 42–57.

Shevtsova, Lilia. 2007. *Russia—Lost in Transition: The Yeltsin and Putin Legacies*. Carnegie Endowment.

———. 2010. *Lonely Power: Why Russia Has Failed to Become the West and the West Is Weary of Russia*. Carnegie Endowment.

———. 2014. "Putin's Perspective Abroad Swayed by Quest for Popularity at Home." NPR. http://www.npr.org/2014/03/21/292471004/putins-perspective-abroad-swayed-by-quest-for-popularity-at-home.

Shirer, William L. 1991. *The Rise and Fall of the Third Reich: A History of Nazi Germany*. Random House.
Shirk, Susan L. 2007. *China: Fragile Superpower: How China's Internal Politics Could Derail Its Peaceful Rise*. Oxford University Press.
Sick, Gary. 1985. *All Fall Down: America's Fateful Encounter with Iran*. I.B. Tauris.
Siegrist, Johannes. 1984. "Threat to Social Status and Cardiovascular Risk." *Psychotherapy and Psychosomatics* 42 (1): 90–96.
Simes, Dimitri K. 2007. "Losing Russia: The Costs of Renewed Confrontation." *Foreign Affairs* 86: 36–44.
Simons, Geoff. 1997. *The Vietnam Syndrome: Impact on US Foreign Policy*. Springer.
Singer, J. David. 1988. "Reconstructing the Correlates of War Dataset on Material Capabilities of States, 1816–1985." *International Interactions* 14 (2): 115–132.
Sivanathan, Niro, and Nathan C Pettit. 2010. "Protecting the Self Through Consumption: Status Goods as Affirmational Commodities." *Journal of Experimental Social Psychology* 46 (3): 564–570.
Small, Deborah A., Jennifer S. Lerner, and Baruch Fischhoff. 2006. "Emotion Priming and Attributions for Terrorism: Americans' Reactions in a National Field Experiment." *Political Psychology* 27 (2): 289–298.
Smith, Eliot R. 2014. "Social Identity and Social Emotions: Toward New Conceptualizations of Prejudice." In *Affect, Cognition and Stereotyping: Interactive Processes in Group Perception*, edited by Diane Mackie and David L. Hamilton, 297–315. Academic Press.
Smith, Eliot R., Charles R. Seger, and Diane M. Mackie. 2007. "Can Emotions Be Truly Group Level? Evidence Regarding Four Conceptual Criteria." *Journal of Personality and Social Psychology* 93 (3): 431–446.
Smith, E. R. 1993. "Social Identity and Social Emotions: Toward New Conceptualizations of Prejudice." In *Affect, Cognition, and Stereotyping: Interactive Processes in Group Perception*, edited by Diane Mackie and David L. Hamilton. Academic Press.
Smith, W. D. 1978. *The German Colonial Empire*. University of North Carolina Press.
Snyder, J. L. 1991. *Myths of Empire: Domestic Politics and International Ambition*. Cornell University Press.
Spears, Russell, Bertjan Doosje, and Naomi Ellemers. 1997. "Self-Stereotyping in the Face of Threats to Group Status and Distinctiveness: The Role of Group Identification." *Personality and Social Psychology Bulletin* 23 (5): 538–553.
Statman, Daniel. 2000. "Humiliation, Dignity and Self-Respect." *Philosophical Psychology* 13 (4): 523–540.
Steele, Jonathan. 1984. *Soviet Power*. Simon & Schuster.
Stein, Janice Gross. 2013. "Threat Perception in International Relations." In *The Oxford Handbook of Political Psychology*, edited by L. Huddy, D. O. Sears and Jack S. Levy, 364–394. Oxford University Press.
Stein, Rachel M. 2015. "War and Revenge: Explaining Conflict Initiation by Democracies." *American Political Science Review* 109 (3): 556–573.
Stengers, Jean. 1962. "L'Imperialisme Colonial de La Fin Du Xix-Siecle: Mythe Ou Realite." *The Journal of African History* 3 (2): 469–491.
———. 1971. "King Leopold and Expansion in the Congo." In *France and Britain in Africa*, edited by P. Gifford and W. R. Louis, 121–166. Yale University Press.
Stent, Angela E. 2015. *The Limits of Partnership: US-Russian Relations in the Twenty-First Century*. Princeton University Press.
Stoecker, H. 1986. *German Imperialism in Africa: From the Beginnings until the Second World War*. Hurst & Co.

Stollberg, Janine, Immo Fritsche, and Anna Bäcker. 2015. "Striving for Group Agency: Threat to Personal Control Increases the Attractiveness of Agentic Groups." *Frontiers in Psychology* 6: 649–665.

Strauss, William Louis. 1971. *Joseph Chamberlain and the Theory of Imperialism*. H. Fertig.

Stürmer, Stefan, and Bernd Simon. 2009. "Pathways to Collective Protest: Calculation, Identification, or Emotion? A Critical Analysis of the Role of Group-Based Anger in Social Movement Participation." *Journal of Social Issues* 65 (4): 681–705.

Sumner, B. H. 1933. "The Secret Franco-Russian Treaty of 3 March 1859." *The English Historical Review* 48 (189): 65–83.

Swaine, Michael D, Sara A Daly, and Peter W Greenwood. 2000. *Interpreting China's Grand Strategy: Past, Present, and Future*. Rand Corporation.

Tajfel, H. 2010. *Social Identity and Intergroup Relations*. Vol. 7. Cambridge University Press.

Tajfel, Henri, and John C. Turner. 1979. "An Integrative Theory of Intergroup Conflict." In *The Social Psychology of Intergroup Relations*, edited by William G. Austin and Stephen Worchel, 33–47. Brooks/Cole.

Tammen, Ronald L., Jacek Kugler, Douglas Lemke, Allan C. Stam, Mark A. Abdollahian, Carole Alsharabati, Brian Efird, and A. F. K. Organski. 2000. *Power Transitions: Strategies for the Twenty-First Century*. Chatham House.

Taubman, William. 2003. *Khrushchev: The Man and His Era*. W.W. Norton & Company.

Taylor, A. J. P., and A. J. Percivale. 1967. *Germany's First Bid for Colonies, 1884–1885: A Move in Bismarck's European Policy*. Archon Books.

Taylor, Alan John Percivale. 2011. *Bismarck: The Man and the Statesman*. Random House.

Thayer, Bradley A. 2000. "Bringing in Darwin: Evolutionary Theory, Realism, and International Politics." *International Security* 25 (2): 124–151.

Thies, Cameron G., and Marijke Breuning. 2012. "Integrating Foreign Policy Analysis and International Relations Through Role Theory." *Foreign Policy Analysis* 8 (1): 1–4.

Thornton, A. P. 1965. *Doctrines of Imperialism*. John Wiley & Sons.

Tiedens, Larissa Z. 2001. "Anger and Advancement versus Sadness and Subjugation: The Effect of Negative Emotion Expressions on Social Status Conferral." *Journal of Personality and Social Psychology* 80 (1): 86–94.

Tiedens, Larissa Z., Phoebe C. Ellsworth, and Batja Mesquita. 2000. "Sentimental Stereotypes: Emotional Expectations for High-and Low-Status Group Members." *Personality and Social Psychology Bulletin* 26 (5): 560–575.

Ting-Toomey, Stella, Ge Gao, Paula Trubisky, Zhizhong Yang, Hak Soo Kim, Sung-Ling Lin, and Tsukasa Nishida. 1991. "Culture, Face Maintenance, and Styles of Handling Interpersonal Conflict: A Study in Five Cultures." *International Journal of Conflict Management* 2 (4): 275–296.

Tir, J. 2010. "Territorial Diversion: Diversionary Theory of War and Territorial Conflict." *The Journal of Politics* 72 (2): 413–425.

Tir, J., P. Schafer, P. F. Diehl, and G. Goertz. 1998. "Territorial changes, 1816–1996: Procedures and data." *Conflict Management and Peace Science* 16 (1): 89–115.

Tomz, Michael, Jessica Weeks, and Keren Yarhi-Milo. "Public Opinion and Decisions About Military Force in Democracies." Forthcoming.

Tooby, John, Leda Cosmides, and Michael E. Price. 2006. "Cognitive Adaptations for N-Person Exchange: The Evolutionary Roots of Organizational Behavior." *Managerial and Decision Economics* 27 (2–3): 103–129.

Torres, Walter J., and Raymond M. Bergner. 2012. "Severe Public Humiliation: Its Nature, Consequences, and Clinical Treatment." *Psychotherapy* 49 (4): 492–501.

Townsend, M. E. 1922. *Origins of Modern German Colonialism, 1871–1885*. Columbia University Press.

Townsend, M. E., C. H. Peake, and W. C. Langsam. 1941. *European Colonial Expansion since 1871*. J.B. Lippincott.

Trachtenberg, M. 1985. "The Influence of Nuclear Weapons in the Cuban Missile Crisis." *International Security* 10 (1): 137–163.

———. 1988. "A 'Wasting Asset': American Strategy and the Shifting Nuclear Balance, 1949–1954." *International Security* 13 (3): 5–49.

———. 2017. "The Soviet Military Buildup." Unpublished Manuscript.

Trager, R. 2012. "Long-Term Consequences of Aggressive Diplomacy: European Relations After Austrian-Crimean War Threats." *Security Studies* 12 (21): 232–265.

Trenin, Dmitri. 2006. "Russia Leaves the West." *Foreign Affairs* 85 (4): 87–96.

Trotter, William R. 2000. *A Frozen Hell: The Russo-Finnish Winter War of 1939–1940*. Algonquin Books.

Tsygankov, Andrei P. 2008. "Russia's International Assertiveness: What Does It Mean for the West?" *Problems of Post-Communism* 55 (2): 38–55.

Tuminez, Astrid S. 2000. *Russian Nationalism since 1856: Ideology and the Making of Foreign Policy*. Rowman & Littlefield.

Turner, Admiral Stansfield. n.d. "Why We Should Build the MX Missile." *The New York Times*.

Turner, Hal Ashby. 1967. "Bismarck's Imperialist Venture: Anti-British in Origin?" In *Britain and Germany in Africa: Imperial Rivalry and Colonial Rule*, edited by P. Gifford, W. R. Louis, and A. Smith, 47–82. Yale University Press.

Turner, John C., Michael A. Hogg, Penelope J. Turner, and P. M. Smith. 1984. "Failure and Defeat as Determinants of Group Cohesiveness." *British Journal of Social Psychology* 23 (2): 97–111.

Uzoigwe, Godfrey N. 1974. *Britain and the Conquest of Africa: The Age of Salisbury*. University of Michigan Press.

Van Evera, Stephen. 1994. "Hypotheses on Nationalism and War." *International Security* 18 (4): 5–39.

Van Zomeren, Martijn, Colin Wayne Leach, and Russell Spears. 2010. "Does Group Efficacy Increase Group Identification? Resolving Their Paradoxical Relationship." *Journal of Experimental Social Psychology* 46 (6): 1055–1060.

Van Zomeren, Martijn, Russell Spears, Agneta H. Fischer, and Colin Wayne Leach. 2004. "Put Your Money Where Your Mouth Is! Explaining Collective Action Tendencies through Group-Based Anger and Group Efficacy." *Journal of Personality and Social Psychology* 87: 649–664.

Varley, Karine. 2008. "The Taboos of Defeat: Unmentionable Memories of the Franco-Prussian War in France, 1870–1914." In *Defeat and Memory: Cultural Histories of Military Defeat in the Modern Era*, edited by Jenny Macleod, 62–80. Springer.

Viaene, V. 2008. "King Leopold's Imperialism and the Origins of the Belgian Colonial Party, 1860–1905." *The Journal of Modern History* 80 (4): 741–790.

Villari, Luigi. 1930. *The Expansion of Italy*. Faber & Faber.

Volgy, Thomas J., Renato Corbetta, Keith A. Grant, and Ryan G. Baird. 2011. *Major Powers and the Quest for Status in International Politics: Global and Regional Perspectives*. Palgrave Macmillan.

Volgy, Thomas J., and Stacey Mayhall. 1995. "Status Inconsistency and International War: Exploring the Effects of Systemic Change." *International Studies Quarterly* 39 (1): 67–84.
Volkan, Vamik D. 1998. *Bloodlines: From Ethnic Pride to Ethnic Terrorism*. Basic Books.
Walker, Julian, and Victoria Knauer. 2011. "Humiliation, Self-Esteem and Violence." *Journal of Forensic Psychiatry & Psychology* 22 (5): 724–741.
Wallace, M. D. 1971. "Power, Status, and International War." *Journal of Peace Research* 8 (1): 23–35.
Wang, Dong. 2005. *China's Unequal Treaties: Narrating National History*. Vol. 43. Lexington Books.
Wang, Zheng. 2008. "National Humiliation, History Education, and the Politics of Historical Memory: Patriotic Education Campaign in China." *International Studies Quarterly* 52 (4): 783–806.
Ward, Steven. 2017. *Status and the Challenge of Rising Powers*. Cambridge University Press.
Wawro, Geoffrey. 2005. *The Franco-Prussian War: The German Conquest of France in 1870–1871*. Cambridge University Press.
Weisiger, Alex, and Keren Yarhi-Milo. 2015. "Revisiting Reputation: How Past Actions Matter in International Politics." *International Organization* 69 (2): 473–495.
Wendt, A. 1999. *Social Theory of International Politics*. Cambridge University Press.
———. 2004. "The State as Person in International Theory." *Review of International Studies* 30 (2): 289–316.
Wendt, Alexander. 1994. "Collective Identity Formation and the International State." *American Political Science Review* 88 (2): 384–396.
———. 2003. "Why a World State Is Inevitable." *European Journal of International Relations* 9 (4): 491–542.
Wesseling, H. L., and A. J. Pomerans. 1996. *Divide and Rule: The Partition of Africa, 1880–1914*. Praeger.
Wetzel, David. 2003. *A Duel of Giants: Bismarck, Napoleon III, and the Origins of the Franco-Prussian War*. University of Wisconsin Press.
Wight, Martin. 2002. *Power Politics*. A&C Black.
Willer, Robb. 2009. "Groups Reward Individual Sacrifice: The Status Solution to the Collective Action Problem." *American Sociological Review* 74 (1): 23–43.
Wilson, Woodrow. "Address to the United States Senate," January 22, 1917.
Williams, Lisa A., and David De Steno. 2009. "Pride: Adaptive Social Emotion or Seventh Sin?" *Psychological Science* 20 (3): 284–288.
Wohlforth, W. C. 2009. "Unipolarity, Status Competition, and Great Power War." *World Politics* 61 (1): 28–57.
Wohlforth, William. 2014. "Status Dilemmas and Interstate Conflict." In *Status in World Politics*, edited by T. V. Paul, Deborah Welch Larson and William C. Wohlforth, 15–140. Cambridge University Press.
Wohlforth, William. 1993. *The Elusive Balance: Power and Perceptions During the Cold War*. Cornell University Press.
Wolf, Reinhard. 2011. "Respect and Disrespect in International Politics: The Significance of Status Recognition." *International Theory* 3 (1): 105–142.
"Xi Jinping and the Chinese Dream." 2013. *The Economist*, May 13.
Yaffa, Joshua. 2016. "Putin, Syria and Why Moscow Has Gove War-Crazy." *The New Yorker*, October 14.
Zacher, Mark W. 2001. "The Territorial Integrity Norm: International Boundaries and the Use of Force." *International Organization* 55 (2): 215–250.

Zaloga, Steven J. 2014. *The Kremlin's Nuclear Sword: The Rise and Fall of Russia's Strategic Nuclear Forces 1945–2000*. Smithsonian Institution.

Zarakol, Ayse. 2011. *After Defeat: How the East Learned to Live with the West*. Cambridge University Press.

Zell, Ethan, and Mark D. Alicke. 2009. "Self-Evaluative Effects of Temporal and Social Comparison." *Journal of Experimental Social Psychology* 45 (1): 223–227.

Zubok, Vladislav M. 2009. *A Failed Empire: The Soviet Union in the Cold War from Stalin to Gorbachev*. University of North Carolina Press.

Index

Abu Ghraib, 9
Afghanistan, 230n107
Aggression
   collective esteem, 64, 72, 77, 95
   defeat and, 79–92, 191*t*2, 193*t*3
   following wars one originated, 199*t*6
   great power, 100, 102
   heightened activity and, 92–93
   material and political incentives for, 95–96
   material recovery and, 78, 85
   motivations for, 72–74, 72*f*3.5, 73*f*3.6
   status expectations and, 80
   target type, 83*f*4.3
   territorial loss and, 100–107
   war, 81–82, 86, 93
Aksai Chin region, 189
al-Nasr, Ahlam, 165
Albright, Madeleine, 179
Algeria
   French conquest of, 111, 116, 118, 232n40
Alsace and Lorraine, 1, 24
Amour propre
   See national confidence
Ampthill, Lord, 126
Andrew, Christopher M., 118
Anger, 16, 58, 64, 67, 73, 75
   authoritativeness, and, 73
   national level, 18, 32, 57
   revenge and, 62
Anglo-Egyptian War, 15
   humiliating effects of, 23
Anglo-Portuguese Treaty, 223n110
Angra Pequeña, 123, 124
Apologies
   German demand for, 125
   humiliation and, 32, 39, 44, 174
   national esteem and, 40
   Soviet demands for, 144–145
Arctic Circle, 66, 68
Assab, 130, 225n156
Atran, Scott, 39, 63

Battle of Dogali, 131
Battle of Sedan, 112
Bay of Pigs, 25

Belgium,
   imperialism, 123, 219n1, 222n80
   Leopold II, King, 121
Berlin Conference, 125, 130, 213n29, 226n187
bin Laden Osama, 165, 213n2
Bismarck, Otto von, 27
   alliance with Italy, 225n149
   Angra Pequeña, 123–125, 127, 223n112
   Berlin Conference, 125–126, 213*n*29, 224n122
   British diplomacy and, 125–126, 132–133
   Franco-Prussian War, and the, 113, 221n52
   imperialism, 122–123, 125, 127–128, 134, 169, 223n101, 224*n*118, 224n133, 224n138, 226n190
   Munroe Policy in Africa, 125, 133
   Tunisia, French annexation of, 116–117, 173, 221n49, 221n52
Bizaine, Francois, 114
Boer War, 212
Bolivia
   anti-Chilenismo, 56
   defeat in Chaco War, 189
Bonaparte, Napoleon, 112, 113
Botswana
   British conquest of, 133
Branscombe, Nyla, 63
Brazza, Pierre de, 120, 222n80
Brezhnev, Leonid, 149–152, 154–156
   Cuban Missile crisis, leadership and, 156
   mental illness, 156
Brezhnev, Leonid, 229n85
Brown, Harold, 158
Brzezinski, Zbigniew, 25

Callahan, William, 7
Cameroons, The
   German conquest of, 123–124
Capabilities, National
   recovery of, 187t1, 195–196, 198t5, 201, 203, 207, 214n63, 219n44
Caprivi, Leon von, 226n191
Carter, Jimmy, 158, 230n107
Century of Humiliation, 4–5, 29
Chaco War, 189

253

INDEX

Chailley-Bert, Joseph, 115
Chamberlain, Joseph, 36, 37, 133, 212
Chile
    War of the Pacific, and the, 56
China
    Century of Humiliation, 4–5, 29, 165–166, 231n14
    Communist Revolution, 5
    decline of, 165–166
    economic growth of, 166
    embassy bombing, 32, 166
    First Opium War, 4
    great power status and, 20
    honor culture, 33
    humiliation of, 165–170, 173
    Japanese defeat of, 165
    National Humiliation Day, 165
    national identity, 166, 173
    Opium Wars, 165
    Sino-Indian War, 189
    Sino-Japanese War, 23
    status expectations, 20
    status-seeking, 219n37
    Taiwan Strait, 68, 71
    territorial aggression, 166–167
    territorial loss, 165–166, 231n8, 231n14
    Treaty of Shimonoseki, effects of, 29
    Twenty-One Demands, 30
Clausewitz, Carl von, 45–46, 101
Clemenceau, Georges, 222n72
Cline, Ray, 163
Clinton, Bill, 25, 166, 210n33, 231n19
Cold War
    See U2 Incident and Cuban Missile Crisis
Collective esteem, 19, 57, 58, 61, 85, 121–122, 210
    See also national confidence
Congo, 222n80
    French conquest of, 111, 122, 135, 136
Congress of Berlin, 116
Correlates of War Dataset, 79, 89, 90
Corti, Luigi, 129
Courcel, Baron de, 117
Crimean War
    effects of, 29
Crimean War, 45
Crispi, Francesco, 131
Cuban Missile Crisis, 147–157
    double standard and, 148
    nuclear asymmetry, 151
    Soviet Union, effects on, 13, 52, 148, 152, 154, 162, 228n58
Cyprus
    defeat by Turkey, 23

de Gaulle, Charles, 141, 177
Defeat
    aggression following, 79–87, 80f4.1
    by weaker states, 197
    diplomatic hostility, effects on, 90–91, 199–201
    dispute initiation and, 79–81
    duration of conflict, and, 24
    failed objectives, 93
    great powers and, 78, 81, 84, 86–87
    hostility levels following, 81–82
    humiliating effects of, 21–25, 79
    in wars one initiates, 23
    loss of territory and, 24
    material recovery and aggression and, 85–87, 198t5
    national morale, decline in, and, 45
    repeated, effects of, 91–92
    revenge, 82–84, 100
    security concerns and, 94–95
    success following, 87–88
    targets of aggression following, 82–84, 194t4
    third-party aggression, 82–83, 100, 192, 193t3, 195, 197, 199, 204, 217n1
    unexpected, 22, 88–90, 196, 197, 187t1, 198t5, 201
Detinov, Nikolai, 152
Diplomatic and Political Hostility, 200t7
Disraeli, Benjamin, 113
Disrespect, 18–19, 26–32
    longevity of, 27
Dobrynin, Anatoly, 142
Dower, John, 178
Duclerc, Charles, 120, 122
Dulles, John Foster, 143
Dulles, John Foster, 178

Efficacy, National, 64, 67, 74, 76, 64f3.1
Egypt
    annexation of, 110, 126
    British and French Dual Control and, 120
    British occupation of, 121, 131, 222n84
    domestic instability and, 110
    Egyptian Crisis, 120, 225n161
    French humiliation and, 135, 136, 222n92
    French loss of influence in, 121,
    Italian interests in, 130
Eisenhower, Dwight "Ike", 138, 141–146, 161 227n23
Eisenhower, Dwight D., 176
Elite incentives
    humiliating and, 60, 61, 77
Embarrassment, 16, 67

INDEX

Emotional Motivation for Aggression, 73*f*3.6
Ethiopia
   Italian conquest of, 129–131
European Coal and Steel Commission, 31
Experimental conditions, 67*f*3.2

Fear, 67
Ferry, Jules, 110, 112, 115, 117–118, 133
Finland,
   defeat in Winter War, 22
First Italo-Ethiopian War, 15, 23, 24
Foch, Ferdinand, 1
France
   Alsace and Lorraine, loss of, 1, 3, 24, 112, 113, 117, 119, 121, 134
   army of, 112, 114, 220n32
   Boulangism, 119, 121
   Chamber, 121
   collective esteem, 121
   Congo, conquest of, 120–122, 135, 136
   decolonization, 176
   demotion of, 135
   Egypt, loss of influence, 121, 135, 136, 222n92
   expansion in Africa, 108–109, 111, 115, 116, 119, 123
   expansion in Asia, 220n44
   Franco-Prussian War, defeat in, 12, 27, 45, 112, 119, 127
   Germany, animosity for, 221n49
   great power status, 108, 111, 113–114, 117, 122, 130
   Italy, diplomacy with, 117
   material recovery of, 112
   Mexico, aggression in, 112
   military reform, 114
   Monarchists, 114
   Napoleonic War, defeat in, 112, 131
   prestige, and, 218n34
   public opinion on expansion, 116–117, 119
   revenge, desire for, 115–116
   Second French Empire, 112
   sphere of influence, 133
   Third Republic, 112, 119
   Tunisia, annexation of, 111–112, 115–119, 121, 125, 132, 221n45, 221n67, 222n72
   World War II, status effects on, 175–177
Franco-Prussian War
   Alsace and Lorraine, 1, 3
   foreign policy, effects on, 1, 3
   Franco-Prussian War, effects of, 45
Franklin, Aretha, 167
Freycinet, Charles de, 117, 120, 121, 223n94

Gaidar, Yegor, 164, 167, 168
Gambetta, Léon, 112–115, 117–118
George, Lloyd, 211n52
Germany
   1940 Armistice with France, 1
   aftermath of World War II, 1, 30–31
   Angra Pequeña, conquest of, 122–124
   defeat in World War I, 26
   defeat in World War II, 219n47
   demotion of, 134
   disrespect by Britain, 123–126, 134–136
   Great Britain, diplomacy with, 124, 133, 226n183
   great power status expectations, 111, 119, 123, 125, 130, 135, 226n183
   imperialism in Africa, 109, 123–124, 132–134, 213n29
   inferiority of, 108
   national resurgence, 45–46
   nationalism in, 224n140
   public opinion on colonization, 126, 223n140
   revenge and, 211n52
   rights and privileges, 123
   Treaty of Versailles, 1, 2, 3, 28–29
   Triple Alliance, 129
   War Guilt Clause, 28
Ginges, Jeremy, 39, 63
Gladstone, William, 120, 121, 125, 132
Gorchakov, Alexander, 29
Granville, Lord, 125, 222n84
Great Britain
   British East Africa Company, 110
   conquest in Arica, 111, 132
   decline of British empire, 220n15
   diplomacy with Germany, 124
   disregard for German status, 124
   disregard for Italian interests, 225n161
   Egyptian Crisis, and the, 131, 222n84
   great power status, 111–112, 130, 131, 226n185
   House of Commons, 225n175
   imperial expansion, 109, 111, 123, 125, 220n17, 223n110
   public opinion and conquest, 132, 219n5
   right to conquest, 124, 125, 133
   security concerns, 109, 201
   status concerns of, 109
Great powers
   See also Status.
   defeat of, 196–197
   humiliation, 26, 33
   third-party aggression and, 48–49
Gromyko, Andrei, 153

INDEX

Group-based emotions, 57–60
  definition of, 9–10
  guilt, 75
  indifference, 67, 76
  intensity of, 76

Hanotaux, Gabriele, 221n45
Harkin, Tom, 25
Harriman, Averill, 141
Hass, Richard, 167
Hideki, Tojo, 178
Hines, Jonathan, 155, 156
Hitler, Adolf, 1, 3, 101
  effects of defeat, 45
  rebuilding of German status, 41, 101
  Treaty of Versailles, reaction to, 29
Hobson, John A., 109
Honneth, Axel, 18
Honor, 33
Howard, Michael, 113
Hugo, Victor, 114
Humiliating international events
  aggression and, 57–58, 71, 75
  defeat as a, 7–87
  denial of rights, 18, 26–32, 49
  foreign policy, relationship to, 60–62
  national confidence, 37
  national failure and, 3, 17–18, 21–26, 79
  national recovery after, 44, 46, 48, 53–54
  non-state actors and, 165
  security concerns, and, 44, 52–53, 57–58, 68, 71–73, 77, 94, 169–171, 175
  success, need for, 62
  territorial compensation for, 174
  territorial loss, 11, 72, 96
  third-party aggression, and, 40–42, 48–49
  timing of responses to, 5, 45, 48, 53–54, 135
Humiliation
  aggression, support for, and, 69f3.3, 70f3.4, 72f3.5, 77, 78
  anger, and, 73, 164, 165, 167, 170–171, 215n17
  avoidance, and, 39, 46, 59
  culture and, 33
  definition, 3, 9, 15–18
  denial of rights, 18, 26–32, 49
  diplomatic practices, 39–40
  domestic politics, 19, 34, 46
  efficacy and, 73–75, 74f3.7
  entrepreneurs, 46
  great powers and, 26, 33, 41, 48, 63, 164, 166–168
  individual level, 15–16
  inferiority, 181
  invoking, 62–63, 71
  longevity of, 5, 9, 16, 19, 38, 56
  mistrust and, 43, 164, 169–170
  national level, 3, 17
  outrage and, 36, 64, 74–75, 79
  physiological effects of, 16
  prevention of, 180–183
  prospect theory, 47
  reduction of, 172–180
  revenge, 4, 36, 41, 43, 115, 119, 121, 135–136, 197, 199, 203, 206
  self-doubt, and, 4, 18, 32, 37, 46, 54, 136, 223n112
  status symbols, 40
  success, importance of, 4
Humiliation entrepreneurs, 46, 61

Imperialism, 110, 202, 212n36, 213n38, 217n11
  domestic rationales for, 110, 226n195
  economic and strategic rationales for, 109–110
In-group bias, 59, 60, 64
  anger and, 64
  identification, levels of, 64
India
  non-aligned status, 174
  Sino-Indian War, defeat in, 189
  status motivations for nuclear program, 139
Inertia effect, 39
Involuntary Territorial Losses, List of, 204t8
Iran
  experimental scenario, 67
  history of US involvement, 2, 3
  humiliation of, 188–189
  Iraq, War with, 189
  nuclear program, 1–2, 68
Iranian Hostage Crisis, 25
Iraq, 188, 203
  effects of 2003 invasion, 212
  Iran-Iraq War, victory in, 188
  honor and, 212
Islamic State of Iraq and Levant, 66–68
  humiliation response to, 165
Israeli-Palestinian Conflict, 39, 63, 210n28
Italy
  Britain, support of, 225n149
  collective esteem in, 130
  conquest in Africa, 128–131
  demotion of, 131
  Egypt, and, 130, 225n161
  humiliation in Ethiopia, 131
  imperialism in Africa, 129–131
  inferiority of, 121, 128–129
  Sixth wheel, as the, 129
  status expectations, 128–129

Triple Alliance, 129
Tunisia, interests in, 129
World War II, status effects on, 175–177
Italy, 175–177
  status decline, 177
  status expectations of, 176–177

Jackson, Henry, 158
Japan
  China's Century of Humiliation, 166
  defeat, effects of, 212n15, 219n47
  nuclear weapons and, 177
  Treaty of Shimonoseki, 29
  Twenty-One Demands, 30
  US postwar treatment of, 140, 177–178, 219n47
  Washington Conference, humiliation of, 30
  World War II, status effects on, 177–178
Jervis, Robert, 150
Jintao, Hu, 169, 170
Johnson, Lyndon, 229n62
Joseph, Franz, 113

Kai-Shek, Chiang, 166
Kanya-Forstner, A. S., 118
Kennedy, John F., 25
  Cuban Missile Crisis, 26, 141, 157, 228m57
Kennedy, Robert, 228n57
Khrushchev, Nikita,
  Cuban Missile Crisis and the, 148–149, 152, 227n35
  nuclear policy of, 141, 152, 156, 158
  overthrow of, 149
  Paris Summit, and the, 141–142
  Soviet status, 153
  U2 Incident and, 142–147, 227n35
  Winter War and, 22
Khrushchev, Sergei, 146, 147
Kissinger, Henry, 152, 153
Kuznetsov, Vasily, 151

Larson, Deborah, 40, 55
Lenin, Vladimir, 109
Leopold II, King, 121, 222n80
Luttwak, Edward, 159

MacArthur, Douglas, 178
Macmillan, Harold, 141
Mancini, Pasquale, 130, 225n157
Mannerheim, Carl Gustaf, 22
Massawa, 131
McNamara, Robert, 22
McNaughton, John, 21–22
Medvedev, Dmitry, 2, 209n5
Melbourne, Lord, 220n15

Menelik II, 131
Mercer, Jonathan, 209n17
Mexico, French aggression in, 112
Milosevic, Slobodan, 172
Mohamed, Mahathir, 165
Moltke, Helmuth von, 113
Morocco, 226n193
Münster, Count, 124, 125
Mussolini, Benito, 131

Namibia
  German conquest of, 123
National confidence, 5, 11, 37, 58, 61, 85, 101
  See also collective esteem
  aggression and, 62
  defeat, and, 45
  national recovery, 53–54
National failure, 34–35
  backing down in a crisis, 25
  defeat in war, 21–25
  territorial loss, 24
National identity, 32, 60, 210n21
  definition and construction of, 19
  perceptions of, 58, 76
  threats to, 60
National security, concerns about, 44, 52–53, 57–58, 68, 71–73, 77, 94, 169–171, 175
Nationalism, 59, 77
Nesselrode, Karl, 30, 37
Niger
  British conquest of, 133
Nixon, Richard, 152, 229n62
North Atlantic Treaty Organization
  bombing of Serbia, 2
  expansion of, 2
Nuclear arms race
  international race for status, as an, 51–52
Nuclear weapons
  arms race, 8, 150, 155, 157
  first-strike capability, 151, 155
  hydrogen bomb, 140–141, 152
  intercontinental ballistic missiles, 139–142, 150, 155–157, 161
  mutually-assured destruction, 150, 153
  parity of, 139, 150–154, 157–163
  status and, 4, 7, 10, 11, 40, 42, 97, 139
  submarine launched ballistic missiles and, 150, 157, 161
  war, and, 149, 151, 155

Obama, Barack, 180, 181
Ottoman Empire, decline of, 20

INDEX

Paraguay
  defeat in Chaco War, 189
Paris Commune, 114
Paris Summit
  expectations of, 141
  failure of, 141–142, 144
Peter the Great, 167
Polyansky, Dmitry, 149
Portugal
  imperialism in Africa, 111
  Congo River and, 223n110
Potemkin, Grigory, 152, 158
Potsdam Agreement, 15
Powell, Colin, 167
Power transition theory, 53, 55
Powers, Gary, 142, 146
Prospect theory, 47, 97
Prussia, 108
  Franco-Prussian War, 112, 127
  imperialism, attitudes towards, 122
  superiority, 220n32
Putin, Vladimir, 2, 66
  Russian humiliation, and, 168–170, 180

Reagan, Ronald, 210n33, 230n107
  intervention in Grenada, 42
Redirected aggression, theory of, 42
Revenge, 41, 43, 82–84
Rhodes, Cecil, 110
Robilant, Carlo Nicolis, 129, 225n156
Romney, Mitt, 180
Roosevelt, Franklin, 175, 176
Roustan, Thèodore, 117
Rumsfeld, Donald, 158
Russia
  Central Asia, expansion in, 107
  Cold War, end of, 179–180
  Crimea, invasion of, 168–169
  Crimean War, effects of, 45, 48, 107
  defeat, effects of, 212n15
  economic recovery, 167–168
  great power status, 30
  humiliation, expressions of, 170
  liberal institutions, 179–180
  NATO expansion, response to, 31, 40
  Russo-Japanese War, 107
  status expectations of, 167–169
  Syria, projection of power in, 168, 213n36
  territorial loss, and, 167
  Treaty of Paris, 29
  US disrespect of, 167–170, 179–180
  War with Georgia, 2, 168
  War with Ukraine, 168, 169
  Yalta Conference, 107

Russo-Japanese War
  humiliating effects of, 32

Saint-Hillaire, Jules Barthélemy, 117
Saint-Vallier, Charles Raymond de, 116
Salisbury, Lord, 1, 113, 116, 131–132
Schevchenko, Alexei
Schlesinger, James, 158, 159, 160
Scramble for Africa, 8, 108–112, 121, 133
  international race for status, as an, 51–52
Semichastny, Vladimir, 149
September 11, 2001, 9, 58
Serbia
  humiliation of, 172
Shame, 16, 64, 67, 73, 76, 101
  avoidant tendencies, and, 59
Shatt al-Arab waterway, 189
Shelepin, Alexander, 149
Shull, John, 155, 156
Sino-Indian War, 189
Six-Day War
  humiliating effects of, 15, 21
Social identity theory, 55
Somalia
  British conquest of, 133
  Italian conquest of, 130
Soviet Union
  See also U2 Incident *and* Cuban Missile Crisis
  collapse of, 5, 218n36, 231n22
  Cuban Missile Crisis, effects of, 13, 52, 148, 152, 154, 162, 228n58
  desire for recognition, 140, 144, 154
  economy, 140, 149, 152
  inferiority of, 142, 144, 147–148, 152–154, 162, 229n62
  nuclear parity, 139, 146, 149–154, 157, 162
  security concerns of, 147, 153, 157–158
  Sputnik, 140
  status expectations of, 138, 140–143, 145, 147, 165
  territorial loss, 167
  United States, relations with, 210n16, 228n57
  Winter War victory, 22
Spain
  inferiority of, 117, 121, 129
  Spanish-American War, effects of, 173
  status decline, 173
  territorial expansion, 111
  Year of Disaster, 172
Spears, Russell, 63
Stalemate, Effects of, 80f4.1, 80–82, 93, 189, 190, 191t2, 192, 201
  status, on, 80

Stalin, Joseph, 210n16
Starabba, Antonia, 131
Status
  See also Humiliation.
  basis of, 19
  collective action, 59
  common knowledge, 42, 144, 159, 161
  concerns about, 7
  definition of, 16–17
  demotion of, 10, 115, 131, 135–136
  diplomatic exchange and, 11
  dynamics of, 50–52
  expectations of, 19
  great power, 11, 18, 19, 20, 26, 83, 116–117, 121–122, 125, 128–129, 131, 133–135, 193, 195, 197, 206, 210n10, 217n11, 221n49
  hierarchies, 59
  imperialism, and, 11
  inconsistency of, 7, 54, 195, 214n61
  influence, and, 153, 160–162
  in-group favoritism, 59, 62
  instrumental effects, 37–38
  international races for, 8, 50–52
  minor powers, 195–196
  non-recognition of, 18
  nuclear parity, 139, 150–154, 161–163
  nuclear weapons, 177
  realist models, and, 52–53
  rights and privileges, 17–18, 41–42, 116–117, 121, 123–125, 129, 133, 138–139, 142, 145, 153, 154, 156, 158, 160, 188,
  physiological effects, 59
  projection of power abroad, 41, 83
  psychological effects of decline, 37–38, 59
  slow decline of, 20
  sphere of influence, 83
  stickiness of, 117, 118, 171–172, 214n59
  superpower, 139, 152–154, 163
  symbols of, 4, 8, 40, 42, 68, 136
Status competition, 8, 50–52
Status inconsistency theory, 54
Status-seeking strategies, 10
  social creativity, 174
Stimson, Henry L., 30–31, 177
Strategic Arms Limitation Treaty I, 152–153, 157, 158, 161
Strategic Arms Limitation Treaty II, 161
Sudan, Italian conquest of, 130
Suez Canal, 120
  British control of, 121
  French control of, 110
Sykes-Pico Agreement, 165

Talbott, Strobe, 170
Taylor, A. J. P., 109
  Bismarck's African policy, on, 223n101
  imperialism, analysis of, 109
Territorial conquest, 98–100
  current era, in the, 102–103
  heightened activity, 104
  political incentives for, 104
  reputation for strength, and, 104–105
  status and, 107
  strategic motivations for, 105–106
Territorial loss
  conquest and, 98–100, 119–120, 202–203, 205t9, 206, 217n5
  contiguous loss of, 99, 106
  defeat, overlap with, 96
  great powers and, 97, 106
  involuntary loss, humiliating effects of, 11, 12, 24, 96, 203, 205, 205t9, 206, 207, 219n45
  material recovery and, 101–102
  revanchist gains in, 203, 205t9
  status, threat to, 96–97, 100–107
  third-party conquest, 100–101
  voluntary loss of, 97–98, 203, 207
Tocqueville, Alexis de, 36
Togo, German conquest, 123, 124
Trachtenberg, Marc, 155
Treaty of Frankfurt, 113
Treaty of Paris, 29
  predicted effects of, 37
Treaty of Shimonoseki, 15
  China, effects of, 29
Treaty of Versailles, 1, 2, 3
  effects of, 5, 28–29, 30
Truman, Harry, 31, 176
Tsar Alexander II, 48, 113
Tunisia
  economy instability in, 221–222n69
  French conquest of, 111–112, 115–119, 121, 125, 132, 221n45, 221n67, 222n72
  Italian influence in, 129
Turkey
  defeat, effects of, 212n15
Turner, Stansfield, 160

U2 Incident, 140–147
  apology for, 144
  Paris Summit and, 142, 144
  Powers, Gary, 142, 146
  Soviet humiliation, 142, 144, 145
Unequal treaties, 27–28

United Nations
  Boutros-Ghali, Boutros, 25
  intervention in Haiti, 25
United States
  Bay of Pigs, effects of, 25
  bombing of Chinese embassy, 32
  collective confidence, 68
  Cuban Missile Crisis, 26
  great power status of, 188, 212
  humiliating loss in Vietnam, 21–22
  influence, international, 68, 71, 72
  international perception, 159–163
  intervention in Grenada, 42
  intervention in Serbia, 31, 40
  Iranian hostage crisis, 25, 53–54
  Minutemen missiles, 155
  national identity, 210
  nuclear policy, 157–163, 229n86
  post-World War II settlement, 30
  Somalia, withdrawal from, 25
  U2 flyovers, 138, 142, 143
  Vietnam, effects of, 53, 210

Valdai Conference, 209n5
Victory, Effects of, 79–82, 80f4.1, 92, 189–192, 191t2, 200, 201
  humiliation and, 87
  status, threat to, 80

Vietnam, 210n33
  humiliating effects of, 21–22
von Bismarck, Otto, 169, 173, 175, 181

Waddington, William, 116
Wann, Daniel, 63
War of the Pacific
  Bolivia, effects on, 56
  territorial loss and, 24
Washington Conference, 30
Weinberger, Caspar, 158
Weisiger, Alex, 93, 190
Wilhelm I, Emperor, 112
Wilson, Woodrow
  humiliating effects of Versailles, 211n52
Winter War, 22
World War I
  aftermath of, 1
  causes of, 1
World War II
  aftermath of, 30–31

Yarhi-Milo, Keren, 93, 190
Yeltsin, Boris, 167, 170

Zanzibar, Italian conquest of, 130
Zemin, Jiang, 166

CPSIA information can be obtained
at www.ICGtesting.com
Printed in the USA
LVHW111655020420
652035LV00005B/50/J